Violence Rewired

This thought-provoking book draws together research from genetics, anthropology, psychology and the social sciences to show that widespread assumptions about the inevitability of human violence are almost entirely a collection of myths. While violence has been a recurring feature of human life, there is no reason to suppose that it is inherent in 'human nature'. On the contrary, patterns of aggressive behaviour are largely learned through experience, and even those individuals who have often acted violently can learn to change. Rejecting the speculations of much contemporary writing about human aggression, *Violence Rewired* presents an evidence-based alternative: a multilevel model of action to reduce violence at both individual and collective levels, linked to public health initiatives developed by the World Health Organization. If humanity is to survive the challenges it faces, a more realistic appraisal of ourselves and our basic tendencies is an indispensable part of the solution.

RICHARD WHITTINGTON is a Professor at the Norwegian University of Science & Technology (NTNU) and is based at the Brøset Centre for Research & Education in Forensic Psychiatry, St. Olav's University Hospital, Trondheim, Norway. He is a psychologist with a focus on violence prevention and mental health and is an Honorary Senior Research Fellow at the University of Liverpool, UK.

JAMES MCGUIRE is Emeritus Professor of Forensic Clinical Psychology at the University of Liverpool, UK. He is also an expert witness in criminal courts and mental health tribunals, has worked as a consultant for criminal justice agencies in thirteen countries and was winner of the 2012 Research Prize from the International Corrections and Prisons Association.

Violence Rewired

Evidence and Strategies for Public Health Action

Richard Whittington

*Norwegian University of Science & Technology (NTNU)
and St. Olav's University Hospital*

James McGuire

University of Liverpool

CAMBRIDGE
UNIVERSITY PRESS

CAMBRIDGE
UNIVERSITY PRESS

University Printing House, Cambridge CB2 8BS, United Kingdom

One Liberty Plaza, 20th Floor, New York, NY 10006, USA

477 Williamstown Road, Port Melbourne, VIC 3207, Australia

314-321, 3rd Floor, Plot 3, Splendor Forum, Jasola District Centre, New Delhi - 110025, India

103 Penang Road, #05-06/07, Visioncrest Commercial, Singapore 238467

Cambridge University Press is part of the University of Cambridge.

It furthers the University's mission by disseminating knowledge in the pursuit of education, learning and research at the highest international levels of excellence.

www.cambridge.org
Information on this title: www.cambridge.org/9781009202275
DOI: 10.1017/9781139086486

First published 2020
First paperback edition 2022

A catalogue record for this publication is available from the British Library

Library of Congress Cataloging in Publication data
Names: Whittington, Richard (Richard Charles), author. | McGuire, James,
 1948– author.
Title: Violence rewired : evidence and strategies for public health action /
 Richard Whittington, James McGuire.
Description: Cambridge, United Kingdom ; New York, NY : Cambridge
 University Press, 2020. | Includes bibliographical references and index.
Identifiers: LCCN 2019038661 (print) | LCCN 2019038662 (ebook) |
 ISBN 9781107018075 (hardback) | ISBN 9781139086486 (epub)
Subjects: MESH: Violence–prevention & control | Violence–psychology |
 Public Health Practice | Behavior Therapy | Models, Theoretical
Classification: LCC HM1116 (print) | LCC HM1116 (ebook) | NLM HM
 1116 | DDC 303.6–dc23
LC record available at https://lccn.loc.gov/2019038661
LC ebook record available at https://lccn.loc.gov/2019038662

ISBN 978-1-107-01807-5 Hardback
ISBN 978-1-009-20227-5 Paperback

The raging stream they call violent
But the riverbed that contains it
No one calls that violent.

Bertolt Brecht, 'On Violence'[*]

Contents

Figures

Tables

Boxes

Foreword
Between Chimpanzees and Bonobos:
The Challenge of Violence Prevention

Between 2001 and 2016, 839,593 people died due to interpersonal violence in my country, Brazil. In less than two decades into the twenty-first century, in a territory that is neither at war nor facing armed internal conflict, there were more than 800,000 homicide deaths. In just one year, more specifically in 2016, 61,143 people died of homicide in Brazil, according to official data from the Ministry of Health. That amounts to a homicide rate of 31.5 per 100,000 inhabitants. More than half of these deaths occurred in the age group between fifteen and twenty-nine years old: 35,995 adolescents and young people were victims of interpersonal violence and died as a result; 92% of the victims were males. Some 56,409 boys and men were murdered in a single year, in a single nation that, I repeat, is neither at war nor facing armed internal conflict. In Brazil, since the end of the 1990s, homicide is in the first position among the causes of potential years of life lost and is the first cause of death among the young population, overcoming all other causes, natural or external. According to estimates by the World Health Organization (WHO), there were around 475,000 homicide deaths in the world in 2012. Brazil accounts for 12.9% of these deaths. It is in this place, this country, which deals with an uninterrupted rising trend in homicide rates since the 1980s, that I write this Foreword. I live in a country that represents an exception in the global trend of homicide decline. Latin America has the highest homicide rates in the world, and Brazil has one of the highest rates in the region.

Violence is a theme that mobilises the interests of a diverse audience. This audience includes practitioners from applied areas, such as health professionals who provide care to victims and perpetrators; law enforcement agents; educators and teachers from elementary and high schools; social workers, psychologists, researchers and academics from different areas such as sociology, anthropology, psychology, medicine, public health, law, and criminology, as well as students in all these fields; victims and their relatives; and the curious in general, ordinary people who live directly or indirectly with violence. Such interest is partly due to the difficulty in understanding its occurrence, even when we can identify possible 'motives' for concrete and singular acts. Why, in a country like Brazil, for example, do so many homicides occur? What explains the use of violence as a form of conflict resolution? If we are rational beings, who live in civilised countries, endowed with systems of justice, in which the monopoly of the use of force is the prerogative of the state, why do so many people not use dialogue, reason and argument to resolve conflicts?

Richard Whittington and James McGuire go to the heart of this when they elect the following investigation as a trigger for their book: Is violence hard-wired? This question leads us directly to that of human nature. To what extent is violence a constituent part of our ethos, a feature rooted in our biology and therefore a feature of our humanity with which we will have to live for the rest of our days (as a human community, even if civilised and rational)? The view that violence is deeply programmed in our brain is frighteningly paralyzing. If we believe it is a trait that connects us to our chimpanzee ancestors – that it is inscribed in our biology, that it is there despite socialising and civilising efforts – what can we possibly do to effectively deal with this problem?

Violence Rewired: Evidence and Strategies for Public Health Action directly confronts and challenges this pessimistic view. First, it shows evidence that through centuries of a civilising process violence is actually declining. We face now less violence than did our prehistoric ancestors. Evidence shows that homicide is declining consistently in different areas across the globe. Following Norbert Elias and his classical theory of the civilising process, violence reduction can be understood as the result of social and psychological changes over the centuries, a social-psychological process that resulted in the creation of modern states, with strong institutions and the consolidation of the rule of law. But the problem is still persistent in some areas, such as Brazil and other Latin American countries, 'high-risk' countries characterised, among other things, by high levels of state corruption, low investment in public education and health, low state stability, and high inequality. To quote the authors: 'effective governance and low homicide rates are really two sides of the same coin'. This is a powerful message, bringing some light and hope for those struggling to build peaceful and violence-free societies.

Many may consider the proposal that humanity is moving toward pacification to be somewhat fragile. In fact, 'pacification' could be a mere effect of external control mechanisms, of the limits imposed by socialisation; but the fragility is shown precisely through the persistence of violence in social relations. We are pacified, but the violence is there, inexorable, as a constant and present threat. *Violence Rewired* then takes us on a beautiful and thought-provoking journey through evolutionary biology, archaeology and anthropology. Throughout this journey, the authors offer us a set of evidences, theories and arguments that allows an alternative reading.

It departs from the reconstruction of our lineage, as members of the great ape family (*hominidae*): we are together with orangutans, gorillas, chimpanzees and bonobos. We are quite close, genetically, to chimpanzees, and this could explain, at least partially, our dispositional aggressiveness. On the other hand, humans are also quite similar genetically to bonobos, and bonobos behave quite differently from chimpanzees: they act prosocially; they do not exhibit violent behaviour; males are subordinate to females; and they share food. Although our history makes it difficult to support the idea of a peaceful human nature, such as that of bonobos, the mere sharing of more than 90% of our DNA with chimpanzees is insufficient to support the thesis of a human nature prone to violence. Maybe we are in the middle.

The questioning of a hard-wired violence, of a violent human nature, does not mean denial of the importance of biology to understanding violence and its causation. Biology is seriously taken into concern here: neurobiology, genetics and epigenetics are deeply discussed; the existing evidence is systematised and scrutinised; and gaps in present knowledge are discussed, as are inconsistencies and advances.

Violence Rewired proposes an ambitious and necessary task: the construction of an integrative theoretical framework, consistent with what the authors call a *biopsychosocial* orientation. As a fundamental part of our puzzle, the aspects related to the processes of socialisation need to come into play. Now, a different question must be posed (not by the authors, but by me!): If violence is not hard-wired, how – and why – is violence wired after all? Violence is not in our nature, but we, human beings, commit violent acts and behave aggressively in many different situations.

To answer, we need to refer to theories that consider the importance of socialisation processes and social learning. We must also understand how the contextual characteristics influence our behaviour. The idea that violence is learned (and not innate) opens a very important door for us to think of ways to tackle the problem that go beyond punishment. We abandon that frighteningly paralysing view and open up to an understanding that it is possible to interfere in a preventive way. We are not born prone to rage: we learn it throughout our lives, through the relationships into which we are inserted. Parental practices and styles, peer groups and school are some of these socialising spaces where violence is learned and reproduced. The macro-social context with shared cultural norms that support gender, race/ethnicity and socioeconomic inequalities and the most diverse stigmas, prejudices and violence are also part of the puzzle and need to be framed in a broad biopsychosocial framework to help us understand violence.

Violence Rewired is integrative from a theoretical point of view, but this is not the main strength of the book. The authors are able to present this discussion and different theoretical currents and scientific evidences using a language that is easy to understand by diverse public audiences. But that too is not the book's main strength.

The main strength of *Violence Rewired* is that it takes us from that frighteningly paralysing view and shows us that there are innumerable ways to face, respond to and prevent violence. There are risk and protective factors that can be the target of preventive actions and programs. To support this optimistic view, Richard Whittington and James McGuire lead us on another journey, now through the actions of the World Health Organization since the Global Campaign for the Prevention of Violence in the 1990s to the current days with the launch of INSPIRE: Seven Strategies for Ending Violence against Children. Yes, preventing violence is possible: let's rewire it.

The reading of *Violence Rewired: Evidence and Strategies for Public Health Action* had a renewing and incentivising effect on me. I really hope it does the same for you.

Maria Fernanda Tourinho Peres MD PhD
Professor at the Preventive Medicine Department,
University of São Paulo School of Medicine
Head of WHO Collaborating Center on Violence and
Violence Prevention in Brazil
Center for the Study of Violence, University of São Paulo

Acknowledgements

It is a pleasure to thank a number of colleagues who have contributed in different ways to the background work and to the thinking that was the origin of this book. Several were members of a research team that carried out systematic reviews of risk assessment methods and of interventions to reduce violence that we have cited in what follows. We are especially indebted in this respect to Maria Leitner for her substantial contribution to the ideas underpinning this book as it developed. Wally Barr and Juliet Hounsome also played a key role in discussions about the nature and quality of evidence in this area. Other colleagues contributed in numerous ways to the review work which prompted this book. We thank in particular Andrew Brown, Ashley Bruen, Gemma Cherry, Rumona Dickson, Yenal Dundar, Rachel Flentje, Alina Haines, Kathryn Harney, Sarah Jones, Beverley Quinn and Abbie Wall. We are grateful to everyone both for engaging in the various research reviews and other activities and for being part of what was a very lively, congenial and supportive environment running through a succession of projects. We thank Maria Fernanda Tourinho Peres for contributing the Foreword and for advising on various specific aspects of the text; and we are grateful to Alex Butchart and an anonymous reviewer for comments on an earlier version of the book. We are indebted to Liz Perkins and Roger Almvik, who were generous in providing time and energy for stimulating discussions during the period spent preparing the manuscript. We are grateful too to the editors and production team at Cambridge University Press who have been supportive and helpful throughout this time. Finally, we thank our wives, Donna and Meredith, for their love and support and for many valuable conversations in the course of our writing.

Alongside various other commitments, this book has been some time in the making, and as time has gone by the shape of it has changed from what we first envisaged. However, the fundamental aim has stayed the same throughout while being enriched by all of these collaborations. Ultimately though, of course, the perspective taken, the conclusions drawn, and any errors that remain here are solely the responsibility of us as the authors.

Introduction and Overview

Consider the following question. What would be likely to happen if a group of humans was returned to a 'state of nature', divested of the elaborate mechanisms of control that we assume restrain our impulses in everyday civilised life? Many people would probably expect that the likeliest result would be a breakdown of order and a resurgence of primeval self-interest, with increasing aggression, possibly spiralling into violence. This is the theme of William Golding's dystopian novel *Lord of the Flies*, published in 1954. It is the imagined story of a group of British schoolboys shipwrecked onto a remote oceanic island. While they initially agree a set of rules for communal living, their behaviour soon deteriorates. Factions emerge, and hostilities erupt, followed by ghastly murderous violence. The book became a worldwide best-seller and was later turned into a stage play and several film versions. It was placed on reading lists in schools and colleges in many countries. The story appears to confirm what many people assume: that once the veneer of socialised conduct is stripped away, human beings naturally resort to 'the law of the jungle' based on evolutionary survival strategies.

In 2018 a Swedish documentary maker, Magnus Lindeen, produced a film about a social experiment which tested this idea. The experiment took place in the 1970s and involved a group of strangers who agreed to be cast away for three months on a specially designed raft, the *Acali*, to be sailed across the Atlantic Ocean from Spain to Mexico. The film included original footage from the journey and interviews with the surviving members of the group who met in Stockholm to recall their experiences of the expedition (Lindvall, 2018). The experiment itself was set up by a Mexican anthropologist, Santiago Genovés, who had previously taken part in the celebrated *Ra* expeditions, led by Thor Heyerdahl. The idea was to recreate a "state of nature" and to examine how the six women and six men in the crew, including Dr. Genovés himself, behaved toward each other as the journey progressed.

The anthropologist fully expected that due to the intense pressure of communal living, and lack of any privacy, relationships within the group, including sexual rivalries, would gradually descend into enmity and violence, a regression similar to the fictional one imagined by Golding. However, the participants initially cooperated happily and showed little sign of mutual hostilities. When Genovés then deliberately tried to incite conflict between them by exposing confidential comments they had made about each other, it had the opposite effect of uniting the group against him.

The course of this "real world" experiment calls into question the prediction above that without the surrounding structures of orderly society, humans will naturally revert to distrust, antagonism, and "brutish" behaviour. This investigation cannot of course on its own disprove the possibility of that happening. But it shows it is by no means inevitable, and that our capacity for cooperation and mutual aid is as firmly rooted, if not more so, than any inclination to resort to selfishness and aggression in order to survive.

This book poses a major question that arises from this debate: Is violence 'hard-wired'? Is the tendency to be violent, in other words, a fixed and elemental feature of the human brain which cannot be significantly changed and which will always exert a destructive influence on human behaviour? This is one of the fundamental questions of philosophy which has been debated over the last two millennia. It is also a key topic for the biological, psychological and social sciences, and any conclusion has substantial implications for how societies organise and police themselves. A decisive answer to this question is still unavailable and may remain out of reach for many years to come. But the persistent and pessimistic tendency to view many people as born with a predisposition to act aggressively toward others and beyond a 'cure' is open to serious challenge. Such a view of human behaviour can lead to unnecessarily restrictive and punitive interventions which are unjust for the individual and needlessly costly for society. Current scientific research and international policy developments actually suggest that much can be done to prevent and intervene successfully with many kinds of violent behaviour. This supports the idea that violence as a concept can itself be 'rewired' to enable new possibilities in constructing a safer and more peaceful world.

This book focuses on that major issue and has three main aims. The first is to draw together and evaluate the implications of recently acquired knowledge about human violence from across the full spectrum of scientific disciplines. This knowledge offers fresh perspectives and a new understanding of why violence occurs and what the main approaches to reducing it should be. The second aim is to address the pessimism which often pervades discussions about this problem by emphasising the potential for greater confidence about effectively intervening with violent people and in violent situations. It is true that we are a long way from eradicating violence, and we may ultimately never succeed in doing so, but nevertheless we have made much progress in the past few decades in designing new ways of successfully understanding and working with those who act violently. The third aim here is to link the full range of interventions currently being developed and tested around the world to a global strategy for tackling the problem, which has been established by the World Health Organization. This strategy offers the opportunity to integrate and implement effective interventions on a scale that has not been considered before. Taken together, the potential synthesis of new knowledge, greater confidence and innovative international policy makes it timely for a 'new look' at the old problem of human violence and offers the prospect of a major step forward in producing a safer world.

I.1 Background

The scientific literature on human violence is now very extensive. As it grows larger on an almost daily basis, any attempt to cover it in its entirety is an almost insuperable task. So we have attempted here to give at least a sense of what the key recent developments have been. While this is not a systematic review of all research relevant to violence, it is an attempt to undertake a comprehensive survey of recent innovations across the breadth of scientific disciplines which can contribute to an improved understanding of causes, and thereby provide potential remedies. The potentially baffling mass of information now available can be summed up using a number of integrative concepts, and here we have used the *biopsychosocial model*. The complexity of violent behaviour and the multiplicity of factors which lead to it mean that the lenses of biology, psychology and sociology are all needed in various combinations to capture the full picture. Any single violent act will have both immediate triggers and background influences which converge to make it more likely a violent response will be elicited. Some violent acts will be primarily driven by neurological damage; different forms of it will arise from powerful emotions or personal conflicts; while other violence will be mostly generated by social conditions. The end point of harm to another person may be the same, but the focus of solutions (from clinical treatment to political change) will be very different according to the immediate triggers and the more distant background factors leading to the act. Adopting a biopsychosocial approach enables an examination of violence which is comprehensive and systematic. It reflects the real complexity of the problem while providing a conceptual structure for the huge diversity of data and theory in this area.

We approach the problem of violence here from a direction which emphasises the potential for real change toward less interpersonal violence in many parts of the world, and in this respect we follow in the footsteps of Norbert Elias and Steven Pinker. Together these authors have developed and revitalised the idea that human beings are becoming less, not more violent, over time (Elias, 2000; Pinker, 2011) and that this improvement has been achieved through concerted action at the level of both society and the individual. Contrary to compelling evidence that the twentieth century was the most lethal period in human history, Pinker provides extensive data on reductions in the frequency and severity of human violence over several thousand years. Thus while there was a high level of lethality in the twentieth century in terms of absolute numbers, it is argued that the proportionate rate of violent death was less than it had been in many previous eras. Pinker (2011) summarises a number of possible explanations for this apparent trend, including the pacification of societies and the empowerment of women. His analysis has been criticised a number of times particularly in terms of the quality of the data which he uses to make the case for a reduction. Inevitably, given his wide historical scope ranging from prehistory to the present, much of the evidence is speculative at best. Estimates of the number of people killed in ancient massacres involve a large element of guesswork, and rely on many assumptions that may be questionable. We in contrast are more closely focused in timescale while remaining broad in theoretical scope and using systematic reviews of the research evidence as much as possible. The emphasis here is only on trends since 1945 but the message is largely the same, and the data, like those presented by Pinker for the same time period, while still flawed in some respects, are generally more robust. We also operate with an awareness of the importance of recent, more nuanced views of these broad historical patterns. Wrangham (2019), for instance, argues that any overall historical trend could mask contrasting processes with a tendency for humans to become less violent in some ways but not in others.

In contrast to these observed trends, the common view of human violence is often pessimistic, tending toward the belief not only that people are more violent now than they have ever been but that the roots of this violence are fixed aspects of 'human nature'. Violence, in other words, is widely seen as 'hard-wired', metaphorically creating a picture of human cognitive and neural structures as primarily if not entirely a result of biological evolution, genetically programmed at the individual level, and in that respect immutable. This 'mark of Cain' perspective ranks nature clearly over nurture and Hobbes's image of short, brutish lives over Rousseau's idea of a natural human capacity for benign social relations. Our contention underpinning the book is that, when the evidence on the psychosocial causes of violence and the effectiveness of violence interventions are considered, such pessimism is unjustified. While we are nowhere near a solution yet, there is plentiful evidence of incremental reductions in the propensity for human violence when a systematic and intensive approach is taken to working with violent individuals and their relationships with those around them.

The potential for change has accelerated in the past two decades because of recent significant developments in global policy toward the problem of human violence. Since 2000 the World Health Organization (WHO) has been actively pursuing a coordinated public health approach to interpersonal violence which, given its remit and global reach, has the capacity to impact the problem worldwide and not only in rich countries. This Global Campaign for Violence Prevention provides a framework for national programmes designed to tackle violence using evidence-based, largely psychosocial, approaches. In this book we attempt to map the elements of the biopsychosocial approach onto this framework and to examine the evidence for various types of intervention which are endorsed by it. Such an integration of science and global policy shows the potential for national governmental action to address the problem.

Taking these elements of knowledge, and slightly recasting the metaphor employed earlier, renewed confidence, and innovative policy together create the possibility of violence being 'rewired'. We are not here proposing any new biological rewiring via novel neural pathways or connections. On the contrary, we wish to rewire the biopsychosocial model itself by rebalancing the emphasis given to each of the different elements within it and the pathways between them.

When initially formulated by Engel (1977) the biopsychosocial model was viewed as an important innovation, even though at that stage the psychological and social elements were in some respects adjuncts to the biomedical domain rather than being assigned genuinely equal weight. The idea's status was later searchingly questioned by McLaren (1998), who did not consider that it possessed the essential ingredients of a scientific model and considered it wholly unsuitable for use in psychiatry, a view shared by Benning (2015). Even when its level of acceptance was appraised twenty-five years after Engel's proposal, that was still within a primarily clinical focus (Borrell-Carrió et al., 2004). More recently its application has been endorsed, though for different sets of reasons, by several authors. Smith and colleagues (2013) argued that the model can be used in a way that is thoroughly evidence-based. Lehman et al. (2017) added 'systems dynamics' elements to it which they considered strengthened its validity and applicability. Wade and Halligan (2017) regarded it as affording the best prospect of viewing healthcare problems from multiple perspectives and of delivering appropriate services accordingly. The last suggestion comes closest to uniting the model with a public health approach to a problem such as violence.

Even within this supposedly integrative approach, the traditional view that violence is hard-wired and built-in remains tenacious. The biochemical or neural levels of explanation are almost always presented as preceding and underpinning the psychosocial levels, and the latter end up assimilated into an overarching biological framework. So biopsychosocial models can superficially appear inclusive and comprehensive, but almost invariably they tend to privilege the bio- over the psychosocial (Boyle, 2013; Johnstone et al., 2018). Reconceptualising this model based on current evidence involves understanding that all three levels are in an ongoing dynamic, interactional, and interdependent relationship with each other and that psychological and social factors can influence the biological just as much as the reverse. Being powerless, for instance, has significant psychological and biological consequences. 'Rewiring' in this way also reminds us that the neural circuitry that exists can be changed by effective interventions, and new pathways can be forged between each of the domains. Rapidly increasing discoveries in the study of neural plasticity are an example offering new insights into the possibilities for change at both individual and cultural levels (Costandi, 2016). In this context, an *ecological model* may be more suitable to capture the intricacies of the interconnections between levels in any comprehensive explanation of human violence and thus as the basis for effective public health interventions (Heise, 1998). This approach complements the biopsychosocial model in some respects by again drawing on factors from different levels. But rather than integrating variables to explain action at an individual level, it also represents an attempt to explain the societal and cultural context of violence, and can thereby lead to proposals for addressing such issues at a far broader level. We draw on this model to complement our overall approach at various points below.

I.2   Defining Terms

Before proceeding further, it is crucial to address the scope of our focus on violence, the important issue of definitions, and the differing forms of violence covered in this book. This is a formidable task: the patterns by which aggression can be expressed are enormously varied. Aggression can be manifested, and violence can ensue, from an almost bewildering array of situations. These range from conflict between siblings, playground bullying, sexual rivalries, family feuds, gang fights, affrays in bars, or road rage to parental abuse of children, partner violence, workplace harassment, street robbery, human trafficking, rape, homicide, familicide, torture, and further onward in scale and seriousness to massacres, war, and genocide. Thus the terms *aggression* and *violence* cover an enormous variety of actions, of the processes believed to underlie them, and of the differing patterns they take. To date, as far as we can discern, no one has produced a satisfactory definition of these terms that has achieved a consensus across the range of fields in which they are studied. The two words are sometimes used interchangeably, despite widespread agreement that they refer to different phenomena. But they are very difficult to separate, and there are several ways in which their meanings overlap. One difficulty central to this is the difference between behaviour – the physical actions people make and the things they say – and the thoughts or feelings that precede or accompany them and may give rise to them. That could be seen as a difference between external (violent) and internal (aggressive) events. But behaviour is also sometimes described as aggressive; and thoughts or feelings are often described as violent.

Aggression is most frequently used to describe the experience or expression of antipathetic reactions on the part of one person toward another, though they may also be directed against the self. In either case they may consist of thoughts, feelings, attitudes, motivations or behaviours, but in each case they typically involve an urge to demonstrate those reactions or to inflict damage or some other unwelcome outcome on the recipient. The latter, in Baron and Richardson's (1994) widely used phrase, is generally 'motivated to avoid' such an occurrence. Words used to depict this include anger, acrimony, hostility, hatred, fury, rage, vengefulness or spite.

The word *violence* is more often, though by no means exclusively, used to refer to observable behaviour. It entails the direct infliction of physical, sexual, emotional or other forms of harm on another person. That can be done by assault on the body of the person, and traditionally, a focus on this has been central to most definitions codified in legal statutes in the criminal law. However, the meaning of *violence* has been progressively extended in recent years to include verbal utterances of the kind linked to some of the feelings just mentioned. It is now considered as also including coercive control of one person by another (as in some forms of partner violence or personal intimidation), and more widely still to encompass any situation in which any person is wilfully deprived of legitimate rights by someone else (as in slavery or human trafficking).

The foregoing outline primarily describes what are sometimes called *direct* forms of violence. The perpetrator acts in such a way as to cause bodily or psychological harm to the victim. Equally however, both aggression and violence can be *indirect*, as when someone spreads a malicious rumour about another person, undermines them by removing beneficial opportunities, ignores or marginalises them 'passive-aggressively' or deprives them of the essentials of life as in child neglect.

The WHO have tackled this issue of definition by characterising interpersonal violence as 'the intentional use of physical force or power, threatened or actual, against oneself, another person, or against a group or community, that either results in or has a high likelihood of resulting in injury, death, psychological harm, mal-development or deprivation' (World Health Organization, 1996: cited in Krug et al., 2002), p.5. Subsequently it has been specified as that violence 'which occurs between family members, intimate partners, friends, acquaintances and strangers' and includes child maltreatment, youth violence, intimate partner violence, sexual violence, and elder abuse (World Health Organization, 2014, p. vii). We follow here the WHO approach of distinguishing interpersonal violence from warfare, which, as a form of collective or organised violence, has its own dynamics and special complexities. This leads us to include all types of physical violence from fighting to homicide occurring between two or more people within an otherwise largely pacified society. Obviously there are areas that are difficult to classify; for example, gang warfare in a fragmented society is a form of interpersonal violence bordering on civil warfare. However, the existing distinctions are worth maintaining.

Our core focus here therefore is on aggression as defined by Baron and Richardson (1994) as any act intended to harm another person who is motivated to avoid such harm. We include many types of violence within this core psychological focus, but a central concern is what creates within a person a tendency toward *aggressiveness* defined by Berkowitz (1993, p. 21) as 'a relatively persistent readiness to become aggressive in a variety of different situations'. We include psychological aggression in the absence of physical violence, especially family abuse which causes suffering in itself but is also a common precursor of future violence. To reflect the biopsychosocial approach, in places we also acknowledge the arguments for expanding this psychological definition to incorporate sociological ideas of structural violence based on wider forms of rights violations, such as economic exploitation. We remain, however, concerned with violence by one person or group toward another. Regrettably we exclude here review or discussion of the problem of suicide, which globally leads to more deaths each year than criminal homicide. We regarded this as requiring discussion of many other factors and as being beyond the scope of the present inquiry.

There is one other important distinction worth noting, in conceptualising the difference between *reactive* and *instrumental* aggression. The former refers to aggression that follows directly from feelings of anger, hostility or other strong emotions, which are discharged in response to perceived threat or provocation; this is sometimes said to have the objective of reducing an unpleasant or aversive internal state in the aggressor. Given its connection to the 'heat of the moment', and the discharge of negative feeling, this is sometimes called 'hot' aggression. Instrumental aggression, on the other hand, denotes situations where aggression is used, or individuals are prepared to use it, in a planned or premeditated way to achieve some other purpose, for example in the crime of robbery. This is sometimes described as 'cold' aggression. While the usefulness and even the validity of this distinction has been criticised by some researchers, mainly because the two patterns sometimes overlap, there is good evidence that it is meaningful to separate them, based on both psychometric (Cornell et al., 1996; Polman et al., 2007) and neuro-psychological (Baker et al., 2008; Tuvblad et al., 2009) research.

I.3   Context for This Book

The genesis of this book was a systematic review which we and others conducted to examine the effectiveness of risk assessment tools and interventions for predicting and managing violence (Hockenhull et al., 2012; Leitner et al., 2006; Whittington et al., 2013). That review was commissioned in 2001 by the main health research funding body in England and was deliberately and unusually broad in its scope while retaining the rigour of 'gold standard' systematic review procedures. Some aspects of the review are discussed below in Chapter 8 in relation to pharmacological interventions for violence. Conducting the review made us aware of both the strengths and weaknesses of the current evidence base in relation to violence prevention and treatment. The literature is very large and contains evidence of some effectiveness in reducing the propensity to act aggressively in both clinical and non-clinical groups of violence perpetrators. Significant improvements have been demonstrated with high-risk individuals who have lengthy histories of violence using psychological, pharmacological, and environmental interventions. On the other hand, some of these improvements are quite short-lived, or at least are only measured over short time periods such as a matter of months, and need to be replicated if they are to be trusted as truly robust. Equally, understanding the changes that occur requires a broader overview of why violence arises, including an awareness of both physiological and psychological factors and a contextualisation of violent behaviour within political structures which generate injustice and persecution. So here we have taken the wide-ranging evidence-based emphasis of the original review and attempted to integrate it within a broad conceptual framework that can be mapped onto national policy objectives. In this way we hope current scientific knowledge can be used to improve and advance strategies to address violence as a public health issue.

We have written this book with two audiences primarily in mind. The first group is policymakers working at all levels within national and local governments who need an overview of the key strategies that can be adopted to address interpersonal violence in their country. Working from a public health perspective which emphasises prevention as much as possible over treatment and management, we discuss here the wide range of potential interventions that can be considered to tackle this problem. Some of these interventions map onto the WHO's 'best buy' strategies identified in Chapter 6, but others with credible evidence beyond this 'menu' are also considered. The second audience we have in mind is practitioners across those disciplines with an academic or clinical interest in the problem of interpersonal violence who wish to locate their expertise within the broader biopsychosocial framework. Psychologists, for example, will likely have a firm grasp of the cognitive and behavioural approaches discussed in Chapters 4 and 9 but may wish to contextualise these in a broader framework. The framework here thus incorporates biological and sociological perspectives within an action-oriented public health approach to the problem of violence. Alongside these two specialist groups, we also hope to interest a wider public audience who are concerned about the issue of human violence. We have therefore aimed to keep the discussion here relatively non-technical and to avoid an over-reliance on specialist terms as much as possible.

I.4   Plan of the Book

The book has two parts – the first concerned with explanations of why people act violently and the second with interventions which have been used to address the problem. We begin in Part I by taking a state-of-the-art look at a range of theoretical perspectives, each of which views the problem of violence differently. Each of these perspectives has generated important evidence which must be considered in designing health-based strategies for tackling the problem. In Chapter 1 we set the scene by examining recent trends in the prevalence of human violence and different health-related ways of viewing the concept of violence. In Chapter 2 we look at the origins of human violence through the lens of evolutionary theory where we start to challenge the view that violence is a 'hard-wired' feature of human conduct, i.e. an element of our biological nature from which we cannot escape. In Chapter 3 we consider the genetics of violence and evaluate the status of evidence concerning the possible role of hereditary factors in creating persons disposed to act violently. In Chapter 4 we consider the various psychosocial processes which can underpin the development of a propensity toward the use of aggression We then end Part I with an examination of the idea of structural violence and its various permutations in Chapter 5. Violence is a multifaceted subject and many other angles could be adopted to view the problem. But we believe these various biopsychosocial perspectives cover much of the field and provide a strong foundation for the public health approach.

In Part II we shift toward an emphasis on potential solutions derived from the fundamental perspectives in Part I. In Chapter 6 we examine the WHO strategy in detail as it provides a policy platform for large-scale evidence-based interventions based on national action plans. In Chapter 7 we examine research-led advances in the field of violence risk assessment and consider how well any proneness to violence can be identified, at least in individuals considered to present some elevated risk. The final three chapters then explore the recent evidence on interventions for violence-prone individuals. These are considered, respectively, at the pharmacological level (Chapter 8), the psychosocial level (Chapter 9) and finally at the broader social level using multilevel programmes tackling structural and other factors (Chapter 10). We conclude with an outlook toward the future in terms of developing effective interventions rooted in a comprehensive understanding of the phenomenon of human violence. Effective interventions for violence are emerging and improving at a steady pace and the potential for an evidence-based solution to this enduring problem has never been greater.

Part I

Origins

1   The Prospect of Human Violence
Pessimism or Realism?

1.1   Human Violence: The Tendency to Pessimism

Violence is a global problem with a history as long as human evolution. It has a recurring presence in our lives, either directly when we are exposed to hostile words and actions by people around us or indirectly through a steady stream of news and frequent portrayals in fiction which turn us into more or less willing witnesses of other people's violence or victimisation. Violence blights our lives through actual harm or through the fear and wariness generated by hearing and seeing what happens to others. Even if we escape exposure to actual violence throughout our lives, our sense of safety in the world will be shaped and distorted by media reports of what is happening nearby and far away. So in trying to think about and tackle the problem of human violence, there is a real risk of despair followed by resignation or calls for a crackdown on whoever is seen as the guilty party. The problem is undeniably complex with multiple inter-related causes and widespread impacts across huge populations and specific vulnerable individuals. Some even see it as beyond definition as a concept (Schinkel, 2010), making prevention efforts ultimately meaningless. But complexity is only part of the problem underpinning our attitude to violence. Deeper social forces are operating which can lead us toward a sense of hopelessness about the future.

Public and media discussions of violence often create a real sense that things are getting worse every year and that violence, like global climate change, is an unstoppable process involving the destruction and disruption of the lives of millions of people. This can come from a basic view that human nature inevitably includes a tendency to use aggression for grasping resources and even just for the pleasure of exerting power. This world view is widespread and shapes our expectations about other people whether nearby or more distant. For instance, youth violence rates dropped significantly in the United States in the 1980s and 1990s, but at the same time media coverage of the issue actually increased. In one case, media articles on juvenile delinquency did so by nearly 700% over the same period that juvenile arrest rates dropped by more than 10% (Nichols, 2011). The dominant narrative of the media coverage at the time also simplistically tended toward an explanation of violent behaviour as a feature of a 'deviant individual' while ignoring the full range of factors influencing any violent act. The daily drip-feed of such a narrative inevitably shapes how the public in Western and other countries view the problem and shows how pressure mounts on policymakers and lawmakers to do something to tackle these 'deviant individuals'.

It has been said before (Pinker, 2011), and we repeat and amplify it here, that pessimism about human violence in contemporary societies is misplaced and should be replaced by evidence-based realism. There are two dimensions to what we consider to be widespread negativity about the problem of human violence and both need to be addressed. First, there is a sense that we live today in historically violent times with more death and destruction than there has ever been before. This could be called *epidemiological* pessimism. Second, there is a repeated message that we as a species are 'hard-wired' to be violent. This message, derived largely from the media but with some reference to serious scientific research, reinvents the old idea that human beings have a genetic propensity to act competitively and, where necessary, violently which has been honed over several million years of hominid evolution. This emphasis on the innate is a form of *causal* pessimism. The first of these ideas, the epidemiological variety, is quite easy to refute and several authors have tackled it (e.g. Pinker, 2011). There is now plentiful evidence of societies pacifying themselves around the world and an increased understanding of how this process of pacification can be extended further. Causal pessimism is more complex and deep-rooted and requires more detailed analysis to test its assumptions against the evidence. Much of this book is an attempt to conduct a sustained enquiry of that kind and to weigh up the evidence for theories of violence which emphasise either internal or external factors in human aggression. The balance of this evidence will enable us to judge the credibility of the 'hard-wired' proposition.

Causal pessimism raises at least three key questions. First: Is violence *inevitable*? Must we accept that, despite every effort to tackle the problem at individual and the societal levels, there will always be a relatively large group of people in any community who engage in attacks on others? Most of the first part of this book (Chapters 1–5) is concerned with this issue. Second, if it is inevitable, is violence *predictable*? For instance, to what extent can we identify who is going to be violent, how they will do it, and when and where? Large strides have been taken in the field of violence risk assessment in the past three decades at the individual level.

But the science of prediction remains incomplete, and this hampers the ability to develop effective prevention programmes. This is a particular focus in Chapter 7. Third, when those at risk have been identified, how successful are different types of *intervention* at reducing the identified risk in the short term or the long term? Again, recent research has generated some potentially effective interventions at the individual and social levels, and many of these interventions will be reviewed in the second part of this book (Chapter 6 and Chapters 8–10) together with the thinking that underlies them and evaluation of their effects.

With all of these questions, there is a political decision to be made about how much resource should be devoted to widescale preventive initiatives which aim to nip many problems in the bud but which potentially will be wasted on an enormous number of other buds who were never going to be a problem. Conversely, what proportion should be spent on those who have already matured into high-risk and dangerous adults, who might benefit from intensive management and intervention but whose management will therefore be extremely costly per head? In short, what is the trade-off between public health and clinical approaches to preventing violence? Our approach to interrogating the evidence in this book is built around the public health model for both preventing and reducing violent behaviour (Mercy et al., 1993) and will examine the effectiveness of interventions at both ends of this spectrum.

These are all large and important questions, and if we adopt a global perspective, we should be aware throughout of the paradox that almost all of the research to be examined here takes place in those rich, mainly Western, countries. They have lower rates of interpersonal violence in the twenty-first century, and have many more resources than those countries where the problem is greatest (Hughes et al., 2014). There are signs of a shift toward more intervention and research in a wider range of cultures driven largely by the World Health Organization's commitment to prioritising this issue (WHO, 2014) discussed here in Chapter 6. But the Western-centric bias in the evidence base must be considered at all times when reflecting on the conclusions that we draw here.

Violence is ultimately an individual act where one person deliberately causes, directly or remotely, physical harm to another. But each act occurs within a particular context and is the outcome of a unique set of circumstances. It is always an action by an individual, but its meaning and expression is always a feature of the society or institution within which it occurs. Contrary to the usual assumptions about a human propensity for violence, most people actually find it quite hard to be violent and experience intense distress when they are forced to (Collins, 2008). This social context for any violent act is the basis on which the grounds for an evidence-based realism about reducing violence in the future can be built. While we as twenty-first-century individuals still have the same biological capacity for violence as our prehistoric ancestors, many of our societies and institutions are less violent now than they were 500 years ago. Something has changed at the social and psychological level to make this possible. As we work out what these changes are and what caused them through patient and often laborious research, we can harness this knowledge to accelerate social development away from conflict toward more peaceful neighbourhoods and societies.

There are, to be sure, many pockets of extreme violence, often very large and deep, in many parts of the world, and we must not be naïve as to how overt physical violence has often mutated into economic and environmental violence. But overall, human society has undergone a historical process of pacification with a move away from large-scale, widespread homicide and warfare. Clearly, our social structures have evolved over the past 10,000 years, while our brains have not changed at all anatomically (having 'plateaued' in size, and as far as is known having had the same internal conformation, from around 100,000 years ago; Striedter, 2005). And if our social structures can change so rapidly in this way, changes in our individual mental structures- which underpin personal perceptions of threat and our choices toward or away from violence- are likely to be changing alongside.

1.2   The Decline in Rates of Interpersonal Violence

To deal first with epidemiological pessimism, numerous reliable data sources can be used to demonstrate that, rather than being a problem that is inevitable and gradually worsening, rates of human violence fluctuate over long time periods and in some ways are decreasing. For instance, with regard to warfare, there is evidence that the traditional type of conflict, large-scale wars between sovereign nations, has become much less frequent since the end of the Second World War. Systematic analysis of conflicts which meet the criteria of an 'interstate war' indicate that in the 1950s and 1960s there were often eight or nine such wars ongoing around the world each year, but by the 1990s this had dropped to fewer than five (Gleditsch et al., 2002). The number of deaths in these wars also fell from approximately 2 to 3 million deaths per year in the 1980s to well under a million per year in the 1990s and the first decade of the twenty-first century (Human Security Report Project 2013, p. 18). This downward historical trend in war deaths is stable despite some obvious upswings during the Vietnam era in the 1970s and the Iran/Iraq/Afghanistan conflicts of the 1980s and 1990s. The probability of war between two democracies was 75% lower in the 1980s than it was a century before and has been close to zero (Cederman, 2001). Wars between developed nations have been so rare in the recent past that some have called war itself an obsolescent institution (Mueller, 2004). Nevertheless it must be acknowledged that new types of hybrid warfare fought by criminal gangs, mercenaries, and freebooters led by warlords within countries lacking effective unified governance have escalated (Kaldor, 2013) and in some cases now cause more deaths than interstate wars of the last century.

Away from war, however undisciplined, our focus here is on interpersonal violence within otherwise largely stable, pacified societies. New international structures and programmes are being developed based on reframing interpersonal violence as a public health problem, as much as one related to criminal justice or community security, and based on delivering social and psychological initiatives built on evidence where they are needed most. The most prominent of these initiatives is the Global Campaign for Violence Prevention (GCVP) led and coordinated by the World Health Organization (2019a). This campaign builds on a number of WHO initiatives and policies produced from the 1990s onward, which are summarised in the Appendix. Two of the key elements in this programme are the World Report on Violence and Health (World Health Organization, 2002) and the follow-up Global Status Report on Violence Prevention (World Health Organization, 2014). Taken together, these initiatives signify that for the first time in human history, a global plan has been adopted at the highest level of world governance to do something about interpersonal violence worldwide. Just as the UN Security Council has been successful for seventy years in helping to prevent international destruction through nuclear conflict between nations and the UN more widely is working toward preventing such destruction through climate change, the WHO arm of the UN is now beginning also to address intra-national destruction through interpersonal violence.

The UN has had a position on the issue of interpersonal violence for more than thirty years. As we discuss further in Chapter 3, the United Nations Educational, Scientific and Cultural Organization (UNESCO) made a declaration (the Seville Statement) clearly advocating the view that violence is preventable and therefore not an inevitable feature of human life. This rejection of inevitability shows its commitment to adopting a constructive perspective on the problem and the potential for change. There is nothing that has been discovered in the years since then to suggest the opposite. If anything, the violence prevention science literature has swollen since the 1980s, and the problem has now become one of selecting (and resourcing) the right approach from many options rather than bemoaning the lack of any options at all.

A starting point for the GCVP has been estimating the size of the problem of interpersonal violence on a global scale and how recent trends might vary across the world. Unlike the warfare casualty estimates discussed above which largely rely on academics compiling data sets from various fragmented sources, the GCVP asked government agencies in UN member states to provide the relevant national homicide figures contained in either police reports or prevalence surveys for the period 2000–2012. In countries where homicide data of a high quality were available, these were directly entered into the analysis, and where the data were poor quality or simply unavailable, estimates were made using statistical modelling. While violence rates are never perfectly reliable and are often very unreliable, homicide rates are likely to be the most dependable aspect because of the seriousness of the crime in all human societies, its high visibility in many cases and the availability of national contacts.

More than 130 countries with a combined population of 6.1 billion people representing 88% of the world's population responded with information. When the data are combined (see Figure 1.1), it is clear that there has been a steady decrease in the recorded homicide rate over this relatively short and recent period. Globally, the rate declined by 16% (from 8.0 to 6.7 per 100,000 population), and while the decline has been particularly marked in high-income countries (39%), the decline was also 10% or more in middle-income and low-income countries (World Health Organization, 2014).

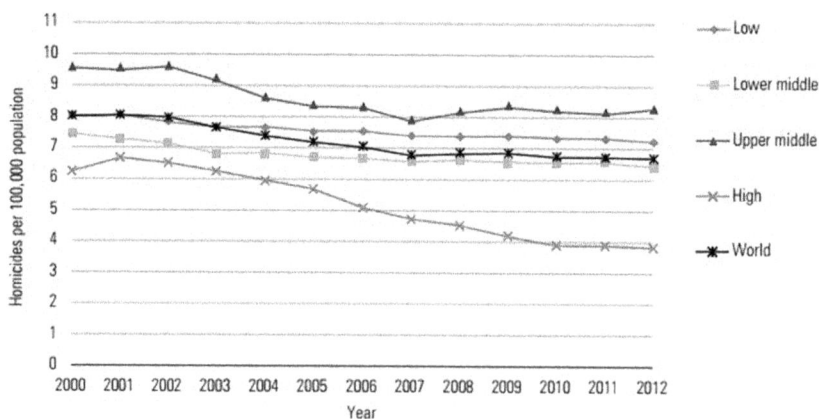

Figure 1.1 Global homicide rates by country income group, 2000–2012.
Source: World Health Organization, 2014.

This global trend fits well with other survey evidence which in some regions of the world can be traced over longer time periods than the single decade here. In the vast majority (>80%) of European countries, for instance, there was an average year-on-year homicide reduction in the two decades prior to 2008 (Marshall and Summers, 2012). This reduction was highest in Albania where it approached an 8% year-on-year decrease, but it also exceeded a healthy 3% in a wide range of other countries. Some of these large, consistent reductions reflect political reconfigurations in Eastern Europe (e.g. Slovenia, Croatia, Latvia, Ukraine, Slovakia) and Northern Ireland, but other rapidly pacifying countries (e.g. Austria, Portugal, Italy) were politically stable throughout and managed to achieve these reductions as part of the normal work of established governments.

There are many examples of further medium-term reductions in and beyond Europe (Eisner and Nivette, 2012). The United States, Colombia, and South Africa all experienced mean annual declines of more than 3% in homicide rates from the early 1990s to 2009–2010, and Japan had a similar rate of reduction from the 1950s to 1990. Again, the reductions in Colombia and South Africa are clearly related to successful conflict resolution at a national or subnational level, but the Japanese and American improvements require other explanations beyond the resolution of civil or hybrid wars and the elimination of internal intergroup strife. Within Europe, the most recent Crime Survey for England and Wales (Office for National Statistics, 2019) noted that, while some concerns about increased rates of assaults with knives are justified, the 2018 homicide rate in England and Wales has resumed a downward trend which has been observed consistently for much of the past two decades.

It is important to acknowledge that this recent drop in homicide rates since 1990 follows a steep increase in rates in the 1970s and 1980s in some countries which in turn was preceded by low rates in the 1950s and 1960s (Mercy et al., 1993). While it would be simplistic to deduce from this that there is a twenty-year cycle of increasing and decreasing homicide rates, it must make us wary of becoming overconfident about the prospects for crime reduction.

Extending the time frame even further, for Europe at least where the records allow, the WHO trend in Figure 1.1 can be seen as the continuation of a long-term process which has been ongoing since the Middle Ages when homicide rates are estimated to have been ten times higher than the figure for the twentieth century (Eisner, 2003; Spierenburg, 2012). This massive reduction over several centuries has been ascribed to a 'civilising process' linked in Europe to the development of nations (Elias, 2000), but its existence and explanation beyond that region are unknown due to the absence of comparable statistical records. Also, nations such as Japan and the United States which have experienced the large reductions noted above over a period when their national integrity remained largely unchanged suggests that something else is contributing and that civilising is a necessary but no longer sufficient basis for violence reduction. However even when two countries have experienced similar trends of pacification like this, it remains very difficult to draw conclusions as the two examples here are so different in many ways, especially in terms of their approaches to gun control.

Whatever the causes, this all contributes a significant counterpoint against the traditional gloomy narrative about human violence and suggests at least that there are grounds for some optimism when considering this seemingly intractable problem. Various points must be borne in mind though to ensure we are aware of the challenges faced when drawing conclusions on this question.

First, the quality of the data varies across countries, and both police records and national prevalence surveys have shortcomings as sources of reliable information. Crime statistics are far from being neutral pieces of information and serve many purposes in addition to simply informing the design or delivery of criminal justice systems or health services (Lysova, 2018). None of these statistics is perfect, and the serious weaknesses of some estimates have been pointed out. This is especially the case for sub-Saharan Africa where estimates in various other WHO surveys have had to be inferred statistically from neighbouring countries (Human Security Report Project, 2013). Also political factors are likely to interfere with the willingness of some countries to provide valid and reliable information.

Furthermore the overall reduction masks some important changes of patterns within types of homicide. In particular, the proportion of all homicide which is due to violence from intimate partners has increased steadily over the long term (Spierenburg, 2012). This suggests certain types of violence remain either stubbornly resistant to intervention at the social or psychological level or have not been seen as sufficiently problematic to merit intervention in the first place.

Whatever the real longitudinal trend, it is clear from Figure 1.1 that, like warfare, homicide is not equally distributed around the world. Middle- and low-income countries clearly suffer high rates compared with their richer counterparts. More than half of all global homicides take place in the 25% most violent countries in the world, and these high-risk countries share certain characteristics. Some of these are listed in Table 1.1 and are compared with those in low-homicide countries. It is clear from this that the likeliest routes toward achieving lower homicide rates, not surprisingly, are through good governance and effective

Table 1.1 *Characteristics of high- and low-rate homicide countries*

High homicide rate
- High state corruption
- Low investment in public health and education
- Low state stability
- Ethnic, ideological, and/or religious cleavages
- High inequality (regardless of high or low national income)
- High divorce rates
- High population growth
- Young population
- Latin-American location
- Predominance of homicides between acquaintances and strangers
- High involvement of elite members
- Predominantly male victims

Low homicide rate
- Functioning and stable state
- State accountable to citizens
- Effective public health, education and criminal justice systems
- Relatively low social inequality
- Citizens who actively engage in matters of shared concern
- High levels of social welfare
- Ethnic homogeneity
- Modernisation and development
- Relatively large proportion of domestic homicides
- Marginalised perpetrators
- Relatively high proportion of female victims

Source: Eisner, 2012; Eisner and Nivette, 2012; Nivette, 2011; Wolf et al., 2014.

policing, for both of which greater prosperity is probably a prerequisite. But effective governance and low homicide rates are really two sides of the same coin. The challenge is to enhance such governance into regions where it is currently absent, and the recent history of imposing such regimes from the outside has been extremely problematic.

1.3   Violence as a Health Issue

Violence is a multidimensional problem. Some of the political and socio-logical dimensions have been introduced earlier, and in later chapters we will consider what we know, for instance, about the genetic aspects as well. The problem also has ethical and legal dimensions largely outside our scope. But the angle we take here is very specifically one which views violence from a health perspective. Violence obviously damages people's health, and some forms of illness are associated with an increased likelihood of violence. It is becoming clear that treating interpersonal violence as a health problem like any other could provide the basis for a potentially valuable new way of tackling the issue. We should emphasise that viewing violence in this way is not the same as defining it as a medical problem. Effective health interventions generally, and public health interventions in particular, require a multidisciplinary approach drawing on social science as much as medicine. As discussed further below, there is a clinical aspect to some violence which requires a more explicitly medicalised approach. But in addressing the overall global problem of violence, this applies only to a small minority of violent acts committed by people with some forms of psychopathology. The bigger problem of worldwide 'violence epidemics' can gain little from focusing on this highly restricted subgroup of people with uncommon problems and behaviours.

This approach means trying to understand the causes of violence in a way that can be used to design specific initiatives for reducing its chances of occurring. The contributing causes can be identified and the potential interventions can be implemented at the national, local or individual levels. That does not mean that there needs to be a diagnosed physical or mental health problem for an individual to be eligible for an intervention to reduce their violence. Alternatively, it may be the overall health of a society or of a particular population that is at risk and would benefit from effective preventive strategies, as for example in a school-wide anti-bullying programme. Individually focused clinical interventions, on the other hand, are designed for individuals who on the basis of previous violent behaviour are assessed as posing a high risk of committing further assaults.

The key point is to distinguish this health-based approach from the other principal way of thinking about and responding to violence which is based on viewing it as a criminal and moral issue requiring punishment. This justice-based paradigm has a pivotal place of course, but viewing violence from a health-based perspective does not mean abandoning that perspective. Any violent act can, and should, be evaluated both ethically and scientifically at the same time, and society undoubtedly needs multiple perspectives in order to respond fully to the problem. But our emphasis here is on intervening with those who have acted violently based on an improved understanding of what has influenced their actions rather than taking a moral position on certain types of behaviour.

Violence has always been a health-related issue in the broadest sense of being a challenge which needs to be understood as well as judged, and in some cases also in the stricter sense of being a manifestation or a result of an individual health problem. Philosophers and scientists have tried to understand human violence at least since the time of Aristotle, who could be said to have adopted a sociological approach in recognising poverty as the source of crime (Aristotle, 2000). In the stricter sense, the role of mental illness in the causation of violence has also been debated since the ancient Greeks, who sometimes saw anger as a form of insanity (Harris, 2004). The reverse relationship, violence as a cause of ill-health (death and injury), has been self-evident since human beings became capable of abstract thought and reflection on the concept of intentionality when harming others.

However, the idea of trying to understand violence, as opposed to just punishing it, became prominent in the West only with the European Enlightenment ideas of the eighteenth century. The systematic study of violence as a manifestation of some forms of mental illness started influencing medicine only in the nineteenth century with the establishment of the asylum system. Recognition of the relationships, and the potential therefore to intervene for prevention purposes, was confirmed when the first criminal asylum in the world was set up at Broadmoor in England in 1863.

Regardless of this growing science of violence and mental illness in a small group of severely disturbed individuals, such as the young offenders whom the child psychiatrist William Healy treated at the Juvenile Psychopathic Institute in Chicago, established in 1909, the wider problem of violence in Western societies was still viewed predominantly in terms of criminality right up until the 1990s (Mercy et al., 1993). But the past twenty years has seen a spreading application of the health/illness perspective beyond the small number of high-risk people incarcerated in Broadmoor Hospital and similar settings to the whole of civil society. Death from interpersonal violence has moved from being seen as a simply a crime or at most a matter of individual illness in certain 'abnormal' individuals to become a matter of public health concern like death from poor sanitation or road traffic crashes. Adopting this public health approach enables all the lessons learned from dealing successfully with previous 'epidemics' such as these to be applied to tackling violence.

However, the public health model being expanded on and advanced here is not the same as a medical or disease model, and needs to be distinguished from those approaches. It is not assumed that there is any single identifiable pathogen at work in causing violence, nor that the underlying explanation is a physical or biological one. Nor is violence considered to be a direct consequence of some form of health deficiency as such, as in behavioural terms it is if anything the opposite: a form of excess. Rather, in this approach, demographic, economic, lifestyle or other types of data are analysed to discover their associations with homicide or other forms of violence. Relatedly, the public health model is not an attempt to formulate a general theory of the causes of violence. Rather, it uses the methodology of epidemiological research to investigate patterns of relationships between contributing factors at national or local levels. Therefore, factors of several kinds – biological, psychological and social/cultural – are taken into account in seeking to address how violence has occurred and thereby how it might be reduced. Its disavowal of a simplistic, merely biological causation and its embracing of a multiplicity of interacting causal factors accords fully with the rewired biopsychosocial approach we are also developing in this context.

The health paradigm thus has much to offer in developing new ways of tackling the problem of interpersonal violence. It has been applied in attempts to develop models for reducing gun violence in the United States (Butkus et al., 2018), and for countering violent extremism (Centers for Disease Control and Prevention, 2000). But human violence and human health are intertwined in many ways. These other interconnections are worth exploring before considering the public health approach more closely.

1.4   Violence, Death, and Physical Injury

The most obvious consequence of a violent assault is physical injury and, at its most extreme, injury resulting in death. Homicide, the intentional killing of another person, is the most serious criminal offence for which an individual can be prosecuted and the one most commonly punishable by death even to this day in some countries. Various trends in homicide over the past few decades and centuries were examined above, and some grounds for cautious were noted. But it is also true that these overall trends mask some important variations between different social groups in terms of exposure to lethal violence.

Homicide itself has a very different profile from other types of violence which are serious but non-lethal. Men, for instance, are four times more likely to die from homicide than women (World Health Organization, 2014), and young people aged fifteen to twenty-nine years are at least three times more at risk than children or those aged sixty years or more regardless of gender. Young males therefore are at huge relative risk with a death rate that is nearly six times that for women in the same age group. Relationships between victims and aggressors also differ by gender as women are at least six times more likely than men to be killed by an intimate partner (Stöckl et al., 2013). Furthermore, use of weapons in homicide also varies geographically, with three-quarters of homicides in low- and middle-income countries in North and South America involving a firearm compared with only a quarter of those in similar countries in Europe.

Beyond homicide, non-fatal violence also causes enormous damage in terms of injury and, in the longer term, illness. Statistics on global rates of non-fatal violence are not nearly as reliable as those for homicide (which themselves are often questionable as noted above), but a variety of regional and national studies illustrate some of the variations. Again, most victims of non-fatal violence are male and the most at-risk age group are those aged under thirty years (World Health Organization, 2014). However, nearly half (42%) of women exposed to intimate partner violence (IPV) suffer physical injury of some sort as a result (World Health Organization, 2013a). The injuries and musculoskeletal disorders caused by such violence are among the top twenty leading causes of disease burden for women, similar in impact epidemiologically to that caused by high cholesterol or a low vegetable diet (Lim et al., 2012). Beyond these immediate injuries, exposure to IPV is associated with long-term physical effects such as significantly raised levels of HIV infection and sexually transmitted diseases, increased abortion rates and a range of health problems for infants including prematurity and low birth weight. Direct exposure to violence as a child can also have a long-term impact on physical health over the life course, including increased rates of sexually transmitted infections, obesity, smoking, arthritis, ulcers and headache/migraine (Norman et al., 2012).

So interpersonal violence causes immediate physical damage, and exposure to chronic violence is linked to ill health for many years afterward. Violence causes injury and illness, but, conversely, illness and physical trauma can lead to violence. Physical pain is both a feature of many illnesses and a well-known trigger for violence. It can lower a person's frustration threshold and thus increase the risk of lashing out in provoking situations (Winstanley and Whittington, 2004). Certain injuries, especially brain trauma, are sometimes linked to a systematically higher risk of violence (Fazel et al., 2009b) because of the reduced inhibition which can often result. This is not to say that afflicted individuals in these groups are at risk, but it does demonstrate that the pathway between physical health and violence runs in both directions.

1.5   Violence and Mental Health

These physical effects of violence on the body are usually visible, but the impact of violence on mental health is more hidden, and the converse relationship between mental illness and a propensity for violence is highly contentious. Exposure to severe violence, either as a victim or as a witness, can be a traumatic event and so can lead to the disabling symptoms of post-traumatic stress disorder. But the perception of traumatic events is subjective, and exposure even to less severe violence can be similarly traumatising for the victim if they perceived their life or physical integrity to be in danger. Sustained exposure to less serious violence is also important as it is linked to a whole range of poor outcomes especially for children. Compared with the general population, women exposed to IPV are nearly twice as likely to have depressive episodes and alcohol use disorders and nearly five times as likely to commit suicide (World Health Organization, 2013a). Exposure to physical abuse as a child multiplies a person's later risk of suicidal behaviour threefold. It also more than doubles the risk of behavioural disorders, conduct disorders and drug use and increases the risk of depression and anxiety disorders by 50% (Norman et al., 2012).

More difficult to establish and controversial is the reverse relationship between mental disorder and a propensity to engage in violence. Mental illness itself is a highly contested and very broad concept covering a wide range of human behaviours and experiences, and most of the forms it takes have no association with violence. In other words, most people suffering from some form of mental illness are no more likely to be violent than people in the general population. People with some disorders, for instance depression, may actually be less likely to be violent, so that mental illness becomes a protective factor against dangerousness in these cases. Nevertheless, about 10% of homicides in England and Wales, for instance, are committed by people who have been in recent contact with mental health services (National Confidential Inquiry into Suicide and Homicide by People with Mental Illness, 2014). This does not in itself reflect an increased risk, but it does indicate the need to examine the pathway between active illness and violent behaviour.

For context, the main diagnostic systems for mental illness, the International Classification of Diseases (Mental and Behavioural Disorders) of the WHO (ICD-11; World Health Organization, 2019b) and the American Diagnostic and Statistical Manual of Mental Disorders (American Psychiatric Association, 2013), list numerous diagnostic categories. Of all these different forms of mental disturbance, most attention in terms of violence research has been focused on just two categories, schizophrenia and personality disorder, with some lesser attention to bipolar disorder, neurocognitive disorders, and substance misuse disorders.

A series of reviews has confirmed the view that experiencing active symptoms of psychosis (a subset of the diagnosis of schizophrenia involving hallucinations and delusions in particular) is associated with an increased likelihood of violent behaviour (Douglas et al., 2009). One estimate is that an active diagnosis of schizophrenia or psychosis more specifically quadruples the risk of violence among men and multiplies the risk for women eight-fold (Fazel et al., 2009a) compared with the general population. The key word here is 'active': historic labels and diagnoses from earlier in life are not relevant if the person is not actively ill. Such unjustified labels are part of the stigma faced by people with mental health problems in everyday life and contribute to the rejection and isolation faced by many.

The inflated violence risk rate that has been linked to active schizophrenia and psychosis becomes multiplied further when combined with certain other factors. In particular, additional clinical problems involving substance abuse and not adhering to prescribed treatment significantly multiplies the strength of the association between psychosis and violence (Witt et al., 2013). In short, taking the wrong drugs, on the one hand, and not taking the right ones, on the other, makes psychosis riskier than it would be otherwise. Similar inflated risk rates have been found when substance abuse is mixed with bipolar disorder (Fazel et al., 2010) and personality disorder (Yu et al., 2012).

It seems indisputable therefore that some specific forms of active mental and personality disorder are linked to an increased propensity for violence in certain circumstances. Nevertheless it is only a propensity: the social and interpersonal circumstances which trigger the actual violence in the context of mental illness are likely to be similar to those implicated in violence by everybody else such as perceived threat, provocation or frustration. So, alternative cognitive and behavioural coping strategies in threatening situations can be developed to minimize the likelihood that the risk and arousal are translated into an assault. Violence in this respect is very clearly a health issue, and pharmacological and psychological therapies to be discussed in Chapters 8 and 9 can play a central role in reducing the risk.

To counterbalance this finding, and perhaps to understand it more fully, it is important to note that individuals experiencing mental health problems are also much more likely to be subjected to violence than are those in the general population. They are at least twice as likely to be victims of crime in general and, for some crimes, more than one hundred times more likely to be victimised (Maniglio, 2009). Roughly one in six (16%) of people with psychosis becomes a victim of violence in the United Kingdom over an average twelve-month period, a rate which is more than double the proportion in the general population. People with a psychosis who are at risk of being assaulted are particularly vulnerable in a number of ways: they tend to be more ill, homeless, misusing drugs and are more likely to have a personality disorder alongside their mental illness. When interviewed about their experience, they feel, perhaps not surprisingly, more threatened and unsafe in their everyday lives as well. The fact that they were also more likely to admit assaulting other people as well indicates again the interactional nature of interpersonal violence and the volatile subcultures that many tend to live within (Walsh et al., 2003).

It is always important to stress in this context that most violence in society is committed by people who have no symptoms of mental disorder and that most mentally ill people are never violent. However, the propensity for some types of mental illness to be associated with violence in certain circumstances is undeniable, and the pathway from mental illness to violence provides an important focus for targeting therapeutic interventions for victims and perpetrators alike.

1.6   Violence as a Clinical Issue

Prior to the 1990s health-based interventions for violence were focused on a small but important group of offenders and patients with severe problems who required intensive individualised interventions of some sort, usually in a hospital or prison. This 'high-risk' group remains a priority even in the new era of public health approaches to violence to be discussed in the next section. Effective prevention was probably never offered to this group of people, and, as a result, they have developed a tendency toward seriously dangerous behaviour and attitudes which are beyond the reach of public health campaigns or advocacy. They are the ones who were left behind in the past in high-risk family and social environments untouched by the sporadic preventive and early intervention approaches of the past.

People with these severe violence problems are often incarcerated but they also can still benefit from a range of evidence-based interventions which have been developed over the past twenty years and which are discussed further in Chapter 9. Effective intervention can lead to discharge and successful reintegration into society, so it is important to seek to achieve the optimal combination of prevention and intervention. Too much emphasis on prevention leaves the lives of those who already have shown evidence of a propensity toward violence untouched. Looking to the future, it is possible to imagine that prevention could be so successful in the coming century that there could be very large reductions in the rates of many types of violence. But any realistic aspiration for a peaceful future must include recognition that there will probably always be some situations that evoke violent responses, and potentially some people beyond the reach of the most intensive and successful prevention programmes.

High-risk people are relatively small in number, but they are account-able for a large proportion of violent events whether in institutions or wider society. In Sweden, for instance, 1% of the total general population were involved in nearly two-thirds of all convictions for violent crime over a forty-year period (Falk et al., 2014). This ultra-high-risk group was predominantly male and had a range of distinct characteristics compared with other violent offenders who were only involved in a small number of violent crimes. These included high rates of personality disorder, convic-tions for violent crime before the age of nineteen, convictions for non-violent crime, drug-related offenses, mental health disorders and sub-stance use disorder.

If we define the very high-risk group as being those people convicted of twelve or more violent crimes (about 2,300 people in Sweden, 0.1% of the population) and they were targeted for sustained and intensive intervention, it is estimated that the number of violent crimes in that country could be reduced by more than 15% (Falk et al., 2014). Targeting a numerically larger high-risk group, those with at least three violent offences (1% of the population), could lead to a reduction in all convictions greater than 50%. Within institutions such as prisons and hospitals, the same pattern emerges (Grassi et al., 2008). In one Italian hospital, seven patients (less than 1% of those admitted, and all with an active diagnosis of schizophrenia) were involved in nearly half of all registered incidents.

Clearly there is a justification for working very hard with these rela-tively small groups to facilitate behavioural changes through support, therapy and effective sanctions which, if nothing else, could reduce the reliance on costly incarceration. Within hospitals, if members of this group can be identified early on during admission, interventions can be introduced to predict and manage potential violence. Then there is scope for more effective use of resources to pacify the atmosphere on psychi-atric wards so that other patients and staff feel safe and able to benefit from a therapeutic milieu.

There are numerous clinical interventions to counter the propensity to violence, many with distinctive 'brand names' but largely overlapping principles. The research literature on this topic is enormous and expanding rapidly year on year (Whittington et al., 2013), but, in general, clinical interventions can be broadly considered as having an assessment phase and an intervention phase. The science of clinical violence risk assessment alone has generated a large number of tools over the past twenty years with less than perfect predictive accuracy but also a small number of tools with an accumulating evidence base for usefulness (Hockenhull et al., 2012). The corresponding literature on interventions for clinical violence is smaller because of the greater challenges in implementing and testing entire programmes rather than relatively brief one-off assessments. A distinction should also be made between treatment of a propensity for violence and management of actual violent acts through restraint or emergency sedation for instance. Treatments are designed to introduce stable improvements in how a person acts in the future, whereas management of violence merely prevents immediate harm to those around the violent person (National Institute for Health and Care Excellence, 2015). Overall such interventions can then be divided according to whether they are primarily pharmacological, psychological or environmental in their approach (Hockenhull et al., 2012). These approaches and the growing evidence base around them will be discussed further in Chapters 7–9.

1.7   Violence as a Public Health Issue

The links between violence and health have long been recognised at this individual level, but more recently there has been a major shift in perspective toward considering the problem instead as a public health issue with multiple widespread causes and effects spread across large populations. This approach draws on the metaphor of violence as an epidemic which is comparable to infectious diseases. In this way the success achieved and lessons learned while eradicating such diseases as smallpox might be creatively applied to the prevention of violence. A new optimism about dealing with a problem that has often been seen as intractable and inevitable then becomes possible.

Reductions in death and injury from road crashes since the 1960s through redesigning cars and roads is an example of how this sort of approach can be used. The metaphor has even been extended to include the idea of violence as contagious in that exposure to it as a child or young person can increase the risk of manifestation in later life (Bellis et al., 2012). Exposure to violence can also interfere with other public health objectives such as increasing physical activity, since fear of violence can lead people to avoid open spaces for exercise and use their cars rather than walking or taking public transport.

This public health approach now dominates national and international strategies for dealing with violence. It underpins the GCVP programme run by the WHO and similar national initiatives run by the American and British governments for instance. The WHO global strategy will be discussed in Chapter 6. At a national level, there are examples of large-scale, well-funded population-based approaches such as the Violence Prevention Programme coordinated by the Centers for Disease Control and Prevention in the United States. In England, the Department of Health has produced a similar strategy to coordinate action addressing a number of problems across the life course of the general population away from institutions. The key idea underpinning both approaches is a shift away from a reactive response focused on perpetrators 'at the sharp end' in prisons and hospitals toward an integrated preventive system coordinated by various state agencies and the voluntary sector but based in local communities. The approach is proactive, targeting those who are seen as more or less 'at risk' of being violent before they commit an offence rather than after the event (Mercy et al., 1993). Changes can be implemented at the level of an individual person's attitudes, skills or knowledge, as in the clinical approach, but also at the level of the person's physical or social environment.

Attempts to reduce violence using a public health approach are often divided into three categories according to their emphasis (Guerra et al., 1994; Limbos et al., 2007). *Primary prevention* refers to projects that are delivered universally to avert the onset of problem behaviour, by providing services to children, families or whole communities. Such actions are widely endorsed in the WHO framework for violence reduction (World Health Organization, 2014). *Secondary prevention* refers to work carried out with those assessed as being at increased risk of becoming involved in delinquency, such as children not attending school, or who are involved in bullying. *Tertiary prevention* denotes work carried out with those who have already committed violent offences of some sort. For instance, in the criminal justice system, adjudicated offenders who have been convicted of offences and are currently under sentence in some part of the penal system (supervision by youth justice or probation services, or detention in prisons or other institutions, for example) would be eligible. Pharmacological treatments are a key element of how some persistently violent people with clinical problems are managed.

Setting up an effective public health programme involves four main steps. These are:

- detecting trends in violence through data collection
- identifying risk and protective factors
- developing and testing interventions based on these factors, and
- widely and deeply implementing successful interventions in communities. (Mercy et al., 1993)

The approach also adopts a multilevel model for understanding the various causes of violence which was originally pioneered in explanations

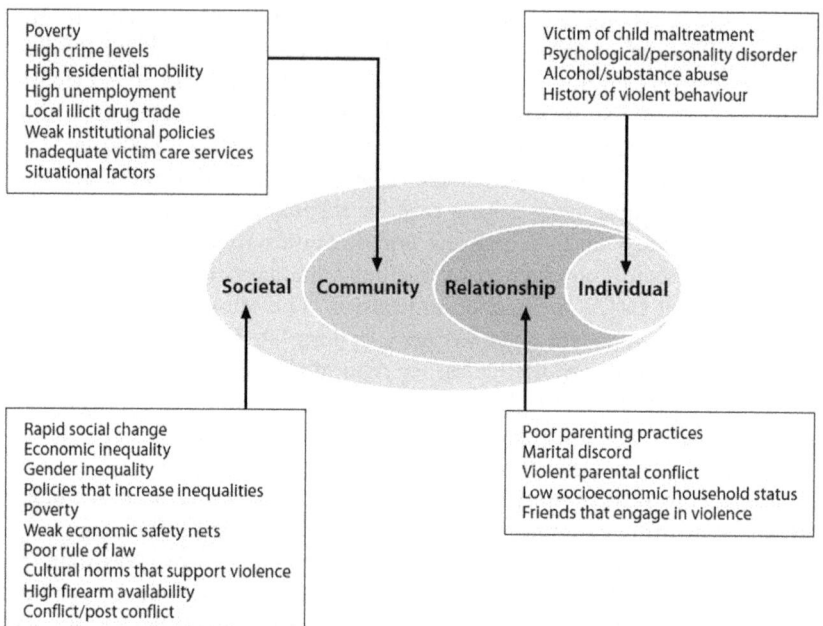

Figure 1.2 Ecological public health model of interpersonal violence.
Source: World Health Organization, 2004.

of violence against women (Heise, 1998). The approach adopted in England (Bellis et al., 2012) is a good example of this overall framework. It reminds us that any person's individual propensity for violence is located within a much bigger context where personal relationships, the community and wider societal influences all work together to shape the overall risk (see Figure 1.2).

The strategy for England reflects the public health approach with its first-stage commitment to tracking violence trends through a variety of data sources. Data collection underpins the planning and implementation of interventions and is collated from national routine data sets supplied by the police and health services. The police data include recorded violence against the person and sexual offences, while hospitals report emergency department attendances, emergency admissions for violence and unintentional and deliberate injuries to minors aged seventeen and under. There are plans to extend the data capture to draw in ambulance data in addition.

In terms of interventions, several options are identified in the strategy for England with varying degrees of evidence supporting them. Some of these interventions target actual violence itself, while others are more indirect and attempt to address the root causes by, for instance, striving to improve parenting or enriching environments. Success in these efforts would have a range of wider benefits in other aspects of public health in addition to reducing violence.

Early intervention from birth to early adulthood with those at risk of becoming violent is the cornerstone of the strategy. Beyond the individual child or young person, however, the social facilitators of violence are also targeted. In particular, this includes restricting the availability and consumption of alcohol and changing attitudes about what constitutes acceptable behaviour in public and private as key elements. Finally, recognising that violence will never be completely eradicated, the strategy includes a focus on the identification of victims and the provision of care and support for them.

The approach has its limitations. The boundary between some of the elements is unclear – why, for instance, is poverty a community issue but economic inequality operates at the society level (see Figure 1.2)? Also, apart from alcohol, there is an absence of possible biological factors which might make a person more prone to violence. There is, for instance, evidence of a relationship between diet and certain types of aggressive behaviour (Simopoulos, 2011), and diet itself is a core focus for public health interventions. The same could be said for lead pollution (Mielke and Zahran, 2012). Nevertheless, this ecological model is an important stimulus for thinking about the relationships between factors at different levels which can mutually reinforce each other in producing violence. It also highlights the range of issues that need to be comprehensively targeted using integrated interventions if the programme is going to be effective.

The public health approach has wider political and economic implications which need to be considered, including questions about the cost-effectiveness of such a 'broad-brush' strategy and the political consequences of mass data-gathering tantamount to surveillance (Foster et al., 2006; Potvin et al., 2005). Conversely, certain types of violence, such as elder abuse, have to date received very little attention. This issue is recognised as a problem in the strategy for England but is absent when it comes to the discussion of interventions. Nevertheless, the comprehensive public health vision embracing both population-wide and targeted interventions has become the dominant paradigm of the present time and provides a powerful platform for launching a new way of addressing the age-old problem of violence.

Ultimately, in balancing the public health and clinical approaches to the violence problem, as in any other health domain, there is a trade-off between prevention and intervention strategies, on the one hand, and between low- and high-risk populations as the focus, on the other. The public health approach indeed acknowledges the importance of identifying and working with vulnerable groups, but these tend to be younger people and children showing warning signs of potential future violence rather than adult perpetrators of serious violence. In contrast, the clinical approach to violence is most often implemented in hospitals and prisons, away from the public eye. These more secure and controlled settings enable highly intensive interventions to be implemented, but new challenges are faced when individuals whose risk of acting violently has been reduced are ready for release or discharge back into the community. In brief, low-risk and occasional potential offenders will benefit from 'upstream' low-cost-per-head environmental adjustments, whereas high-risk and persistent offenders require more high-cost 'downstream' individual, and perhaps pharmacological, interventions. A prevention paradox is as relevant here as in other widespread health problems (Rose, 1981). Since the low-risk population is always much larger than the high-risk population, the majority of violent 'cases' will emerge from the low-risk group rather than the high-risk group. Decisions about the relative weight of resources to be devoted to each of these groups in any particular overall programme therefore are political ones. But policy formation must be informed by the available science, and our aim in the following chapters is to sift through this science to help enable better decisions about the way forward.

1.8   Conclusion

Our overall aim here is to focus on interpersonal violence as a major global challenge for the first half of the twenty-first century and to examine how a public health perspective can contribute to solutions in this area. This perspective can benefit from a biopsychosocial approach to understanding causes and interventions and a public health approach for developing coordinated strategies for action.

2 The Roots of Human Violence
In Search of the 'Hard Wired'

2.1 Introduction: The Standard Narrative of 'Hard Wiring'

We have begun by discussing how, when investigating the problem of human violence, we often encounter a sense of pessimism concerning several aspects of it. This chapter focuses on what we understand to be some of the roots of that attitude. At present there appears to be a consensus of opinion concerning the sources of human violence, which fosters a view that essentially, it is inescapable, as it emanates from fundamental features of us, often collectively referred to as 'human nature'.

Part of the pessimism manifests itself in perceptions of human aggression which appear to be very widely accepted. Despite their currency in this respect, when examined closely it becomes clear that they amount to a misconception about the causes of aggression. While the exact connections within this are difficult to map out, they appear to derive from some basic beliefs about individuals and societies that have acquired a taken-for-granted status. The central idea underpinning them is the view that violence, as part of our natural makeup, has biologically evolved in such a way as to instil within us not just a preparedness to use it but a readiness, if not an eagerness to do so. We therefore all too easily enter into conflict and even physical combat with one another. Those supposedly irresistible tendencies help to explain a wide range of human activities, from the competitiveness of the marketplace and the sports field to the frequency with which organised groups enter into confrontations of different kinds, with results that range from rival gang fights to the carnage of war.

Taking a step back and looking at another branch of science, in physics there is an explicitly named 'standard model' which refers to an integrated theoretical account of matter and energy that is widely accepted. It describes the actions of the elementary particles of which matter is composed, and the operation of the fundamental forces that determine their interactions (Shears, 2012). Though it is beyond the comprehension of many of us without specialised training and knowledge, the model appears universally endorsed by those who possess the requisite skills. It has a sound scientific basis, and is supported by an abundance of research findings, though it continues as 'work in progress' and many questions remain to be answered. When addressing the latter, the model provides a framework for identifying appropriate ways of investigating them and for testing competing hypotheses.

We suggest that the corresponding cluster of beliefs that is applied to understanding aggression and violence bears some similarity to this idea of a standard model, and amounts to a kind of conventional and familiar narrative. It is difficult to ascertain how many people fully accept it, but if public discourse is a suitable guide, it appears to be a prevalent mode of thinking. Some years ago Goldstein (1989) identified a similar constellation of ideas which he referred to as the 'mythology of aggression'. In some instances, the standard narrative of violence seems to be accorded the status of a theory, like the standard model in quantum mechanics. Many people seem to regard the two as more or less equivalent in terms of truth value. Such a resemblance is, however, no more than superficial.

A possible reason for the mistaken perception may be because narratives about human nature are informed by another well-established scientific statement, the theory of evolution. This is widely acclaimed as one of the major accomplishments of modern science (notwithstanding the residual, but still influential activity of creationism in some places). Because of its success in explaining a wide range of observations in zoology and other biological sciences, it has become accepted also as supplying the definitive account of many aspects of human behaviour. But that apparent success may also be because it accords with a number of other core beliefs, unrelated to science, that play a pivotal role in contemporary Western culture.

In a nutshell, the reasoning that sustains this set of beliefs runs along the following lines. The history of all life is one of a struggle for survival: that struggle is the engine of evolution. This occurs not just between but also within species. The units that comprise each species, usually defined as individuals but sometimes as families or sets of close relatives, compete with each other to obtain access to food resources or to the territory that can supply them. In species where there is *anisogamy*, the pattern of reproduction that involves the fusion of two reproductive cells (*gametes*), such as sperm and egg, that are of disparate sizes and procreative 'values', males compete to pass their genes on to the exclusion of those of others (Stearns and Hoekstra, 2005). In evolutionary terms this is known as *sexual selection*, and at the behavioural level it regularly spills over into violent battles between rival conspecifics. Having to fight for both access to resources and reproductive success, the human beings who have succeeded in this contest are inherently and naturally competitive. Within such an immense tournament, aggression and violence have evolutionary value. These behaviours have, it is claimed, thereby become built into who we are. So both between and within species the possibility of conflict is never far away. The accepted imagery is captured in Tennyson's famous poetic phrase representing nature as 'red in tooth and claw'.

Perhaps the bleakest interpretation of the historical evidence of human violence is that forwarded by Nell (2006), who examines our capacity for, and the manifestations of, possibly its most extreme form in *cruelty*. This entails the 'deliberate infliction of physical or psychological pain on a living creature' to the 'evident delight' of those perpetrating it (p. 211), who relish the experience of a 'pain–blood–death complex' (p. 212). The intention to cause pain emanates from our emotional ferocity, which is seen as having its origins in predation that first arose in the Palaeozoic era (250–550 million years ago), and the subsequent evolution of the 'hunting adaptation' across many species. This conferred evolutionary fitness in terms of survival and reproduction, and so was intensely gratifying. Hence much later in the evolutionary chronicle it became and has remained a feature of human behaviour, visible not only in war, torture and personal violence, but more widely in culture and entertainment; according to Nell, 'readiness to commit cruel acts is a human universal' (p. 222). Nell cites a wide range of evidence on other species which hunt, and quotes numerous literary sources, in support of his stance.

This impression of ourselves is commonly believed to have a firm grounding in what we know about our place in evolution. The species usually considered to be our closest animal relative, the chimpanzee (*Pan troglodytes*), resembles us in being prepared to use violence. Patterns similar to human conflict are certainly seen among chimps. This includes both individual and small-group coercion, dominance, and sometimes fatal assault. It also includes intergroup antagonism and conflicts similar to wars, though obviously on a much smaller scale than our own. Ideas of this kind are embodied in a picture of humanity that has been popularised over the last few decades by some eminent primatologists, evolutionary biologists, anthropologists, and psychologists. They are captured in some key phrases now in wide circulation ('killer apes', 'demonic males', 'warrior genes') (Science Daily, 2009; Wrangham and Peterson, 1996). We have not been able to find survey evidence confirming this, but to judge indirectly by the content and tone of many accounts, such as news reports of violent acts, this suite of ideas is widely believed and may even have become deeply embedded in the outlook of large numbers of people (Sussman, 2013).

Belief systems are reflections of the encounter between human minds and the surrounding world, created through interactions between individuals in the groups to which they belong, and their interactions with the physical environment. Many are tempered by information from that world and shaped to be a reasonably reliable and reproducible representation of it. When methodically and painstakingly tested through what is now a well-established set of procedures, they become part of what is called scientific knowledge (Ladyman, 2002). Those tested beliefs describe a world, a set of entities and laws governing their relationship, which as far as we can tell exists independently of human minds. But there are also beliefs which refer to aspects of our world that are not independent of human minds, which instead have been constructed by us. Aspects of the human and social world may come to be perceived mistakenly as if they are part of the natural world: they can become absorbed into an account of how the world is believed to be, rather than being understood as a social construct. Sociologists call such a process *reification* (Berger and Pullberg, 1965). The set of beliefs under scrutiny here arguably has become reified, to an extent that it appears to be an inbuilt and established part of how we understand what is around us. Yet many aspects of it, and some of the assumptions on which it rests, are sharply at odds with available evidence. Others are highly questionable. The standard narrative is a lay theory rather than a well-tested scientific account, and with reference to other aspects of human functioning has been depicted in various terms such as 'folkbiological' (Linquist et al., 2011) or 'vernacular' (Stotz and Griffiths, 2018).

In attempting to place it on a more formal level, the narrative of violence as hard-wired has been ascribed some putative scientific credibility through the set of proposals formerly known as *sociobiology*, more recently recast in a revised form as *evolutionary psychology*. (We will return to some of those concepts later in the present chapter.) The emphasis on comparing us with chimpanzees, as a route to understanding where we have come from, has remained despite this recasting. Some anthropologists have labelled this ostensible cornerstone of our understanding of our evolutionary past as the Chimpanzee Referential Doctrine (CRD; Sayers et al., 2012). Others have characterised it more irreverently as 'chimps R us' (Ferguson, 2011). Satire aside, it is a very powerful metaphor, but it is important to remember again that it is no more than a metaphor. It is not a genuinely scientific model, as many of the propositions that flow from it cannot be tested; they will always remain at the level of conjecture. So there are now many indications that the CRD is a fundamentally misleading guide to understanding modern humans; even more so as a baseline for understanding complex patterns of behaviour such as aggression and violence.

At stake here is one of the most vigorously debated questions across the spectrum of social and biological sciences, one that also reflects some deep-seated social attitudes and orientations. Is there something called human nature, and if so, what does it consist of? Even some of humanity's most destructive acts, however terrible, have been portrayed as being an ineluctable part of the 'human condition'. However much we may try to avoid them, it is assumed that these tendencies are almost certain to emerge.

We note at this point that the concept of human nature is itself vigorously disputed. Most scholars reject what has been called the 'essentialist' version of it, that is, that it is possible to isolate a set of biologically evolved features of humans that are both distinctive and universal, that is, that are unique to our species, separating us from others, can be found in all of us, and have their origins in our genetic endowment. But there is no clear, defensible statement of exactly what such a 'nature' comprises, or of what characteristics or traits should be included within it.

As a result, across evolutionary biology, anthropology, psychology and other relevant fields, there is currently a wide spectrum of opinion regarding whether any alternative version of the concept has a valid meaning and offers any useful explanatory role. Some philosophers defend a more loosely articulated 'nomological' account of the concept in which it is held to be possible that we can find traits that although not definitive of us, are typical of most human beings, and that are products of biological evolution as opposed to environment, learning or culture (Machery, 2018). Other scholars consider this an unsatisfactory position and propose, for example, variant forms of the concept that incorporate developmental processes. As people change over the life course, it is aspects of that growth process that can be used to define what is unique to the human species (Stotz and Griffiths, 2018). Still other writers take a more radical view and reject the concept entirely. They argue that it should be abandoned as it is a social construct that adds nothing to our understanding. On the contrary, it provides a misleading account of the factors that influence human action (Laland and Brown, 2018; Sterelny, 2018).

The finding that we share a very high proportion of genes with our nearest living neighbour, the chimpanzee, has been widely disseminated, and many people are aware of it. It can be seen as further confirmation of the evolutionary storyline just described. However, the implications of the large amount of overlap have been widely misinterpreted, despite some authors' advice against doing do (Marks, 2002). Finding that our ape relatives sometimes behave as nastily as we do is usually taken as an indicator of how we evolved as we did, a core application of the CRD. However, anthropologists have gradually come to question the appropriateness of using chimpanzees as a reference point for studying human evolution. In part this follows the discovery that *Ardipithecus ramidus*, which lived approximately 15 million years ago and was the last common ancestor of chimpanzees, bonobos and humans, had more morphological features in common with modern humans than with any of the other great ape species (Sayers et al., 2012). What has been inferred about its behaviour suggests that its rate of in-group and between-group agonism was low, also closer to that of humans than chimpanzees.

Yet without doubt, much evidence from zoology, anthropology and archaeology certainly seems to fit the grim picture of humanity as a highly and inherently dangerous animal, and so appears to support the standard narrative. All mammalian species are likely to become aggressive under some circumstances, although most have evolved mechanisms such as threat rituals which ensure that fights between conspecifics are avoided, or are brief and not usually injurious (Fry and Szala, 2013). But deadly, collaborative attacks closely resembling murder and other forms of group violence of a kind carried out by humans have been observed only in chimpanzee communities; they have not been reported in other primates. There is also evidence of communal violent death among early modern peoples. So there appears to be a link running across related species and continuing into human evolution. Put together, these different sets of evidence are said to point toward a human proclivity for violence that is as constant as the drive for food and procreation, suggesting that our tendency toward it is 'innate'. To gain a clearer understanding of the extent to which this is true involves a voyage into the fields of evolutionary biology, archaeology, and anthropology.

2.2   Evolutionary Connections

The species to which we belong, modern humans (*Homo sapiens sapiens*), is a member of the family of great apes (Hominidae). Note that the term 'modern humans' does not denote people living in present-day industrial societies, or even those who lived in recent centuries or during the past few millennia. It refers to anatomically modern humans whose origins are dated back to approximately 200,000 years ago, with the emergence of the group to which all currently living humans belong. The hominid family in turn is part of the order known as primates, comprising more than 400 species. Our fellow great apes are orangutans, gorillas,

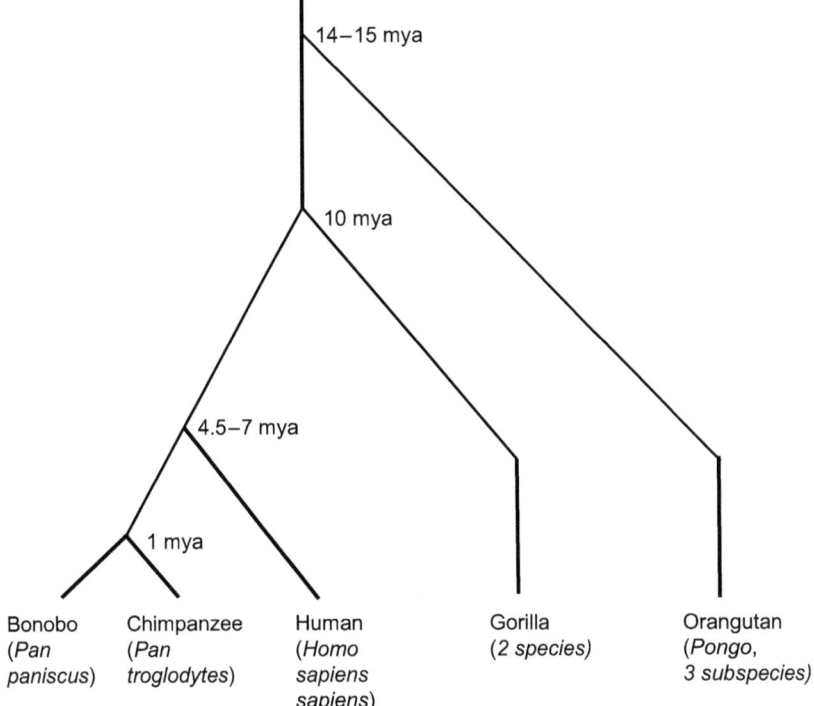

14–15 mya

10 mya

4.5–7 mya

1 mya

Bonobo   Chimpanzee   Human   Gorilla   Orangutan
(Pan   (Pan   (Homo   (2 species) (Pongo,
paniscus)   troglodytes)   sapiens   3 subspecies)
                            sapiens)

Figure 2.1 Simplified evolutionary lineage of surviving hominids (great apes). (mya = million years ago).

chimpanzees, and bonobos. Orangutans diverged from the common ancestor of this lineage in the region of 14–15 million years ago, and humans between 4.5 and 7 million years ago. Chimpanzees and bonobos took separate phylogenetic paths only approximately 1 million years ago. These pathways are shown in rudimentary fashion in Figure 2.1.

Genomics, the investigation and comparison of the genetic complement of different species, has a key role to play in substantiating this evolutionary scheme. The mapping of the human genome was completed in 2003, that of the chimpanzee in 2005 (Chimpanzee Sequencing and Analysis Consortium, 2005), of the orangutan in 2011 (Locke et al., 2011) and of both the bonobo and the gorilla in 2012 (Prüfer et al., 2012; Scally et al., 2012). This confirmed what had been suspected: that we share a very large proportion of our genetic makeup with chimpanzees (although lower than previously thought, in the region of 94%; Demuth et al., 2006). The discovery of the extent of genetic overlap strengthened the drawing of parallels between chimpanzee behaviour and our own. In the study of aggression and violence, many authors have considered that such parallels point to evolutionary origins as explanations (e.g. Wrangham and Peterson, 1996).

Chimpanzee behaviour has been more extensively studied than that of the other non-human great apes. Wilson (2013) noted that observations have been made of as many as fifty chimpanzee communities in different regions of Africa. Communities typically comprise an average of forty or so individuals, but membership may exceed 150. While both sexes of chimpanzees show non-threatening, prosocial behaviour a large proportion of the time, and often groom and protect each other, males compete aggressively for status and for sex. Individuals often form coalitions to redress power imbalances inside their groups. There are recorded instances of violence by males against females, of infanticide by both male and female adults, and of deadly violence against other adults. This was first reported by the renowned zoologist Jane Goodall, whose work in the Gombe Stream National Park in Tanzania is internationally known. For example, there were incidents in which a group of adult males attacked an isolated male from another group. Such attacks have been systematically observed and can be sustained for many minutes, with one male holding the victim while others beat and bite him, often inflicting fatal injury (Newton-Fisher and Thompson, 2012). Wilson (2013) lists a series of studies in which such events have been observed, at five separate sites, in a series of studies published between 1972 and 2008. Some killings were directly observed, others inferred on the basis of indirect but strong evidence.

According to evolutionary psychology this is a type of *adaptation*, a term we will discuss more fully below. Eliminating competitors increases the amount of resources available to support one's own survival, so it increases the aggressor's reproductive success. This in turn increases the likelihood that the next generation will inherit genes for aggressiveness, so continuing the pattern over time. That should ensure that genes for aggressiveness, if such units of DNA exist, are present in successive generations, and potentially that the proportion of individuals with those genes (and so phenotypically predicted to behave aggressively) will steadily rise.

There are several problems with portraying this as an evolutionary adaptation, however. Notwithstanding the evidence of coalitionary violence by chimpanzees reviewed by Wilson (2013), the frequency of such events appears to be very variable. In a review by Wilson et al. (2014) integrating data on eighteen chimp communities studied over five decades, only one showed a rate of killing greater than an average of one per year. In six others it was much lower (between 0.2 and 0.8 per year). In eight it was very low (fewer than 0.2 per year), and in three it was not recorded at all. Boesch and his colleagues (2008) observed four communities of chimpanzees in Taï National Park, Côte d'Ivoire, over a period of twenty-six years. There were only two killings during that time, both of them in the last three years of the fieldwork. Furthermore, there is evidence of prosocial behaviour, in that in the aftermath of non-fatal fights, other chimpanzees come to console the loser, and appear to have an impact in reducing distress (Romero et al., 2010). Moreover, the modal pattern of such killings is very dissimilar to the forms of lethal violence typically found in humans. At some sites the majority of chimpanzee killings involve infanticides committed by a group of males, followed by cannibalism of the victim's body (Watts and Mitani, 2000). This is an extremely rare form of behaviour in modern humans, if it is even known at all.

That simple concept of the transmission of dispositional aggressive-ness is also called into question by evidence from studies of baboons. It is not the case that dominant and aggressive males are uniformly more likely to achieve procreative triumph than their meeker counterparts. Sapolsky (2006) found that male 'nice guy' baboons have just as much reproductive success as their more belligerent peers who have higher status in the hierarchy of the troop.

But in any case, the drawing of parallels between human and chim-panzee behaviour in the light of genetic similarity does not actually tell us a great deal. Humans are as closely linked genetically to another primate species, bonobos (*Pan paniscus*), as we are to chimpanzees. Prüfer et al. (2012) have found that bonobos and humans have an approximately 95% similarity in DNA bases. Yet in crucial respects bonobos' behaviour toward each other differs considerably from that of chimpanzees. Bonobo males show subordination to females and have a far lower rate of competition and conflict with each other than do male chimpanzees. In a pattern quite unlike chimps, bonobo mothers facilitate sexual con-tacts between their sons and receptive females, standing guard during intercourse to protect the encounter from intrusion by other males (Surbeck et al., 2019). Bonobos share food, and do not form group alliances or engage in violent coalitions. They are highly playful and intensely active sexually, with partners of both sexes, in pairs and in groups. When conflicts do occur, bonobos engage in sexual contact as a form of consolation and reconciliation (Clay and de Waal, 2015). For these and other reasons the bonobo has been characterised, or perhaps caricatured, as the 'make love, not war' or the 'Kama Sutra' primate (Weinstein, 2016). Perhaps of closest relevance to the present discussion, lethal attacks of the kind seen in chimpanzees are virtually unknown among bonobos, with only one suspected killing noted over a fifty-year period of observing several communities (Wilson and Wrangham, 2003; Wilson et al., 2014).

In other great apes there is evidence of large differences between groups that cannot be explained simply in terms of genes. Krützen et al. (2011) studied geographic variation in the orangutan, which inhabits the islands of Sumatra and Borneo in Malaysia and Indonesia, and is now a critically endangered species. Although orangutans have a more solitary lifestyle than other great apes, they engage in social exchange for some purposes. These authors compared patterns of behaviour in eleven widely dispersed communities, amassing a total of more than 100,000 hours of observational data over a forty-year period. They found large differences in a series of ten 'conspicuous and frequent' social behaviours including their call repertoires, sizes of social clusters, time spent in party groups, rates of forced copulation and mating strategies. It might be expected that such phenotypic differences could be attributed to genetic *canalisation* within each group. This refers to a process in which, as a result of geographical separation or isolation, sets of genes within a species begin to evolve in different directions. However, analysis of gene variations showed they could explain only a small fraction (<7%) of the behavioural variation, while environmental differences accounted for 25%. Krützen and his colleagues proposed that among long-lived animals, developmental *plasticity* provided a better explanation of the differences that were found than the influence of genes. This refers to the capacity of organisms with the same genotype to vary in their ontogenetic pattern – in phenotype, or in behaviour – according to differing environmental conditions; which can also result in changes in neural pathways. In this case it was thought to include 'social learning of local variations', analogous to what in human society would be called cultural differences. However, the absence of symbolic and linguistic processes differentiates this markedly from human culture. Nevertheless, in summary, the preponderance of evidence points toward the importance of social and cultural learning as more powerful than linear processes of genetic transmission in influencing these aspects of orangutan behavioural evolution.

2.3   Violence in Early Human Societies

For 95% of the time we have existed as a species, human beings lived in small-scale communities of hunter-gatherers or foragers. Despite its obvious physical hardships, and a far shorter lifespan than most people enjoy today, Sahlins (1972/2004) painted a picture of life in the Stone Age in which what we now call the 'work–life balance' was strongly tilted in favour of the latter part of the equation. Extrapolating information from present-day foraging societies, he suggested that early hunter-gatherers probably worked, on average, four to five hours per day, punctuated by frequent rest periods; yet they usually had more than enough food. Kaplan (2000) questioned some aspects of this, and provided data suggesting that work took a higher portion of time each day, and people were often undernourished. Even so, the conditions of life seem less harsh than we might have expected, given the vast gulf between their lives and ours in terms of material wealth and prosperity. Ethnographic evidence also suggests that contemporary forager societies have a high proportion of free time for eating, drinking, playing and socialising (Gowdy, 1999).

However, other aspects of some early communities were probably far from idyllic. Archaeological research over the last few decades has suggested that life in early human groups was sometimes highly dangerous. Apart from the risk of natural disasters, excavations at a number of sites across several continents suggest violent death and injury may have been more common than they are today. Human remains from several locations show signs of brutal death, and in some cases also of cannibalism, though it cannot be established that people were killed specifically for that purpose. Close to the banks of the river Nile at Jebel-Sahaba, Sudan, in a site dated to 12,000–10,000 BCE, the remains of fifty-nine individuals have been found showing signs of having been subjected to multiple blows and injuries. Fragments of arrows or spears were found embedded in bones or sometimes inside the rib cage (Guilaine and Zammitt, 2005). The earliest European site showing clear evidence of a concerted massacre is in Ofnet, Germany, dated at 7,720 years old, where a series of thirty-eight skulls have been found with wounds indicative of having been bludgeoned to death, and also of decapitation. Nineteen of the skulls were those of children. Most of the rest were of adult females and only two were of adult males, suggesting a large group was attacked when most of its men were away. The skulls were daubed with red ochre and arranged in neat circles. Another site at Talheim, Germany, contains remains of thirty-four bodies (eighteen adults and sixteen children) with evidence of having been attacked with adzes and axes, two types of cutting tool associated more with farming than with hunting.

The human bones and the artefacts found in these and other sites have been examined in detail. Using the techniques of forensic science, it is possible to deduce whether or not deaths were a result of violence (based on patterns of injury and the configuration of bodies), whether they were immediately fatal (based on the presence of any signs of tissue repair), what kind of implement caused them, and many other details (Walker, 2001). Patterns of striations on bones suggest that cannibalism was not unusual. Alongside this direct evidence, some early rock paintings, such as those found at a number of sites in Sicily and in eastern Spain, respectively dated up to 12,000 and 9,000 years ago, display scenes of torture, execution or sacrifice, and of persons having been struck by arrows or spears (Guilaine and Zammitt, 2005). These and other sets of data have been drawn together by Pinker (2011), who combined tables from previous reviews of violent death rates in different types of society. He collated twenty-one data sets from prehistoric archaeological sites yielding an average death rate from violent conflict of 15%. If that figure was applied to England and Wales today, we would be counting an annual total of nearly 7 million murders.

Findings of this kind have led many authors to conclude that both individual and collective violence have been features of human activity since ancient times (LeBlanc and Register, 2003; McCall and Shields, 2008). The net result has been the impression that, despite the very high casualty rate from all forms of violence in the twentieth century, in proportionate terms the rate in premodern groups was considerably higher (where *modern* here refers to the period since the agricultural revolution, approximately 10,000–12,000 years ago). People seem to have been killing each other concertedly for a very long time. We might again easily conclude that extreme violence is almost natural, in line with what we earlier called the conventional narrative, and we have evolved to engage in it. Extrapolating from this, we might accept that it is only strong social or state control that stops many more people from carrying out lethally violent acts.

However, other anthropologists have questioned the accuracy of these datasets and argued that they are not representative of human societies in the premodern era. Ferguson (2013a) analysed the list of violent death rates assembled by Pinker (2011) and shows that in several cases they are overestimates and include other kinds of error (several are counted twice, for instance). More importantly, the sites themselves are an extreme selection: there are many other sets of remains where there is no evidence of violence. Indeed overall, Ferguson shows that the sites listed by Pinker are ones with an exceptional rate of violence, and are not typical of what archaeologists have found in many other places. The conclusion that early modern humans were habitually violent is based on 'a selective compilation of highly unusual cases, grossly distorting war's antiquity and lethality' (Ferguson, 2013a, p. 126). Furthermore, evidence of inter-group violence only began to appear circa 10,000 BCE. Prior to that, though many human remains and artefacts have been found, there are none resembling the skeletons of Jebel-Sahaba, Ofnet, or Talheim; and those at the first of these sites are the oldest with signs of a mass killing ever to be found (Ferguson, 2013b). Of course, those remains appear to be the effects of intergroup violence rather than individual homicide. It seems almost inconceivable that there would not have been individual acts of violence farther back in time. Other forms of killing (e.g. by strangulation, disembowelling) would not be identifiable from skeletal remains. The central question of whether violence is somehow built into the human behavioural repertoire to an extent that makes it part of our 'nature' remains open.

Against this, some anthropologists insist that there is convincing evidence of widespread violence, at both and individual and collective level, in early human communities. Australia has been described as the closest example of a 'hunter-gatherer continent', because until the arrival of European colonists from the late eighteenth century onward it was inhabited exclusively by small-scale aboriginal groups widely spread across its area. Gat (2015) collated evidence of violence in these communities. Several of the sources are historical accounts by nineteenth-century European settlers, often written several years after the events they describe, and their accuracy may be questionable. Others, however, are based on archaeological examination of skeletal remains from various sites in different regions of Australia. Pardoe (2014; see also Allen, 2014) compared the Murray-Darling river basin, where due to reliable availability of water there were higher population densities, and signs of agriculture and of settlement including burial grounds, with arid or semi-arid regions where survival was much harder and lifestyles were likely to have been entirely nomadic. Contrary to the expectation that evidence of violence would be higher in the more settled, densely populated areas, indications of rates of violent death were similar in both environments. Based on findings such as these, Jones and Allen (2014) took the view that 'to accept the long chronology of war … is to accept that humans likely do have an innate biological propensity to engage in conflict' (p. 362).

However, much of the Australian evidence is drawn from work by Webb (1995), who found sizable variations in evidence of violent injury across different regions. In a detailed analysis of types of injury by geographical area, all forms of injury varied in frequency. Webb (1995) viewed the evidence as posing numerous 'interpretative uncertainties' concerning the relationship between injuries and behaviour. For example, many injuries, especially to lower limbs, could have been sustained through falls or from accidents when hunting. Nevertheless, some remains showed signs of cranial injury, while others indicated forearm 'parry fractures', sustained when a victim raises an arm in an attempt at self-protection from an attacker's blow. These types of injury, thought attributable to aggression, were more common among female than male remains, suggesting domestic assault and femicide.

Findings that parallel these were obtained from detailed analysis of communities in California in the period prior to European settlement (Schwitalla et al., 2014). These authors analysed data from 329 archaeological sites including a total of 16,820 sets of human remains. The overall rate of evidence of 'sharp force/projectile trauma' was 7.4%. But here too rates of all forms of injury showed markedly uneven distributions. Also importantly, evidence indicated temporal as well as spatial variations in injury rates, indicating that there had been two major episodes of escalation in violence. Findings of this kind suggest that an upsurge in conflict is in part a result of events including environmental change.

A core and recurrent difficulty in arriving at meaningful rates of violence is the lack of population data for the periods from which most skeletal remains have been dated. This has been called the 'denominator problem' (Milner, 2015, p. 787), as information is not available on the 'population at risk'. There are more remains available from more settled communities during the Neolithic period (since approximately 12,000 years ago) than for earlier periods when human groups were mostly nomadic. Proportions of remains showing traumatic injury are generally higher for later than earlier eras, hence it is crucial not to extrapolate from the former backward to the latter (Estabrook, 2014).

A pattern in which collective or inter-group conflict fluctuates over time is in accordance with a broader set of relationships identified by Ember and Ember (1992). Based on analysis of data from 186 pre-industrial societies, these researchers found that conflicts of this kind were most reliably predicted, independently and significantly, by two types of factors. One was the threat of natural disasters that would have serious impacts on the availability of food resources. The second was what they labelled 'socialisation for mistrust'. Both of these factors generate states of uncertainty and fear. Thus the occurrence of warfare was a function of external events and of cultural processes rather than of any inbuilt predilection for engaging in aggression that was selected through a primarily biological process. Clearly, we have capacities for different types of response, but Jones and Allen (2014) appear to go beyond the evidence in depicting some of them as 'innate propensities' more firmly embedded than others.

Overall, notwithstanding what has been found at some burial sites, a large quantity of archaeological evidence does not support the suggestion that human communities have been unremittingly violent throughout their history; excavations at many sites found no evidence of violent death. The pattern is more complex and variable. Furthermore, in all the groups where evidence of violent death has been found, periods of conflict have alternated with periods of peace (Kelly, 2005). There is also evidence that where conflicts arose they were often precipitated by environmental events, including climate change, that caused abrupt variations in living conditions (Hsiang et al., 2013). The bulk of evidence points to major intergroup conflicts having emerged after populations became more sedentary, in the period from 10,000 BCE onward (Ferguson, 2011; Fry, 2012; Kelly, 2005). The fatality rate from intergroup aggression is higher among subsistence farming communities, which are of relatively more recent origin, than among the older hunter-gatherer cultures (Wrangham et al., 2006). Alongside this there is evidence that some neighbouring societies with a history of rivalry and conflict went on to develop 'peace systems', what today would be called treaties, to avert a return to violence. Fry (2012) lists a number of such systems which have emerged across different parts of the globe. For example, groups of neighbouring societies indigenous to what are now Australia, Brazil, Canada, Greenland, India, Malaysia, and the United States set up formal agreements of this kind. The European Union, although nowadays dominated by economic concerns, was instigated and founded as an agreement designed to foster peaceful co-existence, to 'make war unthinkable'.

2.4   Violence in Small-Scale Societies Today

These historical data are linked to controversies within the field of anthropology regarding the level and the pervasiveness of violence in contemporary subsistence economies. These societies have declined in number, but there are still several dozen of them around the world pursuing lifestyles that once were the norm for the entire human species. They continue in some parts of the globe such as the Amazon basin, central southern Africa, southern Asia, New Guinea, and on several oceanic islands. Some now have mixed economies that include elements of horticulture.

A particularly vociferous academic dispute arose over studies of the Yanomami, an Amazonian people of Venezuela who have been depicted as habitually fierce and warlike, and almost routinely prone to murderous violence (Chagnon, 1988; Wrangham and Peterson, 1996). This was said to be associated with the belief that being a warrior brought greater success in producing children. Another group initially described as prone to frequent homicidal violence are the Gebusi people of Papua New

Guinea. When first systematically studied during the 1980s, this group was found to have one of the highest rates of homicide reported in a society of this kind. In the years 1940–1962, it has been estimated that almost one-third (32.7%) of deaths were due to homicide (Knauft et al., 1987), which often followed accusations of sorcery or involved revenge for earlier attacks. If correct, both of these patterns could be claimed to fit comfortably into the mainstream narrative outlined earlier.

But there are still difficulties with these suggestions that humanity in general or even some societies are habitually violence-prone. The account of the Yanomami given above was later challenged by other anthropologists. Ferguson (2011) described the violence as more sporadic, and attributed much of it to pressures on the tribe from outside forces, notably, encroachment on their land by mining interests. This enforced displacement by vastly more powerful economic forces is an example of *slow violence* as we will discuss more fully in Chapter 5. In addition, data from elsewhere contradict the simple evolutionary view that the more aggressive 'warrior class' will have an evolutionary fitness advantage in passing on their genes over those who less often engaged in killing. When first researched by anthropologists, the Waorani people from the Amazonian rain forests of Ecuador were recorded as having the highest rate of homicide on earth, exceeding that of the Gebusi: a study across five generations found 42% of deaths were due to homicide. Women were victims almost as often as men, a pattern unlike that of the Yanomami, and when first studied in the 1970s the population was gradually declining as a result. The rate of internal killing was such that if the pattern had continued, this society was on a path toward complete self-extinction. Working in this community, Beckerman et al. (2009) compared the reproductive success of high-status warriors with their less bellicose peers. If the conventional narrative is correct, zealous warriors who carried out more raids or killed more enemies should have had more wives and children than their less zealous counterparts. In fact, the reverse was the case, with a particularly large difference showing in the numbers of children who survived to age fifteen; this was far higher in the 'non-zealous' than the 'zealous' group.

Similarly among another reputedly warlike group, the Cheyenne of the Great Plains of the United States, Moore (1990) found a historical pattern whereby men more inclined toward peace had a higher reproductive success rate than those who became war chiefs and were renowned for their bravery and aggressiveness. Like the findings of Sapolsky (2006) with 'nice guy' baboons mentioned earlier, this casts doubt on the thesis that aggressiveness is an evolutionary adaptation because it increases reproductive success.

An alternative and radically different view is that evolutionary adaptation proceeded by the selection of communicative abilities and skills in cooperativeness, and that these processes also drove human cognitive evolution. What Hare (2017) has called 'intragroup prosociality' became the central feature in a process he has called 'human self-domestication', similar to that of the domestication by humans of other animals, but which in the first instance we applied to ourselves. Living in small groups, modern humans acquired patterns of tolerance, mutual aid and cooperation, changes that were facilitated by the evolution of self-control, including the ability to inhibit aggression (MacLean et al., 2014). The human fossil record supports the view that the 'explosion of cultural artefacts' which began approximately 80,000 years ago 'occurred due to selection for temperament that allowed more cooperative communication and promoted rapid transmission of innovations' (Hare, 2017, p. 167). Essentially, evolutionary fitness depended on selecting not for aggressiveness, but for friendliness.

Such a thesis, that human aggressiveness has reduced due to selection pressures, has been taken a stage further by Wrangham (2019). Recalling the distinction between *reactive* and *instrumental* aggression outlined in the Introduction, Wrangham postulates that the former has reduced through human *self-domestication* mentioned above. We have become progressively less likely to react violently on an individual level, indeed have essentially become more docile than our ancestors. However, alongside that process, our tendency to use aggression and violence in ways that are planned and premeditated, such as in war and other forms of organised inter-group conflict, has increased.

One of the factors which Wrangham (2019) considers has led to selection against reactive aggression is the use of one or other form of capital punishment. He cites many instances of how he believes this reduced the proportion of violent people in the population. However, many of the illustrations he employs are not evidence of this. Examination of historical records, for example, of responses to witchcraft, sorcery, bestiality or other abhorred practices, shows that in many cases the people who practised these or who were suspected of having acted in 'evil' ways had not committed any actual violence, yet were eliminated; and often very brutally. On the other hand, the individuals who killed them were themselves far more violent in how they dealt with the perceived threat. It is difficult to see how the net effect of this could have been to reduce the proportion of aggressive genes in the population.

The process of self-domestication through which Hare (2017), Wrangham (2019) and others consider human aggressiveness has evolutionarily declined is almost entirely a biological one. Domestication through natural selection is thought to have occurred in bonobos and humans, and through artificial selection in other species such as dogs, cats, and horses. Thus whether natural, or occurring via imposed breeding, we and other animals have become less emotionally reactive and more socially tolerant of each other, in sum more 'prosocial'. This is accompanied by changes in brain structure and volume, and a range of other physical adaptations, which some researchers believe can be detected in alterations in the human genome over time (Theofanopoulou et al., 2017).

The concept of self-domestication, which has been considered as an approach to understanding human evolution for some time, is however contentious, and there have been some strident criticisms of it (Brüne, 2007). In contrast to that explanation, other anthropologists consider that the fundamental driver of increased prosociality has been cultural evolution, in which increasing human cooperativeness, which greatly magnified prospects of survival, was strengthened by the development of communication, social learning, and other advantages. On this analysis a clear understanding of human evolution can be obtained only by introducing cultural variables into models of how these changes occurred (Laland and Brown, 2011; Lewens, 2015). Human neuroanatomical evolution involved a growth in brain volume relative to body size, accompanied by a proportionately greater expansion in association and specialised executive areas. There is evidence that this was linked to increasing abilities for conceptual processing and for the use of language, for social interaction, learning, and cooperation (Reader and Laland, 2002; Rilling, 2014; Verendeev and Sherwood, 2017).

There are other anomalous patterns emerging from anthropological research that do not fit the 'violent human nature' perspective. Contrary to what would be predicted by the evolutionary idea of *inclusive fitness*, that a person would be more likely to murder someone biologically unrelated to them (thereby preserving relatives with shared genes), the reverse was found among the Gebusi. In this society, close relatives were three times more likely to be killed than others. Even more counterfactually, perhaps, for violent human nature expectations, Gebusi society underwent a major shift in ethos after a large proportion (84%) of the population was baptised as Christians, not by missionaries from overseas but by evangelists from elsewhere in Papua New Guinea. They also embraced education, and beliefs in the power of sorcery rapidly declined. Knauft (2011) reports data showing that over a twenty-year period, the rate of homicide among the Gebusi people decreased remarkably, falling to 5.1% in 1982–1988 and with no reported cases from then onward.

Focusing on extant forager societies (hunter-gatherers), Fry (2011) and Fry and Söderberg (2013) analysed parts of a worldwide dataset, the *Standard Cross Cultural Sample*, containing information on 186 societies, including twenty-one hunter-gatherer groups classified as mobile forager band societies. The available evidence here again dispels the commonly believed stereotype of 'man the warrior', including, for example, the idea that boys are assimilated into a closed-off patrilineal, masculine-oriented culture. That did occur in some groups; but the majority (86%) of the twenty-one societies did not show any such pattern. Where homicide does occur, it is most often motivated by revenge, with sexual relationship conflicts running close behind. But seven of the twenty-one societies on this list have very low levels of violence. Analysis of other material from the same dataset showed large variations in the numbers of homicides. Of 148 lethal events recorded, almost half occurred in just one society. Three societies had none at all and a further nine had three or fewer. This picture is markedly at odds with one in which humanity is pervasively or regularly engaged in serious interpersonal violence, as implied in the dominant portrayal of our species.

Separately, the Department of Anthropology in the University of Alabama at Birmingham (2019) has maintained a website concerned with peaceful societies. This describes a series of twenty-five societies in which there is 'significant scholarly literature' describing a way of life that promotes social harmony and respect for persons, and eschews aggression and conflict. They include for example the Paliyan of southern India, who moved from a nomadic to a sedentary lifestyle approximately 150 years ago. While, as noted above, this is sometimes associated with a rise in violence, the Paliyan have highly developed systems for managing disputes, and have maintained a non-violent cultural ethos throughout (Gardner, 2000). When studied they were found to have a very low level of feuding and a complete absence of homicide.

These communities often have a range of methods for conflict resolution. The Semai of Malaysia have a well-established peaceable lifestyle in which violence is regarded as abnormal. Their definition of it includes both physical assault and emotional injury causing psychological stress; both are regarded as impermissible (Dentan, 2004). Homicide is extremely rare; Dentan was able to find only four instances over a forty-year period. Even physical fighting is highly unusual. The Semai regard counter-violence, hitting back at someone who has wronged you, as pointless; anger is expressed in a verbal harangue against the person who has caused offence, or to a third party. An aggrieved person can go to the home of someone who has harmed their interests and demand a gift in compensation in order to settle the matter.

In other societies, processes for resolving conflicts have included public wrestling matches with rules to avoid serious injury, or appointment of conciliators to oversee specially arranged hearings. Perhaps the most unusual innovation is the use of elaborate song duels in which adversaries sang insults to each other face to face in front of an audience. The process energised an audience reaction in a way that enables the disputants to resolve their differences and channel hostile feelings without engaging in violence (a forerunner perhaps of some television programmes with audience voting that are popular today). These ritualised events are perhaps best known among the Iglulik, Netsilik and other peoples of Greenland and northern Siberia (Eckert and Newmark, 1980), groups where high levels of conflict often led to violence, but where it was sometimes solved in this manner rather than through homicide. But song duels and related practices have also been found in societies in many parts of the world (Pim, 2013).

Variations in rates of non-sexual violence, both lethal and non-lethal, are paralleled by societal and cultural differences in rates of rape. There are instances of rape in all societies, but there are groups among whom its rate of occurrence is reportedly very low. In a survey of 156 tribal cultures, Sanday (1981) coded a series of cultural variables including the extent of taboos restricting sexual contact, overall rates of interpersonal violence, the amount of fathers' involvement in childrearing, and indicators of male dominance such as the level of female involvement in political decision-making. There were strong correlations between rates of rape, levels of violence in general and an ideology of male toughness and dominance, as contrasted with a more even balance of power between the sexes in other societies. In later work, Sanday (2004) chronicled the almost complete absence of rape among the Minangkabau people of Western Sumatra, which she attributed to the structure of male–female relations within that society. Minangkabau culture has been described as the most explicitly matrilineal form of society on earth. For example, in contrast to the conventions of many other societies, land and property are passed through female lineage, and there is a pattern of near-symmetrical male–female status and relationships, differing markedly from that found in most other locations. Sanday (2004) suggests that the lower rate of male-on-female violence is explained by the fundamental difference in power relations and the greater respect in which women are held.

Summarising some of the findings discussed here, Knauft (2011, p. 222) concluded that

human patterns of lethal violence are extremely variable and malleable in character and in degree, and in their intensity or absence. Given the adaptability and diversity of humans in many other regards, this should not be surprising. These trends contravene the notion that humans have an inborn, genetic, or otherwise deeply predisposed nature to be violently aggressive.

Similarly Ferguson (2011, p. 257) suggests that

the same human infant has the potential for being a pre-industrial hunter-gatherer or an astronaut, for being a genocidal slaughterer or a pacifist monk. That is pretty darn flexible, and humans can do it because culture *is* our nature. It is culture that made possible human beings' spectacular reproductive success.

2.5   Evolutionary Forensic Psychology

Psychology itself has contributed to the idea of hard-wired violence propensity through its close association with evolutionary theory. It is incontrovertibly the case that like all other species, human beings are a product of biological evolution (Coyne, 2009). This is unanimously accepted within the scientific community, so much so that alongside the atomic theory of matter it is seen as one of the cornerstones of modern science. As the philosopher John Searle (1995, p. 6) has remarked, these 'two features of our conception of reality are not up for grabs'. The importance of the mechanism of natural selection described by Charles Darwin (1809–1882) is supported by an overwhelming quantity of evidence as an account of how species differentiated and developed. It can explain not only the structural features of animal anatomy but also many aspects of the functions served by various sequences of behaviour. But there is less agreement about the degree to which the process of natural selection described by Darwin can explain the variations of human behaviour that can be observed across cultures and situations and over time. According to one view aligned closely with evolutionary theory, culture is propagated by 'memes', units of language or thought that replicate themselves in a manner analogous to genetic transmission at the microbiological level. Critics have discarded this, however, as too simplistic, in favour of a more 'kinetic' emphasis in which culture is reproduced across generations by multiple processes that include social learning and other patterns of interaction that are both direct and symbolic (Lewens, 2015).

In criminology, where patterns of violence have been studied extensively, there have been several attempts to explain both violent and acquisitive crime in terms of evolutionary biology (Barak, 2009; Cohen and Machalek, 1988; Vila, 1994). In psychology, those ideas have been taken even further, to the extent that there is now an identifiable subfield of *evolutionary forensic psychology* (Duntley and Shakelford, 2008; Durrant and Ward, 2011; Shakelford and Weekes-Shakelford, 2012).

Several researchers, most notably Buss (2012) and Tooby and Cosmides (1992; Cosmides and Tooby, 2013) have proposed that evolution can explain a far wider range of human behaviour than had previously been thought. In doing so they challenged a position which they have called the Standard Social Science Model (SSSM), which dominated thinking from the 1950s onward. At its core, this is the view that because human adults show so much variation across different societies, there is clear evidence for the primary influence of environment, learning, and culture on behaviour. It is the opposite of the conventional narrative under examination here. Within the SSSM, the individual mind was viewed as a product of those processes, and had no inherent structure of its own; it was the figurative 'blank slate' (*tabula rasa*). Tooby and Cosmides (1992) argued that this conception was scientifically unfounded, out of date, had held back the progress of psychology, and kept it separate from the other sciences. They argued instead that the mind had developed its own internal structure through the process of evolution, and that that structure was passed from one generation to the next through genetic transmission.

According to this view, the internal mental structure resides in a set of 'adaptations' or 'adaptive specialisations'. These mechanisms evolved during an earlier phase of human history, and enabled us to survive and reproduce as they served particular purposes or solved specific problems. In evolutionary psychology these structures are called 'modules'. This refers to cognitive information-processing programmes that 'were sculpted over evolutionary time by the ancestral environments and selection pressures experienced by the hunter-gatherers from whom we are descended' (Cosmides and Tooby, 2013, p. 203).

The idea of the modular mind has been likened to the evolution of other bodily organs (e.g. heart, lungs, liver), each of which has a special-ised function. It has also been likened more metaphorically to the design of a Swiss Army knife, which has separate tools for specific purposes that can operate independently of each other. In evolutionary psychology, the entire human mind is viewed as having this modular structure. The modules that compose it produce patterns of reaction or perform a variety of tasks essential for survival and procreation. They range from fear of snakes to mate selection, activation of sexual jealousy, and detec-tion of cheating in our fellow humans. There are held to be many thousands of such modules, a pattern called 'massive modularity'.

This is a very different view of cognitive evolution from one accepted by most neuroscientists, which says that the human brain has a wide-ranging, general-purpose ability to adapt flexibly to novel situations, and that there is communication between its components across different functional domains. In this broader view, while some of the brain's processes may be localised to a degree, it has enormous *plasticity* or ability to change through learning, such that for example when part of it is damaged, an adjoining area can to some extent take over its role.

Evolutionary psychologists dismiss the latter concept of brain functioning, and propose instead that modern humans are endowed with a set of modules that evolved during the phase of history when we emerged as a species. Earth scientists call this the Pleistocene era, a period of geological time from approximately 2.5 million to just over 11,000 years ago. The structure of the mind was given shape in what evolutionary psychologists call the *Environment of Evolutionary Adaptedness*, which is not described precisely but is sometimes identified as the savanna of Eastern Africa, where humans are thought to have emerged from the primate ancestral line.

For Buss (2012), these ideas are eminently applicable to the understanding of crime, including violence. He considers that evolutionary psychology offers a 'powerful set of tools' (2012, p. 91) for studying human behaviour in general and criminal acts in particular. The argument takes the form of a syllogism. All human behaviour requires psychological mechanisms and environmental input into them. All such mechanisms owe their existence to evolution by natural selection. Criminal behaviour is a subset of human behaviour, *ergo* there must be evolved adaptations underlying it. 'If another causal process exists that can create complex functional psychological adaptations, it has not been made known to the scientific community' (Buss, 2012, p. 92).

Pursuing these basic principles has led some psychologists to make specific proposals about how evolution shows through in different kinds of aggressive behaviour. Two proposals have attracted particular attention. The first is the finding that children are more likely to be maltreated and on occasions murdered by step-parents than by biological parents. This finding is attributed to the idea of inclusive fitness, briefly described earlier, here familiarly referred to as the 'Cinderella effect' (Daly and Wilson, 1985, 2005). The second is the suggestion that rape is a form of evolutionary adaptation which has its origins in the difficulties that 'low status' males have in securing opportunities to reproduce, to an extent that they therefore resort to sexual violence. Their limited or perhaps non-existent access to sexual partners through socially acceptable channels leads them to use coercion instead (Thornhill and Palmer, 2000). In addition to these proposals, other authors have applied similar principles in offering explanations of intimate partner violence (Goetz, 2010; Kaighobadi et al., 2009).

While all of this may appear superficially plausible, evolutionary psychology has been subject to very trenchant criticisms, targeted on some specific proposals such as those just mentioned; its basic assumptions have also been called into question. The following are some of the key issues in this dispute.

First, from the viewpoint of the philosophy of science it has been said that the central ideas of evolutionary psychology cannot be subjected to proper empirical testing; they cannot be verified or falsified. The difficulties arise from the nature of the data sources used to support core arguments. These are often either indirect (extrapolations from other species to humans) or distant and vague (interpretations of a largely unknown past). Conway and Schaller (2002) suggested that adding a historic layer to any theory lowers its credibility by making it harder to test. The net effect is that many of the explanations informed by this approach are based on drawing inferences from sources that have extremely low reliability. As a result, they are inevitably highly speculative. Even before the inception of evolutionary psychology, Gould and Lewontin (1979) called the concept of adaptation a series of 'Just so stories'. That is, the idea could be used to suggest almost anything someone wanted to say about the human past, as the necessary data could not be obtained and methodically examined. Of course, that criticism can be levelled at many of the hypotheses concerning the lives of humans in the remote past, including those discussed in the preceding sections of this chapter. However, the anthropological research cited here characteristically stays closer to the available data than the typically less disciplined approach found in much evolutionary psychology.

For example, earlier we encountered a particularly disturbing vision of the postulated rewards of some violence through cruelty (Nell, 2006). But evidence relating that phenomenon to more frequent forms of human aggression is virtually absent. Many of those who commented on Nell's article[1] considered that a description of a particularly lurid form of violence, which most would class as sadism, had been extended and applied beyond its meaningful range. Some also noted contradictions, for example that very few people find cruelty inherently pleasurable, and expressions of pain more often inhibit aggression (Bandura, 2006). Others questioned how it makes evolutionary sense for adults to inflict cruelty on their own children (Swain, 2006). We might expect, instead, that they would seek to protect them as far as possible, to maximise their potential to continue the genetic line of their parents.

Second, the existence of adaptive modules as posited by evolutionary psychology has been described as neurologically implausible, indeed 'farfetched' (Janskepp and Janskepp, 2000, p. 125). The posited modular

---

[1] The format of the journal *Behavioural and Brain Sciences* in which the article appeared consists of a main article followed by a series of commentaries, then the author's response.

structure is notionally one where there are vertical connections between regions of the midbrain that regulate basic emotional and survival functions with cortical areas dedicated to higher-level processing in concert with them. At the same time, to preserve the independence of these units, 'horizontal' connections that would result in more generalised functioning should be absent. However, no neural structures exist that actually fit this description; indeed, it departs markedly from the way the brain operates (Buller and Hardcastle 2000; Ferguson, 2012; Gannon, 2002). Recent reviews of research on brain structure and function show enormous distribution of information flows in multiple directions at the cortical level (Buckner and Krienen, 2013). There is a growing recognition in the neurosciences of the importance of this individualised network of neural interconnections within the brain, a concept captured in the term *connectome* (Seung, 2012; Sporns et al., 2005). Processes of this kind occur at several levels, and underpin the brain's capacity for different kinds of rewiring, including learning (Bennett et al., 2018). This does not correspond at all well to a model based on massive modularity.

A third major objection, running contrary to the remarks of Buss (2012) quoted above, is that there is another causal process that is well known to science, which is empirically well validated, and provides a more coherent and better substantiated account of the available data. This process is *neural plasticity* (Costandi, 2016) and it underpins a model of the human brain very dissimilar to the one forwarded in evolutionary psychology. What emerged during evolution was not a brain or mind that was crammed with specialised modular adaptations, but one whose principal fitness advantage was the capacity for adaptability itself. The human brain evolved to be openly responsive to our diverse and changeable environments through learning. A process of that kind is far more capable of producing complex psychological functions than the types of modularity proposed within evolutionary psychology.

2.6   Conclusion

We have dwelt on these issues at some length because of what appears to be a widespread trend toward accepting a view of human violence that while appearing plausible, is actually at odds with large amounts of information from primatology, archaeology, anthropology, psychology, and neuroscience. To summarise: there is no evidence which convincingly demonstrates that humans have an intrinsically violent nature. Clearly, we have a capacity to act in this way but we also have a complementary capacity for avoiding violence, for reducing and resolving conflicts. The relevance of data from other species for explanatory purposes is questionable, and there is no reason why chimpanzees rather than bonobos should be taken as exemplars of our evolutionary past. The proposal that the human mind consists wholly or largely of evolved adaptive 'modules' is not corroborated by any clear evidence and is incompatible with what is known about neural structure and networks. There is far better evidence for a general multipurpose model of brain structure and function, in which the developing brain responds flexibly and adaptably to its environment. Furthermore, that idea also corresponds better to what is known about how the genome operates. Genes code for proteins in neurotransmitter systems which, although produced in one area of the brain, are distributed across many other areas in regular functioning. The unique and unprecedented learning potential of humans as a species is associated with the massive growth of the cortical areas, and is a product of biological processes acting in synergy with cultural development.

Where does that leave the orthodox narrative of hard-wired human violence? Arguments for it come from joining together three sources of information that supposedly provide evidence for it. One is that chimpanzees, our closest biological neighbours with whom we have a large shared genetic makeup, show violence with some patterns in common to that seen in humans. A second is that early peoples not only committed homicide but did so at a far higher rate than seen anywhere today, and also engaged in collective violence (massacres). A third is that groups of modern humans with the closest similarity to Paleolithic peoples, that is those who have continued the practice of foraging (hunting and gathering) as their sole means of subsistence, have high rates of both individual and communal violence.

We have seen that the evidence forwarded in support of each of these three core contentions in actuality shows considerable variation and so is far from conclusive. The frequent reference to the sometimes-violent chimpanzee as the most meaningful human analogue, on the basis of genetic similarity to us, is called seriously into question on the basis that the bonobo, another species with whom we share a similar proportion of genes, exhibits very different patterns. Equally there is extensive variation in the amounts and in the patterning of violence among early modern humans, insofar as that can be researched, and among contemporary human societies with foraging lifestyles. These historical and contemporary societies show both large differences from each other and sizable changes over time. In our view these findings call sharply into question the view of violence as hard-wired in the human behavioural repertoire.

3   The Biology of Violence
Possibilities and Limitations

3.1   Introduction

There is general agreement among scientists that biological factors form an essential ingredient of a comprehensive explanation for human violence. As we have already noted, displays of aggression, fighting, and other forms of violent behaviour are easy to find across many species, and it is mostly the case that aggression pays off when survival is at stake, if there are no other means of ensuring it. It is deployed in acquiring and protecting resources, for self-defence and to promote chances of reproductive success. Yet the public health approach in this area often appears to shy away from the issue of biological factors in human violence, especially from the potential role genes might play in a tendency toward such behaviour. One of the WHO's key statements, the World Report on Violence and Health (Krug et al., 2002), gives only brief consideration to the possible role of genetic biomarkers as risk factors for *self-directed* violence, but notes that what individuals may inherit is a risk of mental disorder linked to suicide rather than a propensity toward suicide in itself. The subsequent Global Status Report on Violence Prevention (World Health Organization, 2014, p. 27) in contrast acknowledges that 'violence is a multifaceted problem with biological, psychological, social and environmental roots'. However, neither of these two landmark publications allots any space to detailed consideration of biological processes, and neither mentions genetic factors in relation to violence at all. Both reports depict violence as a problem which encompasses biological as well as the other identified influences. Yet could it be that simultaneously they render genetic influences on human aggression as something of an 'elephant in the room'? At issue again is the question of whether we consider this strategy to be integral to our biologically evolved makeup, to an extent whereby as humans we are incapable of refraining from it. Can we leave that history to one side in explaining and addressing violence, and is the WHO on secure ground in paying minimal attention to biological influences?

What makes this apparent gap additionally curious is the fact that as we have seen, the WHO initiative is firmly and explicitly located in the discourse of the public health model of prevention and intervention. Such a model is underpinned both historically and currently by an epidemiological account of causation, prevention, and intervention which is itself fundamentally biological in nature (Elliott et al., 2000). The emphasis on the epidemiological does not go entirely unacknowledged in the WHO reports. For example, the 2014 report claims to bring 'violence prevention in line with other issues such as alcohol and health, climate change, mental health, road safety, tobacco, and tuberculosis' (p. 46). Yet with the exception of climate change and road safety, advances in the understanding of genetic contributors to cause and outcome have been a major component of attempts to address the other public health issues listed. Pursuing the epidemiological analogy lying at the heart of violence as a public health issue a step further, a substantial proportion of the factors highlighted in both the 2002 and 2014 WHO reports as major contributors to aggression are considered by some researchers to be mediated by genetic influences. On the face of it, that consideration seemingly rather belies the WHO report's goal of drawing close parallels between the proposed approach to violence as a public health issue and other issues which have to date been addressed using this model (World Health Organization, 2014).

Placing this in a still broader context, the initiative toward addressing violence as a public health issue began with the explicit exclusion of genetic factors. Specifically, the 1986 Seville Statement on Violence, issued during what was designated as the United Nations International Year of Peace, asserted among other things that 'It is scientifically incorrect to say that war or any other violent behaviour is genetically programmed into our human nature' (Adams et al., 1994, p. 845). The Statement, signed by twenty leading scientists from twelve countries, including Dr Santiago Genovés, originator of the *Acali* experiment (as described in the Introduction), was subsequently adopted by the United Nations Educational, Scientific and Cultural Organisation (UNESCO), and that same year a full book expanding on it was edited by Groebel and Hinde (1989). The Statement was subsequently endorsed by a number of professional bodies such as the American Psychological Association and the American Anthropological Association. However, the Statement has also been the focus of some criticism. Beroldi (1994) contended that in essence it was a political rather than a scientific document and cast doubt on the credentials of some of the authors. Pinker (1997, p. 46) dismissed it as propounding a 'moral certainty' that was misguided and unwarranted. Blanchard and Blanchard (2000) argued that behaviours similar to war are found in several non-human species and interpreted the Seville Statement as discounting any role for biology in contributing to aggression. Gat (2019) argued that the abilities to cooperate, or to compete, or on other occasions to wage war were all inherent dispositions of, or tools available for use by, human beings, that we found 'handy' from time to time. Others have defended the Seville standpoint. Scott and Ginsburg (1994) responded to Beroldi's (1994) comments by indicating the strong scientific backgrounds of the contributors. Ramirez (2013) insisted that the Seville Statement took account of the role of biological and evolutionary factors in behaviour and rejected the claim that this had a predetermining effect on human violence or warmongering.

But these discussions do not take the form of reviews of research bearing on the Statement, and of the role of biology in general, or of genes in particular. Given these sizable inconsistencies of standpoint, therefore, in this chapter (which given the complexity of the material covered, is the longest in the book) we consider whether the alleged neglect or at least the seeming marginalisation of biological – including genetic – levels of explanation is justified. We therefore address the questions: What do we know about the role of biology, and especially of genes, in the occurrence of violent acts and events? Is there anything we can say about this that genuinely advances our ability either to understand the causes of violence or to identify possible ways of reducing it?

3.2   Neurobiology of Violence

A biologically informed model of aggression and violence, which is one constituent of the biopsychosocial orientation adopted here, itself involves integrating several levels of evidence. We will briefly examine each of them in turn but will apportion more time to the genetic aspects. In terms of basic neurobiology, a working model of human aggression requires an understanding of three 'substrates' involved in its occurrence: the roles of specific brain anatomical structures, neurotransmitters, and hormones (Mehta et al., 2013; Nelson and Trainor, 2007; Patrick, 2008; Portnoy et al., 2013; Rosell and Siever, 2015; Waller et al., 2018). At a more foundational level, the operation of neurotransmitters is in turn underpinned by the action of genes, which code for amino acids that initiate the production and action of these 'chemical messengers' in the brain.

Brain structures. Information bearing on the roles of different neural structures comes from several sources. At an earlier stage, what was understood about the functions of different areas of the brain was largely inferred from the study of individuals who had sustained injuries at specific sites. With the advent of neuroimaging techniques, it has been possible to study how levels of activity vary within and between separate 'regions of interest' (ROIs) in the brain when performing different kinds of tasks.

This needs to be viewed in an evolutionary context. Looking at what we might call the 'big picture', there is an association between a number of features of animal brains and intelligence, defining the latter broadly as the 'degree of mental or behavioural flexibility resulting in novel solutions' (Roth and Dicke, 2005, p. 256). These features include overall brain volume, *encephalisation quotient* (the extent to which the brain exceeds the size expected relative to body size), but more importantly 'information processing capacity' which is a function of the number of cortical neurons and conduction velocity. In each of these respects, human brains emerge with significant advantages compared with most other species, though not always by a large margin compared with some. Of potentially closer relevance to aggression and violence, MacLean et al. (2014) investigated the performance of 567 individuals from thirty-six species (mammals and birds) on two tasks that entailed the ability to exercise *self-control*, defined as 'the ability to inhibit a prepotent but ultimately counter-productive behavior' (p. E2141). While this study did not include humans, it did show that brain volume and dietary breadth (an index of the variety of foods a species consumed) were the strongest predictors of capacity for self-control. Humans possess both of these features to a greater extent than the other great apes studied (bonobo, chimpanzee, gorilla, orangutan) and show correspondingly greater ability to restrain impulsive urges.

Among humans, while many different parts of the brain are involved in most activities, with respect to researching aggression most attention has focused on the *amygdala*, part of the limbic system which processes emotional states and especially reactions to threat, and several ROIs in the *frontal cortex*, which is generally viewed as a centre for executive functions such as decision-making and inhibitory control. Within the latter, the *orbitofrontal* and *dorsolateral frontal* areas of the cortex have both been investigated to varying degrees.

Some studies have searched for *structural* differences between the brains of those who have shown aggression, have committed violent acts, show poor impulse control, or have mental disorders of different kinds associated with elevated risk of these problems. Studies have included adolescents diagnosed with conduct disorder, convicted offenders, and adults diagnosed with psychotic illnesses such as schizophrenia, with personality disorders of antisocial or borderline types, or who were classified as 'psychopathic' (Yang and Raine, 2009). This involves use of brain imaging techniques to search for evidence of thinning of designated cortical areas. Other studies have investigated *functional* differences, meaning variations in the level of activation shown in different neural areas when performing a task expected to involve those areas. Brain scanning techniques used in this research have included functional magnetic resonance imaging (fMRI) and positron emission tomography (PET), among others.

The overall findings from such research show some consistency in the patterns of activation associated with aggressive arousal (McLernon et al., 2018). When individuals become emotionally agitated, there are alterations in the levels of activity within all these systems. But it is difficult to discern whether there is any recurrent pattern within this that is unique to anger, aggression or violence, as opposed to fear, grief, sexual excitement or other states of arousal. Taken together with the inclusion of different populations who have varying patterns of difficulties, and inconsistencies among the findings obtained, this precludes the drawing of any exact conclusions about the neural structures involved in violence.

Neurotransmitters. There are more than 100 chemicals known to act in communication between cells of the central nervous system, but only a small number of them have been studied closely in relation to their effect on behaviour. Most prominently in relation to aggression, they include dopamine and serotonin, while others such as noradrenaline (norepinephrine) and vasopressin have been studied to a lesser extent (Niv and Baker, 2012). Realising that findings from previous studies and reviews had been equivocal, Duke et al. (2013) conducted a meta-analysis of 144 studies of 175 independent samples on the relationship between serotonin and aggression, anger, and hostility. (This method of combining findings from a series of similar studies to calculate a more robust estimate than that which can be obtained from a single study is explained further below in Chapter 6.) There was a mean overall effect size of -0.12, indicating a small negative association. That is, lower levels of serotonin were associated with higher levels of aggression – although strangely, in a subset of analyses using third-party reports of aggression, correlations were in the opposite direction. This scarcely makes the serotonin–aggression relationship 'perhaps the most reliable finding in the history of psychiatry', which one of the authors cited by Duke et al. (2013) had proclaimed it to be. They labelled that view instead as a 'demonstrably false belief' (p. 1163).

In what follows, we will look closely at evidence concerning the action of genes in these neurotransmitter systems, which would be the foremost biological route in influencing human aggression. Meyer-Lindenberg et al. (2006) assembled evidence concerning the routes through which a specific gene, the 'low expression' variant of *monoamine oxidase A* (MAOA) could affect impulsivity, a factor in some forms of aggression, via a sequence of neural circuits. Based on fMRI analyses, they noted the impact of this gene variant on levels of amygdala activity during emotional arousal, on hippocampal activity during retrieval of aversive (but not neutral) emotional material, and on levels of functional activity in cingulate cortex and other ROIs. While the changes in the amygdala were observed in both sexes, the other patterns were observed only in men.

These substances are also, of course, often the targets of pharmacological therapies used to ameliorate agitation and aggression, with effects that can be beneficial, but which are often diffuse and may detract from other areas of people's functioning. We will review and discuss evaluation research in this area more fully in Chapter 8.

Hormones. More than seventy chemicals in the human body are known to act as communicators between different organs, but again only a few have been investigated for their possible relation to behaviour such as aggression and violence. The most frequently analysed for this purpose are cortisol and testosterone. These are undoubtedly activated in relation to aggression, but the relationships between them show numerous intricacies. They appear to act interdependently, but the mode of interaction between them varies according to numerous other influences such as age, gender, level and type of aggression, levels of stress, and the presence of other clinical problems (Rosell and Siever, 2015).

The coordinated action of certain brain structures, of neurotransmitters operating within them, and of hormones linked to other bodily systems form the biological substrate for all forms of behaviour including aggression and violence. The relationships of these processes to each other, and to variables on psychological levels and to events in the outside world, are exceedingly complex, and to date it has not proved possible to map out any definitive causal pathway that is unique to aggression such that it can be established that it is the exclusive origin of aggressive impulses or actions.

3.3   Genes and Behaviour

At a deeper level of the biological process in explanatory terms, we encounter the action of *genes*. Let us turn therefore to the more specific question of what role they play in the occurrence of violent behaviour. The question is one that has been asked many times, forming one strand of the 'nature versus nurture' debate in the biological and social sciences. This is a long-running and at times acrimonious dispute with numerous facets, within which the origins of a wide range of behaviours have been discussed. Here we focus specifically on what is known about the role of genetic factors in aggressiveness, and as potential causes of violence: whether genes directly control those behaviours or influence them along- side other factors, and if so, to what extent. This has been a recurrent theme in what is still an ongoing controversy (Beaver et al., 2015; Ferguson and Beaver, 2009). The issue generally centres on the extent to which different aspects of the *phenotype* – observable variations in the *traits* of a living organism – are *heritable*, that is, traceable to its comple- ment of genes.

Several routes have been found through which genes can influence the activity of neural circuits, operating primarily by their effects on the transport of neurotransmitters or on their reception and breakdown after transmission from one neuron to another. To the extent that aggression and violence are thought to have had survival value in human evolution, the link between genes, neurotransmitters, and the action of neural systems is viewed as critical and provides the biological underpinning both of our supposed general predisposition to violence and of individual differences in the strength of such a predilection. In what follows we will explore the light that can be shed on this by surveying findings from three broad areas: (1) quantitative genetics, (2) molecular and biochemical aspects of gene expression, and (3) gene–environment interactions and epigenetics.

Eminent scientist and Nobel Laureate Francis Crick, one of the dis- coverers of DNA, portrayed the 'central dogma of molecular biology' in a simple statement, sometimes represented as DNA → RNA → protein (Crick, 1970). This is shorthand for describing the action of *deoxyribo- nucleic acid* (DNA), the complex arrangement of molecules in the lengthy chains that form our chromosomes. A *gene* is a section of DNA at a fixed position on this chain. Genes operate through intermediary molecules known as *ribonucleic acid* (RNA), and thereby code for the action of a protein or part of a protein inside the cell. This process is essential in determining how cells behave and thereby how our bodies develop and function. According to the central dogma, this process was viewed as unidirectional and irreversible: information did not and could not flow the other way. Some genes have specialised roles in the formation and action of neurotransmitters in the human brain. However, a single gene can have multiple effects, or effects at more than one site, a pattern known as *pleiotropy*.

There are some firmly established examples of direct, linear, causal relationships between identified genes and certain aspects of the human phenotype. Research over recent years has also identified a number of 'candidate' genes thought to have a function in controlling the action of neurotransmitters with respect to particular traits or patterns of behaviour. Some examples of both of these processes are discussed below. In what could be regarded as an expanded version of the central dogma, Knopik et al. (2017) set out a core doctrine for behaviour genetics, which using the same format as above can be summarised as: DNA → RNA → protein → brain → behaviour. This shifts the focus of genetics research from the study of the extent to which a trait or pattern of behaviour may be inherited to an investigation of the mechanisms through which that occurs.

3.4   Quantitative Genetics: Studies of 'Heritability'

The first broad area of genetics which can provide insight into the alleged human propensity for violence is quantitative genetics. Research in this area, for a long time the fulcrum of all work in behaviour genetics, was primarily focused on producing a statistic called *heritability*. This is an estimate of the amount of variation in an attribute of the phenotype (meaning a personality trait, pattern of behaviour, or risk of disorder) that is accounted for by heredity (meaning by the action of a selected gene, or set of genes). Heritability estimates, sometimes denoted as h^2 and reported as a correlation coefficient or as a percentage,[1] have been arrived at using three main strategies. They entail:

- *Family or sibling studies,* in which children varying in their degree of biological relatedness (for example, full versus half-brothers and sisters) are compared in their behaviour.
- *Twin studies,* in which comparisons are made between the traits and behaviours of identical (monozygotic, MZ) and non-identical (dizygotic, DZ) twins. As the former share 100% of their genes, and the latter on average 50%, this affords a test of the importance of heredity as an influence on phenotypic differences.
- *Adoption studies,* in which children are compared in terms of their degree of similarity to their natural versus adoptive parents. One design takes the twin method just described to an additional stage in which MZ and DZ twins who were brought up by their biological parents are compared with other sets of twins who grew up in families into which they had been adopted.

Twin studies, the most frequently used methodology, have yielded extensive evidence of a high degree of genetic association with many features of

---

[1] The forms of reporting heritability estimates given in the text correspond to those used in each research study under discussion.

human makeup at the somatic level. In a very elaborate undertaking, Polderman et al. (2015) drew together results from no fewer than 2,748 such studies published over a fifty-four-year period (1958–2012). The research they reviewed came from thirty-nine countries, integrating results based on an aggregate sample of more than 14.5 million pairs of twins, on the heritability of a total of 17,804 features of individual differences. The latter were condensed into twenty-eight major categories. The majority of the traits so examined referred to bodily features such as height, weight, metabolic or endocrine gland function, the structure of the mouth or the eyeball, and physical illnesses of many types; but some aspects of mental health and behaviour were also included. This review reported an average heritability across all traits of 0.48, and researchers found considerable support for a simple additive model of genetic factors, so providing 'compelling evidence that all human traits are heritable: not one trait had a heritability estimate of zero' (p. 706). At the same time, for most of these traits there was some variation that was not explicable in terms of genetic factors alone.

Aggressiveness was not included within this review, and the closest phenotypic 'trait' associated with it, conduct disorder (CD), departed from the dominant pattern in some important ways.[2] For example, it was among the approximately one-third of the traits that did not conform to a pattern in which there was a mean ratio of 2:1 between correlations for MZ and DZ twins, respectively. For CD indicators, DZ twin correlations were higher than half of the MZ twin correlations, suggesting a 'substantial contribution from shared environmental factors' (p. 706) and that 'shared environmental effects are causing the deviation from a simple additive genetic model' (p. 708). A 'shared environment' refers to, for example, growing up in the same household. Hence evidence of a direct or additive genetic influence on CD is not strong. We should note that aggression can be manifested in CD, but the diagnosis includes several other features, so we cannot be certain that it was present. One criterion involves different types of aggressiveness, but the diagnosis also includes deceitfulness, rule-breaking and destructiveness. Each of those in turn can take a variety of forms. In total there are fourteen features, and an individual can be diagnosed with CD if they manifest any four of them. A person could therefore be diagnosed without having shown physical aggression at all. That being said, in a fraction of cases CD is a precursor of antisocial personality disorder, a frequently found correlate of violent criminality where that emerges in adulthood.

---

[2] Dissocial personality disorder was also included, but information concerning it was very limited.

Though not included in the review by Polderman et al., studies of heritability have been undertaken in regard to many types of behaviour other than conduct disorder. The three methods outlined above have been applied in the behaviour-genetic study of crime in general, to specific forms of it such as violence and to features that are thought to contribute to it such as impulsivity, low self-control, antisocial personality and alcohol abuse. Given the accumulation of findings, there are also several systematic reviews and meta-analyses.

The first review that was concerned with a general gene–crime relationship was carried out by Walters (1992), who expressed scepticism regarding whether research of this kind could tell us anything of practical usefulness. What he concluded to be the best heritability estimates, obtained from adoption studies, ranged from 11% to 17%. In contrast, Mason and Frick (1994) reviewed twelve twin studies and three adoption studies with criminality, aggression or antisocial personality as the dependent variables, and found an average heritability of 48%, far higher than that found by Walters. Miles and Carey (1997) collated results of studies on the scores of MZ and DZ twins on clinical personality inventories that included traits thought to be associated with criminality; they concluded that genetic factors accounted for 50% of the variance.

In a subsequent more extensive meta-analysis, Rhee and Waldman (2002) integrated results from fifty-two samples, comprising 149 groups and a total of 55,525 participant pairs. These authors reported their findings in terms of four main categories of influences on antisocial behaviour (ASB). The effect sizes for each of them were as follows: for additive genetic factors, 0.32; for non-additive genetic factors, 0.09; for shared environmental factors, 0.16; and for non-shared environmental influences, 0.43.

Reviewing the available research, Moffitt (2005) concluded that overall there was evidence that genes influence roughly 50% of the variation in human ASB; shared environmental influences within families account for a further 20%, and unique environmental influences explain the remaining 30%. These figures give somewhat more weight to the genetic component than found in Rhee and Waldman's (2002) study which was the largest available at the time of Moffitt's (2005) overview. However, a few later studies produced still higher heritability estimates than those just mentioned.

- One twin-based study of the genetic contribution to 'psychopathic' traits (grandiosity, callousness, impulsiveness, irresponsibility) obtained values of up to 0.56 (Larsson et al., 2006).

- In a survey of twins, Baker et al. (2007) obtained a figure of 0.96 for the heritability of antisocial behaviour.
- Ferguson (2010) suggested that on average, 56% of the variation in antisocial personality and behaviour could be explained through genetic influences.
- Burt (2009) reported a meta-analysis of nineteen studies of aggressive rule-breaking behaviour, yielding a heritability statistic of 65%, though in fifteen studies of a separate and 'etiologically distinct' form of non-aggressive rule-breaking, h^2 was lower at 48%.
- As part of a longitudinal study, Barnes et al. (2013) compared rates of intimate partner violence (IPV) between MZ and DZ twins aged twenty-four to thirty-four. Analysing data on three forms of violence, they reported that genetic factors explained 54% of the variance in *injuring partner*, 51% in *forcing sexual activity*, but a lower figure of 24% for *hitting partner*.

Using a different methodology, Beaver (2011) reviewed twenty effects from sixteen studies of adopted children. The objective was to test whether having one parent or both who had a history of criminal convictions was associated with greater likelihood of 'being processed' in some way by the criminal justice system – getting arrested, placed under probation supervision or sentenced to prison. Having biological parents with a criminal record was significantly associated with such processing, and this held when the analysis was limited only to those who reported having not been reared by their biological parents. This study has weaknesses, however, in that all the data were based on the children's self-reports, including their accounts of criminal histories of parents with whom they had little contact; and as the ages at which they were adopted were unknown, the possible influence of socialisation by birth parents prior to adoption could not be eliminated.

There are also studies that produce more mixed or ambiguous results, reporting h^2 estimates that are lower and indeed at odds with an analysis supporting marked impact of heritability. For example, as regards personality traits in general, an adoption study by Plomin et al. (1998) found a complete lack of evidence for any genetic influence, reporting an average heritability figure of 0.01 with children assessed annually between the ages of nine and sixteen. Examining factors linked with aggression, Johansson et al. (2010) investigated self-reported control of anger when sober and after drinking alcohol among a large sample of adult twins ($n = 8,964$) in Finland. Using the *State-Trait Anger Expression Inventory* (STAXI) they found heritability estimates for self-reports of anger and its control, among males and females, respectively, to be 27% and 34%

when sober, and 29% and 37% when intoxicated. A comparison of IPV rates among MZ and DZ twins by Hines and Saudino (2004) found that shared genes explained 16% and 22% of the variance in physical and psychological aggression, respectively; somewhat below the figures reported by Barnes et al. (2013) just cited. In a study we will revisit later, Sullivan and Newsome (2015) investigated the possible associations between a series of what are called 'candidate genes' and delinquency. This study found no evidence of significant relationships. There are likely to be variations and inconsistencies in any set of scientific results, and while this is not a fatal flaw, uneven or incompatible outcomes suggest there are other sizable influences on the phenotype. Heredity may not be as dominant an influence as is often claimed in the standard narrative.

A further layer of data collection has been added to the familiar twin-study design by examining correlations between features of twins and those of their own children, using what are known as *children-of-twins* (COT) studies. Logically this rests on the assumption that the progeny of MZ twins are genetically as close to their parent's twin sister or brother as to the parent themself. This has been pursued as a possible methodology for disentangling the respective roles of genes and environment in child development. A review by McAdams et al. (2014) of forty-three studies that employed COT methodology found two studies that focused on some aspect of ASB as a phenotypic outcome (D'Onofrio et al., 2007; Silberg et al., 2012). However, in both of these studies, the dependent variable was conduct disorder, which as we saw earlier includes a range of behaviours and may not necessarily entail aggression. Results from both studies showed patterns of both genetic and environmental influence.

Dhamija et al. (2016) reviewed the field of quantitative behaviour genetics, drawing together results under a conceptual framework of the *externalising spectrum*. This encompasses a range of interrelated psychiatric diagnoses: attention-deficit hyperactivity disorder (ADHD), oppositional defiant disorder, conduct disorder, and antisocial personality disorder. It also includes substance use disorders as they are frequently found to be comorbid with the other types of problem. For the disorders of childhood and adolescence, estimates of heritability typically ranged between 0.50 and 0.70, though there was also variability among the findings located; but very little emerged as attributable to shared environmental factors. For antisocial behaviour defined within this spectrum, the findings of Rhee and Waldman (2002, cited above) were considered the best estimates.

Hence overall, when investigated using traditional MZ–DZ twin comparisons, together with adoption studies, there is evidence of heritability for a variety of personality traits or other aspects of individual differences commonly associated with aggression. On the basis of findings of these kinds, and appearing to repudiate several decades of criminological research, some researchers have gone on to suggest that the actions of parents are only tangentially relevant to the outcome of children's development of capacities such as self-control, usually thought to be instilled through socialisation (Beaver et al., 2010b; Wright and Beaver, 2005). The net import of these results has been to create an impression that alongside many other aspects of the human phenotype, aggressiveness is moderately to highly heritable and genes are the largest single influence on its appearance in someone's life. But there are difficulties with these claims, which we now turn to examine.

Evaluating Quantitative Genetics of Aggression and Violence

The results just surveyed are represented by their authors and widely accepted elsewhere as providing firm evidence for heritability of the tendency to be aggressive. However, in determining what they are believed to reveal about the inherited nature of aggression, these studies are beset by a number of methodological and interpretative difficulties. There are several grounds for concluding that this body of evidence is not as solid and convincing as it ostensibly looks.

First, there is often a marked lack of specificity in the phenotypic variable. It is not possible to say what has been transmitted genetically, and it may not be aggressiveness as such. Given the overlap between different types of emotional and behavioural problems, it might (for example) be a proneness to some type of physiological reactivity, or personal disorganisation, the actual form of which then reflects familial, environmental, peer-related or other types of influence.

Second, some findings leave major interpretative issues unresolved. Analysing data from the National Longitudinal Study of Adolescent Health (ADD Health) in the United States, Beaver et al. (2010a) compared youths with low and high levels of the MAOA gene with respect to whether they became members of gangs or carried weapons. Across the study sample of 1,041 males and 1,155 females, 440 and 201, respectively, showed low MAOA. Among males only, it was found that those with low MAOA were 1.94 times more likely to be gang members and 1.82 times more likely to use weapons than those with high MAOA. But in the overall study population, only seventy-seven were gang members and only fifty-eight used weapons. Thus 96.5% of the sample were not in gangs, and 97.4% did not use weapons. The authors do not present data separately by gender, MAOA status, gang membership, and weapon use. The reported odds ratios for males are impressive and there was a statistically significant difference between those low and high in MAOA in the likelihood of using a weapon in a fight. However, among the males who used a weapon in a fight, the numbers who had high and low MAOA were 4 and 15, respectively. Notwithstanding the statistical significance reported, given that a large majority – in the region of 90% – of the 641 participants with low MAOA did *not* join gangs or use weapons, it is unclear what we can conclude about the association between the gene and the dependent variables.

Third, there have been numerous methodological critiques of twin and adoption studies. Interpretation of twin-based research rests on acceptance of the *equal environments assumption* (EEA): that MZ and DZ twins differ only in the proportion of genes shared, but grow up in similar environments in terms of how they are treated. Almost all identical twins are of the same gender (exceptions are extremely rare), whereas DZ twins can be the same or mixed gender. We might expect the latter to be more likely to elicit differential responses from those around them. For these and other reasons, critics argue that MZ twins are probably treated more similarly by their parents (and others) than DZ twins. A considerable quantity of research shows that 'MZ co-twins experience more similar social environments than DZ co-twins' (Burt and Simons, 2014, p. 231). Thus estimates of heritability might be inflated by the greater similarity in how MZ twins are treated. Very few twin studies report data on environmental variables, so the extent of similarity within them usually goes unmeasured (Burt and Simons, 2014).

In a direct study of this in relation to externalising behaviour problems, LoParo and Waldman (2014) found that MZ, same-sex DZ, and opposite-sex DZ twins did inhabit significantly different 'rearing environments'. In addition, correlations between dimensions of externalising symptoms (such as inattention, hyperactivity-impulsivity, oppositional, and conduct problems) were significantly higher for MZ than DZ twins. Correlations between environmental similarity and externalising symptoms were, on the other hand, very low. The authors concluded the EEA was still intact, as when a combination of rearing similarity and one twin's externalising scores was used to predict those scores for the other twin, none of the correlations proved significant. But that might hardly be surprising: none of the environmental variables recorded (such as whether twins dressed alike, played together or slept in the same room) was a 'trait-relevant' one with an established relationship to problem behaviour. Fosse et al. (2015) reviewed eleven twin studies on schizophrenia, containing 5,187 MZ and 3,932 DZ twin pairs, where aspects of child social adversity (maltreatment, neglect, victimisation, traumatic events) were recorded. For each of the comparisons made, there was significantly greater similarity (at $p < .001$) among these variables for MZ than DZ twins. Felson (2014) examined twenty-five studies to test how much heritability estimates were altered if environmental similarity were taken into account. He found an average reduction in heritability of 14%, concluding that 'it seems unlikely that the EEA is strictly valid, but it also seems likely that violations of the EEA are relatively modest' (p. 196).

Adoption studies too have been criticised on methodological grounds. Deciding to adopt is a premeditated, positive choice, and those who seek to do it are carefully screened. Adoptive family environments tend to be unrepresentative of the environments from which many adopted children come. Thus there are several selection biases operating, and by narrowing the range of environments, those correlations are reduced, again potentially amplifying h^2 estimates. Collectively, these points throw into doubt some aspects of the design strategy and the reliability of conclusions. Twin researchers reject these criticisms and argue, among other things, that genes may influence individuals' environmental pathways, meaning the latter are in that sense also a genetic effect.

Interpreting Heritability

But a more profound difficulty arises from considering what exactly heritability means. To place this issue in a broader perspective, let us examine two related aspects of it. One is the part played by genes in some phenotypic differences that are widely accepted as being wholly or largely attributable to their action; the other is an analysis of the concept of heritability itself. Let us look first at the relationship between inherited and other influences on differences customarily accounted for by genetic mechanisms.

Cystic fibrosis. Some variations are related to health problems that have serious implications throughout individuals' lives, and that are well established as being primarily genetically induced. One example is *cystic fibrosis* (CF), an inherited condition affecting the lungs and other organs. CF causes significant difficulties in breathing together with a range of other symptoms, and leaves individuals open to risk of lung infections. The expression of the gene variant responsible for this, a mutation known as *delta F508*, results in incomplete synthesis of an essential regulatory protein, which affects metabolism of salts and reduces the body's ability to cope with an accumulation of mucus. But that process has been found to be remarkably complex. While genes play the pivotal role in causing CF, they have been found to be influenced by other factors in addition. The severity and rate of progression of CF are influenced by other factors alongside the specific mutation itself. They include the action of other genes, the level of air pollution, and the responses individuals make when trying to control their symptoms, such as their use of exercise (Lewis, 2011). These phenotypic variations arise in relation to a physiological process despite its being traceable to a known number of missing nucleotides at specific loci on a single identified gene, where there is little or no role for learning, experience, interaction or culture.

Handedness. A different example is that of *handedness.* Indicators of left- or right-handedness can be observed some time before birth, as early as at ten weeks' gestation, and it is commonly regarded as an inherited characteristic. It is thought to be one index of *cerebral dominance,* reflecting an asymmetry of roles between the two hemispheres of the brain (Somers et al., 2015). Behavioural asymmetry in the form of handedness has been discovered in chimpanzees and other great apes (Hopkins et al., 2013). This appears to be an elementary and might seem a straightforward and relatively uncomplicated feature of individual differences. However, the determination of handedness is again more complex than we might expect.

Part of this derives from the fact that there are different ways of measuring handedness. When they have been used with the same study populations, in research projects comparing individuals with their first-degree relatives (fathers, mothers, and siblings), they have produced different estimates of the degree to which variability can be accounted for by genetics (Lien et al., 2015). That applies also to other indicators of cerebral dominance. Somers et al. (2015) investigated two hypothesised aspects of this, hand preference and degree of language lateralisation. Results showed that these two indicators are not correlated, and while some gene loci were found that suggested there may be linkage between the two, researchers concluded that it is likely that each of these differences is *polygenic,* that is, influenced by the independent action of a number of genes.

There is research suggesting that a person's handedness can be influenced by environmental factors such as parental influence, culture, differential experience of hand–eye learning, and even season of birth. While there is consistent evidence of genetic contribution, forty or more genes have been identified as being involved, and they interact with one another. Thus estimates of heritability obtained from one sample are not applicable to another (Ocklenburg et al., 2014).

Hence, the role of genes in the development of handedness is not at all clear. The largest analysis of this to date, by Medland et al. (2009), with a combined sample size of 54,270 individuals from families in the Netherlands and Australia, found that genetic influences accounted for just under 24% of the variance in phenotype, with the remainder accounted for by environmental factors. Analysis of historical data suggests there have also been variations over relatively short timescales, and that the proportion of people who are left-handed rose during the course of the twentieth century (McManus et al., 2010).

A second crucial point to recognise when interpreting heritability is that the h^2 statistic quoted in research studies applies at the aggregate or population level. In other words, whatever its numerical value, it cannot tell us anything about the reasons why any given individual acts as they do. Furthermore, even when heritability has been calculated, the results 'apply only to the specific balance of genetic and environmental variation in the time and place in which its participants grew up' (Moffitt, 2005, p. 58). Carrying out a similar study at another time or in a separate population could produce a different heritability estimate. Heritability estimates cannot be extrapolated from one study to another. 'Heritability is the property of a population, not of the characteristic or disorder itself' (Joseph, 2015, p. 78). Putting this another way, 'attempts to measure the relative contributions of genes and environment to a particular characteristic are highly dependent on who is measured and the conditions under which they are measured' (Bateson and Gluckman, 2011, p. 14).

This is a vital point as heritability statistics are often interpreted to mean something that they do not. The figure that is obtained describes the amount of variability within the selected study population that can be attributed to the operation of *their* genes. But as Lewontin (2006) explained, the design of heritability research essentially entails analysis of variance or related statistical techniques. Analysis of variance is not, and should not be taken to be, an analysis of causes. It might be possible to find a heritability estimate of 100% in a study, but that would not mean that the phenotypic feature was entirely determined by genes. It might be obtained because the environment was uniform. Where that (hypothetical) situation occurs, the differences that are observed between individuals will be wholly due to heritable factors. If the environment were more variable, heritability estimates would go down. An example of this is given by Bateson and Gluckman (2011). There seems very little doubt that humans have evolved to have two legs, and have genetic mechanisms that bring this about. But a small number of individuals have fewer than two legs; where that occurs, it is always due to external events or factors (such as toxicity or accidents). Thus any variation that occurs in leg numbers is 100% environmentally induced and heritability is reduced to zero. But it is clearly absurd to discount the role of genetic control over this aspect of the phenotype.

Results illustrating this point with regard to the heritability of intelligence quotient (IQ) were reported by Turkheimer et al. (2003). This aspect of individual differences is usually regarded as highly heritable. This study, however, found that the extent of IQ heritability diverged as a function of socioeconomic status. The h^2 coefficient was higher in middle-class families with more resources, in which case there was lower environmental variation, than in families from more deprived backgrounds, where environments were more variable. Another example of such variation came from a study of gender differences in spatial intelligence, which are often considered to have a sex-linked, genetic basis but have been found to be moderated by culture. Hoffman et al. (2011) used a test of spatial ability with 1,279 villagers from two societies in northeastern India with a shared genetic background but different patterns of social organisation: patrilineal as compared with matrilineal. While in the former they found a significant gender difference in spatial task performance, in the latter no such difference materialised.

Thus a heritability coefficient reflects a pattern of variation. It needs to be seen in the context of the sample from which it was obtained. It cannot be generalised elsewhere, and it is not an indicator of a cause–effect relationship. As Feldman and Ramachandran (2018, p. 7) remark, 'It is almost 50 years since heritability of human traits became discredited as an indicator of genetic causation.' Accepting heritability estimates outside the context of sample variability has been a repeated error in the interpretation of their meaning (Crusio, 2012; Rose, 2006). It makes no sense therefore to calculate average heritability statistics; the result is analogous to being given a figure for the average size of houses in Europe.

How Much Does Heritability Matter?

There is an additional dimension to this, which has to do with the implications of heritability. They are evidently far-reaching, for example, when we can identify a specific genetic cause of an illness, as in cystic fibrosis, phenylketonuria, sickle-cell anaemia, or Huntington's disease. As regards behaviour, on the other hand, even where it appears to be under the control of genes, the pattern can be reversed. Contemplating that prospect, in this context (as compared with medicine) one wonders why so much effort is expended in searching for heritability. Consider two examples from research with laboratory animals.

In a classic series of studies in the behaviourist tradition, Tryon (1930, 1931, 1940) carried out a succession of experiments on the ability of rats to find their way through mazes, a widely used test in behavioural research. This involved selective breeding of two groups differing in ability – referred to as 'maze-bright' and 'maze-dull' rats - over a series of twenty-one generations. After the seventh generation, there was no overlap in the error rate of the two groups. The difference remained a fixture from that point. The laboratory environment was kept equivalent for both groups, so it was concluded that the difference between them was attributable to hereditary factors.

But in a study conducted twenty years later, Cooper and Zubek (1958) found that within a single generation, the differences between bright and dull rats can virtually disappear. When rats differing in selectively bred maze-running ability were placed in 'enriched' as compared to 'restricted' environments for five weeks, their performance was significantly altered by their learning experiences. In the more stimulating conditions of an enriched learning environment, the maze-dull rats' performance equalled that of the maze-bright rats.

A similar pattern of effects has been found for aggression as well, this time with mice. Hood (2005) summarised a series of experiments, also using selective breeding, in which aggressiveness was measured by speed or frequency of attacks by one mouse on another when any two were placed together. To elicit and assess aggression, mice were placed in isolation shortly after weaning. More and less aggressive mice were selected and bred separately for five generations, an experience found to increase attacks in many mice. By the sixth generation, their respective levels of aggression were significantly different. There was no crossover between their attack scores. Each group was then divided, with the descendants of one-half of each continuing to be reared in isolation, while those in the other half were reared in group conditions. For the groups bred in 'social' conditions, the level of aggression by the high-attack mice became similar to that of the low-attack mice. High-attack mice that continued to be reared in isolation continued to show high aggression. When this was repeated after a series of thirty-nine generations, the same effect was found. What had been passed between generations, and was thereby apparently fixed, was actually altered by experience and learning.

3.5   Molecular Genetics

The second broad approach for examining the relationship between genes and violent behaviour focuses on specific genes and combinations of genes. Given its relatively recent inception, *molecular genetics* has been referred to as the youngest discipline to address the foundations of basic human emotion (Reuter, 2010). Rather than comparing the phenotypes of people with different degrees of genetic relatedness, in molecular genetics researchers compute correlations between single genes or their variants and phenotypic variations within a study population. While many research methods are used, two principal approaches have been employed for investigating possible relationships between genes and many aspects of phenotypic variation, including aggression (Gizer et al., 2016a):

- *Candidate gene studies*, in which research populations differing in a characteristic are compared with reference to selected genes or *alleles* (alternative forms or variants of genes) of interest; similar to a group comparison or 'case-control' study in which those with and without a problem are investigated to detect key differences between them.
- *Genome-wide association studies* (GWAS), in which genetic and phenotypic data are collected from very large samples and then systematically searched for associations between gene variants and variations in the phenotype (in this context, in relation to aggressiveness, history of violence, or antisocial personality).

Candidate Genes

In 2012, Niv and Baker (p. 25) noted that approximately two dozen genes had been studied with respect to their possible connections with aggression or violence. More have been added since then. We limit discussion here to only a few of the most intensively investigated in relation to aggression: mainly occurring in the *dopaminergic* or *serotonergic* systems, in other words, genes that respectively affect the activity of dopamine or serotonin, though other circuits have also been investigated. Genes may operate on the transport, reception or breakdown of the neurotransmitter. Portions of this research have been carried out with mice, rats, monkeys or other species. Experimental animals such as mice can be engineered by deactivation ('knock out') of a gene that acts on these systems, and then tested for changes in levels of aggression.

Many studies, however, have been undertaken with humans. Genes may be assessed by direct analysis of DNA obtained from mouth swabs or blood samples, or by detecting leftover metabolites that can be found in cerebrospinal fluid. Participants may be healthy individuals, clinical groups with various diagnoses, or, in some cases, prisoners. Groups are identified as differing in levels of the candidate gene (low versus high) and they are then compared with respect to a phenotypic variable such as self-reported aggression or criminal convictions. Many studies have employed brain imaging while individuals perform tasks such as responding to faces showing (for example) hostile or neutral expressions. The genes most frequently researched are known as *DAT1, DRD2, MAOA,*

COMT, and *5HTTLPR.*[3] Some are parts of larger configurations, but only some of their variants have been studied closely.

For children aged five to sixteen who were described as highly or pervasively aggressive, having scored in the top 10% on scales used to assess this, Zai et al. (2012) investigated possible roles of candidate genes involved in dopamine transport and reception. Three *polymorphisms* of dopamine system genes (i.e. patterns in which variant forms of genes (alleles) were found at the same locus in a strand of DNA), were found to be significantly overrepresented among the group. Hirata et al. (2013) examined the COMT gene. While there was a nominally significant finding for one allele among children of European origin, after required statistical adjustment there was no evidence of genetic differences between the children and controls. On the basis that DNA does not change during development, the control groups in both these studies consisted of healthy adults.

For adolescents and young adults there have been several studies from the National Longitudinal Study of Adolescent Health, which has involved four waves of data collection. Guo, Roettger and Shih (2007) investigated dopamine transporter genes among those in the age range of twelve to twenty-five who reported involvement in serious and violent delinquency. Significant differences were found for alleles of genes DAT1 and DRD2. But the difference showed only in males – there was no similar pattern among females, and findings were not specific to violence: they also emerged among those who reported serious non-violent offending. Vaughn et al. (2009) investigated the DAT1 and 5HTTLPR genes and found a significant association for the former, but only among youths with lower as opposed to higher numbers of delinquent peers, a gene–environment interaction. In a later study of 2,573 young people (with a mean age of sixteen) from the same project, concerned with the same three genes but also including DRD4 and MAOA, no significant associations emerged (Sullivan and Newsome, 2015).

There are several reviews drawing together candidate gene studies thought to be associated with aggression or other forms of ASB. Ficks and Waldman (2014) reported a meta-analysis of thirty-one studies of the MAOA-*uVNTR* gene and eighteen of the 5HTTLPR gene. In both cases there was a significant association between the gene and phenotype, but because the effect size was small to moderate, and there was a large

---

[3] DAT1, dopamine transporter gene; DRD2, dopamine receptor gene; MAOA, monoamine oxidase A (neurotransmitter metabolism gene); COMT, catechol O-methyltransferase (neurotransmitter breakdown gene); 5HTTLPR, 5-serotonin-transporter-linked polymorphic region (serotonin transporter gene).

amount of heterogeneity – in other words, the studies showed a wide spread of results – the authors concluded that 'the magnitude of their effects suggest that each plays only a modest role in ASB phenotypes' (p. 438). No obvious reason could be found for the varied effects. Godar et al. (2016) reported a systematic review of seventy-six studies of MAOA published over a thirty-year period (1985–2015), many based on research with mice. The most frequent association with aggression was produced by an interaction between the low-MAOA gene variant and external stress.

For the COMT gene, Qayyum et al. (2015) collated findings on a total of fifty studies on an allele known as *Val158Met*. The outcome variables here were very varied, however, and included a wide range of mental health and substance misuse as well as behavioural problems. In addition, studies used numerous different methods of assessing aggression. Possibly as a consequence of these issues, findings were very mixed with no clear pattern evident. They were also difficult to interpret because the associations of COMT were in opposite directions among different groups – something also found in research on MAOA (Schlüter et al., 2016) – and due to 'confounding' problems of medication use in some study samples. Attempting to explain the incongruities arising in this research, in overviewing studies of MAOA, 5HTTLPR, COMT, and DRD4, Iofrida et al. (2014) concluded that gene effects were not direct, but a function of an interaction with emotional stress to which some individuals may be particularly vulnerable as a result of neurotransmitter levels modulated by genes.

Among adult offenders, several studies not included in these reviews have found associations between histories of violent offending and levels of the MAOA gene. In a comparatively small study in the United States, Stetler et al. (2014) found low MAOA in 61% of prisoners with convictions for violence, but in only 20% of those convicted of non-violent offences. That difference emerged, however, only for Caucasian and not African American prisoners. In a far larger study in Finland, Tiihonen et al. (2015) compared three groups of prisoners, 203 convicted only of non-violent offences, 430 convicted of violent offences, 78 individuals who had committed at least ten violent offences, and 3,424 individuals in a non-offender control group. Alongside these was an additional replication cohort of 114 offenders, all of whom had committed homicide, and on whom data had been gathered between 1987 and 1998. Two gene variants distinguished the most highly recidivistic violent group from others: low MAOA, and a gene called CDH13, which has a role in the adhesion of external molecules to neurons. The authors considered that up to 10% of serious violent assaults in Finland may be traceable to the effects of these genes, and given that 80% of homicides were 'impulsive, non-meditated crimes' (p. 791), they considered it plausible that a proportion of them may be attributable to an impulse control deficit resulting from this genotype.

Researchers regularly report results pertinent to the central hypotheses under test about links between candidate genes and violent phenotype, and as noted these have received varying levels of support. Beyond this, often many other analyses are conducted and results can be very complex. This occurs, for example, for other relationships that are expected but not always found, such as between the designated gene and personality disorder diagnoses or alcohol abuse. Most studies involve male samples only, but where females are included, often the gene–phenotype relationship does not emerge for them.

A meta-analysis of 185 studies that were published between 1992 and 2011 examined a total of 277 independent associations between thirty-one candidate genes and aggression outcomes. The studies that were included involved a total of 60,000 participants spread across twenty-nine countries. Only studies in which there were at least two replications of an initial finding were retained. Applying this standard for the consistency of findings, there was no reliable evidence of significant associations between any gene and measures of aggression (Vassos et al., 2014). There were primary studies in which significant associations were found: in ninety-two publications (almost exactly half of those located) one significant association was found. But unless the pattern emerged with some consistency, the authors questioned the validity of these studies and excluded them from the review. As Vassos et al. (2014, p. 474) noted, 'the lack of confirmed associations with candidate genes appears to contrast with the expectations in the field, based on the confirmed heritability of aggression'.

The net outcome of this research is that a number of associations have been found. Some of the results appear compelling, probably the most striking being those of Tiihonen et al. (2015). If a cohesive body of evidence emerged along such lines, it would add great weight to gene-based explanations of violence. But there are several difficulties that would need to be overcome for that to happen. First, in some studies the phenotype that is studied is broadly defined ASB-embracing behaviours such as alcohol abuse or rule-breaking other than violence; very few focus on direct measures of violence. Second, only some of the results are reliably duplicated: evidence supporting the hypothesised differences is not consistent. Third, as a result of *pleiotropy*, many of the candidate gene associations discovered are not unique to aggression or even to ASB; typically, they are also associated with other types of difficulty. To take just one example, the COMT *Val158Met* allele has also been linked to depression, schizophrenia, post-traumatic stress disorder, panic disorder, and cocaine dependence. Perhaps the common thread connecting them, if there is one, resides in some subcomponent of emotional lability or reactivity. A similar story could be told about each of the other genes that have been researched in this context. Finally, the amount of variance explained by the gene associations is generally rather low, and with the exception of the study by Tiihonen et al. (2015), effects are usually the product of an interaction with external stress.

As we saw with heritability statistics, there are other complications here that should act as caveats against the mistake of viewing gene discovery as generalisable. Having a genetic architecture that includes a gene or variant thought to be a risk factor for aggression does not mean that the gene will be expressed. Also, a gene found to be present and linked to aggression in one population might not predict it in another, either not to the same degree or possibly not at all; alternatively, it might simply be absent. Allele frequencies vary substantially across different ethnic groups (Spielman et al., 2007). Furthermore, the action of genes often occurs in conjunction with environmental variables, in what are called gene–environment (*GxE*) interactions. Variables such as child maltreatment or adverse backgrounds often have a larger effect on their own, with genes acting in a moderator role.

The limited success of candidate gene research in relation to violence propensity gave rise to mounting and recurrent concern over what was called 'missing heritability'. This denotes the discrepancy between the heritability reported in twin or adoption studies and that accounted for in molecular genetics research. Even when gene variants were located that differed between those people affected and unaffected by a problem, they usually explained only a very small percentage of variance in the phenotype. This was a problem not only in behavioural and psychiatric genetics but across many areas of medical research (Joseph, 2015; Manolio et al., 2009).

Genome-wide Association Studies

The movement from quantitative genetics research (focused on heritability) to the use of more refined techniques of searching and testing for candidate genes was expected to lead to major advances in gene identification. The pace of work accelerated following the advent of microarray techniques (Plomin, 2013). Rather than looking at a solitary gene for possible association, within one study it became possible to explore hundreds of thousands of *single nucleotide polymorphisms* (SNPs) – small variations in the DNA bases of genes – across each individual participant's genome. This provided an extremely efficient and cost-effective mechanism for exploring the hypothesised genetic basis of behaviour.

We therefore focus next on the second of the methods listed earlier, *genome-wide association studies* (GWAS), which include some of the most powerful techniques devised so far for tracing the evolution of human genes. This has been used to map the historical movement of our populations across the globe, and the changing epidemiology of diseases. In the context of researching aggression, the focus of molecular studies has been on the pathways from genes to proteins that then affect the action of neurotransmitters such as dopamine and serotonin, or enzymes such as monoamine oxidase which break down neurotransmitter molecules after they have passed across the synapse.

This approach has been applied to a number of variables with possible links to aggressive behaviour. Two studies have searched for genes associated with conduct disorder (CD). Dick et al. (2004) assessed the genomes, and obtained information on behavioural histories, of three members from each of 1,227 families. No significant associations between any gene and CD emerged, but five genes were identified as having possible linkages. In a later analysis with 1,899 individuals who met criteria for alcohol dependence, and 1,946 in a non-clinical control sample, Dick et al. (2011) found four genes with significant associations to CD. However, there was no overlap between the two sets of findings; none of the genes was the same in both studies, indeed they were not located on the same chromosomes.

A large UK-based study of child behaviour problems used a specific type of GWAS known as *genome-wide complex trait analysis* (GCTA). Trzaskowski, Dale and Plomin (2013) analysed data from 2,500 twin pairs at the age of twelve, examining a total of 1.7 million DNA markers. The phenotype variables measured covered a wide range including ADHD and negative moods, but also antisocial features such as impulsivity, narcissism, and callous/unemotional personality traits. However, no evidence of significant genetic influence was found. For all the variables assessed, there were large drops in heritability in GCTA analyses as compared with twin heritability estimates.

Tielbeek et al. (2012) reported a GWAS of adult antisocial behaviour carried out in Australia. This included 3,167 individuals having a diagnosis of antisocial personality disorder, for which the diagnostic criteria stipulate that an individual had conduct disorder before the age of fifteen; and 1,649 others who took part in a telephone psychiatric assessment interview. Thus genomic and phenotypic data were collected for a total of 4,816 participants from 2,227 families. 'No genes met the criteria for

genome-wide significance' (p. 4), and the top fifty genetic markers showing the strongest association with the phenotype explained less than 1%
of the variance in it. One gene that emerged as having a possible association was already linked in other research to risk of intellectual disability.
The authors also conducted specific searches for potential links with
candidate genes that had been investigated in other studies; however,
none reached a statistically significant level.

Gizer et al. (2016b) brought together a wide range of molecular
genetics studies concerned with problems on the externalising spectrum
described earlier. This suggested possibilities in relation to several genes
that may be linked to the spectrum, but no indication of any identifiable
pathways from specific genes to specific problems or disorders. However,
there was very little overlap between the genes identified through different methods of investigation (of the kinds listed earlier). Notably, there
was a 'lack of overlap between candidate gene and GWA studies'
(p. 159). Gizer et al. raised the prospect of some communality potentially
emerging as sample sizes are further increased. However, the difficulty in
finding recurring or consistent patterns may be a consequence of the
multiple ways in which genes or alleles combine in influencing the
emergence of traits, because those differences are a function of as yet
unknown gene switches that are responding to environmental conditions, an issue we will return to later.

The largest meta-analysis to date of genome-wide genetic variants with
potential relevance to aggression and violence was conducted by an
international group of researchers, the Broad Antisocial Behavior
Consortium (*BroadABC*), and reported by Tielbeek et al. (2017). The
review combined data from five 'discovery' study samples (from
population-wide exploratory studies) and three 'target' samples (target
populations specially selected for testing hypotheses), making a total
participant pool of 25,781 individuals. All were of European descent.
The phenotypic trait of interest was a broad-spectrum definition of
antisocial behaviour, which in the samples that were studied encompassed rule-breaking, conduct problems as reported by teachers or
parents, and criteria for personality disorder. No genome-wide significant associations were found across the amalgamated discovery sample,
but three 'promising' gene loci were found, two among females and one
among males.

Boccio et al. (2018) drew together evidence on the molecular genetics
of aggression and violence and with reference to GWAS expressed
several concerns about the realistic chances of locating genes linked
to aggression. First, like candidate gene studies, this research is

inconclusive; there are sometimes positive, sometimes negative associations; no firm or consistent pattern of findings has emerged. Second, again the identified genes usually explain only a very small portion (<1%) of the variance in the phenotype; very large sample sizes are needed to increase this proportion. If there were a strong causal pathway operating, surely it should become discernible without a resort to study samples in the tens of thousands. Third, the upshot of this is to leave the problem of missing heritability wholly unresolved. Researchers recommend that further studies be conducted with larger samples, in the hope of finding rarer gene variants, and gradually explaining more of it. That may succeed in relation to some disease traits, but the evidence so far raises the question of whether any combinations of genes are going to be found that will be reliable risk markers for aggression.

In a similar exercise, Gard et al. (2019) gathered together the findings of six genome-wide association studies of different aspects of antisocial behaviour. They include the studies by Dick et al. (2011) and by Tielbeek et al. (2017) just outlined, together with reports by Viding et al. (2010) on conduct problems and callous-emotional traits, Pappa et al. (2015) on children's aggressive behaviour, and Salvatore et al. (2015) and Rautiainen et al. (2016) on antisocial personality disorder. Across the last four studies with samples in the hundreds or thousands, only one genome-wide significant association was found (by Pappa et al.). A suggestive association in the Salvatore et al. study did not reappear in a replication sample. There were, however, some suggestive associations in the study by Rautianen et al., and a proportion of the 'hits' in stage 1 of the study by Viding et al. yielded significant associations in stage 2.

Some other GWAS are of note as they were concerned with factors often linked to aggression. Two were concerned with *behavioural disinhibition*. McGue et al. (2013) defined this in terms of alcohol or other substance misuse but also included conduct disorder and aggression, obtaining data from 7,188 individuals in 2,300 families. The study 'failed to yield any significant associations' (p. 370), though one genetic marker fell just below the significance threshold, and several others were noted as candidates for further study. Derringer et al. (2015) searched for similar associations between genes and a composite measure involving substance misuse, novelty seeking, and conduct problems in a sample of 1,901 adolescents with a mean age of 16.5. Here too no locus reached genome-wide significance. A third GWAS by Warrier et al. (2018) is a study of *empathy* with a participant sample of 46,861. This was investigated because people with limited capacity for empathy are considered to be potentially more prone to violence given their relative difficulty in responding to other people's feelings, or their lack of concern for the hurt caused to them. The measure of phenotype here was the *Empathy Quotient*, derived from a self-report questionnaire administered online, comprising cognitive and affective dimensions of empathy. This identified eleven potential or 'suggestive' gene loci, but none reached statistical significance.

Yet fundamentally, research in this area is still plagued by measurement issues. When researchers identify a gene, they are referring to a cluster of molecules (DNA) typically with a breadth of just 2.5 nanometres (billionths of a metre). Using computerised microarray techniques, this task can nowadays be carried out with fastidious precision. By comparison, the measurement of almost any aspect of aggression or violence involves methods that are both highly varied and notoriously imprecise. As Duke et al. (2013, p. 1152) have commented, what have been called the *jingle fallacy*, using the same label for different constructs, and the *jangle fallacy*, applying different labels to the same construct, are both 'rampant in aggression research'. To make matters worse, the phenotypic variables of interest here are rarely if ever unitary constructs with formal definitions to begin with. They are assessed by a plethora of methods that often correlate very poorly with one another. For example, the level of agreement between different measures of low self-control (what is called their *convergent validity*) is well below satisfactory, as found in a meta-analysis by Duckworth and Kern (2011). More worryingly, expert psychometricians have questioned whether variables of this kind can be meaningfully quantified in the manner that is widely applied in psychological research and practice (Borsboom, 2005; Salzberger, 2013).

On the basis of the foregoing compilation of studies, placed against the background of results from research in quantitative genetics, if there are genes that confer an increased risk of aggressiveness, they have proved elusive. Itemising the gene loci highlighted in each of the fourteen GWAS discussed above, and including not just the small number that emerged as statistically significant but also those considered promising or suggestive, no single gene emerged more than once from the collected analyses. The most common finding of reviews in this area is that very little is discovered that is of any real substance. If genetic influences were a main driver of human aggressiveness, it would be reasonable to expect there to be more persuasive results from the sequence of studies just reviewed. The discrepancy between the conclusions of heritability studies and the outcomes of both candidate gene and genome-wide studies gives rise to some uncertainty over existing models of how genes work in influencing features of the human phenotype.

Parallels in Research on Mental Disorders

When considering the roles of genetic influences on aggression, there are illuminating parallels we can draw with research on the genetics of schizophrenia and other major psychiatric diagnoses. As with aggression and violence, the definition of many of these involves a mixture of sometimes quite dissimilar phenomena. There are high levels of heterogeneity within disorder categories and of comorbidity between them. There are consequent disagreements as to the scientific validity of some of the constructs employed (Hyman, 2010). Nevertheless, evidence from the type of twin and allied studies outlined above has indicated a high level of heritability for schizophrenia, and many psychiatric texts and research papers refer to it as a heritable brain disease. At an individual case level, clinical reports almost routinely include information on a patient's first- and second-degree relatives who have been diagnosed with mental disorders. Given those presuppositions, there has been extensive research into the genes that might be responsible for schizophrenia.

In recent years that work has extended to encompass several other diagnostic categories in addition to schizophrenia itself, coordinated by a worldwide research group, the Psychiatric Genomics Consortium (PGC), which as of 2018 included more than 800 researchers from over forty countries (Plomin, 2018). In the first wave of the studies, the other disorders that were investigated were autism, ADHD, bipolar disorder and major depressive disorder. In a later development, more were added: anorexia nervosa, obsessive-compulsive disorder, Tourette syndrome, post-traumatic stress disorder and substance use disorders (Sullivan et al., 2018).

Population-based research in mental health has required very large samples for the purpose of discerning gene associations. For example, a study of genes related to the first five disorders just listed was based on a sample of 33,332 individuals diagnosed with schizophrenia, plus 27,888 controls (Cross-Disorder Group of the Psychiatric Genomics Consortium, 2013). There is an eventual aim of achieving 100,000 participants per disorder category. The broad outcome of this massive research effort is that numerous genes have been identified, each of which confers a small and nondeterministic additional risk for the development of schizophrenia. Many of the same genes, sometimes in combination with others, can also be risk markers for a variety of other disorders.

As compared with the early years of genetic research on schizophrenia, when one after another rather simplistic theories as to its genetic cause were forwarded but not long afterward discounted, the notion that there is any specific gene or set of genes responsible for any single disorder has had to be wholly abandoned. In the case of schizophrenia, more than 700 genes have been probed as to their potential significance (Farrell et al., 2015). By 2018 the list of candidate genes being researched by the PGC had reached 155.

The position today therefore is one in which it appears likely that a large, indeed potentially very large, number of genes may each contribute a small additive effect to the development of one or more mental disorders. Their contributions may be independent, but they may also be combinatorial. Some of the genes are implicated in a wide assortment of different problems including not only mental disorders but also physical diseases such as diabetes. Others are rare variants of different genes whose action in each case is itself variable. Researchers have produced an 'atlas' showing significant correlations of different permutations across a series of twenty-four aspects of individual differences or 'traits'. These include basic features such as birth weight, age at menarche, years of education, and presence or absence of certain physical diseases and mental disorders (Bulik-Sullivan et al., 2015).

Alongside this, on the grounds of genome-wide research conducted by the PGC, heritability estimates reported in twin studies have all been revised downward, as shown in Table 3.1.

As mentioned, most of the mental disorders discussed here have complex presentations. For schizophrenia they include features in multiple constellations: positive symptoms such as hallucinations and delusions; negative symptoms such as social withdrawal; cognitive dysfunction such as thought disorder; and altered mood states. At an individual level the pattern of experience may be very variable. Consider then the variation in the kinds of phenomena that are classified as aggression. Even when employed in psychiatric diagnosis, the range of disorders that include some variant of aggression as a potentially defining feature is wide. It is associated with ADHD, oppositional defiant disorder, and conduct disorder in childhood and adolescence and with

Table 3.1 *Heritability estimates in twin studies and genome-wide studies*

	Twin studies (%)	Genome-wide studies (%)
Schizophrenia	81	45
Bipolar disorder	80	21
ADHD	70–80	22
Substance use disorders	50	8

Source: Sullivan et al. (2018).

antisocial/dissocial personality disorder in adulthood. Yet the links between each of these remain poorly understood, and none has been validated as a clear, naturally occurring category separated from others (Hofvander et al., 2009). The definition of the phenotype when discussing these disorders is therefore highly varied and refers to different behaviours at different phases of the lifespan.

Returning to genetic research on aggression, a similar position prevails, as described by Craig and Halton (2009). These authors reviewed a range of candidate genes and possible pathways through which they might influence behaviour. This entailed examination of sex differences in hormones associated with aggressiveness, various neural axes through which genes might operate, and the roles of serotonin, tryptophan enzymes, and other neurotransmitter and receptor mechanisms. Studies on each of these do not yield consistent results, and 'the overwhelming conclusion from both linkage and candidate gene studies is that there are few, if any, loci with large effect sizes' (p. 108). Craig and Halton propose that any such connections need to be understood as part of a 'multifactorial miasma' probably including a wide range of gene–environment interactions to which we now turn.

3.6   Gene–Environment Interactions and Epigenetics

The net conclusion from the research we have perused thus far is that no gene has been detected that directly causes aggression or violence. Nor to date are there any dependable clues as to a combination of genes that fits that description. It looks highly doubtful whether such a gene or network of genes exists. How then can we account for the heritability estimates discussed earlier in this chapter, and assertions to the effect that approximately 50% or more of individual differences in aggression are due to the action of genes?

Several possibilities arise in trying to understand this. They need to be placed in the context of developments in the genetics of antisocial behaviour (ASB) as described by Niv and Baker (2012, p. 26, emphasis in original):

Although there is much interest in candidate genes, molecular biologists now understand that DNA sequences of various polymorphisms do not tell the whole story. Especially when considering the profound influence of environment on ASB, it is important to consider how environment interacts with DNA on a molecular level. A new field of genetics has emerged that examines an additional level of complexity in genes ... this field is called *epigenetics*.

Part of this consists of cellular-level modifications to DNA that do not affect the sequencing of its bases but determine the frequency of translation into proteins. There is evidence that the environment is involved in this and can influence whether or not a gene is transcribed. This highlights the potential for rewiring our theories of violence to ensure the reciprocal relationships between levels in the biopsychosocial model are fully incorporated.

Thus one widely discussed possibility with increasing evidential support is that the effects of genes occur mainly through interaction with environmental variables (often labelled *GxE*). The impact of this is probably not directly on aggressiveness itself but on temperamental factors which, depending on socialisation experiences, could place people at risk of using aggression as a frequent means of responding. Research in this area needs to be approached with caution, as in an initial extensive review of candidate GxE studies in psychiatry, Duncan and Keller (2011) found evidence of publication bias and failures to replicate. Their review, however, did not cover studies of aggression or antisocial behaviour.

Byrd and Manuck (2014) reported a meta-analysis of the interaction effect between the low MAOA gene and childhood maltreatment in relation to later antisocial behaviour. The effect did not appear among females, but was found in sixteen of twenty studies with males. We will discuss this in a little more detail in Chapter 4. Weeland et al. (2015) reported a meta-analytic review of fifty-three studies of interaction effects between candidate gene polymorphisms (DAT1, DRD2, DRD4, 5HTTLPR, MAOA, COMT) and environmental variables (family adversity, child neglect/abuse, harsh parenting or neighbourhood disadvantage) in relation to externalising behaviours. They found an inconsistent pattern of results, and that methodological differences between studies, including poorly specified environmental and ASB measures, made comparisons difficult. To address those deficits, they recommended the articulation of clearer, testable models of the process through which GxE interactions have an impact, suggesting emotional reactivity, or sensitivity to punishment and reward, as possible mediating variables. This has similarities to the *differential susceptibility* model proposed by Simons and Lei (2013) as a formulation of GxE processes leading to aggression. Subsequently, Gard et al. (2019) provided a tabulated summary of studies in which interactions between different genes and environmental factors have been found to have effects on antisocial behaviour.

Non-coding Genes

How do such interactions occur? A potential resolution of the missing heritability puzzle, if we regard it as such, given reservations expressed about it earlier, could emerge from the recognition that a large portion of the human genome consists of genes that do not directly code for proteins. This is what was at one time known as 'junk DNA'. Finding that this has an active and perhaps focal role may call into doubt the generality of the central dogma (DNA → RNA → protein). Evidence continues to mount that 'the number and repertoire of protein-coding genes remains relatively static across the metazoan lineage, despite enormous increases in developmental and cognitive complexity' (Mattick, 2011, p. 1601). (Metazoan refers to any organism with a multicellular body containing differentiated or specialised cells, essentially referring to all animals). By contrast, the proportion of what are called 'non-coding' genes varies widely across species. In the period since completing the analysis of the human genome, research has produced some momentous surprises. One is that there are many species which, despite showing immense phenotypic differences, have roughly the same number of coding genes and even share many of them in common.

For example, an organism often studied in genetics research is the nematode *Caenorhabditis elegans*, a soil-dwelling worm just one millimetre long. This animal has only 1,000 cells in its entire body. Of those, 302 are neurons, with 7,000 connections between them. It was the first multicellular organism to have its genome sequenced (Wilson, 1999), and also the first to have the 'circuit diagram' or *connectome* of its entire nervous system fully mapped (Seung, 2012). Notwithstanding its structural simplicity compared to humans, *C. elegans* has 20,470 protein-coding genes, not far short of the number possessed by *Homo sapiens*.[4] On what we can only call a different order of magnitude, human brains are calculated to have in the region of 86 billion neurons (Azevedo et al., 2009).

Running counter to the relative uniformity in numbers of genes that assign proteins, there are major differences between species in the proportion of *non-coding* DNA, which refers to sections of DNA with functions other than transcription for proteins. One of those functions involves regulating the action of coding genes, governing whether or not they are *expressed* (transcribed and translated), and their interactions with one another. The number of such non-coding genes steadily increases with the developmental complexity of organisms. Mattick (2011) has graphed the proportions for 86 species. Humans have the

---

[4] When the space shuttle *Columbia* was destroyed on re-entry to the earth's atmosphere on 1st February 2003, killing all seven astronauts on board, several hundred *C. elegans* which had been part of an on-board experiment were later found to have survived (BBC News, 1st May 2003). (To be accurate, as *C. elegans* has a lifespan of only three weeks, the ones found were descendants of the originals).

highest known proportion, at 98.8%. In other words, only 1.2% of our complement of DNA is of the coding type, the genes that have direct expression as proteins.

Non-coding genes act as 'switches' of protein-encoding genes. It is therefore conceivable that there are routes of genetic transmission other than by direct transcription of protein by coding genes, where the extent to which that is implemented is a function of non-coding genes. The latter are attuned to and responsive to signals from the environment, such that from the moment of conception when two strands of DNA meet, the subsequent path of development represents a convergence of genetic and environmental influences.

Tremblay, Vitaro and Côté (2018) provide an outline of how this may happen in relation to aggression. This drew initially on laboratory research with animals, in which it was found that higher levels of maternal care provided by mother rats towards their offspring affected a process known as DNA *methylation*.[5] This results from the action of a non-coding *promoter* gene, which was activated in response to the mother's efforts to soothe the pup following stress (Weaver et al., 2004). Testing whether anything similar occurred in humans, in their research in child development Provençal, Booij and Tremblay (2015) found that chronic aggressive behaviour by a small proportion of boys may be a result of epigenetic changes during pregnancy and early childhood, that were the joint effect of genetic risk, early-life adversity and maternal stress. Another study found that men with a long history of aggression dating from childhood had significantly lower blood levels of immune molecules called *cytokines*, and a distinctly different pattern of DNA methylation, as compared to others with a less aggressive behavioural profile. Numbers in both these studies were however relatively small.

On the basis of these and other studies, Tremblay et al. (2018) forwarded a multi-stage model of the first six years of life, supported by research, showing channels of interaction between the environment, DNA expression, brain functioning and behaviour - from conception, in utero, in infancy, and early childcare, to the start of schooling and formation of friendships. Earlier, Szyf (2009) formulated how early-life experiences 'reset' the epigenome to anticipate the likely environment at later stages of life, and proposed that epigenetic processes

---

[5] Methylation is one of a number of processes in which a chemical change is induced in DNA bases by the action of promoter molecules, located in a non-coding region of DNA. This has a decisive effect on whether a gene is transcribed. An explanation of how this occurs is given by Roth (2012).

dynamically influenced the extent of gene expression, possibly at all stages of the lifespan. This is a genuinely multi-level, biopsychosocial approach and integrates data from each of the three planes, producing a more soundly balanced and more firmly evidence-based account of the roles of genetic factors.

3.7   Conclusion

In response to these and other kinds of advances, many geneticists and theoretical biologists now agree that there is a clear need to advance our thinking beyond what has been called the 'protein-centric' view of how genes operate. Partly stemming from the highly influential work of Jablonka and Lamb (2005), they consider that there are more processes involved in evolution than those specified in the central dogma that revolves around the action of DNA, RNA, and proteins (Bonduriansky and Day, 2018; Moore, 2015). They propose that other mechanisms are needed to make sense of the evidence, which is more complex than can be explained by what is called the 'neo-Darwinian synthesis'. Genetic transmission as specified in the core doctrine (DNA → RNA → protein) is just one route. Evolutionary change also occurs through epigenetics, behavioural learning, and cultural dissemination.

This is an increasingly influential perspective that goes beyond the atrophied clash of ideas on the relative importance of heredity and environment, and supersedes the concept of 'innateness'. One approach involves analysing the relationship between those aspects of development that are robust alongside those which exhibit some form of plasticity, and how such processes interact (Bateson and Gluckman, 2011). It has also been contended that an approach of this kind can explain the gap between quantitative and molecular genetics results (missing heritability). The perspective is that of *postgenomics* (Charney, 2012; Panofsky, 2015), and is illustrated in the following statement by Keller (2015, p. 25):

I am proposing that today's genome, the postgenomic genome, looks more like an exquisitely sensitive reaction (or response) mechanism – a device for regulating the production of specific proteins in response to the constantly changing signals it receives from its environment – than it does the pregenomic picture of the genome as a collection of genes initiating causal chains leading to the formation of traits.

Probably the most controversial suggestion within this, forwarded by Burt and Simons (2014), is that heritability research is misleading, flawed, and should be discontinued. Researchers working within the paradigm of heritability were critical of and resistant to such a proposal (J. C. Barnes et al., 2014) and the debate has continued. While contemporary research in medical and behavioural genetics has in many ways now moved far beyond that issue, the backdrop of evidence from heritability studies still functions as a cornerstone of reasoning about the proportion of our makeup that passes routinely and pristinely from one generation to the next.

But drawing together the research reviewed here alongside that discussed in Chapter 2, the extent of malleability of human behaviour is signally its most outstanding feature. Of course, there are biological necessities and limits on our abilities. Yet many patterns of behaviour that we usually regard as, if not determined, at least genetically highly influenced, can be modified or completely overridden by environmental changes. What is described as innate or inherited in human behaviour is not a tendency to act in any specific way, but a capacity to adapt to diverse situations, and to develop neural connections that become the foundation for subsequent modes of response (Costandi, 2016; Elman et al., 1996). Recognition of this has led to proposals that what has been called the 'modern synthesis' is in need of radical revision or replacement. This term refers to the combination of evolutionary theory, genetics, and studies of population variance that dominated biology from the middle of the twentieth century onward. Laland et al. (2015) have suggested that such a position needs to be broadened and reformulated in an *extended evolutionary synthesis* which takes into account evidence concerning cultural and social learning, and the construction of 'developmental niches' which have a considerable impact on the phenotype through non-genetic processes.

Having devoted this chapter and parts of the preceding one to biological aspects of aggression and violence, we return to the general position that these problems can be understood only within a multifactorial framework, which includes biological, psychological and social factors, placed in their environmental context. Our interest in the biopsychosocial orientation is an authentically integrative one. We have devoted considerable space to the biological component, but it is not construed in such a way as to 'privilege' biology over the other components, as has happened in some previous iterations of similar models (Johnstone et al., 2018). Biological influences are evidently fundamental and far-reaching: we are products of evolution, and are constructed by the action of our genes. But our careful search through the evidence reviewed here suggests, if anything, that the role they have in explaining the occurrence and patterning of aggressive or violent thoughts, feelings or actions is often overstated. The view that we are genetically programmed toward using violence is scientifically unfounded. That is in essence the substance of the Seville Statement. We consider that the material brought together in this chapter and elsewhere in the present volume amounts to a strong vindication of the precepts contained in that Statement.

4 Developmental Factors in Violence Propensity
The Learning of Violence

4.1 Introduction

So far we have been reviewing evidence for and against the idea that human beings are 'hard-wired' for violence. We have been suggesting that there is limited evidence for the strong proposal that acting violently is an integral part of 'human nature' and that there is plentiful support for the alternative perspective. At the very least, the charge of biological determinism for human violence remains unproven. To be sure, this is not to discount the plentiful evidence that violence has obviously been a recurrent feature of human life at both individual and societal levels for millennia. It is awareness of this long-standing characteristic that may sustain the seemingly widespread but as yet unjustified assumption that we are inherently motivated toward violence, or that we cannot stop ourselves from engaging in it. However, we must remind ourselves again that the simple occurrence of violent events even if frequent does not on its own confirm or deny the supposition that the cause of them lies in our basic nature, or that such a pattern is inescapable and we are perennially bound to repeat it. All that counting violent events can ever do is support the self-evident position that we have a *capacity* for violence that in some circumstances is expressed. The extent and manner of that expression shows large variations, between individuals, between social groups, and over time, as a function of developmental, cognitive, situational and historical factors. These variations provide the key to understanding the more likely reasons for human violence and the degree to which environment and culture counterbalance any hypothetical innate drive toward aggression and destruction.

Rejecting the widely taken-for-granted narrative, of course, leaves a large question unanswered. If we are not by nature violent, yet we often perpetrate it – despite the obvious damage it does, and contrary to the claims of most people to abhor it – where does it come from? Acts of violence do not appear out of nowhere. They are a product of a convergence of factors. A tendency to act aggressively or to resort to violence on repeated occasions is a result of numerous influences operating in combination. Some of them are immediate and directly precede the situation where it occurs ('proximal factors'), while others have longer-term antecedents ('distal factors'). Both types of factor can operate at any level: biological, psychological or social. It is the time lapse between the cause and the violent effect which is relevant, not the type of factor. All of the causal or contributory factors considered here in the first part of the book can be proximal or distal.

In this chapter we will address the question of causation from a psychosocial perspective by surveying research on human development from birth to adulthood, investigating individual differences in whether and to what extent people show aggression or violence. This indicates strongly that the likelihood of engaging in violence is largely a product of experience and learning. This review will underpin the discussion later in Chapter 9 which focuses on the question of whether individuals who have acted violently are susceptible to change through psychological interventions which can reduce the extent of it in their lives, with benefits both for others and for themselves. Adopting a developmental perspective indicates that what has been learned can also be unlearned; alternatives to violent behaviour can be adopted to replace it. The next chapter on structural violence will take this argument one step further by showing that similar processes of learning and of social interaction can be seen operating within both individuals and societies, at micro- and macro-levels of human behaviour.

An important preliminary point is worth noting before we proceed. Reviews of research on 'criminal careers', the study of human development with an emphasis on when and how individuals break the law, indicate that the majority of offenders do not act violently. Violent behaviour is a rare event in most crime careers, forming only a small portion of the criminal 'repertoire' of most offenders, with the exception of a small group of prolific or chronic individuals who are more likely to have committed violent offences. This clustering of violence in a small group of perpetrators was noted in Chapter 1 and occurs in part because they have committed a far larger number of offences of several kinds: across the population of convicted offenders, the larger the total number of convictions individuals have, the likelier it is that some of them will be for violence. Even among those labelled as violent offenders, the majority commit only a single violent offence during an offending career (Piquero et al., 2012). Although one-fifth of the prison population of England and Wales comprises those who have been convicted of violence against the person (Allen and Dempsey, 2016), that proportion results from the greater likelihood of being given a custodial sentence after being found guilty of such an offence. The key point is that very few offenders 'specialise' in committing violence, and members of that group tend to commit a first offence at an earlier age, and to commit more crimes overall, than other offending groups. They also acquire a much higher public profile through media reports, which tends to skew our perception of the problem.

4.2   Becoming Violent

The process through which some individuals turn into adolescents or adults who are prepared to use violence to secure their goals or to resolve conflicts is a complex one. Psychologists and others use the term *multifactorial* to describe how an outcome is produced from the inter-action of numerous variables, which can also influence each other in multiple ways through feedback loops. Thus, other than in a very small minority of cases, there is no direct line from early childhood experiences to adulthood, along which we can easily trace the growth of a tendency toward acting aggressively or violently.

In the study of development, the intricacy of the paths that a growing child might take is reflected in two interconnected terms. *Equifinality* refers in general to the possibility that 'organisms may reach the same end-point via many different pathways' (Bateson and Gluckman, 2011, p. 25) and, in this context, to how 'the same antisocial outcome can accrue from disparate sources' (Dodge and Pettit, 2003, p. 354). Along-side this is another tendency called *multifinality*, in which 'specific risk factors can be associated with a variety of outcomes' (Dodge and Pettit, 2003, p. 354). Putting this more concretely, adults who act aggressively could have got that way due to varying combinations of predisposing influences. Conversely, children or young people exposed to similar adverse experiences do not all turn out the same. The number of specific variables that can affect this process is large, and given varying permutations of them, the range of possible outcomes is enormously wide. In what follows we examine some of the main categories of factors that have been established as playing a contributory role. We consider them under five headings: biology and temperament, socialisation, cultural context, situational factors, and cognitive processes.

4.3   The Influence of Temperament

Not long after birth and before any significant opportunity is available for learning, newly born infants show individual differences in several features, including how much they sleep, their level of activity when awake, or how easily they become distressed. In the following days some become more restless, while some may appear calmer, or perhaps more fearful than others. Parents often discuss how well their babies sleep, how much they react to changes in their surroundings, and how easy they are to soothe if they become upset. In the ensuing months, some children cope better than others with short periods away from their parents or other key caregivers. Developmental scientists call these differences aspects or features of *temperament*. The term refers to patterns of behavioural activity and emotional responding rooted in biology, which are evident soon after birth and remain relatively stable for some time afterward, at least for the first few months of life and sometimes for longer (Kagan and Snidman, 2004; Rothbart, 2011). These tendencies are clearly to some degree influenced by or under the control of genes and epigenetic factors, but at this early age none of them constitutes aggression in most of the ways it is defined. Some temperamental differences remain relatively stable and are maintained into the first few months and even perhaps the first few years of a child's life, and in some cases they continue into the early adolescent years (Kagan et al., 2007). These patterns were discovered through longitudinal research designs in which large cohorts of individuals are followed up and assessed on successive occasions over a period of years. In some of the best work of this kind, developing children have been studied for decades across successive phases of the lifespan: from birth or early childhood well into adulthood or, in some studies, even into their forties.

Studies of this kind, following children over extended periods, have uncovered noteworthy consistencies in temperament variables over quite lengthy timescales. For example, in the Dunedin Multidisciplinary Health and Development Study in New Zealand, Caspi et al. (1995) compared observations of 800 children when aged three with independent descriptions of them at age fifteen. Some three-year-olds were described as 'under-controlled' and were thought to manifest irritability and impulsiveness; when aged fifteen, these same children were more likely to be described as having externalising (or 'acting out') problems; that is, they were more likely to be aggressive or to show outwardly directed displays of negative feelings. In the Concordia Longitudinal Risk Project involving 1,770 children in Montreal, Temcheff et al. (2008) found a significant correlation between childhood aggression in primary school, based on children's descriptions of their peers, and self-reported violence toward a spouse or partner almost thirty years later. In a wide-ranging integrative survey of the correlates of crime, Ellis et al. (2009) located fifty-nine studies of the association between aggressiveness in childhood and general adult criminality (i.e. including both violent and property offences). They found that a large majority of the studies showed a positive correlation between the two variables, with a high degree of consistency between the studies, although as we might expect the size of the correlations declined gradually over time as additional influences came into play.

Initial temperamental differences of the kind just described are very likely under some degree of genetic control, though conditions (such as maternal nutrition or trauma) during the period of gestation and other epigenetic processes are probably also involved. As we described in Chapter 3, a large UK-based study of child behaviour problems using genome-wide complex trait analysis could find no evidence of significant genetic influence (Trzaskowski et al., 2013); and a systematic meta-analysis of 185 studies of a series of thirty-one candidate genes found no evidence of significant associations between any of them and measures of aggression (Vassos et al., 2014). A direct route from genetic causes to behavioural outcomes appears gradually less plausible the more research that is done. Temperament is likely to be the primary route through which genes play a role in the later potential for aggressiveness and other characteristics as the principal pathway through which we inherit personal dispositions from our parents. As infants develop through early and middle childhood, environmental factors interact with and can overlay and modify these differences, in some cases narrowing them but in others widening them.

An important question that arises in this context, closely connected to the issues we addressed in Chapter 3, is whether it is possible to identify an 'age of onset' of aggressive behaviour in human development. Ascertaining this could be an important contribution to the debate concerning whether that behaviour is innate or acquired (Tremblay et al., 1999). If it appeared very early, that could imply it is inborn, a ready-made or built-in part of us. If it did not appear till much later, we might feel justified in claiming that learning had some role in it, even a major one.

Some researchers conclude on the basis of parents' reports that children show physical aggression from a very early age. This is also based on the findings of longitudinal studies, which track children's development from birth to adulthood, often collecting information from multiple sources including parents, teachers, and at a later stage children themselves. These studies suggest that aggression appears only a few months after birth and that the 'peak age' for acting aggressively is between two and three years old, after which its rate steadily declines for the rest of the lifespan. That may appear surprising and even implausible, as other statistics suggest the peak age for antisocial behaviour of most kinds is in the mid- or late teenage years. What is the basis of this claim?

In a study by Tremblay et al. (2004), researchers contacted and assessed a cohort of more than 500 Canadian families when their babies were just five months old, then measured children's aggression at the ages of seventeen, thirty and forty-two months. Reports of behaviour were obtained from the 'person most knowledgeable' about each child, usually their mother. Using maternal reports children were divided into three groups with respect to aggression: high, just under 14% of the cohort; medium, 58%; and low, 28%. This study was repeated on a much larger scale, with ten cohorts each of roughly 1,000 children, producing a total sample of 10,658, who were followed for a period of six years, in an *accelerated longitudinal design*. This means that data were collected from parallel groups spanning the ages from two to nearly twelve (Côté et al., 2006). The same measurement of physical aggression was used and findings followed a similar pattern in which aggression appeared early, reached a peak between age two and three, and gradually declined thereafter.

Reaching earlier into infancy, studies carried out in Cardiff extended the age of observation down to six months, using an assessment called the *Cardiff Infant Contentiousness Scale* (Hay et al., 2010, 2014). Hay et al. searched for the earliest signs of behaviour that could be described as aggressive, and for evidence of continuity of those patterns of individual differences from early infancy into toddlerhood. A strength of these studies was that the aggression items were embedded in a broader scale covering a variety of other behaviours linked to developmental milestones.

In all these studies, there was evidence of continuity over the first few years of life, but the number of children repeatedly showing behaviour classed as aggressive was relatively low. In the Canadian research, for example, the high aggression group had a mean score at seventeen months of slightly over 2.5, rising to 3.5 by forty-two months. For the low group scores were close to zero at all three measurement points. For the medium group, mean scores rose from 0.5 at seventeen months to 1.75 at forty-two months. To put these scores in context, a child could obtain a score of 3 on the aggression scale if they 'sometimes' hit, bit, kicked, fought or bullied. This was not anchored to any specified frequency, so could mean that a child did each of those things only once or twice. So the 'high aggression' group might not be high in the sense most people would use that word. Looking at this another way, with the single exception of sometimes taking away things from others, more than half of the children are not recorded as showing any aggression, and indeed for most forms of behaviour the proportions of children in the non-aggressive category is 75% or more. With regard to *often* acting in these ways, the prevalence rates are such that well over 95% of children can be placed outside this category. Also in the Canadian research, the strongest predictors of membership of the 'high' group were having younger siblings, low income, early motherhood, high family dysfunction, and mothers who use coercive parenting. The Cardiff studies involved a cohort of more than 300 first-time mothers, so there were no siblings present, but aggression was associated with other aspects of family disadvantage.

These findings contrast with observations of Kagan (1998), who noted that despite having conducted research with hundreds of two-year-old children, he had never seen a child strike out in an encounter with an unfamiliar child. Certainly, young children can be demanding of caregivers' attention and when distressed their movements lack fine control. But looking at this from an evolutionary perspective, they cannot achieve anything by threat or force, so it is difficult to see what function aggression would serve for them. On the contrary, aggressive behaviour could put a child at risk by eliciting antagonistic responses from adults. Maltreatment of children is not uncommon, and those who experience it may respond in a number of maladaptive ways including displays of hostile aggression. But it is questionable to what extent behaviours of these kinds can properly be classed as aggression that is unfolding in a natural developmental sequence.

Another sometimes more direct effect of biology on behaviour, including the likelihood of violence, is, as we saw in Chapter 1, associated with traumatic brain injury (TBI). Williams et al. (2018) reported a large-scale review of the evidence pertaining to this. For example, when incarcerated young offenders or adult prisoners are screened for evidence of TBI, the proportions of them with a history of it is invariably higher than among the general population. Some of the reviewed studies found that having had a TBI increases the risk of involvement in some type of crime by a factor of two or three times; the risk of violent crime specifically is sometimes higher, sometimes lower than this. The association is more marked where an individual lost consciousness for thirty minutes or more following brain injury, or where there has been more than one incident of TBI. Analysis of several sets of data concerning this suggests that TBI is a risk factor for violence independently of other variables that might affect it. However, the roles of these variables are very difficult to distinguish. For example, having had a TBI appears to increase the likelihood of other problem behaviours with a link to crime, such as substance misuse. Furthermore, the main cause of TBI in young offenders is having been a victim of assault, suggesting that those individuals grew up in violent families or neighbourhoods; and adolescents with brain injuries were more likely to have been physically abused. Thus the causal pathways that may connect TBI to increased violence remain unclear due to this complex confounding of factors. Head injury often results in repeated headaches, memory problems and difficulties in anger control. As Williams and colleagues comment, TBI is embedded in a 'constellation of socioadversity factors' (2018, p. 5), and there is a need to 'explain how TBI is situated within the criminogenic life histories of offenders' (p. 6). Hence while TBI may be a separate, biologically based causal factor in a proportion of violence, it is often intercorrelated with other environmental (and especially familial) variables.

In a wide-ranging review of the role of neuropsychological factors in violence, Séguin et al. (2018) concluded that there is a lack of evidence on clear links between the specificity of neuropsychological deficits and violent behaviour. Research has overused global measures, with the result that assessments are not sufficiently specific to different forms of violence. Because this behaviour occurs in many different patterns and circumstances, they recommended that research studies should assess the specific nature of actual violent acts, and not assume links with ADHD, substance use or other forms of challenging behaviour that are not violent:

Neuropsychological impairments, even in executive function, are not necessarily specific to physical aggression.... lesions among frontal lobe patients, despite their poor executive function, rarely lead to physical violence, though these lesions may lead to explicit forms of violence in the context of other risk factors ... Neuropsychological variables tend to explain at most 8–10% of the variance in measures of violence. (p. 152)

Thus while neuropsychological events and processes presumably play an essential role as the basis of cognition, emotion, and behaviour, their explanatory power in relation to specific classes of action such as violence, while important, is somewhat limited.

4.4   Socialisation

The people surrounding us as we grow up have crucial and far-reaching influences on the course of the rest of our lives. The processes involved in this are usually brought together under the general heading of *socialisation* and this has several strands. Research on the emergence of aggression and violence has highlighted the relevance of several of them: in particular, the central role of parents, the occurrence of maltreatment (abuse or neglect), and the influence of peer groups.

Parenting. Probably the most powerful influence on the environment into which any child is born and which will have profound effects on the course of their development is the immediate social surroundings of the family of origin, and the key figures within it: parents and other family members. In this context several forms of learning take place: imitation and modelling; the shaping of behaviour by positive and negative reinforcement, extinction, punishment, and other types of behavioural learning; attachment and the development of security; witnessing how family members treat each other; and, at later stages, following language acquisition, the formation of attitudes and beliefs.

Findings from several large longitudinal studies indicate that the overall environment within families and the difficulties they face have a major impact on the prospects of children developing within them. In the United Kingdom, the Millennium Cohort Study followed up a sample of more than 18,000 children born in the years 2000 and 2001 (Sabates and Dex, 2012). Researchers collected information on a total of ten 'risk indicators' within families based on parental reports. These were:

- Depression
- Disability or long-term illness
- Substance abuse
- Alcohol dependence
- Domestic violence
- Financial stress
- Worklessness
- Teenage parenthood
- Lack of basic skills
- Domestic overcrowding.

The larger the number of these risk factors to which a growing child was exposed, the greater the likelihood of various adverse effects in the child's life. In particular, children who were subject to more risks were significantly likelier to have conduct problems and hyperactivity, two characteristics that are generally among the strongest correlates of later delinquency. Families in the lowest income bands showed significantly higher levels of these problems than those at higher income levels, as their circumstances are marked by greater disadvantage. Similar findings were found in the United States, for example in the Pittsburgh Youth study. Here, young males with four or more risk factors were fourteen times more likely than those with fewer than four to go on to commit homicide (Loeber et al., 2005).

Apart from difficult domestic circumstances, some parents engage in behaviour that has been found to increase the likelihood that their children will become aggressive. Perhaps the most widely recognised of these behaviours is the corporal punishment of children. Many studies have found that this has numerous negative effects on children's development, but there is also an association between it and children's later aggressive behaviour. Many research studies have been undertaken that demonstrate this particular link. While it has been objected that corporal punishment is a response to children's aggression, used with the aim of reducing it, research finds that after controlling for levels of aggression at the starting point, the reverse occurred. For example, in a longitudinal study of 2,461 children across twenty American cities, Taylor et al. (2010) examined the rate at which parents spanked their three-year-old children (this was not perceived by study participants as a form of abuse). The outcome variable in the study was the children's levels of aggression at age five. Even after other variables that could affect the outcome were controlled for, more frequent use of spanking at age three was significantly associated with children's levels of aggression two years later. The net outcome of such studies has been to show that the idea that it is necessary to teach children not to be aggressive by physically hurting them in effect produces the opposite result. Furthermore, although the authors described the age of three as a 'peak age' for spanking use, clearly the impact is likely to be greater if this is present over a prolonged period of a child's life.

Other less obvious but thereby perhaps more insidious processes inside families that can foster the development of aggression were investigated in a series of studies by Patterson and his colleagues at the Oregon Social Learning Center (OSLC). Parts of their work involved the direct observation of families of 200 children who already had histories of aggressiveness alongside a comparison group of sixty non-violent families. These observations led to the identification of a cyclical process the researchers called *negative microsocial exchange*, whereby parents and children reciprocally influence each other's aversive behaviour. Their responses are mutually interdependent and result in a particular reciprocal pattern with 'mixed schedules of *positive* and *negative* reinforcement plus frequent punishment' (Patterson et al., 1984, p. 256).

Within such cycles, the child engages in (for example) minor unwanted behaviours such as antagonism toward a sibling. This elicits the attention of an irritated parent, who admonishes the child, but soon turns attention away again. To regain attention, the child then repeats the behaviour or gradually escalates to more problematic acts, even if doing so could produce a sharper reaction from the parent. This response and feedback loop continue in an ascending spiral, until eventually the parent focuses more attention on the child. In another scenario, a similar cycle enabled children to resist unwanted attention of parents, for example by showing hostility when asked to carry out a household chore (Reid et al.,

2002). Although these actions often involve some punishment along the way, in due course the achievement of a desired goal reinforces engagement in aggressive behaviour.

While parents probably want their children to be able to defend themselves, few if any will say that they consciously set out to teach them to be aggressive. The contradictory net effect of these sequences, however, is that parental reactions that are intended to *reduce* the likelihood of a behaviour in the short term in fact serve to *increase* its likelihood in the long term. Patterns like this, once learned within families, can carry into situations elsewhere (Dishion et al., 1992). Essentially, through such a *coercive family process* parents are inadvertently training their children to find that aggression works, with that learning potentially then being transferred to the child's interactions with others outside the home (Patterson, 1982; Patterson et al., 1984). By the onset of adolescence, what might be called the individual's 'aggressive traits' are well established; but they are actually the product of a series of hundreds of parent–child interaction sequences in an extended social learning process. Large-scale reviews of research on parenting have confirmed the role of coercive, inconsistent, negligent, hostile or rejecting forms of parenting as predictors of children's later involvement in delinquency (Hoeve et al., 2009; Leschied et al., 2008).

The relationship between attributes of parenting and the emergence of involvement in delinquency is a *bidirectional* one, as found in a study of 12,505 children and youth from the US Add Health longitudinal study (Gault-Sherman, 2012). This study measured general, property and violent delinquency separately, and followed adolescents over a period of five years, from age twelve to age seventeen. Violent delinquency referred to a set of behaviours that included fighting, group fighting, robbery, pulling a knife or a gun on someone, and shooting or stabbing someone. At the start of the study period, 36.7% of the study sample exhibited one or more of these behaviours. The higher the level of parental involvement, the lower was the rate of all types of delinquency. But alongside this there was a significant effect in the reverse direction: over time, violent delinquency reduced levels of parental involvement and attachment. These effects were stronger than parental monitoring alone, that is, than parents' setting of rules for their teenage children and checking their adherence to them. Reciprocal effects of these kinds are consistent with what is known as the *interactional* or *transactional* model of development (Dodge and Pettit, 2003; Sameroff, 2009).

Maltreatment. If the processes just outlined are compounded by an additional layer involving maltreatment, the likelihood of some deleterious effect on developing children is magnified. Following definitions used by the WHO (Butchart et al., 2006), maltreatment of children is usually divided into four broad categories: physical abuse, sexual abuse, emotional or psychological abuse, and neglect. Where maltreatment occurs, it can lead to any of a wide range of adverse outcomes, including mental health problems as well as crime and violence.

One of the earliest and most frequently cited investigations of the sequelae of abuse and neglect was reported by Widom (1989), who compared official arrest records of a sample of 908 abused and neglected children with those of 667 matched controls. Following these groups over a twenty-year period, she found that members of the abused and neglected group were 55% more likely to have had a record of juvenile delinquency, 35% more likely to have an adult criminal record, and 42% more likely to have been arrested for a violent crime. Having been arrested for violence was associated with physical but not sexual abuse during childhood. Widom forwarded what became known as the 'cycle of violence' hypothesis, but was careful to point out that the different kinds of maltreatment were *risk factors* for later violence. That is, the observed associations were *probabilistic*, and while 11% of the abused and neglected individuals were later arrested for violence, eight times as many (89%) were not. As with all risk factors an adverse outcome is not inevitable. Recalling the patterns of *equifinality* and *multifinality* described earlier, it is by no means the case that those who have been victimised will automatically go on to victimise others. As a later review found, while there appears to be support for a 'cycle of maltreatment' model, weaknesses in the research relevant to this mean that no clear conclusion can yet be drawn (Thornberry et al., 2012).

However, there is consistent evidence that childhood maltreatment is one of the main precursors of later aggression and of involvement in violent crime. Several studies have obtained findings very similar to those found by Widom. For example, Lansford et al. (2007) reported results of the Knoxville-Nashville-Bloomington Child Development Project, a longitudinal study of 574 children followed between the ages of five and twenty-one. Those who had been physically victimised in early childhood (before the age of five) were significantly more likely to be convicted of an offence over the period up to age twenty-one. Although convictions were more likely to be for a non-violent than a violent offence, the latter association with violent offences was also significant. Maas et al. (2008) reviewed findings from eight longitudinal studies in this area with an aggregate sample of 8,659. They found 'compelling evidence of a link between child maltreatment and later violence in youth' (p. 62), and they suggested that physical abuse may be the most consistent predictor of youth violence.

Braga et al. (2017) confirmed and added weight to this overall picture by carrying out a meta-analysis of thirty-three prospective longitudinal studies containing thirty-seven samples, with a cumulative participant population of 23,973. The advantage of this type of study design is that data collection is planned in advance and individuals are followed from a baseline prior to the emergence of problems of the type being researched. Braga et al. examined the overall effect of maltreatment, but also the separate effects of its four main types (physical, sexual, or emotional abuse, and neglect) on later delinquency including aggression. The overall main effect of maltreatment was highly significant on general delinquency, with a similar effect size for aggressive antisocial behaviour. But 'physical and sexual abuses were more strongly associated with aggressive behaviours rather than general antisocial acts' (p. 46).

There is also evidence that maltreatment is associated with the likelihood of carrying a weapon. Lewis and her colleagues (2007) investigated this in a longitudinal study of 797 children followed to age twelve. Boys were eight times more likely than girls to carry a weapon. Boys and girls who had been physically abused were 2.8 times more likely, and those who had been sexually abused 4.4 times more likely, to carry a weapon than those with no abuse history. Similar findings have emerged from other studies. Note again, however, that several factors are also involved, and this is a risk or probabilistic relationship rather than a direct causal one. Of those who had experienced childhood abuse, the majority did not carry a weapon in later years.

The study of child maltreatment is additionally important as its impact has been investigated in conjunction with that of genetic factors in research on the *gene–environment interactions* discussed in Chapter 3. This has focused principally on the MAOA gene, which influences the levels of activity of the monoamine oxidase (MAO) enzyme and so in turn modulates the activity of certain neurotransmitters. Lower levels of MAOA activity mean that these neurotransmitters are more active, and this has been associated with higher levels of aggression (Ellis, 1991). Some research has reported higher levels of the low-activity MAOA allele (gene variant) among violent as compared with non-violent adult prisoners (Stetler et al., 2014). Indeed, it has been argued that the presence of this gene variant on the X chromosome may explain the difference in violence-proneness between males and females.

The first, widely regarded as ground-breaking, study in this area was part of the Dunedin longitudinal research project mentioned earlier. From its total sample of 1,037 participants, Caspi et al. (2002) collected and analysed data on levels of MAOA for 442 children. Within that group, they compared children with higher and lower levels of MAOA.

They also classified them into three subgroups according to suspected levels of maltreatment before the age of eleven (severe, probable, or absent). Data were collected on aggressiveness at the age of twenty-six, using a composite index of antisocial behaviour that included records of conviction for violent crimes.

Analysis revealed a striking interaction effect. Those with low MAOA activity and a history of severe ill-treatment were found to have significantly higher antisocial behaviour scores than the other two groups. But the effects of maltreatment and the differences between the groups were most marked among those with low MAOA activity. While evidence pertaining to this has not been wholly consistent, and the finding emerges primarily among boys, subsequent meta-analyses of studies have confirmed the original trends (seven studies reviewed by Taylor and Kim-Cohen, 2007; twenty-seven studies reviewed by Byrd and Manuck, 2014). This remains the clearest demonstration available of the moderating influence of a gene on an environmental variable linked to violence. In the largest review to date of a total of fifty-three studies, Weeland et al. (2015) located thirty-one studies of the links between MAOA, family adversity and externalising behaviour, and noted that the original pattern found by Caspi et al. (2002) had been confirmed sixteen times in subsequent research. However, the review did not include a large-scale study by Haberstick et al. (2014) with a total sample of 4,316 adult males that did not find any significant main or interaction effects. Moreover, studies of other types of family dysfunction, and encompassing research on other genes, found more heterogeneous effects. Methodological differences between the studies has potentially obscured underlying consistencies.

Weeland et al. (2015) proposed that there may be different mechanisms at work in producing the observed gene–environment interaction. For example, the gene may influence emotional reactivity, or degree of sensitivity to rewards or punishments. Subsequent studies have searched for other relationships of this kind. Simons et al. (2012) offered support for a complex model in which three genes, MAOA, 5-HTT, and DRD4, in combination produced a type of *response plasticity*, that is, greater responsiveness to environmental variation. They suggested that in a hostile and demoralising environment during the initial adolescent years, this plasticity mediated the extent of adoption of the 'street code', which was subsequently associated with the likelihood of involvement in violence in early adulthood. The greater the number of plasticity alleles (variant forms of genes) present (one, two or three), the higher the level of absorption of the code and perpetration of violence. More tentatively, Lu and Menard (2017) suggested that the MAOA gene may moderate susceptibility to peer influence within groups of male adolescents.

Peer influence. Through attending school and meeting other people of similar age, developing children become exposed to another layer of socialisation influences, those of peer groups. Given that when young people initially become involved in lawbreaking of almost any kind, they do so in groups – a proportion of which evolve into gangs – the process of peer influence has been the focus of a substantial amount of research. This indicates that both initial predispositions (resulting from a convergence of earlier factors) and group influence processes both play a part in the onset of participation in delinquency (see, for example, Matsueda and Anderson, 1998). There is also evidence of the process of 'differential association', whereby individuals are influenced by the predominance of the attitudes expressed by those around them (Rebellon, 2006). That is, the same processes of social influence that draw youths on street corners into gangs also operate in corporate environments where there are other, usually more lucrative crime opportunities available. Perhaps not surprisingly, many young people attribute their involvement in crime to the malign influence of others. Where this is claimed as a mitigating factor, there might be reasons to doubt whether it is always genuine despite the firm evidence that such an influence process occurs.

To overcome this potential interpretive obstacle, Conway and McCord (2002) examined 60,821 court records, extending over an eighteen-year period, and extracted 200 cases of individuals who committed a crime alone, and 200 cases of others who did so with an accomplice. They then analysed the types of offences committed by offenders and co-offenders in the same and subsequent crimes. What emerged from this was clear evidence that regardless of age, an initially non-violent individual who co-offended with someone who acted violently was more likely to go on to commit violent offences, more so than other types of offence: 'exposure to violence during a first co-offense appears to have increased propensity to violence specifically' (p. 104).

Maimon and Browning (2010) investigated the potential importance of 'unstructured socialising', defined as 'activities that carry no agenda for how time is spent' (p. 445), in the onset of violent offending by young people. In the absence of supervising adults but with the presence of opportunities for deviance, youths who spend time loosely in this way show more involvement in several forms of delinquency. Maimon and Browning analysed data from the Project on Human Development in Chicago Neighborhoods, a community survey and longitudinal cohort study, involving 842 children and youths aged three to eighteen (drawn randomly from a total study population of 6,500) in eighty 'neighbourhood clusters'. In-home interviews were conducted with children and their primary caregivers at three points over a six-year period. Violence was defined as having carried out one or more of a series of seven types of acts, from hitting someone or throwing objects at them, to acts of arson, assaults with a weapon or participation in gang fights. These data were analysed by means of multilevel modelling, to test the relative importance of individual, family and neighbourhood-level characteristics. Analysis showed that unstructured socialising had a highly significant effect on the likelihood of violence: 'Specifically, a 1 standard deviation increase in an adolescent's unstructured socialising with peers increases the likelihood of violent offending by 37 percent' (pp. 461–463).[1]

Individual violence was also positively associated with deviant peers and impulsivity, and negatively with family attachment and support. Conversely, where neighbourhoods possessed features of 'collective efficacy' (evidence of social cohesion, local participation, monitoring, and trust), this reduced the strength of the link between unsupported socialising and violence.

Adolescent peer groups are often considered to have negative effects on their individual members. But they can also serve protective functions. In a study of children followed from age ten to age sixteen, there was evidence that even for those children who previously had been maltreated at home, attachment to parents and lower levels of delinquency among friends decreased their risk of violent offending (Salzinger et al., 2007).

4.5   Cultural Context

There are large variations between societies in levels of violence, and even within the same nations there can be sizable variations as a function of differences in cultural contexts. These contexts include patterns of beliefs that affect individuals' expectations concerning conflict, and their readiness to resort to physical violence as a response to it. These are very difficult variables to capture in research as clear definitions of them remain elusive, and measurement or recording of them poses a daunting task. However, in two sets of studies carried out in the United States, cultural differences when successfully assessed have been found to have an influence on several forms of violence, including homicide and rape.

Baron et al. (1988) explored the relationship between social attitudes concerning aggression and the rates of rape in all fifty American states. These authors designed a composite measure, the *Legitimate Violence Index*, to provide an indirect indicator of the extent of tacit social

---

[1] Standard deviation is a widely used statistic indicating the degree of spread of a data distribution.

approval of violence. The Index incorporated contemporaneous data on the proportion of violent content of television programmes, rates of readership of magazines with a high violence content, the extent of laws permitting corporal punishment in schools, the numbers of hunting licenses issued, and levels of National Guard enrolment. They also extracted historical information on the numbers of incidents of lynching in each state in the period from 1882 to 1927.

The rate of rape across states varied by a factor of eight, and Baron et al. analysed the relationship between this and scores on the Violence Index. Broadly speaking, there were large differences between different regions of the country. Several types of demographic information were also entered in the analysis, for example, the age distribution, the level of urbanisation, extent of income inequality, and proportions of single and divorced males in the population. These are similar to some of the features identified as characteristic of high homicide rate countries in Chapter 1. However, in addition, as a third data source they also interviewed people on the extent to which they explicitly approved of violence in some contexts (the *Violence Approval Index*), for example, whether they believed it permissible to punch a stranger under certain circumstances (e.g. if a drunk person bumped into you in the street).

Analysis showed that the rate of rape was most strongly predicted by demographic variables including the level of urbanisation and percentage of divorced males in a state. But it was also highly correlated, and significantly and independently in statistical terms, with the Legitimate Violence Index, and there was a lower but still significant correlation with scores on the Violence Approval Index.

American regions and cities also vary considerably in their rates of homicide and other serious violence. There are large differences in this, for example between southern and south-western states, on the one hand, and those of the north-eastern United States, on the other. Nisbett and Cohen (1996) analysed rates of violent crimes, including homicide, across US regions, and examined them in relation to beliefs concerning violence. In southern and south-western states, there was greater endorsement of a shoot-to-kill policy in law enforcement, stronger backing for the exercise of violence in the defence of male reputations, a greater tendency to ruminate over personal insults, and more support for physical discipline of children. Addressing such attitudes is a key part of the public health anti-violence campaigns run by WHO and others, discussed further in Chapter 6. In other parts of their research, Nisbett and Cohen (1996) set up an experimental situation in which participants were subjected to a contrived insult. They found significantly higher increases in the levels of some hormones (cortisol and testosterone) among residents of high-homicide regions (mainly southern states) than was the case for citizens from other parts of the United States.

To explain these findings, Nisbett and Cohen proposed that the observed differences are a function of a residual attachment to values arising within a culture that, prior to emigration to the United States, was traditionally centred on the herding of animals. They suggested this had its origins in the high proportion of people of Scottish and Irish descent in some southern American states. Historically in such economies, a group's livelihood was dependent on the management of herds of animals. This produced a need for individuals to project an intimidating image that signalled a preparedness to make speedy resort to violence for the protection of property and of self. Such a 'culture of honour' thesis as depicted by Nisbett and Cohen has been subjected to wider comparisons. Baller et al. (2009) analysed historical and crime records from 479 counties in the thirteen states of what is sometimes called the 'old South' and found solid support for the proposal. Altheimer (2013a) also found supportive evidence in an analysis of international homicide data for fifty-one nations. This employed WHO homicide rates for different countries for the period 2002–2005. The independent variable was a composite *culture of honour proxy* measure combining different factors obtained from data indicating the 'economic precariousness' of a country and the extent of the government's role in providing protection for citizens. The resultant association was stronger than that found for a measure of economic inequality. It is important to keep in mind, however, that these differences arise between cultural groups, rather than with respect to modern state societies, which often include a spectrum of culturally diverse groups. Thus when Altheimer (2013b) tested the same idea with a larger set of 186 states, no association was found. This may have been because the second analysis was concerned with modern politically identified states rather than culturally identified 'nations'.

Another societal factor showing a strong association with homicide rates is the ease with which individuals have access to firearms. Countries differ widely in rates of gun ownership. In England and Wales, on a worldwide scale the proportion is relatively low at 6.2%. In other countries there are higher rates, for example, 15% in Australia, just over 30% in Germany and Canada, and 45.7% in Switzerland. Highest of all is the United States, where the figure is 88.8% (Graduate Institute of International and Development Studies, 2007). Bangalore and Messerli (2013) reported a survey of twenty-seven countries and found that the number of guns per capita was a direct and significant predictor of firearm-related deaths. The United States has the world's highest rate of gun homicide and suicide, and also by far the highest rate of mass shootings. What appears a crucial factor in these differences, however, apart from the ready availability of guns, is the set of beliefs concerning what they represent, as a means of personal protection rather than to be brought out in situations of national emergency (Killias and Markwalder, 2012).

Cultural forces play a powerful role in many types of violence, and examples can be found in many societies. In Japan, particularly during the 1950s and 1960s, there were several thousand cases of *oyako shinjū*, a form of murder–suicide in which a parent killed themself with a child or in some cases several children (Iga, 1996). This was influenced by strong internalised values, shame, guilt, and a sense of responsibility following a misfortune such as bankruptcy or divorce. Honour killings, in which individuals are murdered by their relatives because they are viewed as having broken important social taboos and thereby brought shame on their families, continue to be carried out in a number of countries. For example, in Pakistan in the period 2004–2007 nearly 2,000 deaths of this kind were reported (Nasrullah et al., 2009). The most common reason given for these events was alleged sexual infidelity. Executions were usually carried out by close family members, most often by shooting. But in some other cultures very brutal methods are used for these particular types of killing, such as stoning or burying alive. The cultural preference for boys over girls is so strong in several societies that, as a consequence of selective abortion (in countries where termination is legally allowed in specified circumstances), it has resulted in a marked imbalance in the gender ratio. This has been found, for example, in India: in the period from 1980 to 2010 there was an estimated minimum of 4.2 million more abortions of female foetuses, and possibly as many as 12 million more. In the census for 2011 this is estimated to have produced a discernible gender population differential in the age range from zero to six years (Jha et al., 2011).

4.6   Situational Factors

While the importance of situational determinants of behaviour is often endorsed at a theoretical level and we are very aware of external provocations when understanding our own feelings of anger and hostility, all too often when explanations are forwarded of some specific behaviour such as crimes of violence by other people, those factors are overlooked. Instead, dispositional accounts emphasising the individual and their temperament are relied on when they only partially explain what occurred. There is, however, extensive evidence that aggressive and violent behaviours are a function of environmental conditions and of situational and contextual factors and that awareness of such external influences generates a clearer understanding of them. At the simplest level, the likelihood of aggressive reactions increases as a function of rising temperature. Studies of what has been called the *heat hypothesis* show that uncomfortably hot conditions heighten hostile feelings and aggressive cognitions. This conclusion is based on triangulation from several different types of research in field and laboratory settings (Anderson, 1989, 2001). Similarly, for some individuals, having lost significant amounts of sleep or being sleep-deprived is associated with increased risk of feeling or acting aggressively (Kamphuis et al., 2012).

Pubs and bars and other drinking venues are common locations for displays of aggression and for violent assaults or affrays, especially given their function as part of the 'night time economy'. Part of this tendency is attributable to the role of alcohol itself, which may have direct physiological influences on aggressiveness (Tomlinson et al., 2016). But part is also associated with a range of psychological effects including disinhibition (loss of control), narrowing of selective attention, anxiety reduction, or changes in outcome expectancies, which may indirectly contribute to it (McGuire and Duff, 2018). There is clear evidence that alcohol is associated with many different types of offence but especially with violence (Felson and Staff, 2010), including that against intimate partners (Foran and O'Leary, 2008). Access to alcohol is thus often regarded as a key mechanism of the public health approach to violence reduction.

But research also suggests that some features of drinking environments, such as the level of comfort in bars, their state of repair or the behaviour of door staff or of serving staff, are conducive to an increased likelihood of aggression. In a study based in 118 large-capacity bars in Toronto, Graham et al. (2006) measured aspects of the environment and their relationships with levels of recorded aggression. The frequency and severity of aggression was associated with the rowdy or disorderly nature of bar atmospheres, the extent of sexual permissiveness and competition, the accumulation of drinks near to closing time especially when large numbers of people lingered afterward, and with poorer coordination by staff. There is also evidence of an interaction between features of bar surroundings and characteristics of their typical regular customers. Quigley et al. (2003) compared groups of violent and non-violent bars, and found that they differed in levels of noise, temperature, ventilation, and staff behaviour. But they also attracted different clienteles, with those who gravitated to violent bars showing higher levels of alcohol dependence and trait anger. Bar environment, however, was a stronger predictor of levels of violence than customer profile.

Thus violent offences do not arise solely as a result of aggressive dispositions or intentions, but are in part a function of everyday events and circumstances in offenders' lives. Using statistical modelling, Horney (2001) and Horney et al. (1995) found an association in which following some adverse life events, the likelihood of violent offending doubled. The possibility of violence is greater among those living certain lifestyles, and living a large portion of life 'on the street' increases risks of becoming either a victim or a perpetrator of violence (and in some instances both). Kennedy and Baron (1993) and Kennedy and Forde (1996) analysed violent incidents involving homeless youths. These individuals claimed not to be violence-prone but to have been drawn into violence by situations that arose in that environment. Findings of this kind have led to the development a *criminal event perspective* designed to counter the overemphasis on individual variables that often dominates how offences of violence are understood (Meier et al., 2001).

Violence obviously constitutes only a small proportion of all the social exchanges in which people engage on an everyday basis, but there are certain circumstances in which it is more likely to occur than in others. Some are influenced by prior unfavourable events as just noted. But disputes themselves appear to follow certain sequences with implicit but nevertheless recognisable rules. Although these are hard to identify, they can be uncovered in detailed research. This reveals not only that acting violently is more likely to follow certain types of untoward events, but that the offences themselves unfold through a sequence of stages. At each stage, the responses of those involved are pivotal influences on what happens next and whether violence will occur. This has been found in analysis of robbery offences, non-lethal assaults, fights and homicide (Felson and Steadman, 1983; Luckenbill, 1977, 1981). Many homicides involve a series of exchanges between the eventual offender and victim, who exchange insults, and sometimes issue what are construed as 'identity attacks'. As the encounter proceeds, each continues to interpret the actions of the other and to respond in ways that can lower the level of tension and lead to negotiation, or cause the confrontation to escalate to lethal assault.

Employing detailed analyses of crowd and other forms of group violence, using a variety of source material including film and video footage, police and CCTV recordings, news photographs, mobile phone images and in some cases forensic reconstructions, Collins (2008, 2009, 2013) proposed that most people in potentially violent confrontations are primarily in a state of fear rather than one of anger. He considered that this is the case because, contrary to the standard narrative of hard-wired violence, most people are actually very reluctant to initiate violence or to assault others, even in extreme circumstances. In any case, most people are poorly coordinated and inept when highly anxious or agitated. This research suggests there are specific pathways along which violence becomes more likely to erupt. The crucial factor in determining whether disputes spiral into violence is the ongoing pattern of exchanges between the antagonists, and their appraisals of each other's emotional states and intentions. Applying what he called *micro-sociological analysis*, Collins suggests it is an error to look for types of violence-prone individuals, as features of situations have a more powerful effect on whether acts of violence are committed. At any one moment, there are many more people who, as a function of demographic, developmental or personality factors, are available to commit crimes than actually do so. The crucial variables influencing whether they do so or not is the confluence of those factors with situational variables and sequences of events (Collins, 2009).

Finally, even inside institutions that contain individuals with proven histories of violence, their behaviour is not unremittingly aggressive, and such problems are more likely to arise at identifiable 'flashpoints'. There are detectable patterns in the locations or the times at which aggressive incidents are more likely, whether in prisons (Gadon et al., 2006; McGuire, 2018) or in secure psychiatric units (Welsh et al., 2013). Effective management of such institutions usually involves focusing attention on features of the environment or of daily routines, alongside monitoring the mental states or current preoccupations of those who are detained. Such features can provide a major focus for violence prevention measures.

4.7   Cognitive Processes

All the above sets of factors – individual differences in temperament, learning through socialisation, the effects of maltreatment or of peer pressure, the extent of cultural support for aggressiveness, and situational or contextual variables, operating through each person's history – come together inside the cognitive processes that are activated in every situation that person enters. At the level of cognition, however, it is difficult to isolate features that differentiate individuals who commit violent offences from those who break the law in other ways. That may be because, as we saw from the work of Piquero et al. (2012) at the beginning of this chapter, other than among a small minority of offenders, committing violent offences is in most cases a product of 'criminal versatility' – of having committed more offences overall, rather than something that signals that we are dealing with a different category of person. This has been a repeated finding in criminological research.

Many variables have been investigated, and many hypotheses formulated concerning them, in efforts to find either personality features or recurrent patterns of thought or feeling that characterise those referred to as 'violent offenders'. Those that have been substantiated by evidence include the presence of hostile beliefs and attributions, of automatic angry thoughts, neutralizations or self-justifying inner messages ('self-statements'), distorted perceptions of threat from victims, moral disengagement, and hypermasculinity (for an overview of research pertaining to those and other related variables, see McGuire and Duff, 2018). For the most part these are tendencies rather than stable aspects of functioning as they are not exhibited across all situations but are triggered by specific circumstances or personal crises. An individual's internal processing of information and of emotional reactions to events may be the 'final common pathway' prior to acting violently (McGuire, 2008), but it is a joint product of the other dimensions of experience we have discussed in this chapter.

The areas we have reviewed have been centred on attempts to understand violence at the individual level. But in some respects, despite obvious differences in scale and severity, they have parallels in the diverse forms of collective violence in group conflicts ranging from 'gang wars' to episodes of genocide. Thus in summarising and integrating the multiple factors that influence violent acts on the individual plane, we want to emphasise the close connection this often has with other forms of violence that are acted out on a far larger canvas.

Even the most extreme manifestations of collective violence in episodes of genocide result from a convergence of factors. They range from distant historical grievances, sometimes distorted to fit selected in-group concerns, to self-serving, often nationalistic, present-day narratives. Such events occur where the ultimate perpetrators have lived through difficult economic circumstances, and there are pressures on populations, rising discontent, and the popularisation of discourses focusing on injustice and maltreatment. In the wake of triggering events, often followed by extensive, sometimes deliberately contrived, campaigns of misinformation which further feed the existing resentments, the sense of threat escalates to a point where systems of belief in existential threat are activated and lethal violence is unleashed. Historical analyses of such extreme events including the Holocaust, and the Cambodian and Rwandan genocides (Jones, 2017; Staub, 1999, 2000; Waller, 2007) all demonstrate these processes.

Klusemann (2010, 2012) applied Collins's micro-sociological model, discussed earlier, to an analysis of the 'emotional dynamics' of the period immediately preceding atrocities such as the 1994 Rwandan genocide and 1995 Srebrenica massacre. Such an analysis illustrates how, when communities are already in the throes of painful conflict and disarray, fear and anger can further escalate in individuals as a reaction to messages they are given that affect how they perceive another group of people, in those cases with appalling results. These actions were the outcome of the accumulation of the learnt experiences of the individuals who were involved. Like acts of violence carried out by individuals, they can be made comprehensible when seen as emerging from a combination of factors and processes, rather than attributed to any presumed inbuilt tendency to which we have to resign ourselves as part of our 'nature'. This is again far removed from a picture in which humans are metaphorically beset by having a 'dark side', buried deep in our evolutionary histories and evolved mentalities, predisposing us toward violent and destructive behaviour.

4.8   Conclusion

Let us draw together what in our view can be concluded from the ground covered so far. To summarise, the fullest understanding we can obtain of how and why a violent attack, fight or homicide has occurred will be one in which we combine both *distal* and *proximal* information about the perpetrator with information about how the event itself unfolded and the context in which it occurred. The former includes possible genetic, temperamental, socialisation and attitudinal influences, and processes of social learning that result in some individuals developing a pattern in which they more readily resort to violence than others. The latter includes perceptions of the current situation and pressures from others, operating within and then driving sequences of events that increase levels of both experienced and perceived hostility. While the capacity for acting violently is present in potential form, it is only when these factors converge in particular combinations that violence is likely to occur.

5 Structural Violence
Social and Political Factors in Understanding Violence

5.1 Introduction

As we have now seen, any act of violence is a result of many factors in the perpetrator's life. The most obvious of them are immediate and concrete situational triggers such as a perceived insult or attack. The trigger here is proximal, closely linked in time and space to when and where the act of violence occurs. Such factors are usually not difficult to discern and their relationship to the act of violence is clear and specific, so they are relatively easy to identify, isolate, and address. But many other factors, just as important, are far removed in time and space from the moment when the violent act takes place. Time-wise, they may lie far back on a lifelong pathway of shaped behaviour, acquired beliefs and restricted choices. We have seen in the last chapter how developmental experiences set up some people for a future of potential violence. Attitudes, assumptions, emotional impulsivity, and violent tendencies all come from a person's history based on where they grew up and who, if anybody, cared for them. Space-wise, these factors form the micro- and macro-environment the person inhabits at the moment of violence and act as less obvious influences channelling, as Brecht says, the flow of behaviour. Poverty, gender, education, and inequality are not easily perceptible amid the firecrackers of the immediate violent encounter, but they are present nevertheless and play a crucial part in making violence almost inevitable in some circumstances and for some people.

As with the distinction of proximal and distal factors, an integrated public health approach to violence distinguishes 'upstream' explanations which focus largely on social influences relatively removed from the actual manifestation of the violent behaviour and those direct triggers which are more 'downstream' (Gehlert et al., 2008). The clear implication of this language is that one set of causal factors precedes the other, and a range of tributary factors combine, feeding into a growing momentum toward violent behaviour. Upstream factors such as education are distal in relation to the actual manifestation of the problem behaviour, removed in time and even space from its occurrence. Downstream factors such as intoxication are more proximal, present only at the time and place that they actually occur. Such a distinction can be simplistic and misleading especially when distance in time and space between exposure to the factor and the manifestation of the behaviour is confused with levels of explanation and the strength of the causal link (Krieger, 2008). But it remains useful as an overall framework to organise the extensive empirical data and theoretical literature on violence.

The public health approach to violence prevention is a novel application of a well-established approach to reducing disease. This approach has had some spectacular successes in saving lives and protecting whole populations since its inception in the nineteenth century. The eradication of cholera in Western countries is just one example of how a large-scale lethal 'condition' can be tackled through concerted political and social action. But when considering the larger picture of premature death around the world, homicidal violence actually forms a comparatively small proportion of it. The commonest killer is still disease resulting either from lifestyles in rich countries or from infection in poor countries (World Health Organization, 2018). Fifty-three million people died prematurely in 2010, and, in that context, the half-million deaths from interpersonal violence annually are a fairly limited part of the problem of premature death, making up less than 1% of the total. While every violent death is an individual human tragedy, numerically, the death toll from violence is much lower than that from HIV/AIDS, tuberculosis, malaria and other infectious diseases (Lozano et al., 2012). So perhaps the UN and other international organisations should be focusing all their resources on tackling these challenges first and then turning later to address the issue of violence. After all, problems rooted in physiology alone like malaria could be seen as easier to address than a problem like violence which, as we are seeing, has multiple proximal and distal causes located on a wide spectrum, from physiology to sociology.

It should be acknowledged that there are indeed significant global efforts to address these bigger killers through international programmes run by the UN and other organisations. The UN Sustainable Development Goals (SDGs), which were set in 2015 to stimulate and coordinate activity in priority areas over the period up to 2030, place a strong emphasis on factors contributing to these major causes of premature death (Griggs et al., 2013; United Nations, 2016). The programme has a wide range of objectives for tackling social structures around the world which underpin variations between countries in premature death rates from disease, and changing these structures could directly or indirectly affect violence rates as well. The ambitious goals include, for instance, ensuring access to clean water and sanitation for all and ending hunger. Competition for such basic resources as food and water will increasingly drive violent struggles between individuals and groups. Other sustainable development goals such as gender equality will also likely have wide-spread implications for conflict reduction, including a decline in gender-based violence.

Beyond this, however, the microbial killers can also be seen as inherently part of how the human violence problem is construed. From one point of view exclusion from resources and exposure to disease is seen not just as a cause of violence but as a form of violence itself. The capacity of some societies, organisations, and powerful individuals to impose economic and political systems on their less powerful neighbours is a violent act in itself if, as a result, many are killed even without a shot being fired. This perspective, broadened to include what is now called structural violence, enables a more socially critical approach to be developed and opens up a new vista on the problem which challenges the narrow individually focused interpretation of violence dominant in much of psychology and criminology. It can be a strong underpinning for the public health model of violence prevention, though it has potentially radical implications for some governments around the world. Beyond biology and psychology, it offers the widest possible context for understanding violence and providing ideas for future solutions.

5.2   Beyond Direct Violence

The idea of structural violence offers a redefinition of violence far removed from the everyday idea of an intentional physical assault. It focuses instead on the underlying structures within society which create the conditions where preventable injury, ill health, and death occur. Unlike the traditional vivid image of one person striking another, this approach shines a spotlight on insidious processes of invisible, slow, or silent violence which are tolerated, encouraged or even deployed either by the state in order to ensure its smooth functioning or by non-state actors in pursuit of profit or power.

While a 'political' approach to understanding and preventing violence is inevitably controversial and open to debate, certain key elements of the idea are beyond question. It is, for instance, undeniable that we have constructed a world built on social, political, and economic structures where power and resources are highly clustered in certain geographical areas and, within these areas, further concentrated within specific elite groups. Some 82% of the global wealth created in 2017, for instance, was owned by 1% of the world population (Oxfam, 2018). The higher we go in the wealth pyramid, the steeper the gradient and the greater the concentration: the richest ten people in the world, for instance, hold assets worth more than the annual GDP of a country like Nigeria with a population of over 170 million people (Institute for Policy Studies, 2017).

This grossly uneven distribution of power and resources has clear consequences for both the rich and the poor. People lower down the pyramid will die through acts of both omission and commission by those at the top. They may be actively killed through military action to preserve the current balance of power and ownership of resources. But, less obviously, they may die as the result of lethal working practices in industries such as mining or construction work or as a result of untreated diseases or environmental catastrophes from which they could have been protected. The concept of structural violence invites us to consider the latter as forms of violence that are in principle not morally different from military action or murder. Individuals in multinational corporations and voters for popular governments which create the necessary conditions for premature death likely have no conscious intention of inflicting that fate on unknown people far away and largely out of sight. Nevertheless, governments and companies may deliberately calculate a cost–benefit ratio including actual or likely fatalities.

This broader view of violence also shifts perspectives on how violence is defined and what factors are considered part of the solution. In terms of definition, it incorporates that which is hidden or out of sight as well as the obvious and direct physical blow. Social structure shapes the way we look at the world, and thus what we call violence, and also shapes the ways in which the violence itself is expressed in different times and places. In terms of causation, this broader view highlights the complex political background to any act of violence, reminding us of the social constraints which create people who act aggressively on repeated occasions, as considered above in Chapter 4, and societies with high levels of violence. Overall it foregrounds the idea of structure as a core aspect of violence in contrast to the traditional ideas of intentionality, individualism, and physicality.

The definition of violence underpinning the WHO Global Campaign for Violence Prevention considered in Chapter 1 is clearly not structural in this sense. The specified categories – armed violence, gang violence, youth violence, child maltreatment, intimate partner violence, sexual violence, and elder abuse – are all overt acts in the traditional, nonstructural sense. There is no scope here for the wider definitions of violence which include deaths from treatable diseases or the consequences of negligence in designing safe workplaces. On the other hand, the WHO recommendations for interventions to tackle the problem, which will be discussed further in Chapter 6, do clearly embrace the need for structural approaches. The recommendations for governments (World Health Organization, 2014) emphasise the development of national action plans, the integration of violence prevention programmes with other public health initiatives such as school health programmes and improving anti-violence leadership across communities. To complement these approaches the recommended 'best-buy' intervention programmes are less focused on wide-ranging and fundamental structural change. They are preventative but operate largely at the individual and family levels. Only the microfinance initiatives and social norm-changing that are recommended to tackle intimate partner and sexual violence really reflect this wider perspective. Their great potential and implementation challenges will be discussed further in Chapter 10.

A rich strand of critical thinking in the twentieth century led to the development of this new perspective, which balances the traditional focus on individual and biological causes of violence with a growing awareness of social and political factors. Structural violence is an alternative form of aggression which in the magnitude of its effects is far worse than the violence of which we are conscious and with which we live in our daily lives (Roberts, 2008). It is impossible to understand and start to tackle the problem of interpersonal violence from a global perspective, as we are now in a position to do, without some consideration of the social structures which underpin its expression and too often put people in lethal situations. Certain types of social organisation facilitate violence and, since social systems are human creations which are open to change, it is possible to imagine and plan other types of social organisation which will reduce or perhaps even eradicate the problem. This requires a political as much as a purely scientific approach which shifts the emphasis toward an awareness of our collective rather than our individual responsibilities for any particular violent act.

Structural violence first and foremost is a collective rather than an individual phenomenon. While it often has no obvious perpetrator in the sense of a visible, active agent intending to cause harm, it arises and resides within collective social entities. This may be an entire society which imperially imposes its power and values on 'inferior' societies, or, within societies, it may be particular groups which consciously or unconsciously hold power over others. First social class, then gender and race, have been identified as characteristics which divide societies and provide a platform which privileges the perspective of one or more groups over others. More recently, characteristics such as disability, gender identity, pregnancy, sexual orientation, and marital status (Hepple, 2010) have been identified as vulnerabilities increasing risk for exposure to violence and discrimination. All of these status categories embed a set of social structures which may be triggers for direct overt aggression by others or lead indirectly to more insidious violent effects. Indirectly, being a member of the category may, for instance, be associated with an increased risk of premature death due to political decisions about the deployment of social resources. The high level of AIDS-related deaths among gay men in the early 1980s is an example where a 'minority' problem was deemed invisible by society and thus starved of resources. 'Silence = Death', the gay activist slogan from the time, tersely captures the formula underpinning this form of structural violence.

Within societies, there are also certain types of organisations which can facilitate the operations of structural violence. In the public sphere, large institutions have a power to damage people physically and psychologically without engaging in overt violence, by controlling their access to resources and their expectations of what is normal. These can be institutions with a physical presence such as hospitals or prisons, where the power is most concentrated, or more dispersed organisations such as the media or community social services. Employees may be subjected to this form of violence through bullying and a passive acceptance of dangerous working conditions (Tombs, 2007), and patients or prisoners may suffer institutional abuse. In the private sector there is growing awareness of the driving force of corporations to damage the environment and disrupt the political and economic arrangements of client states, the wider population and even their own employees.

5.3 The Concept of Structural Violence

The idea underpinning contemporary views of structural violence was first proposed by Johan Galtung in the 1960s (Galtung, 1969). This Norwegian sociologist radically expanded the concept of violence then accepted by proposing that it is present whenever any aspect of a person's physical or mental potential is unrealised because of social influences which could be changed. This occurs when access to health and other resources are clustered in higher or elite social groups and thus is made unavailable to those in less powerful groups as a result of the way a particular society is constructed. More concisely, it is the difference between optimal and actual life expectancy or 'any avoidable impediment to self-realization' (Galtung, 1980, p. 67). This far wider conception encompasses a huge range of social situations previously not taken into account in the study and prevention of violence.

It is worth carefully examining the elements of these definitions in order to evaluate this original notion of structural violence. Optimal life expectancy is that which could be achieved if all the resources within a society were used most effectively for the benefit of all, and there is an assumption that this can best be achieved by organising society in a way which maximises economic equality. So, death from tuberculosis in the twenty-first century is a form of structural violence because the means to prevent it are available now, whereas such a death in the fifteenth century was not an example of such violence as it was virtually unavoidable once the disease was contracted then. The idea of prematurity of death thus shifts over both historical time and geographical space. It moves from being unavoidable to becoming avoidable, and, if it is avoidable, it must be tolerated in some way within a society making overt and specific political choices about how resources should be distributed. Another example Galtung gives, in the language of the time, is: 'when one husband beats his wife there is a clear case of personal violence, but when one million husbands keep one million wives in ignorance there is structural violence' (Galtung, 1969, p. 171). This is what we now refer to as coercive control in domestic relationships, and here the issue is as much the loss of unrealised potential as it is the risk of premature death. In both cases, the assumption of patriarchy, the cultivation of ignorance and the diversion of resources are not just causes of violence as, perhaps, people struggle against their oppressors; they *are* the violence. In neither case, tuberculosis nor coercive control, is somebody necessarily subjected to overt aggression. Indeed, they do not really need to be as they are either too ravaged by disease or too mentally controlled to put up any significant resistance. Structural violence is thus successful inasmuch as it neutralises the potential for actual overt violence.

Life expectancy as a metric for structural violence is worth considering in more detail. Clearly it varies enormously around the world and within countries. Measured from birth, people in Europe currently live on average sixteen years longer (to seventy-seven years) than people in Africa (sixty-one years) (World Health Organization, 2016a) and it differs by eight years even just comparing the most affluent and the most deprived areas of the United Kingdom, for example (Office for National Statistics, 2015). A strong case can be made that this variation is almost entirely due to the relative distribution of health resources in the differing areas, and, thus, as an avoidable form of premature death, it is a manifestation of structural violence against the poor. However, other variations in life expectancy are more difficult to attribute to structural violence. Female life expectancy in the United Kingdom, for instance, is on average three years longer than that for males in the same area with comparable socioeconomic conditions. Here the case for claiming this as a form of structural violence is less clear and reminds us that numerous factors are at play which make it difficult to establish what is truly avoidable through redistribution of resources and what is not. This reconceptualisation of violence, drawing in a range of other avoidable ways of dying, exposes the relatively small scale of the problem of direct violence in comparison. Roberts (2008) estimates that there are fifty deaths by structural violence for every one by direct violence.

Altogether, this is an extremely broad reconceptualisation of what violence is, and, as such, it has both positive and negative consequences. Undoubtedly the idea of structural violence has provided a theoretical tool which enables us to think about social and health problems in a completely different way. Now the capacity of political institutions, commercial companies and social practices to prevent people meeting their basic needs or realising their potential through marginalisation or exploitation are subsumed as part of the larger violence phenomenon.

At the same time there are real difficulties with this expanded approach, despite its widespread adoption and endorsement by many social scientists and policy analysts. Galtung himself has acknowledged that it is very challenging to define the 'potential' that is blocked by the structures and that, even if they can be defined, it is harder still to gain consensus on what potentials should be valued over others. Literacy, for instance, is widely accepted across the globe as a desirable goal for societies to strive toward and is a major priority in the UN Sustainable Development Goals agenda. It is clearly linked to the availability of educational resources, so literacy rates in a population are easily construed as an important measure of structural violence. Other social values are more contested around the world. Adherence to a particular religion, for instance, is esteemed very differently in different countries or during successive periods, so the proportion of the population subscribing to a particular religion at any one time (e.g. 'Christianity rates') is less meaningful in this context. Even when agreement is reached on the key deficits within a society that need to be addressed, there will be differing views on what is and what is not actually avoidable. We have seen this already in the 'standard narrative' of hard-wired violence which accepts that violence is a problem but which minimises or rejects the relevance of resource distribution to its causation.

More broadly, if violence is viewed in such wide terms, it becomes difficult to distinguish it from related ideas such as 'power', 'coercion' or 'domination', which are hard to define and encompass even greater levels of complexity. Some see this conceptual breadth as a real impediment to analysing the various distinct phenomena and thus as an obstacle to developing ways of counteracting each or all of them (Parsons, 2007). Violence is distinct from, say, domination through power, and it is misleading to mix up the two things in a way that will limit our ability to deal with either. The key issue is about the effects of an act and whether or not it causes harm. Parents have power over their children but generally act in their best interests, so power can be benign. Violence occurs when we cause someone harm or force them to act against their will, when we have no justification for doing so, or when we do so in our own self-interest as opposed to theirs.

Linking violence to the idea of structures also implies that it is something very fixed and stable within a society. The original Marxist idea informing Galtung's work was that the relevant structures, especially social class, are more or less static, unchanging features of social relations requiring enormous effort by subjects to confront and overthrow them (Galtung, 1969). But structures are rarely completely fixed in this way, with many at least evolving slowly over time and some transformed rapidly at moments of revolutionary change. Gender is a good example of a key structure clearly linked to both overt violence and, as noted above, to structural violence. Women's hugely disproportionate exposure to domestic violence, for instance, can include both restricted opportunities and actual violence. Yet gender roles have changed slowly but significantly in the past forty years, and so even this deep-seated core structure is evolving within the lifetime of a single individual. More recent conceptions of structural violence attempt to incorporate this more fluid element into the idea and will be discussed further below.

5.4   Inequality as the Engine of Violence

The idea of inequality is fundamental to the concept of structural violence, with Galtung's original definition highlighting the issue of resources being concentrated in one group rather than another. Structural violence is therefore rooted in unequal access to social and economic resources, and this inequality can be estimated empirically using a specific metric, the Gini index. This statistic calculates the proportion of national wealth held by those in the poorer levels of a particular society and estimates how much this proportion diverges from a notional level of complete equality. In a hypothetical situation of such equality, everybody in a society would earn or own exactly the same amount (Gini coefficient = 0). Conversely in a society where one person owned 100% of a nation's wealth and everybody else owned nothing, the Gini coefficient = 1. Most estimates of global inequality from 1970 onward report a Gini coefficient of about 0.6 or 0.7, but one study estimated that there was greater equality in 1820 than at any time since 1970 (Hillebrand, 2008). In 2009 the global average Gini coefficient was estimated at 0.68, representing a slight increase in inequality since 2005. The amount of inequality within countries also changes over time, of course, according to economic developments and social policies. The United Kingdom was a more equal society than Norway in 1960, but since the 1980s opposing political approaches have reversed the relative profiles of these two countries.

Given that the observed relationship is a correlational one, cause-and-effect pathways are difficult to examine. Inequality itself can take many different forms and does not always just mean income or wealth inequality. For example, power was unequally distributed in the former Communist societies in a system which engineered income equality. Also, wealth inequality is not to be confused with wealth itself since both wealthy countries and poor countries can have high or low levels of inequality. Norway and the United States are examples of rich countries with very different income distributions, but low income countries can also be very different. There are major variations between, for instance, Ghana (relatively equal) and Namibia (relatively unequal). Bangladesh and the Netherlands have very similar equality levels but very different average wealth. Even within the group of developed countries, the income gap (comparing the richest 20% with the poorest 20%) varies massively, for example between the unequal societies of Singapore and the United States and the more egalitarian ones of Japan and Finland.

There is strong empirical evidence of an association between violence and inequality when comparing countries. Nations with unequal societies tend to have higher rates of violence than those with more equal distribution of resources. Pickett and Wilkinson (2010) show that inequality is associated with a wide range of social ills but that the relationship with violence, particularly homicide and assaults, is stronger than with any other factor. There is a clear trend in their analysis for homicide rates to increase as inequality increases. The United States and Portugal have the highest homicide rates and the highest inequality rates in the OECD countries; Japan and Norway have the lowest (Pickett and Wilkinson, 2010). But the relationship is complex. The United Kingdom and Australia are relatively unequal but relatively peaceful, while Finland is relatively equal but violent.

Wolf et al. (2014) go beyond this focus on homicide in high-income countries to include non-fatal assault rates in a much wider range of rich and low income countries. Combining data from various UN, WHO, and other sources they found that income inequality significantly predicted homicide and assault rates both overall and when rich and poor countries were considered separately. While having a relatively young and highly urbanised population was predictive of violence in some analyses, none of the other variables they examined had such a strong and persistent association with violence rates as income inequality. The tentative conclusion is politically loaded but unavoidable: to reduce violence, societies must implement measures to reduce income inequality. Clearly inequality plays a role in violence rates globally and represents a key element of structural violence, so political and economic actions are likely to have an effect if adopted and sustained. These actions potentially include labour market reforms, redistributive fiscal policies and expansion of financial markets for small enterprises.

5.5   Developments in the Idea of Structural Violence

Structural approaches to understanding violence have been developing for several decades now and the idea has been elaborated in a number of new ways. The impact of structures on the environment, the global economy and human health and the violence inherent in these processes, in particular, have been explored over this time with a number of novel applications proposed.

Growing awareness of the accelerating environmental crisis has led to a keen interest in considering environmental problems as manifestations of structural violence which, in turn, trigger more overt, direct violence. The idea of *slow violence* (Nixon, 2011) is one such conceptual refinement of the basic structural violence approach we have been considering. It shares with the original concept an emphasis on the relatively hidden nature of structural violence, but, in contrast to the original portrayal of highly stable, almost static social structures, it moves toward a more dynamic perspective, taking into account speed of change. Setting up a mining operation in a low-income country, for instance, will require relatively little overt violence, and such violence may even be viewed as counterproductive to the economic goals of the corporation. But it will also involve numerous small-scale human and environmental violations to get the job done. None of these on their own will seem particularly significant, especially to consumers many thousands of miles away, but they may, over time, have a cumulative effect on human health and mortality in the chosen location. Unlike the spectacle and visibility of what is usually considered 'real' violence (i.e. direct physical assault), slow violence is insidious and incremental, with a cumulative effect on individuals, societies and the landscape. There is no blood, so it remains formless and imperceptible, at best obscurely perceived. As the originator puts it: 'Chemical and radiological violence … is driven inward, somatised into cellular dramas of mutation that – particularly in the bodies of the poor – remain largely unobserved, undiagnosed and untreated' (Nixon, 2011, p. 6).

From this perspective the environmental crisis currently gripping humanity is a 'long emergency' with a series of 'scientifically convoluted cataclysms in which casualties are postponed, often for generations' (Nixon, 2011, p. 3). The effects of slow violence can be exponential, spreading out from a central location to generate new and wider overt conflicts. The key to its invisibility is a wide dispersion of individual actions and effects over lengthy time periods and large geographical spaces so that the culprit is never explicitly recognised and cannot be called to account. Even when it is visible, our traditional perspective means it is not really seen as violence at all. It is furthermore virtually impossible to capture in traditional media 'snapshot' terms and so never gets relayed back to those who live in either those societies which are affected or those countries which host the decision makers.

Srikantia's (2016) description of the destruction wrought on traditional societies when a hydroelectric dam was built in a rural area of South America is a good illustration of this. The dam made perfect economic sense in many ways to many people, most of whom lived far away from the site. National politicians, international investors and consumers were all rewarded with increased profits and reduced costs to such an extent that an extension to the work is now planned. But the reservoir contained by the dam flooded the gold mines and agricultural land which underpinned the economy of the local people who were neither consulted about nor compensated for their loss. Nor, in an ultimate injustice, did they even receive the benefits of reduced energy consumption prices. The flooding led to people being displaced to less fertile agricultural lands with inevitably reduced incomes and the importation of drug problems, which had been unknown before.

Alongside this structural violence and driven by the money to be made, various enforcers have emerged who deploy direct, overt violence to intimidate, and in some cases kill, opponents to the project. A paramilitary group targeted various community leaders with threats and 'disappearances' to minimise opposition: 'I call [the dam] a cemetery because many people have disappeared in this pool. And all that this has brought us is problems. Beginning in the 1980s, people who went down to where they were building the dam wall started to disappear' (Srikantia, 2016, p. 244; brackets in original). Environmental destruction by powerful forces is not restricted to the countries of the 'global south' of course. The Dakota pipeline dispute and recent US presidential decisions to reduce the size of national parks in Montana both involved similar kinds of environmental violence.

Farmer (2005) has also applied the idea of structural violence to health and infectious disease in developing countries. He focuses especially on tuberculosis and HIV/AIDS in Haiti and sees the death rates there as evidence of a 'war on the poor'. He describes being called by a woman queuing outside the clinic where he worked as medical director. She had advanced breast cancer and had visited fourteen clinics before seeing him but underwent no biopsies and received no meaningful treatment. Farmer maps this catastrophic healthcare failure onto the material conditions of Haiti as a former slave colony which was later punished economically and politically by the United States for the offence of establishing its independence as a black state less than fifty years after the American Revolution. Racism and rejection of the poor mean that the money and political will to eradicate infectious diseases is absent. This is obviously avoidable death, as originally conceived by Galtung. As a result, '[t]he distribution of AIDS and tuberculosis – like slavery in earlier times – is historically given and economically driven' (Farmer, 2005, p. 317).

Put this way, with these examples, it is hard to avoid the need to take action in some way. Both Srikantia and Farmer write from a position of engagement, partway between analysis and activism. Both advocate explicit actions which should be taken by those who are persuaded that structural violence is based on political and ethical choices made mainly by those in power in developing countries, often abetted by their counterparts in the rich West. Farmer sees the issue of health as inextricably woven with the issue of human rights, so that without adequate human rights there can be no real protection from ill-health as a manifestation of structural violence. There is no lack of consensus around lofty ideals expressed in documents such as the Universal Declaration of Human Rights, but the persistence of systematic and population-wide abuses indicates that a stronger commitment is needed on the ground. An agenda for action would aim to improve both health and human rights together and includes the need for health professionals to be fully engaged in pushing for human rights around the world and building services based on principles of excellence and inclusiveness rather than just cost effectiveness and sustainability. Some of these actions are on the WHO agenda for violence reduction, which will be considered in the next chapter, so the potential for change and a concerted response is growing.

The most explicit analysis of structural violence in economic terms is the identification of various advanced commercial relationships as forms of 'necrocapitalism' (Banerjee, 2008). This violent underside of capitalism includes a modern form of colonialism sometimes enforced by privatised military forces and often generating conflicts over natural resources. We saw evidence for the emergence of these hybrid wars as a substitute for traditional international warfare in Chapter 1. Necrocapitalism is often masked by benevolent language about 'development' and rescuing impoverished societies from economic 'backwardness'. Even in a world of apparently sovereign states, there are some geographical zones of 'exception' where the application of national laws is suspended in order to allow the development of resources for the benefit of global organisations rather than the local economy and people. To take one example, according to media reports in 2005 there was a massive increase in suicide among farmers in southern India with over 4,000 dying in this way after agricultural trade liberalisation was introduced and a genetically modified cotton crop failed. Banerjee (2008) notes that while six journalists were covering this suicide story in February 2006, more than 500 journalists were in Mumbai in the same month to cover a fashion event at which the finished products of the cotton crop were being revealed. Another example he gives is 200 deaths from cholera in South Africa after access to water and sanitation services was restricted for people who could not meet the 'cost recovery' prices driven by World Bank recommendations.

5.6   Violence, Structure, and Public Health

Social structures such as inequalities in gender and in wealth often exist outside the conscious awareness of many people, and even when they are recognised they may seem immutable. By the process of reification they are seen as part of human nature and just 'the way things are'. Emphasising the social dimension of violence alongside the more individualistic components of the biopsychosocial approach enables us to shine a light on these hidden structures and to emphasise the scope for changing them in the cause of violence prevention and more peaceful societies. The public health model then adds the potential scientific basis for understanding regular patterns in the relationship between social structures and violent outcomes. The primary prevention element of this approach highlights how changes in remote 'upstream' causes can have dramatic effects downstream on violence. Its focus on whole populations also leads to an emphasis on the sociodemographic factors which constitute some of the core social structures, such as gender and class as noted above. The WHO approach, rooted as it is in this model, therefore places great emphasis on addressing structures in societies around the world which facilitate or cause direct violence. It has the potential also to connect up with the other UN Sustainable Development Goals for 2030, particularly those for tackling infectious diseases, and thus to contribute to the reduction of structural violence in its widest sense.

We therefore live among the structures we have created with or without awareness of their existence, and, while they shape our behaviour,

our everyday actions also constantly reshape them to a degree. While there is always some scope for human agency and freedom to make choices outside these structures, the extent of that freedom varies across different contexts. The constraints that structures, again such as gender and wealth, place upon people in choosing how to live their lives are often ignored in psychological interventions such as those considered in Chapter 9. Some psychological models underpinning interventions implicitly assume that people are purely rational beings who will make a conscious calculation when faced with a choice (Sheeran et al., 2013) and who need only to be provided with adequate knowledge, information, and education to choose the right option. The moderate effect sizes of many psychological interventions, while commensurate with the magnitude of effects found for many widely accepted medical interventions, could perhaps be increased if more consideration were given to these powerful constraints external to the individual.

5.7   Conclusion

All of these approaches based on the original idea of structural violence provide a powerful perspective, which reminds us of how limited the traditional viewpoint of violence really is. As some criminologists have argued at least for the last forty years, whether deliberately or just through laziness, we are encouraged to see violence as simply, at root, just one person physically striking another. Stopping that form of violence is difficult enough given the complexity of human minds and the limitations of our currently quite basic psychological and pharmaceutical armoury. It is even more daunting to try and tackle the formidable social and political interests served by the status quo. The various conceptualisations of structural violence discussed here highlight a massive problem and emphasise the scope we have for addressing a system for which we are all partly responsible.

Part II

Solutions

6 Advancing a Global Public Health Response to Violence

6.1 The Global Status Report on Violence Prevention

We are now in a position to consider some of the possible new approaches which are showing promise and might contribute to a truly international programme for tackling the scourge of human violence. We have overviewed a range of biological, psychological, and social factors which play a role in causing violence, and knowledge gained from each of these perspectives can be drawn upon to devise interventions within the overall public health framework. As described in Chapter 1, this approach has encouraged and underpinned a growing global perspective on violence. Governments in virtually every country around the world have seen it as a core part of their role to establish national laws which maximise safety within their jurisdiction. Some richer countries have gone further and developed extensive national public health and clinical programmes to tackle the problem. Public policies at the national level are now seen as a key element of an effective prevention programme (D'Inverno et al., 2018), and instruments to convert these policies into effective programmes are increasingly available (Centers for Disease Control and Prevention, 2018). However, concerted and synchronised international action to deal with violence has appeared only in the past twenty years since the UN and its constituent body, the WHO, turned their attention to the problem.

The starting point for developing a global approach to interpersonal violence was the Seville Statement in 1986, noted already in Chapter 3, which strongly argued against the standard narrative we have been interrogating throughout here. The statement, signed by biological scientists as well as social scientists including the renowned anthropologist Richard Leakey, explicitly challenges 'a number of alleged biological findings that have been used to justify violence and war [and] have contributed to an atmosphere of pessimism'. The scientific basis for a series of incorrect claims is then rejected, including any evidence for an inherited human tendency to make war, genetic programming of violence, or any special evolutionary process for selection of aggressiveness over other tendencies. The authors of the statement also rejected the idea of the 'violent brain' and any 'instinctual' basis for war. Instead, they argue that science provides the basis for moving away from biological pessimism toward a social and psychological transformation that will enable peaceful societies to develop and thrive. The Statement has been controversial since it was first made more than thirty years ago, and the biological science it was attacking in particular has developed almost beyond recognition as outlined in Chapters 2 and 3 above. Nevertheless, the principle of a coordinated evidence-based international approach to building peaceful societies was first articulated in this statement and thus it has influenced policy and governmental actions ever since, as this chapter will illustrate.

The adoption of a resolution by the World Health Assembly (WHA) in 1996 has been seen as a step change in how the violence problem is framed internationally and how this public health framing could form the basis for a coordinated and sustained transnational approach to the problem. The WHA is the main decision-making body for the WHO and has been convening annually since 1948. The 1996 resolution called for violence to be prioritised as a problem to be addressed by all member states and emphasised the need for a formal scientific and evidence-based approach to tackling it (WHO, 2002). This was not the first international attempt in this area, as shown by the various initiatives listed in Box 6.1 and the Appendix, but it is recognised as the starting point for a programme of actions over the two decades that followed up to the current time.

The first step in this programme was to develop a World Report on Violence and Health through consultation with experts in more than seventy countries around the world (Krug et al., 2002; World Health Organization, 2002). That Report, the first of its kind, was published in 2002 with powerful endorsements by global leaders including former South African President Nelson Mandela and former UN General Secretary Kofi Annan. It stands out as a landmark document and a platform for strategic and coordinated action across all the various domains of violent behaviour. It set out a number of key challenges at the start of the new century, and these make up the components of the new global public health approach. Governments were given a clear set of recommended high-level actions to consider and implement. These included creating national action plans for violence prevention, improving monitoring systems, supporting relevant research and strengthening services for victims of violence (see also Box 6.2).

Since 2002, the new approach has been widely adopted in theory but less so in practice, and the challenges remain (World Health

Box 6.1   Selected UN initiatives to address interpersonal violence, 1986–2018 (see Appendix for complete list)

1986: **Seville Statement: 'violent behaviour is not genetically programmed into human behaviour and is therefore preventable'.** Adopted by UNESCO in 1989.

1994: UN Special Rapporteur on Violence against Women appointed

1996: World Health Assembly declared violence a 'leading worldwide public health problem' and called upon the WHO Director General to develop a science-based approach to understanding and prevention (WHA49.25)

2002: World Report on Violence and Health

2009: Appointment of the UN Secretary General's Special Representative on Violence against Children

2014: Global Status Report on Violence Prevention published

2015: UN General Assembly adopted the 2030 Sustainable Goals Agenda linking sustained peace to sustainable development

2015: Preventing Youth Violence: An Overview of the Evidence

2016: Global Plan of Action to Prevent Interpersonal Violence (WHA 69.5)

2016: Global Partnership to End Violence against Children

2018: INSPIRE Global Partnership to End Violence against Children launched Implementation Handbook and Indicator Document

Note: Bold entries refer to key 'cornerstone' texts which are referenced repeatedly in the text.

Source: Lee, 2015; World Health Organization, 2014; M. Peres and A. Butchart, personal communications.

Organization, 2014). In particular there is still a need to shift the emphasis away from managing the violence problem purely through incarceration of high risk offenders and toward preventing potential violence through much earlier community interventions. Clearly, despite its relative expense, imprisonment as the endpoint of a criminal career remains a major plank of justice systems around the world, and little more than lip-service is paid in many countries to early intervention with at-risk families, for example, as an alternative. National and local health organisations need to fully embrace violence prevention as part of their remit, but again, with so many competing demands in a context of limited resources, this remains an ongoing struggle. Advocacy for

> **Box 6.2   Recommendations from the World Report on Violence and Health**
>
> - Create, implement, and monitor a national action plan for violence prevention
> - Enhance capacity for collecting data on violence
> - Define priorities for, and support research on, the causes, consequences, costs and prevention of violence
> - Promote primary prevention responses
> - Strengthen responses for victims of violence
> - Integrate violence prevention into social and educational policies, and thereby promote gender and social equality
> - Increase collaboration and exchange of information on violence prevention
> - Promote and monitor adherence to international treaties, laws, and other mechanisms to protect human rights
> - Seek practical, internationally agreed responses to the global drugs trade and the global arms trade.
>
> Source: World Health Organization, 2002.

resources is made even harder because of the disquiet among many taxpayers toward the idea of violent perpetrators as worthy recipients of health funding. Communities also need to feel a sense of ownership at the local level for change to be promoted and implemented, and effective leadership in cities and elsewhere is the key to this. A local champion such as a mayor can be the essential catalyst for driving through essential changes and new initiatives that make the crucial difference, regardless of top-down directives from national governments. A final challenge is the need for robust information systems through which patterns of violence and the effectiveness of interventions can be tracked. On this there have been substantial advances over the past decade with various new national and international datasets established around the world.

The 2002 World Report was given impetus through being endorsed by many international bodies such as the African Union, the Council of Europe and Médecins Sans Frontières, which helped to galvanise many countries in the international community into taking action. More than thirty countries, for instance, developed a National Action Plan from 2002 onward to tackle violence against women based on the principles of the Report (UN Women, 2012). More than half of these national plans were developed in low- and middle-income countries where resources may be extremely limited. Other countries convened national policy discussions and produced national reports modelled on the original approach. All this activity culminated in the production of a second major WHO document a decade or so later reviewing progress around the world following the publication of the World Report. This 2014 Global Status Report provides an update on what was achieved in the first decade of the international programme and, inevitably, what remains to be done in the future. The 2014 recommendations are set out in Box 6.3.

These recommendations are more detailed than the previous set and distinguish national policy tasks from those required at a higher level of global collaboration. But the direction of travel stays much the same within the public health framework, and for the first time the 2014 report provided data from each country on what actions had been taken in the

---

Box 6.3   Recommendations from the Global Status Report on Violence Prevention

At the national level:

- Strengthen data collection to reveal the true extent of the problem; develop comprehensive and data-driven national action plans
- Integrate violence prevention into other health platforms
- Strengthen mechanisms for leadership and coordination
- Ensure prevention programmes are comprehensive, integrated, and informed by evidence
- Ensure that services for victims are comprehensive and informed by evidence
- Strengthen support for outcome evaluation studies
- Enforce existing laws and review their quality
- Implement and enact policies and laws relevant to multiple types of violence
- Build capacity for violence prevention.

At regional and global levels:

- Strengthen the global violence prevention agenda
- Strengthen support for comprehensive and integrated violence prevention programming
- Strengthen the efforts of regional and subregional organizations to work with national offices to coordinate data collection and disseminate data gathered
- Increase collaboration between international organizations and donor agencies
- Set baselines and targets, and track progress.

Source: World Health Organization, 2014.

intervening period. As such it provides a progress report on the achievement of the original aims and thus enables us to gauge the success in implementing a global programme of action to tackle violence. These data will be examined further below.

6.2   National Action Plans for Violence around the World: Coordinating Law, Policy, and Interventions

The keystone of the new approach to preventing violence is the National Action Plan (NAP). This is an overarching framework produced by a national government as the basis for a coordinated prevention programme targeting one or more of the main types of violence identified in the WHO definition cited in the Introduction: child maltreatment, youth violence, intimate partner violence, sexual violence, and elder abuse. Judging from information provided by the 133 countries which responded to the 2014 Global Report, success in developing NAPs across the various types of violence has been highly variable (World Health Organization, 2014). One-fifth of them had developed a NAP for all the types of violence, and nearly half, covering a combined population of more than 5 billion people worldwide, had a NAP for at least one type. Most commonly, NAPs have been developed to tackle child maltreatment, intimate partner violence (IPV) or sexual violence, with about half of the countries in the world having NAPs in these areas by 2013. Fewer countries had developed plans for addressing youth violence despite this age group being more at risk of homicide than children. Fewer still had started thinking about elder abuse, with under a third of countries having a coordinated plan in this area. It is highly noteworthy that despite having access to significantly fewer resources, low-income countries are no less likely to develop NAPs than high-income countries, which might suggest the importance of having a national coordinator with statutory responsibility to lead on action. Cambodia and Guinea, for example, have both developed NAPs in five areas despite having a gross national income per capita which is one-fifth or less of the global median. Once again, equality, as noted in Chapter 5, may be a factor – both countries are poor but the resources they do have are spread relatively evenly, as both are close to the global average for income equality.

Inevitably there are still definitional issues here, especially related to the individual approaches taken by different countries. Responding to the broader agenda set out by the UN, and with an awareness no doubt of the interconnectedness between multiple factors, many countries have developed NAPs for violence against women and girls overall rather than according to different types of violence. These NAPs cut across the various violence categories but are probably intended primarily to cover prevention of the three categories most relevant to females specifically: sexual violence, IPV, and child maltreatment.

What does a NAP look like and what should it cover? A model exists to guide the design of such Plans for violence against women, which can be used for further developments in this area and for NAPs to deal with other types of violence (UN Women, 2012). The guiding principles of the model emphasise the need for adoption of a human rights–based perspective on violence which includes recognition of violence in this context as a form of sex discrimination and as a manifestation of gender inequality more broadly. So violence against women is seen as both a reflection of sexist attitudes which view women as subordinate and as an instrument used actively to enforce that subordination. The model also stresses the need to recognise that violence, or at least aggression, can be manifested in many different ways driven by a multiplicity of root causes. It adopts, in other words, the equifinality concept discussed earlier (Chapter 4). The prevalence of exposure to violence and the impact it has are also highly variable, reflecting multiple, and intersecting forms of discrimination and disadvantage.

A NAP should be designed as a national programme of activity which is coherent, comprehensive, and sustained, cutting across all the relevant government departments and going beyond government to include other relevant national agencies. In reality, many of the violence NAPs have been designed as part of even wider public health initiatives, most commonly including promotion of safer sex activities as part of HIV prevention programmes. This is logical since the gender norms which underpin violence against women also provide justifications for engaging in unsafe sex, and, in any case, deliberately inflicting HIV exposure on somebody else is, in itself, a form of violence. Existing social structures enable this to happen unthinkingly if a genuine universal human rights approach is not adopted. On the other hand, unsafe sex and interpersonal violence are different social phenomena involving distinct social dynamics, and a complete overlap in terms of strategy might obscure these differences and reduce the effectiveness of the programme.

Guided by the NAP, national agencies, such as health ministries and criminal justice systems, should work together to meet agreed objectives across a wide range of social domains, and the activity must be sustained despite the many other inevitable demands on resources in both high- and low-income countries. There needs to be a combination of 'ground up' involvement to harness the energy and insights of local groups in any civil society, on the one hand, with clear accountability through 'top down' governance protocols, on the other. National political leadership is an absolute essential – if there is no meaningful, sustained endorsement, and support at the top, then the NAP becomes yet another paper exercise with no impact on society.

A good starting point for any national anti-violence programme is a rigorous review of how current national laws and policies either strengthen or impede activities which would maintain progress toward the overall goal. An example of such an analysis is the Readiness Assessment for the Prevention of Child Maltreatment (World Health Organization, 2013b). The national leadership role should be held by one high-level agency which then provides all the necessary elements of support, monitoring, and coordination across the relevant government departments. Independent research and data collection have a key role to play in regular monitoring of progression toward the programme objectives. On the ground, it is important to identify what skills are needed by those who work directly with victims or perpetrators to do their job effectively and to contribute to the overall programme. Where there are skills gaps, there should be sustained implementation of relevant training to build capacity among key workforces such as community nurses and police officers, who will be tasked with delivering the relevant services and initiatives.

Reflecting again the underpinning public health approach, interventions in the women's NAP model are divided into those designed to prevent violence being perpetrated and those designed as responses to support those who have been attacked. The emphasis is on primary prevention, spreading activity across whole populations in order to tackle the underlying attitudes which facilitate gender-based violence and which are presumed to be held by all or most of those, women and men, within the chosen society. These norms and attitudes can be challenged through public awareness–raising campaigns and by agencies working with the local and national media to sensitise them to the issues.

There are various examples of this around the world. Couples applying for marriage in Turkey, for instance, are sent information on gender equality, domestic violence, and reproductive health as part of the national awareness-raising campaign according to the national plan there. A 'Machismo Is Violence' campaign in all the provinces of Ecuador was funded by a range of government agencies working together; and in Portugal, a large campaign challenging domestic violence was implemented at football matches. In terms of media sensitisation, Box 6.4 sets out some key strategies that were adopted in Spain to change the way the media portrayed women in general and violence against women in particular.

Box 6.4 Strategies to sensitise the media to social and cultural norms underpinning violence against women in Spain

- The creation of an Advisory Committee on the image of women to analyse how women are treated in advertising
- Extension of self-regulation agreements in advertising
- Development of agreements with publicly owned media to promote non-sexist content and the active participation of women in all areas of life
- A self-regulation pact that will guarantee that news items are treated objectively and that they transmit the values of equality and reject this type of violence
- Extension of the Self-Regulation Agreement for television operators on the subject of the protection of minors to include gender-based violence and discrimination for reasons of sex
- Conventions with Audiovisual Regulatory Authorities to establish collaboration procedures to eradicate from programming and advertising all direct or indirect encouragement of gender-based violence.

Source: UN Women, 2012.

These community-wide initiatives can be supplemented by more targeted campaigns in various settings where people gather to learn and work, including schools, workplaces, sports clubs, religious buildings, and military settings. Schools are, of course, a major focus because early attitudes learned at home can be reinforced or challenged before they become more fixed in early adulthood. In Jordan, for instance, school curricula have been rewritten and teachers have been trained to be more aware of the issue. Given their significant role as agents of socialisation and as sites where opportunities for violence and violence prevention outside the family are first opened up, schools are important sites for communicating attitudes toward the resolution of personal conflict. We will consider school-based anti-bullying interventions further in Chapter 9.

Beyond institutions, the particular risks faced by many women in public spaces are also recognised, with significant efforts in many NAPs to change attitudes and behaviour. Taxi drivers in Lesotho, for instance, have been encouraged to adopt a gender-sensitive code of behaviour, and architects in New Zealand have been given training to enhance urban planning and their design of the relevant physical environment. Again, as with HIV prevention, these initiatives often go hand-in-hand with a country's broader crime prevention agenda. Such synergy could be seen as either enhancing or weakening the impact on the specific issue of violence against women as a distinct problem, but it is tempting for governments to bracket these efforts together.

As well as targeting specific settings, the NAP guide advocates a focus on specific groups within society whose attitudes and behaviour are either relatively influential positive role models within their communities or, alternatively, who are at a particular risk of perpetrating the violence itself. Since violence against women is seen as a function of broader gender inequalities which enhance the status of men relative to women, changing the attitudes of men and boys is fundamental to any sustained programme to eradicate the problem. Some men are more influential than others, and these individuals can be co-opted to act as ambassadors or champions for the programme within their specific communities. Male celebrities, athletes, and religious leaders are all examples of high-status individuals whose words and behaviours carry a weight which can be deployed to influence other men who listen to and watch them. In Australia, for instance, MPs and others have been encouraged to make public statements rejecting violence against women at every opportunity. Parenting, as we have seen, plays a central role in developing attitudes, and anti-violence messages can be incorporated into more general pro-grammes supporting parents in the early years of their role. Fathers of male children are likely to play a particularly important part in this if, of course, they are attending the classes in the first place.

An example of a "celebrity effect" comes from a study by researchers at Stanford University of the impact of the rapid rise to success of Egyptian footballer Mohamed Salah (Alrababa'h et al., 2019). Following his transfer to Liverpool Football Club in the summer of 2017, Mr Salah became one of the team's key players, scoring a large volume of goals in the following two seasons. As a devout Muslim, his behaviour on cele-brating having scored a goal was to prostrate himself in prayer (*sujood*). The Stanford researchers investigated whether the prominence of Mr Salah as a top goal-scorer might have influenced how Muslims were perceived more widely. They analysed records of hate crime in the Merseyside area of England (where Liverpool FC is based) over a thirty-six-month period and compared them with equivalent data else-where. They found evidence of a significant drop (18.9%) in hate crimes within Merseyside, but not in other counties, nor in other types of offence, associated with Salah's arrival. Alongside this, examining a set of fifteen million tweets sent by football fans across England, there was an almost 50% reduction in the proportion of them with anti-Muslim content sent by Liverpool football fans, but no change among fans of other English Premier League clubs. A separately conducted survey of more than 8,000 Liverpool fans suggested that the increased familiarity

with Islam, rather than other factors, was the principal change influencing the encouraging results on hate crime and Islamophobic tweets.

All these prevention strategies have a whole-population approach
which views the attitudes supporting violence as endemic across entire
societies to varying degrees. It is true that certain groups and settings
are targeted for special efforts in this approach, but the capacity for
perpetrating violence is seen as evenly spread across the male population in any society and widely embedded in the attitudes of the public.
However, evidence suggests that, due to the vagaries of development,
some groups in society are more at risk of growing up with antisocial
attitudes and are then at risk of becoming the violence perpetrators of
the next generation. So primary prevention needs to be supplemented
by secondary prevention strategies focusing more intensively on these
smaller high-risk groups. Children and young people who have grown
up in violent households and who may already be expressing attitudes
which support violence are a cause for particular concern. In Denmark,
for instance, a digital network has been set up which is designed to
enable children and young people in violent families to talk with each
other and share their experiences in a way which helps them to avoid
developing a mindset which leads them to growing up into adult perpetrators. This sort of approach needs to be developed carefully with
suitable mentors, as it is possible unintentionally to amplify negative
rather than positive attitudes (Granic and Dishion, 2003). Contacts
between separated children and parents from some violent families in
France are restricted to secure, purpose-built centres where their interaction can be assessed and managed.

Responding to current violence is just as important as preventing future
violence, and a range of victim support services is essential to the comprehensive anti-violence strategy in the NAP model. Some of these are
standard practice in many countries and have been so for several decades,
but for other countries they will be a novel prescription. Table 6.1 sets out
some key potential elements of a national response strategy with noted
examples of countries which have introduced such initiatives as part of
their national service model or are planning so to do.

Examples of NAPs for violence against women are widely available from
around the world,[1] and it is noteworthy that low- and middle-income

---

[1] Australia: www.dss.gov.au/our-responsibilities/women/programs-services/reducing-violence/
the-national-plan-to-reduce-violence-against-women-and-their-children-2010-2022;
Cambodia: https://drive.google.com/file/d/0By4DrHxo3C94Skx4VmZUN2JoMmc/
view?pli=1; Czech Republic: www.mpsv.cz/files/clanky/12194/5_material_NAP_15-04-
2011_en.pdf.

Table 6.1 *Key components of recommended national best practice for supporting victims of violence against women*

Recommended response strategy	Noted national model
Care support and empowerment of victims/survivors	
Emergency physical and mental healthcare	
Identify and respond without charge Access not conditional on police reporting Formal protocols for joint working	Denmark, Liberia, Morocco, Papua New Guinea, South Africa
Safe accommodation	
Accessible, immediate, and secure emergency and short-term accommodation, with children, including at home if safe	Albania, France, Liberia, Norway, Sweden
Counselling and support services	
Immediate and long-term access Telephone hotline	Albania, Belize, Cambodia, Cape Verde, Denmark, France, Honduras, Lesotho, Morocco, Norway, Turkey, United Kingdom
Advocacy and legal services	
Free legal assistance, court support etc. Free interpreter	Belize, Lesotho, Liberia, Morocco, Peru, Tanzania
Support and care for accompanying children	
Appropriate services Safety of women and children to override father access rights	Ireland, Palestine NA, South Africa, United Kingdom
Longer term empowerment	
Ensure economic independence Promote reintegration	Dominican Republic, Georgia, Haiti, Palestine NA, Portugal, South Africa, Tunisia
Protection and justice	
Police/prosecution practices	
Review of police practices and associated legislation Specialised police and prosecutor units	Belize, Denmark, Liberia, Norway, Sri Lanka, Sweden, United Kingdom, Yemen
Protection orders	
Immediate availability, no charge, without a hearing; cross-border enforcement Criminalisation of violations	Denmark, Sri Lanka
Legal processes	
Review of practices Review of legal processes	Palestine NA, Papua New Guinea, United Kingdom

Table 6.1 (*cont.*)

Recommended response strategy	Noted national model
Specialised court systems	
Creation of specialised training	Palestine NA, South Africa, United Kingdom, Uruguay
Intervention programmes for perpetrators	
Statutory and non-statutory programmes	Germany, Honduras, Philippines, Portugal
Minimum standards	
Review and monitoring	

Source: UN Women, 2012.

countries have adopted them as part of national policy to the same degree as high-income countries. More detailed mapping studies of WHO regions have indicated that three European countries (Sweden, Hungary and Ireland) had NAPs covering all the main forms of violence in one document, and another twenty-seven had separate NAPs covering specific forms of violence against women (European Women's Lobby, 2011). A 2011 African mapping study indicated that of the fourteen countries surveyed, three (Lesotho, Mauritius and Seychelles) had costed and budgeted plans or had made substantial progress on implementation (Gender Links for Equality and Justice, 2018). It is also worth noting that the widespread adoption of NAPs across both rich and low income countries of the world is in contrast to the concentration of research activity for generating evidence on this problem in a tiny group of rich Western countries.

National Action Plans exist around the world for other types of violence, but it is in this area of violence against women, broadly defined, that the greatest efforts have been made to recognise the problem and devise a coordinated strategy to deal with it. The lessons learned from reviewing the numerous NAPs in this area must be used to guide the development and refinement of the programmes needed for other types of violence such as elder abuse and youth violence.

6.3   Laws to Deter and Prevent Violence

Beyond coordinated NAPs and the specific issue of violence against women, it is possible to discern a lot of other activity which is ongoing through examining other responses to the 2014 Global Status Report survey. Some 80% of homicide victims worldwide are male, and the strategies required to deal with this form of violence may be different.

The 2014 survey asked for information on the degree to which a wide range of individual strategies dealing with any of the main types of violence had been implemented in each country. Much of this activity consists of the responses which might be part of a NAP, but there is still a high level of concerted action even in countries with no relevant NAP. At the moment many of these strategies may have been introduced *ad hoc* and would benefit from coordination as part of a national plan, but for now they can be considered separately in four domains: legislation, prevention programmes, victim services, and data gathering.

The legal framework governing crime definition and the sentencing of those found guilty is presumed to be essential to the deterrence of violence in the short and long term, despite considerable evidence which draws that expectation seriously into question (Honderich, 2006; McGuire and Duff, 2018). Sentencing frameworks do, however, reflect what a society deems as being wrong and sufficiently important to be worthy of legislation. Some laws are universal, while others vary and reflect national priorities and cultural values. It can be seen in Table 6.2 that firearm use and rape were the most consistently regulated aspects of violence across almost all countries responding to the WHO survey. Laws regulating other behaviours are not universal and largely reflect local priorities and values.

Controlling access to the lethal power of firearms is a core strategy for any serious attempt to tackle violence internationally, and legal regulation of civilian access to firearms is the one area of law which is almost universal. Loss of this control is part of the process which leads from interpersonal violence to social breakdown and hybrid wars. It should be noted, of course, that enacting a law and enforcing it are two different processes and having a law does not necessarily mean that it is implemented fully or even partly. Every country responding to the survey had some form of firearms regulation, but a small number of countries had various, sometimes disturbing exceptions. Rwanda, for instance, reported no legal regulation of the use of handguns or the carrying of arms in public, while Zambia reported unregulated use of long guns, automatic weapons, and handguns. Nor is the relationship between legal regulation and violence rates across countries very straightforward. Two countries with no handgun regulation logged in this survey, Panama and Tajikistan, have wildly different homicide rates. While the 2013 rate in Panama was nearly ten times the global median (1.75 per 100,000 population), the rate in Tajikistan was lower than the global average. Clearly, legal restrictions on firearms are a necessary but insufficient strategy to pacify societies.

Laws on rape, statutory rape, and other forms of contact sexual violence are also almost universally implemented, though again a few

Table 6.2 *Percentage of countries with specific types of anti-violence legislation*

	All countries (*n* = 129)	High-income countries (*n* = 40)	Low- and middle-income countries (*n* = 89)
Regulation of civilian access to firearms	100	100	100
Regulation of carrying firearms in public	99	100	99
Law against statutory rape	99	100	99
Law against rape	98	100	98
Regulated use of long guns	98	100	97
Mandatory background check for access to firearms	98	100	97
Regulated use of automatic weapons	97	100	96
Regulated use of handguns	95	100	93
Law against contact sexual violence without rape	95	100	92
Law against child marriage	91	93	90
Law against non-contact sexual violence	88	98	84
Law against weapons on school premises	84	85	83
Law against gang or criminal group membership	80	75	82
Law allowing removal of violent spouse from home	73	80	70
Law against rape in marriage	68	78	64
Law against elder abuse	62	75	56
Law against female genital mutation	50	70	42
Ban on corporal punishment	47	55	43
Law against elder abuse in institutions	45	60	38

Source: World Health Organization, 2014.

countries have no fully-framed laws against it. Cameroon, Mauritania, Nigeria, Uganda, and Vanuatu all report currently lacking laws specifically governing one or more aspects of this type of violence. This is perhaps more surprising than the non-universal regulation of firearms, since carrying a gun can be a facilitator of violent offending, not an act of violence in itself, whereas rape is in itself an act of violence. Firearm regulation is concerned with violence prevention, while sexual violence regulation is concerned with denunciation and punishment of an actual crime.

Certain types of violence and facilitators of violence in Table 6.2 are relatively unregulated when considered from this global perspective. Gang membership, corporal punishment of children, rape in marriage, forced removal of violent spouses and female genital mutilation are not legally regulated, at least through specific laws, in a large minority of countries. This clearly reflects ongoing cultural debates in different countries and the lack of a global consensus of what exactly counts as violence in certain areas. Elder abuse is the least recognised form of violence as far as legal regulation is concerned, with fewer than half of the countries around the world having laws governing abuse of elderly people within institutions. This does not necessarily mean that assaults on elderly people are legally permitted, of course. It may be that this, and the other unregulated violent acts above, are covered by broader legislation, while many countries have decided instead that this form of violence requires its own specific powers.

Legal regulation is in general slightly more common in high-income countries than middle- and low-income countries, with regulation of many types of firearm noticeable as a universal feature of richer societies. The difference between relatively rich and poor countries is particularly stark, however, for laws on elder abuse, corporal punishment, and female genital mutilation. Patriarchal social structures in some poorer countries may explain the lack of commitment to outlaw violence against children and women, but, by the same token, it might be expected that violence against older people would therefore be a priority for legislation. Perhaps such elder abuse is actually rarer than it is in richer countries with their common emphasis on 'youth worship' and so is not seen as a sufficiently big enough problem requiring special laws. On the other hand, in one area the legislative emphasis is reversed. Low- and middle-income countries are more likely than high-income countries to have legislation tackling gang violence. Clearly such violence is a major problem in many countries, rich and poor, but there may be a greater instability in poorer countries, forcing national governments to step up their response to this particular type of violence.

6.4   Social, Educational, and Therapeutic Prevention Programmes

Legislation is the platform for national action on violence, but it is a blunt instrument, largely reactive, awaiting occurrence of the violent acts before the law can be activated. The primary and secondary prevention approach advocated in the NAPs for violence against women emphasises the need for proactive prevention programmes across whole populations and more specifically with high-risk groups. But which prevention programmes should be adopted and rolled out? What works best and provides the best value for money? After fifty years of research effort in the field of violence prevention, there is a myriad of answers to these questions, but, unfortunately, many of the answers are contradictory and any single recommendation is highly contestable. We will consider an array of social, educational, and therapeutic interventions in greater depth in the following chapters but for now it is worth considering the WHO approach to provide a context for these later discussions. Overall, a number of strategies are considered 'best buys' by the World Health Organization (2014) in terms of the balance of economic cost and therapeutic effectiveness. These can be divided into a number of areas.

Developmental/educational
- Developing safe, stable, and nurturing relationships between children and their parents and caregivers
- Developing life skills in children and adolescents

Legal/environmental
- Reducing the availability and harmful use of alcohol
- Reducing access to guns and knives

Cultural
- Promoting gender equality to prevent violence against women
- Changing cultural and social norms that support violence

Victim-focused
- Victim identification, care, and support programmes

First, it is clearly desirable to intervene as early as possible with at-risk groups of children and young people, and we have already considered some of these strategies as part of the NAPs addressing violence against women. These interventions can be implemented via parents and caregivers to maximise the opportunities for the child to grow up in an enriching relationship with their family or through direct individual work with the child or young person themselves to improve and foster effective life skills such as anger management, resisting peer pressure, or conflict resolution.

Second, access to two key facilitators of violence, alcohol, and firearms, needs to be regulated and in some cases minimised. We have considered firearm legislation above and also noted the increased association between violence and mental illness in the context of substance misuse. Alcohol use alone is a well-established risk factor for intimate partner and other types of violence (Foran and O'Leary, 2008), and the main tool specified in the WHO survey is taxation of alcohol, with the majority of countries (70–80%) levying such taxation. There are other approaches in addition, including restricting opening hours, reducing the density of alcohol outlets and minimum pricing policies (Bellis et al., 2012).

Third, there is the potential for broader social and educational programmes which are designed to empower vulnerable groups and to change attitudes among those at risk of perpetrating violence. Inequality has been linked to many types of antisocial behaviour, including violence (Eisner & Nivette, 2012; Pickett and Wilkinson, 2010; Vieraitis et al., 2015).

Therefore, at the broadest level, political and social changes which improve the status of women in a society should lead to reductions in gender-based violence. Such changes should be, and are likely to be, accompanied by attitudinal changes which shift from seeing certain types of violence as acceptable and even praiseworthy toward progressively reducing tolerance of such behaviour. The most obvious example of this currently in many Western societies is the growing rejection of homophobic and transphobic hostility and violence. Laws in this area are not considered in the WHO survey, but the percentage of countries enacting them is likely to be significantly lower than that for IPV and elder abuse, and they remain contested in some countries.

These broad best-buy strategies are a good start for planning what types of activity need to be prioritised and commissioned by governments, but it is important to consider this more fully and specify more clearly the range of options which are available so that they can be implemented and monitored systematically. The WHO survey attempted to do this by asking about the degree to which each of eighteen particular types of prevention programme had been implemented in each country. These programmes map onto the six best-buy strategies in some ways but in other cases do not fit well into the framework. For instance, prevention through improving physical environments, highlighted already in the NAPs for violence against women, are not obviously listed among the most highly recommended (best-buy) strategies; and others, such as interventions to reduce dating violence, are not clearly specified. Despite these definitional issues, however, again the survey provides us with a valuable insight into progress in running prevention programmes around the world, listed in Table 6.3.

Most of these programmes are variations on a theme of behavioural change through skills training and reflection on attitudes and values, and they will be considered more fully in Chapters 9 and 10. While they may be delivered in group settings, the focus is largely on the individual. Only the few focusing on changing the physical environment or providing economic empowerment through microfinance can be considered as structural in the sense of addressing the larger, more stable and largely hidden influences behind adoption of particular individual ideas and behaviour. It is clear that, unlike legislative responses to the problem, there is no universal adoption of any particular prevention programme. The most popular programmes aim to change social and cultural norms toward sexual violence and intimate partner violence. Such programmes are probably relatively cheap to deliver, but the relevant attitudes are often thought to be intractable and it is unclear what degree of change can be achieved. As with legislation, richer countries are somewhat more

Table 6.3 *Percentage of countries implementing specific types of violence prevention programmes*

	Domain	All countries (n = 129)	High-income countries (n = 40)	Low- and middle-income countries (n = 89)
Social and cultural norms change	SV	88	93	87
Social and cultural norms change	IPV	87	90	85
Life skills and social development training	YV	86	90	84
Parenting education	CM	84	90	81
Training to recognise/avoid sexually abusive situations	CM	84	85	83
School and college programmes	SV	81	80	81
School anti-bullying	YV	80	88	76
Home visiting	CM	75	80	73
Mentoring	YV	74	85	70
Physical environment changes	SV	74	75	74
Professional awareness campaigns	EA	66	73	63
Caregiver support	EA	66	90	55
Public information campaigns	EA	65	78	60
Pre-school enrichment	YV	64	68	63
Residential care policies	EA	63	80	55
After-school supervision	YV	60	75	54
Microfinance and gender equity training	IPV	58	30	71
Dating violence prevention in schools	IPV	52	63	47

Note: CM, child maltreatment; EA elder abuse; IPV, intimate partner violence; SV, sexual violence; YV, youth violence.
Source: World Health Organization, 2014.

likely than poorer countries to have adopted these programmes, but even in countries with relatively few resources there has been widespread implementation of various training programmes. An outstanding difference between rich and poor economies is the popularity of microfinance initiatives in low- and middle-income countries. While there are financial inequalities between the genders in rich countries, perhaps the gradient is steeper in poorer countries, or a bigger impact can be made with relatively few resources.

6.5   Victim Services

The final best-buy strategy for violence in general and a core element of the NAPs for violence against women in particular is implementation of

Table 6.4 *Percentage of countries implementing specific types of victim services programmes*

	All countries (n = 129)	High-income countries (n = 40)	Low- and middle-income countries (n = 89)
Child protection services	96	98	96
Medico-legal services for sexual violence	93	95	92
Laws providing for victim legal representation	88	78	93
Mental health services	88	95	84
Adult protective services	58	75	51
Laws providing for victim compensation	56	78	47

Source: World Health Organization, 2014.

effective victim support services. Priorities in this area again vary across countries around the world (Table 6.4). There is near universality in the provision of child protection services and medico-legal services for women subjected to sexual violence. Mental health services for victims and laws supporting legal representation for victims are also widely implemented. In contrast, adult protective services and laws enabling financial compensation for victims are available in only half of the countries and are, perhaps unsurprisingly, fewer in number in poorer countries.

6.6   Monitoring Violence: National Prevalence Surveys

Data collection and population surveillance are the foundation of the public health approach to violence prevention in general (Mercy et al., 1993) and also a key element in the WHO approach. Without an accurate estimate of the size of the problem and its spatial and demographic patterns, it is futile to start devising interventions which might be effective. Unfortunately, the further one moves away from the problem of homicide, the more difficult it is to measure violence levels validly and reliably. Dead bodies are difficult to hide in any society, but bruises are easy to cover up and psychological damage is often invisible. Police records of crime are inadequate alone as a data source for accurate estimates as crime levels (Office for National Statistics, 2016), and self-reports of exposure to violence are needed at least to complete the picture obtainable from them. The necessary surveys are expensive, intensive, and imperfect in their own way, but trends in self-reported exposure to violent and other crimes can be picked up through repeated longitudinal

Table 6.5 *Percentage of countries implementing specific types of national prevalence surveys for non-fatal violence*

	All countries (*n* = 129)	High-income countries (*n* = 40)	Low- and middle-income countries (*n* = 89)
Intimate partner violence	60	58	61
Sexual violence	57	50	60
Child maltreatment	47	50	46
Youth violence	31	53	21
Elder abuse	23	40	16

Source: World Health Organization, 2014.

surveys such as the American National Crime Victimization Survey, run annually since 1972, and the Crime Survey for England and Wales, run since 1982 (initially as the British Crime Survey). The International Crime Victims Survey also collates data on violent victimisation from a number of countries for comparison.

National prevalence surveys are seen as the basis for any meaningful monitoring of how any national action plan is working. Inevitably, the further we move away from homicide, the more definitions of relevant behaviours will vary, but at least some attempt is being made for systematic collection of data to examine trends. Despite their key role in NAPs, surveys are lagging in terms of implementation especially in some areas and with respect to some forms of violence, with about half of countries having set them up for IPV, child maltreatment, and sexual violence but only one in five for elder abuse (see Table 6.5). Youth violence and elder abuse again lag behind in terms of monitoring particularly in poorer countries.

6.7   The Logic and Procedures of Evaluation Research

Many of the interventions discussed in this chapter are recommended because they have some degree of evidence to support the claim that they are effective in reducing the likelihood of violence occurring. They should all, to some extent at least, have been tested in an evaluation research project or, ideally, a series of projects. Many of these claims for effectiveness will be examined in the next few chapters, so it is important to set out briefly here the logic of such evaluations and how they are usually conducted in real service settings.

Typically, in evaluation or *treatment-outcome* research in this area, a cohort of people who have been violent or are deemed as at risk of being violent is divided into two groups. Ideally, they should resemble each other in important respects that could affect the outcome of the study, so efforts are made as far as possible to ensure they are *matched* on key characteristics. One group, denoted the experimental or treatment group, is then provided with some form of intervention that researchers or policymakers think might have a beneficial effect, and which they want to evaluate. This could be any one of a wide range of activities. In trying to address problems such as aggression and violence, it might consist of education, vocational training, psychological therapy, skills training or, indeed, drug treatment. Alternatively, it might comprise some type of punitive sanction, for example, longer prison sentences or a physically demanding regime in an institution such as a boot camp. The second group is dealt with in the conventional way that is accepted as standard or routine in the agency where the work is being done. This is sometimes called the 'business as usual' or 'treatment as usual' condition, and some standard services may be provided to its members. Alternatively, this group may receive nothing at all and be described as an 'untreated' control group. A few studies employ more elaborate designs in which there are two or even three treatment groups, each receiving a different type of intervention.

After the intervention has been delivered, the study groups are compared on the designated dependent or outcome variable. Usually the key outcome of interest is the rate of violence or *recidivism* after a fixed follow-up period – which might be anything from one month to several years, though one year is more common in studies of psychosocial interventions. But many other variables can be and have been measured. In research on aggression and violence, they have included numbers of reconvictions for violent offences, the time lapsed until their occurrence, their degree of seriousness, self-reports of offenders or victims, or, in institutions, changes in numbers of disciplinary incidents over time. There might also be assessment of indirect factors linked to violence propensity such as attitudes, coping skills, self-control or other personal attributes through self-report or as reported by professionals or family members. The object of the exercise is to test whether the two groups differ at the end of the study: whether the activity that was being experimentally tested had a measurable impact.

This is a very brief account of the process and there are many features of doing this that can vary a great deal between studies. The rigour of the design that is used can be a crucial factor when interpreting the results. What is regarded as the strongest evidence is usually based on research where individuals are allocated to the experimental and control conditions on a random basis, in a *randomised controlled trial* (RCT), as this should eliminate the influence of extraneous between-group differences that might affect the outcome. This is not always possible in the sometimes very pressured world of the criminal justice system, for instance, given the emphasis there on punishment and on security, and the inevitability that key decisions on allocation are made by sentencers (judges, magistrates, or sheriffs). When random allocation of participants to the treatment or control group is not possible, other types of research design can be employed, but the conclusions that can be drawn based on these non-randomised studies are weaker. In these quasi-experimental, case-control or before-and-after studies, factors other than the intervention alone cannot be ruled out as possible influences on the outcome, or there may even be no 'untreated' group against which to make a comparison. Researchers spend a lot of time thinking about the quality of the evaluations that are done, and whether the findings constitute a fair test of the intervention that was being evaluated.

For any given research question, it is important to wait until a series of primary studies (those in which original data are collected and reported) have been done, before attempting to draw conclusions regarding it. Following agreed procedures, researchers employ methods of *systematic review* and *meta-analysis* (or *statistical review*) for this purpose. The idea underlying this is essentially that of attempting to see the 'big picture' of what a set of findings can tell us. Within each study, there will be a measure of the difference between the groups (experimental and control) at the endpoint; this is called the *effect size*. In a meta-analysis, the effect sizes from different studies are collected together and analysed; this generates a *mean effect size*. There are several ways of computing these statistics. In discussing outcome effects, we will at times quote them, using a statistic called the *standardised mean difference*, which, when zero, means there was no effect – no difference between experimental and comparison groups. Different studies use plus or minus signs when reporting the size of effects, thus when interpreting any number we need to keep in mind that a positive outcome can be represented by either sign depending on how an analysis was done. Researchers often adopt a convention proposed by Cohen (1988) for classifying mean effect sizes, considering those of 0.20 or lower as small, in the region of 0.5 as moderate, and 0.8 as large.

Many other analyses can be conducted to test the robustness of findings, for example, comparing studies with different designs, sample sizes, populations, lengths of follow-up time and so on. If the groups were not well matched at the outset, to some extent that can be adjusted for in statistical analysis. Often, however, no clear conclusions can be drawn and the only solution is to carry out more and higher quality basic research. Where enough research is available, some researchers go to the next step and conduct 'reviews of reviews', collating the findings from groups of systematic reviews or meta-analyses. Ultimately this procedure provides the most credible estimate of effectiveness, but clearly it relies on substantial efforts by many research teams beforehand to generate such extensive basic data to work from, and so relatively few interventions have this degree of support.

6.8   Conclusion

The WHO has taken huge strides in the past twenty years first in recognising the scale of the problem of interpersonal violence and then in initiating and organising a strategic approach to tackle it. The emphasis on evidence-based policy rooted in a coherent public health model has enabled a framework to be established which can guide individual countries in the right direction, taking account of resource availability. The evidence base itself is constantly evolving, and, while it is often contradictory, there is a growing consensus on 'what works'. The following chapters will consider in more detail how the evidence is shaping up in each of the biopsychosocial domains which contribute to violent tendencies and will discuss how work in each area can bolster the elements of the overall approach.

7 Risk Assessment
Can Violence Be Predicted?

7.1 Introduction

Prevention of violence before it occurs is the cornerstone of a public health approach, but whole-population strategies delivered through the media and education channels address only part of the problem. Effective tertiary prevention of further violence by those who have already perpetrated it requires careful appraisal, as far as is possible, of the likelihood of its recurrence. Effective secondary prevention with those deemed at higher risk than the general population requires successful identification of those who would benefit from targeted interventions. Each of these in turn relies upon the development of effective risk assessment tools, and this aspect of violence prevention has developed rapidly over the past three decades. The recognition of separate factors that are associated with the occurrence of violent acts, such as those we surveyed in Chapter 4, has opened up the possibility of using that information to predict when such acts might occur. Attempts to do this usually focus on whether there may be some individuals who are more likely than others to behave this way. As a result of some combination of temperament, upbringing, attitudes, personality traits, poor self-control or other influences, are there people who are likely to resort to violence more readily than most others? More worryingly, are there some who might do so repeatedly, or might commit very serious forms of it? If we can identify them, we might be able to go a stage further and forecast when or against whom they are about to commit an assault.

If we possess such information and we could predict and thereby avoid an event that would cause serious harm, it is understandable that people will search for ways to do this. The study of risk and how to assess it is based on that simple premise, and in this chapter we will describe the empirical foundations and the practical applications of the idea. Being able to do this successfully is clearly desirable, but it means that a series of challenges need to be overcome. One daunting aspect of them is the simple fact that, however much we may fear them and be preoccupied with the possibility of them, violent events are relatively rare. Compared with the number of other things people do, the proportion of the time even the most aggressive people spend behaving violently is not high. Indeed, what statisticians call the *base rate* of an offence such as assault is comparatively low, and for offences such as homicide it is extremely low. Very infrequent events, such as solar eclipses, are of course perfectly predictable, since they follow orderly and discoverable patterns. For several reasons, that cannot be done with violence. Although we have a general understanding of why it happens, the factors that we know contribute to it can interact in almost limitless ways (*multifinality*). To compound matters, the risk factors are often private events, hidden from view in the minds of individuals, some of whom may themselves not even know what they might be about to do.

The damage that can be done by violence, however, is such that the importance of trying to predict it and to stop it happening is not in doubt. The case for making the effort to do this is supported by several strands of evidence.

- Large and well-established sets of data which show a broad patterning of criminal and other antisocial behaviour over time, such as the 'age–crime curve'. There are grounds for expecting that age is a strong predictor of the likelihood of committing violence. Close examination often shows a number of different trajectories or pathways within this. If behaviour was entirely erratic, prediction would be impossible. Fortunately, patterns can be discerned within it, though they have to be extracted from varying amounts of distracting 'noise', or information that will have no bearing on the outcome.
- There is a pattern of some continuity in *aggressiveness* (the tendency to use aggression in a range of situations) over time. It shows relative stability across periods of several years, though the relationship between measurement of it at two time points declines as the gap between them widens. This has been found in many longitudinal studies and also in meta-analyses (Olweus, 1988; Piquero et al., 2012; Zumkley, 1994).
- It is now fairly widely accepted that it is possible both to predict general criminal recidivism and to use information gathered for that purpose in the design and delivery of interventions to reduce it (Andrews, 1989; Andrews et al., 2006; Bonta and Andrews, 2017). This discovery led to the formulation of the 'risk principle': that the amount and intensity of intervention should be tailored to an individual's measured risk of reoffending. Large-scale reviews have shown that criminal justice programmes informed by that principle have yielded higher success rates than those not so informed (e.g. Andrews and Dowden, 2006; Lowenkamp et al., 2006).

7.2   The Development of Risk Assessment

Like other sets of data and research results, the findings above were not obtained speedily but amassed progressively over time. Awareness of possible threats to our safety and calculating whether any given individual might pose a danger to us are long-standing, evolved habit mechanisms for both humans and many other species, but investing the responsibility for this task in a designated group of professionals is a fairly modern phenomenon. The route along which we have travelled to arrive at the position that currently prevails has entailed several changes of direction in terms of the main focus of activity.

There are separate strands in the emergence of the kinds of risk assessment instruments in use today. One major source is based in criminological and penal research and has often entailed analysis of very large databases held by justice departments. Grove (2005) traced the attempt to employ what we would now call risk assessment in criminal justice as far back as 1928, when the criminologist Ernest Burgess tried to predict success or failure of 3,000 men paroled from prisons in Illinois. Later research of this kind is illustrated, for example, in the work of Glaser (1987), and criminal justice agencies expended considerable investment in developing better ways to assess, classify, and allocate prisoners according to risk of reoffending. Hollin (2002) reviewed some specially designed risk scales, including the *Salient Factor Score, Reconviction Prediction Score*, and *Client Management Classification* system, which were devised in that context.

The other source is located at the interface between criminal justice and (what is today called) forensic mental health. The major growth in attention to the issue of prediction is usually attributed to the publication of a landmark book by Meehl (1954) . Within these fields, both the study of risk assessment and its practical application in individual cases have been described as having passed through several phases (sometimes referred to as 'generations') in their development. This suggestion needs to be interpreted rather loosely, as the boundaries between the identified phases are not neatly defined. But looking back over what has been published in the past forty to fifty years, it is possible to see a series of innovations in the appraisal and prediction of violent behaviour (Andrade et al., 2009; Bonta and Wormith, 2008).

Unstructured Clinical Judgement (UCJ)

The earliest research in this field comprised what have been called naturalistic studies of 'unaided' professional clinical judgement. Individuals released from secure institutions were retrospectively followed up in the community, and their rates of reconviction or of return to institutions were recorded. Melton et al. (2007) portrayed this phase as occupying approximately the period from 1960 to 1980. Most assessments undertaken during this phase, and probably for several decades before, were founded primarily on the exercise by experienced practitioners of their own judgement drawing on their own accumulated experience and recall of past cases. But when this was subjected to rigorous evaluation, it proved to be fairly weak in two respects:

- Reliability (agreement between different clinicians judging the same case), and
- Validity (predictive accuracy in relation to the outcome).

Without any specially provided training or formal assessment procedures, this approach is nowadays considered inadvisable. It is over-reliant on the use of professional discretion, lacks transparency and accountability and does not lend itself to replication. As regards its outcomes, it was frequently found that rates of predicted 'dangerousness' made in this way were often far higher than the rates of violence that actually occurred (Monahan, 1984). This emerged most notably in what have become known as the Baxström cases, where as a result of a legal loophole a large number of compulsorily detained patients had to be transferred to civil hospitals and many were discharged. When followed up, they were found to have a far lower rate of reoffending than anticipated.

In an attempt to systematize the task of assessing risk, researchers were therefore urged to move toward an approach centred on the measurement of variables for which there was an empirically demonstrable association with a violent outcome (Monahan, 1981). In terms of research, the discovery that a methodology of this kind was superior to individual judgement had been shown when Meehl (1954) published his groundbreaking study comparing the relative accuracy of the two approaches. But it was some time before the impact of these findings was felt in criminal justice and forensic decision-making. On the predictive weakness of unstructured judgement, numerous studies, and reviews in ensuing decades have solidified support for the conclusions originally drawn by Meehl (e.g. Grove and Meehl, 1996; Sawyer, 1966). This has been further amplified using meta-analysis, replicating and extending the original conclusions (Ægisdóttir et al., 2006; Grove et al., 2000).

Actuarial Risk Assessment Instruments (ARAIs)

Evidence of the error-proneness of clinical judgement alone led to the emergence of the 'actuarial' approach, entailing 'use of formulas that are experimentally derived' (Melton et al., 2007, p. 308), markedly contrasting with the 'clinical' approach that preceded it. In actuarially based risk assessment, specified variables that have been found to be correlated with the occurrence of adverse events (offending in general, or offences of a particular type) are measured, and predictions are then made, based empirically on discerning the combination of them with the greatest prognostic accuracy. The key feature of this process is grounding predictions in a systematic empirical study of relationships, usually recorded in a database, where the scores obtained in an individual case are compared with that database, rather than drawing on the judgements of individual clinicians working independently. The result consisted of a statistical formula, algorithm, table, graph or other formal quantifiable procedure which produced a probability estimate (Grove and Meehl, 1996). The distinguishing feature of ARAIs is the use of explicit rules for combining items into a global risk score of some kind (Bonta, 1996).

This approach is also believed to make the reasons for risk decisions more explicit. Many practitioners would probably find it difficult to articulate how or why they arrived at their conclusions regarding someone's level of risk. It could often be based on how much an individual reminded them of someone else they had assessed previously. But of paramount importance, the use of an actuarial approach results in an impressive increase in predictive accuracy. Loza (2003) estimated that it led to an improvement in predicting general recidivism from 60% to 80%, and violent recidivism from 40% to 53%. Hanson and Morton-Bourgon (2009) also found actuarial measures unequivocally superior to clinical judgement in the prediction of sexual and violent offending.

Structured Professional Judgement (SPJ)

But the tendency of actuarial risk assessments to focus almost exclusively on 'static' factors has in turn proved to have its limitations. Such factors are insensitive to change over time and to the fluctuations in variables that have clear potency as contributing to risk. The resultant picture is inevitably incomplete as many aspects of individual functioning are excluded from the process. In a further development, therefore, 'dynamic' factors were reintroduced in risk assessment. This also allowed the reintroduction of some elements of clinical judgement, as there are recurrent situations on which little or no systematic data can be brought to bear. However, rather than being based on intuitions formed by experience, here clinical judgement is structured or guided according to reproducible criteria, and where possible is anchored in statements or observations that can be made explicit, so facilitating calibration between assessors. Thus, these risk assessments combine actuarial and clinical methods of prediction, though in clearly designated and systematized ways. Some approaches represent 'dynamic risk factors', using alternative terminology, that of 'criminogenic need', and therefore call this model 'risk-needs assessment' (Andrews et al., 2006; Wong et al., 2007).

Thus, this method is empirically based but avoids the possibly restrictive reliance on a formulaic procedure for combining information. The element of judgement within this approach can also be applied in a number of ways. In some methods, clinical judgement can be used to supplement or modify the information gained from actuarial assessments. In others, judgement is exercised in a way that is anchored to specified descriptors contained in the assessment process. The inclusion of dynamic factors also means this approach can be employed in risk management, in treatment/ intervention planning and in evaluation of progress.

For practitioners to use the majority of these methods, training is required, usually designed and sometimes provided by a scale's authors. Not long ago Guy et al. (2012) identified a total of nineteen extant SPJ tools for violence, and several of them are in routine use in many settings.

From Risk Assessment to Risk Management

In current standard practice, the process of risk assessment is often closely conjoined to the complementary process of *risk management*. This builds on all the findings of previous approaches, but adds a further ingredient in which a plan is prepared and implemented, designed to reduce the level of risk by containing the factors that influence it (Heilbrun, 2003). Information on broad risk categories may be used for allocating individuals to different levels of security or to varying types and intensities of treatment and support. Information on dynamic risk factors is then added, focusing on those variables associated with new incidents, and attempting to reduce their potential impact, monitoring progress over time and adjusting interventions as necessary. Thus a 'feedback loop' is built into risk assessment procedures.

This procedure is sometimes supplemented by what is called *anamnestic* risk assessment, as proposed by Melton et al. (2018). This entails examining details of events, most importantly in this case such as violent offences, including the circumstances in which they occurred, with a view to mapping the combinations of risk factors that appear to be associated with their recurrence. This might entail behavioural or offence analysis using semi-structured interviews or witness statements. This could more accurately inform future risk management, but to date has little separate evidence to support it.

As noted earlier, with the exception of the move from unstructured clinical to actuarial methods, the above progression does not always mean there are aggregate improvements in terms of predictive utility. For example, Hanson and Morton-Bourgon (2009) found the accuracy of structured professional judgement was intermediate between unstructured clinical judgement and actuarial measures. The choice of method is probably best guided by the nature of the task to be addressed. What is still very often neglected in risk assessment is the environment: the circumstances in which an individual finds themself and the influences to which they are exposed. In the earlier generations of research, when the language of 'dangerousness' was more commonly used, most risk assessments were almost entirely *dispositional* in their orientation; that is, they located the likely causes of potential future violence almost exclusively within individuals (Otto, 2000). Although some approaches to prediction place emphasis on environmental factors at a theoretical level, proposals, and methods for recording information about it and incorporating them in risk assessments have remained relatively undeveloped. Most risk assessment therefore retains its internal, intrapersonal emphasis.

7.3   The Continuum of Risk Assessment Approaches

Running through the above account is a key distinction between two main approaches to risk assessment, which has been a central feature of research, debate, and discussion in the area for more than fifty years. The distinction and the terms initially used to make it come from the seminal work of Paul Meehl (1954), who distinguished 'clinical' and 'statistical' approaches to making predictions of future behaviour. What Meehl called the *clinical* approach, in its most basic form, referred to the judgement by an individual clinician or practitioner of the likelihood of a future pattern of someone's behaviour (such as offending or some type of it, e.g. violent, sexual), based on the clinician's previous experience of such cases. The *statistical* approach, by contrast, denoted a systematic, quantified attempt to base predictions on an evidence base containing data on previous cases, where information about the present case is compared with outcomes shown in the database.

The studies Meehl reviewed were mainly located in the fields of personality and mental health, though some were concerned with criminal offending. Meehl showed that using a structured assessment that was converted into a numerical scale (statistical prediction) produced a more accurate forecast of outcomes than unstructured clinical judgement. In a set of twenty studies, the statistical approach proved considerably better than the clinical one in sixteen of them; somewhat better in three; and fared worse only in one, where the available information was found to be unreliable.

What Meehl initially called 'statistical' prediction is nowadays more often known as 'actuarial' prediction, or in the fields of criminal justice and mental health, actuarial risk assessment, as described above. The reason for this is that while an actuarial approach entails the use of numerical scores and statistical analysis, its pivotal feature resides in the use of a specially devised formula for combining information, and of a pre-existing data bank containing assessment and outcome information, against which the current case can be compared. A true actuarial approach requires no exercise of professional judgement: scoring could be done by an untrained person or by using a computer programme, and still prove better than individual judgement, regardless of the amount of experience that lay behind it.

However, in contemporary research and practice these two approaches can be combined in a number of ways, and the boundaries between them have become somewhat blurred. Thus the clinical/statistical distinction has been superseded by a fuller set of categories. Following the suggestion of some researchers (e.g. Conroy and Murrie, 2007; Tardiff and Hughes, 2011), it is more appropriate to consider risk assessment methods as lying on a continuum, with wholly unstructured, subjective judgement at one end and fully mechanised, automated procedures at the other, as described above. Most risk assessment methods in current use occupy a position somewhere along this continuum.

Risk and Protective Factors

All risk assessment methods depend on the gathering of information concerning what are defined as *risk factors*. In essence, these are simply variables that are significantly correlated with the occurrence and likely recurrence of a targeted problem, such as a violent crime. They do not have to be causes of it: properly confirming a causal link can be extremely difficult. They simply have to be correlated with it sufficiently well to qualify as useful predictors. Single variables taken in isolation may do this only to a limited degree. So risk assessment entails combining such correlates in an effort to maximise predictive power.

In risk assessment in criminal justice, a distinction is usually made between *static* and *dynamic* risk factors as noted above. The former generally consist of demographic or criminal-history variables which at the time of assessment are fixed or determined by prior events. Some are permanently fixed, such as the age at which someone was first convicted of an offence, or having a parent with a criminal record. Others, though fixed at a given moment, may gradually alter over time, such as the total number of previous convictions, or types of offences committed. Together these can determine an individual's overall 'risk status'.

Several of the most widely used risk assessment measures available today have been developed through analysis of large databases of criminal history and allied information held by criminal justice departments. When someone is arrested, charged with or convicted of a crime, that is recorded by the police. In the United Kingdom that information is entered into the Police National Computer, and portions of it are used in the Offenders Index developed by the Ministry of Justice. This led to the possibility of developing and testing a risk assessment tool, the *Offender Group Reconviction Scale* (OGRS), introduced in 1994 but which has since gone through several iterations (Howard, 2018). By contrast, some clinical risk assessments, used in forensic mental health services (secure hospital units), are based on much smaller numbers, but often contain richer and more detailed information on individuals.

Dynamic risk factors, by contrast, typically fluctuate over time and reflect temporary circumstances or internal states of the individual. They include, for example, influences of antisocial companions or associates; attitudes and cognitions; impulsivity, self-management and control (or its absence); and the pattern or extent of substance misuse. Dynamic factors vary in their rate of fluctuation. Moods and emotional states such as anger, sexual arousal or feelings of rejection can change very rapidly over time, whereas attitudes or habits of self-regulation usually change more slowly. These factors can indicate an individual's 'risk state' and may also correspond to criminogenic needs that should be addressed (Wong et al., 2009).

Protective factors are variables or influences that are likely to lower the likelihood of aggression or violence (or other problem) occurring. Sometimes called *resilience* factors or simply *strengths*, they consist of individual features or aspects of environmental support that can mitigate against the likely impact of forces that heighten risk. With reference to violence, there is growing evidence of the importance of these factors (de Vries Robbé et al., 2013; Dubow et al., 2016; Hemphill et al., 2016; Kim et al., 2016; Kuin et al., 2015; Ttofi et al., 2016; Vassallo et al., 2016). On the basis of a large-scale, longitudinal research project, the Pittsburgh study, Loeber et al. (2008) developed a set of more finely tuned definitions of different aspects of risk and protective factors, for example delineating *hindering risk factors* as ones which predicted a lower likelihood of desisting from violence among those already convicted – such as having no accommodation on release from custody.

The number of separate risk assessment scales and other instruments now available is quite large. Contemporary practice in this area generally relies on a combination of actuarial risk assessment instruments (ARAIs) and structured professional judgement (SPJ) methods. It remains unclear whether there is any difference between these two approaches in overall predictive accuracy. While most systematic reviews find ARAIs performed at a slightly higher level (e.g. Hanson and Morton-Bourgon, 2009; Whittington et al., 2013), a side-by-side comparison by Guy (2008) found them to be more or less equivalent. Similarly, there is no firm and consistent difference favouring any single risk assessment tool over any of the others, though there are some with very little convincing support. But it should be borne in mind that the volume of research is very variable across the different available tools.

However, evidence points toward different kinds of approaches as offering value for different purposes. Heilbrun et al. (2010) envisaged the application of risk assessment at three stages of management of offenders, at successive points in the criminal justice/penal process: the initial prediction and classification decision, monitoring change in risk level over time, and risk management planning in the later phases of a sentence (or period of detention) prior to release. For the first of these stages, actuarial or SPJ methods are the most appropriate; SPJ approaches are more valuable in the intermediate phase; and 'anamnestic' methods are most useful for future planning.

7.4   Elements of Risk Assessment Research

Risk assessment requires a sound empirical basis if it is to maximise its likelihood of being effective. That evidence is crucial in determining both its practical usefulness and its credibility in legal proceedings or for informing penal decisions. To evaluate risk assessment instruments, several indicators are used, and before employing any single method it is advisable to check on how well supported it is in this respect. Within this, the study and assessment of risk of violence employs some specialised terms.

In principle, a simple *correlation coefficient*, a statistic indicating the extent to which two linear variables are associated, if it was sufficiently high and was consistently obtained, could act as a risk predictor. Most studies of risk factors consist of examining correlations between such variables and levels or rates of offending. Given the complexity of serious crime, however, no single variable meets this criterion sufficiently well to be used on its own. Predictions are superior when based on combinations of variables. But making decisions about which ones to combine can mean resorting to some complex statistics.

The following are some of the statistics that are commonly cited as evidence that any given assessment is worth using. There are three pairs of definitions and an additional, more elaborate concept combining one of the pairs in a single measure.

- *Positive* and *negative predictive value*: These terms refer, respectively, to the proportion of a study sample predicted to be violent or not to be violent for whom the outcome is correctly predicted.
- *False positive* and *false negative rate*: The former is the proportion of those who are actually non-violent who are incorrectly predicted (i.e. who were predicted to be violent), while the latter is the proportion of those who are actually violent who were incorrectly predicted (i.e. were predicted to be non-violent).
- *Sensitivity* is the proportion of those who are actually violent who were correctly predicted to be, whereas *specificity* is the proportion of those who are actually not violent who were correctly predicted to be.
- The last two measures can be combined in a statistic developed from a 'signal detection' model of appraising accuracy. This involves the use of *receiver operating characteristics* (ROC) curves, where the relative accuracy of prediction is computed across the range of possible scores on an assessment. As a risk prediction score increases (on whatever scale we are testing), the proportion of those who are actually violent should increase, while the proportion of those not violent should fall. A perfect predictor would (by definition) get this right every time. The extent to which an actual predictor falls below this ceiling can be plotted graphically. The resultant statistic is therefore known as the *area under the curve* (AUC) (Mossman, 1994), which can range in value from 0 to 1. An AUC of 0.5 or less indicates a tool is predicting violence no better than chance, for example by flipping a coin.

For approximately the last twenty years or so, based on recommendations of some experts, the AUC has been widely used as the key indicator of the predictive validity of most risk assessment scales. However, this was not a universally supported recommendation. Several recent reviews have questioned some aspects of it (Mossman, 2013; Singh, 2013). One important suggestion is that it is not advisable to use the AUC on its own and that other indicators (such as positive and negative predictive value) should also be included in research and evaluation reports. Another is that published manuals of risk assessment instruments should include cut-off values and other material as essential reference points for interpreting risk scores. Most of the risk assessment tools in current use have been evaluated and compared using one or other of the above parameters.

Classification and Decision Trees

In technical terms, all the methods described so far are derived from a *linear model*. That is, they involve numerical analysis of continuous variables meeting certain statistical assumptions. However, risk assessment can also be undertaken via a quite different route, entailing the use of what is called a *classification-based* or *decision tree* approach. Here, cases are assigned to risk levels, using specified features, and classed as high or low in violence propensity in a succession of dichotomous (yes/no) decisions (Gardner et al., 1996; Glaser, 1987). A sequence of such binary comparisons ('recursive partitioning') thereby generates a tree-like structure.

The more features an individual possesses that are associated with violence, the likelier it is they will emerge in the higher-risk branches of the tree. This type of procedure was employed to analyse data from the first twenty weeks of the MacArthur Risk Assessment study, in which a total sample of more than 1,000 psychiatric inpatients from three sites was followed over the course of one year after discharge (Monahan et al., 2001). Where some research participants were not neatly classified at the first attempt, the procedure was repeated until all had been allocated to a risk-level group. This is known as an iterative classification tree (ICT). Using a total of 106 potential risk factors, individuals were ultimately allocated to one of five groups. As risk levels increased, the numbers in a group declined.

Banks et al. (2004) have described a still more elaborate analysis in which the MacArthur study sample was successively classified using as many as five different risk assessment 'models' (where a 'model' means a selected combination of risk factors). The authors argued that rather than trying to identify a single 'best' model, a preferable approach might be to combine prediction models, employing different sets of variables each time. Such analyses have been conducted converging data from up to ten distinct models. The *Classification of Violence Risk* (COVR) developed within the MacArthur study employs this approach in its design and evaluation.

7.5   Reviews of Risk Assessment Research

Risk assessment for the purpose of appraising the likelihood of future violence has become standard practice in many locations. Singh and colleagues (2016) have noted that more than 400 different instruments have been developed for this purpose, and while some are used only 'in house' in the services where they were devised, others are widely available. Singh et al. have reported the findings of a survey of 2,165 mental health professionals from forty-four countries spread across all continents of the world, on their level of usage of these tools. They comment that 'the routine assessment of violence risk has become a global phenomenon' (p. 122). At an average age of 43.9 years, their respondents (60% of whom were women) reported having conducted an average of 435 violence risk assessments in their careers, of which a mean of thirty-four had been conducted in the previous twelve months. Just over half of these assessments were carried out using some form of structured risk assessment instrument (SRAI), using either an ARAI or SPJ approach. The converse of this, examined more fully by Nicholls et al. (2016), is that almost half were still being conducted using UCJ, notwithstanding plentiful evidence of the questionable value of that practice.

Several reviews published in recent years have provided comparisons of the level of usage and the predictive accuracy of different risk assessment methods. The AUC offers particular advantages in providing a common metric developed from the relative balance of an instrument's sensitivity and specificity which can be used to compare across studies, and it is independent of sample size. This provides an indicator of the comparative success of each measure, that is, its accuracy as a means of predicting rates of violent, sexual or other criminal recidivism. Note that in the following reviews, data from studies of offenders with and without mental disorders are often combined.

Farrington et al. (2008) compared a number of risk assessment methods for criminal recidivism in terms of the average AUC of each, generated across a number of prediction–outcome studies. The highest mean AUC figures were obtained for measures that had been developed using large databases in criminal justice systems (England and Wales, and Canada), though there were only a few published studies on these. For several other measures, there was more published research (e.g. eighteen studies each on the *Violence Risk Appraisal Guide* [VRAG] and the *Psychopathy Check List* [PCL-R]). But none of the obtained AUCs was particularly high: the range across the six most extensively researched scales was from 0.64 to 0.73.

Campbell et al. (2009) undertook a similar task but confined their main analysis to those measures on which data were available from ten or more effect-size calculations, focusing therefore on just five instruments. It is not necessarily the case that each successive, generation, of tools represents an unequivocal improvement on the one before. The choice of method should be guided by the assessor's objective. Campbell et al. (2009) found that actuarial risk assessment instruments were best for predicting institutional violence, whereas structured professional judgment methods were superior predictors of long-term post-release outcome.

Yang et al. (2010) ranged more broadly and analysed data on nine separate tools. These authors concluded that 'there is no appreciable or clinically significant difference in the violence-predictive efficacies of the nine tools ... if prediction of violence is the only criterion for the selection of a risk assessment tool, then the tools included in the present study are essentially interchangeable' (p. 759). That conclusion is perhaps not surprising given the findings of an earlier factor-analytic study by Kroner et al. (2005). These authors separated out the items from four established scales and then recombined them in a series of random selections. The resultant permutations yielded predictions of post-release recidivism or revocation of parole as accurately as their formal counterparts, suggesting that all assessments tap into essentially the same pool of predictor variables.

Singh and Fazel (2010) reported a 'meta-review', a sweeping survey of previous efforts at evaluation of the field of violence risk assessment. They identified forty reviews (nine systematic reviews and thirty-one meta-analyses) of this area, encompassing 2,232 primary studies and no fewer than 126 separate risk assessment instruments. Again, no single measure emerged as consistently superior to any of the others in terms of its predictive validity. In many other respects, there was sizable inconsistency among the findings. However, there were 'significant methodological weaknesses' in many reviews, among them the problem that moderator effects were rarely analysed, such as the differential impact of settings on results (e.g. differences between prison, secure hospital, and community samples).

Singh et al. (2011) and Fazel et al. (2012) reported two related systematic reviews also comparing nine risk assessment tools (though a different selection from Yang et al., 2010). Singh et al. integrated a set of sixty-eight studies, involving eighty-eight independent samples with a cumulative total of 25,980 participants; Fazel et al. did the same with a set of seventy-three samples with an aggregate of 24,827 participants. Unlike the other reviews above, these authors found wide variation in the predictive accuracy of the selected measures. They concluded, somewhat disappointedly, that 'even after 30 years of development, the view that violence, sexual, or criminal risk can be predicted in most cases is not evidence based' (Fazel et al., 2012, p. 5). They recommended that risk assessments be combined with other information, and should be used only to 'roughly classify' individuals in different risk categories.

Whittington et al. (2013) reviewed studies of formal violence risk assessment scales published in the period 2002–2008, used in either mental health or criminal justice settings. Integrating data from sixty-five studies where AUCs were reported, these authors too found a wide range of predictive values. The mean AUC across all studies was 0.69, with a range from 0.44 to 0.88. However, the upper reaches of this range (above 0.75) were populated by only five studies derived from four different assessments, with the two highest figures obtained from a far shorter follow-up interval (eighty-four days) than for the other instruments (which varied from 350 to 4,143 days). Average AUCs for actuarial scales were higher than for those based on structured clinical judgement.

Rossegger et al. (2013) conducted a review of studies on three ARAIs reported to be the most widely used in clinical practice. They located eighty-four replication studies based on 108 separate samples. They discovered that there was a sizable gap between the reporting of an evaluation study by an instrument's developers and evaluations conducted by other researchers. Insofar as some studies were designed as replication tests – to check the validity of ARAIs – the level of matching between how measures were implemented in original (developer-led) as compared with later (replication) studies was often found to be rather poor. Rossegger et al. concluded that without independent evaluations of measures, that is conducted by researchers other than their developers, the validity of those instruments remains in doubt. However, where replications were conducted in a manner that diverged from the original studies, the meaning of any apparently positive results obtained from them also remained unclear. Findings obtained under these circumstances do not provide corroboration of the predictive value of a risk assessment.

Singh et al. (2013) reported a 'second order' systematic review of forty-seven predictive validity studies published in the period 1990–2011, dealing with twenty-five risk assessment instruments, some of them ARAIs, the remainder based on the SPJ approach. The principal aim of this review was to evaluate the standards of reporting in risk assessment research, and in particular to examine how predictive validity had been measured. The latter procedures were found to be very variable across studies; AUC values were reported in only one-third (34%) of the studies and possible limitations discussed in fewer than one in five (19%). Most studies reported only global outcome data for total samples, rarely examining different outcomes for those at higher and lower levels of risk. Based on these and other observations, the authors identified a need for more standardised forms of analysis and reporting across the field of risk assessment research.

Nicholls et al. (2013) conducted a review of risk assessment approaches in the specific area of intimate partner violence (IPV). From a search of three relevant databases, a set of thirty-nine studies was located, published in the period 1990–2011, encompassing nineteen different risk assessment measures. The authors cited studies showing that most professionals working with IPV 'continued to rely on their intuition and subjective judgement despite the limitations' of that approach (p. 87). Results showed there was a wide variability in the quality and rigour of the studies that were found. On average, predictive validity was in the moderate range, though assessments with a specific IPV focus performed slightly better than those with a general violence focus. As elsewhere, no measure emerged as superior to any of the others for risk assessment purposes. There were few prospective outcome evaluations, in which a plan for all data collection is formulated in advance, and in some the selected measures were not used as directed by their developers. Some relatively high AUCs found in 'construction samples', the group studied in the initial research, were not reproduced in cross-validation studies (i.e. when transposed to other settings), a result paralleling that reported by Rossegger et al. (2013) as described above. Overall, the authors characterised the usage of risk assessment methods in IPV as being in need of considerable development and refinement of methods.

Tully et al. (2013) reported a systematic review of risk assessment tools used in the area of sexual offending. In a large-scale literature search of six databases and very painstaking meta-analysis, they integrated data from forty-three studies on fifteen measures, with a cumulative sample size of 31,426. After applying extensive quality-control procedures, data were collated on nine measures, with relevant studies also being assigned quality scores. Most assessments showed predictive success that could be considered in the moderate range, with two measures performing at a higher level than this, but unfortunately based on only two studies in each case. Several of the other measures had reported high AUCs in some studies but far lower ones in others. As in some of the other reviews cited here, Tully et al. were particularly interested in the difference between developer-led versus other evaluations, and the possible influence of 'developer bias' was noted in some of the reported evaluations.

Desmarais et al. (2018) reported a meta-analysis of fifty-three studies on the validation of risk assessment instruments used in the United States, on which research was published in the period from 1970 to 2012. They found results on nineteen different instruments, the majority employing only static risk factors, with little usage of dynamic risk or protective factors. No single scale emerged as yielding the consistently highest predictor scores. In this review, different scales outperformed each other in different settings, implying that a well-equipped agency in this field needs a suite of measures (and suitably trained personnel) to be able to adapt to all circumstances. However, there was a major deficit of all scales in having very little information on the usability of scales for members of different ethnic groups, leaving open the possibility of bias in their use. The measures that were surveyed, being used mainly in penal settings, took insufficient account of possible mental disorders and, perhaps more surprisingly, of substance misuse.

It can be seen that an enormous research effort has been conducted over the past thirty years in this area. As Mossman (2013) has suggested, there have been remarkable positive developments in the field of risk assessment particularly over the past two decades. Numerous advances have been made in both methodology and generating a wide array of findings. Having acknowledged that, predictive power appears to have reached a ceiling, and no risk assessment measure has been found that regularly outperforms any of its comparators. It may be that risk assessment research in this area has reached a stage of diminishing returns. Overall, drawing on these reviews, there is no firm and consistent difference favouring any single risk assessment tool over any of the others – although there are some with very little convincing support. But as previously noted, the amount of research varies considerably across the different published scales. There also remains a proportion of the variance (the extent of variability in recorded outcomes), due to unmeasured or perhaps even unmeasurable factors, or maybe simply 'noise', that cannot be captured by any of the methods in present-day use.

While many risk assessment tools can yield average estimates that are accurate at well above chance levels, their predictive accuracy nevertheless remains limited at the individual level, which is where they are intended to be used in practice. For these reasons, as discussed later in this chapter, some commentators on the process have continued to express significant concerns and recommend that caution needs to be exercised in the importance attached to the results. There is probably no consensus regarding this, but a majority message appears to be that despite its shortcomings, structured risk assessment adds value and it would be wasteful to dispense with it; but at the same time its users and promoters should be careful not to overstate its effectiveness.

Many of the risk assessment tools currently available are concerned with prediction of criminal reoffending in general terms rather than violence as such. Some, such as the *Violence Risk Appraisal Guide*, was specifically designed for the latter purpose, and others, such as the

Offender Group Reconviction Scale, have been extended to yield a violence and *risk of harm* score. There are several that are specifically designed for assessing risk of sexual offending or of intimate partner violence. A conclusion that often emerges from many reviews of research on risks of violence, however, is that the variables that are associated with risk of offending in general and those associated with risk of violence are fundamentally the same.

More broadly, some experts have contended that research on anti-social behaviour itself has generally become 'stuck at the "risk-factor" stage' (Moffitt and Caspi, 2007, p. 97). The next major improvement is likely only to be through the development of causal models through which the occurrence and possible recurrence of criminal acts is better understood.

In criminal justice, it may be that risk assessment tools are most useful for classification purposes at the early phase of a sentence, where individuals are placed in categories or allocated to regimes or to interventions on the basis of that information (as suggested by Fazel et al., 2012). Given limits in predictive power at the individual level, that may also avoid the problems that prediction is likely to encounter at the parole or pre-discharge phase. During those later phases, when monitoring change and forward planning, while structured risk assessments may be useful, detailed offence analysis might generate more valuable information. That could involve the development of individual *case formulations,* which comprise explanatory accounts, amounting to individualised theories, of the causal factors involved in the origin and maintenance of a person's pattern of difficulties, and the use of anamnestic assessment. In a study of sexual offending in Germany, crime analysis has been shown to enhance predictive validity using risk scores based on behaviour at the time of the index offence (Janka et al., 2012).

Reviewing the current status of risk assessment research and its translation into practice, Taxman (2018) identified a series of areas on which it appeared more work is required or improvements are needed. They included questions over the accuracy of prediction; whether methods of assessing and scoring items were sufficiently consistent to allow comparisons to be made between sites, populations, and agencies; whether the assessments in use were neutral or contained biases with respect to race, gender, and other important demographic features; and how satisfactory are the other statistical and psychometric properties of the available measures. Taxman (2018) also questioned to what extent the use of the instruments actually contributed to practice, that is, whether research findings can be translated into meaningful information and communicated clearly to support decisions.

7.6 Ethical Questions Raised by Risk Assessment

The development and continually expanding use of risk assessment raises some fundamental ethical issues and moral dilemmas for practitioners and decision makers and for the agencies within which they work (McGuire, 2004).

First, there is a continuing and troubling ethical problem, foreseen by some early commentators on the growth of risk assessment, characterised by Pfohl (1979, p. 57) as the likelihood of 'error through over-prediction'. That is, risk assessment may lead more or less unavoidably to some individuals having their risk of committing violence overestimated and being detained in a prison or secure hospital when they need not be (Litwack, 1993). Grisso and Appelbaum (1992) considered that, provided accuracy was reasonably high, the use of risk assessments was ethically acceptable. On the other hand, it might be contended that as long as predictive accuracy fails to achieve 100% (a position unlikely to change), inevitably some individuals will be wrongly classified. In reality, predictive values are generally well below their theoretical maximum, and even with an AUC in the region of 0.80 (which few measures reach) the numbers of people wrongly classified is potentially quite large. Szmukler et al. (2011) examined data from a prediction study where there was a fairly respectable AUC value of 0.77 and showed that this led to a sizable group of wrong predictions and consequent violation of some individuals' rights. Unfortunately, even some of the most carefully designed research, involving large samples and thorough data collection and analysis, may generate prediction scores in a similar range (Fazel et al., 2016).

Observers of the use of risk assessment may retort that the safety of the community takes precedence over individual rights. Others would reject that position in principle, and many others would not accept it as justifying such a high level of error. Shepherd and Sullivan (2017) suggest that while risk assessment has beneficial uses, including the possibility it offers of reducing cognitive bias in individual assessments, its limitations have not been adequately acknowledged. There are covert and 'furtive influences' at work in seeking to preserve the image of some agencies or practitioners as being able to forecast accurately and protect society from unwanted events.

Second, some researchers have been concerned about standard error and confidence intervals of risk scores. These statistical terms reflect the fact that all measurement in this area and elsewhere is inevitably imprecise, and are estimates of the amount of inaccuracy that is typically expected in a given assessment and of how close we believe we can get to a prediction that provides a sound and justifiable basis for decision-making. Hart et al. (2007) contended that the likelihood of achieving this is low, and called the entire risk assessment enterprise into question in arguing that the scope for error when scores are considered at the individual level is unacceptably wide. They described margins of error that undermine the possibility of meaningful risk assessment. Their arguments constitute virtually a wholesale rejection of the possibility of evidence-based prediction on a case-by-case basis. Other researchers have responded that in arriving at these conclusions Hart et al. misapplied statistical techniques. For example, the notion of confidence intervals around the score for a single individual was described as meaningless (Gendreau and Cullen 2008; Harris et al., 2008; Mossman and Sellke, 2007). However, Hart and Cooke (2013) responded vigorously to rebut these and other criticisms, sustaining their argument with an empirical study of ninety convicted male sexual offenders followed up over a three and a half to five-year period. On the basis of their analyses they concluded that 'it was virtually impossible to make meaningful distinctions among subjects based on individual risk estimates made using ARAI scores' (p. 93). Other researchers, however, have defended the use of risk prediction in individual cases (Hanson and Howard, 2010; Imrey and Dawid, 2014; Mossman, 2015).

Third, there can be a temptation to employ risk assessment instruments outside their appropriate sphere of applicability. It is essential to ensure prediction instruments have been validated on a population similar to the one with whom they are to be used (Otto, 2000). Thus assessment tools that had been developed for use in mental health settings and validated on relevant populations are not suitable for use with other groups on whom no comparable data are available, such as persons convicted of terrorist offences (Devernik et al., 2009; Pressman and Flockton, 2012). As different factors influence different types of violent offending, a measure developed for one population could give highly erroneous results when applied to another.

7.7   Conclusion

Taken together, these ethical issues and the research evidence considered here have led to some concerns over the whole violence risk assessment undertaking. According to Szmukler and Rose (2013), for example, it gives rise to a range of problems including possible conflicts in the roles of practitioners, perhaps more so in forensic mental health than criminal justice, where there is simultaneously an obligation to carry out both supportive or therapeutic and custodial roles. The 'base rate problem', the fact that the kinds of serious events that risk assessment is intended to prevent have a relatively low rate of occurrence, alongside the limited predictive accuracy of assessment instruments, means that decision-making in this area raises recurring ethical questions for which at present there are no clear answers.

A balanced and defensible position on these questions is likely to recognise the following points. Over recent years there has been a considerable level of success in isolating the correlates of violent behaviour of different kinds (risk and protective factors), and reasonable progress has been made too in identifying causal pathways within them. Risk assessment methods now in widespread use present a statistically significant improvement over chance in making valid predictions, and are a major advance on the well-intentioned but faulty clinical judgement of the past. Further improvements seem unlikely to be made through the route of recombining risk-related variables in new assessment tools. They are more likely to come from clearer understanding of causal factors and of situational contingencies at the individual level, possibly through the use of the procedures of case formulation. But at a higher level, so to speak, what we can broadly conclude is that in principle acts of violence are predictable; they do not emerge from nowhere; their patterning can be understood; and, on that basis, steps can be taken to reduce the likelihood of their recurrence.

8 Pharmaceutical Interventions
Medication, Violence, and the Public Health

8.1   Introduction

Effective risk assessment, when it occurs, ideally leads to decisions about effective interventions. The multifactorial nature of violence, with its origins in biological, psychological, and social processes operating separately or together, means that interventions at all of these different levels are available for those who present an identifiable violence risk. The challenge is to identify which intervention, or combination of interventions, is most suitable in each case and to find the necessary resources for successful implementation. The next three chapters will consider interventions at each of the levels and examine some of the evidence currently available with regard to their effectiveness. In public health terms, the medical and psychosocial interventions to be considered, respectively, here and in the next chapter, mainly represent tertiary but also some secondary prevention efforts deployed with at-risk populations, or with relatively high-risk individuals who have already acted violently. In contrast, the integrated interventions considered in Chapter 10 often incorporate a primary prevention element in addition, as part of a truly comprehensive approach to the problem.

To begin with pharmaceutical and psychosocial interventions, there are large research literatures on both types of approach, and some conclusions can be drawn about which drugs and psychological therapies might work for which types of problem. But when weighing up the evidence available in these two domains against each other, a number of key differences need to be emphasised at the outset. For instance, the psychological evidence tends to be designed more for the problem of violence specifically and as it occurs in everyday life than the comparable pharmacological literature. Violence itself is rarely the primary focus of drug trials, and almost all the evidence on pharmacological effectiveness is based in psychiatric settings, usually with people who have severe and less common problems. Usually, if violence outcomes are included in such trials, they are secondary and the main focus is on clinical

186

symptoms such as hallucinations or mood fluctuations, which may or may not accompany changes in violence. In contrast, the comparable studies evaluating psychological interventions tend to be designed explicitly to address violence as the main problem. They are also implemented in a much wider range of settings such as at home with families; in schools, prisons, and secure mental health units; and across various services such as youth justice and probation.

Also, even when a significant drug effect is found, there is rarely a detailed theoretical explanation for why this might have occurred through directly linking neurochemistry with behaviour. Some psychiatrists have argued that this 'theoretical poverty' applies to all the observed effects of pharmacological interventions on mental health problems (Moncrieff, 2008). They argue that there is no clear mechanism explaining how drugs work in psychiatry and that even the broad labelling of drugs as, say, antidepressants or antipsychotics wrongly implies that they have a specific effect. Psychological research, on the other hand, tends to develop and test theoretical models of a causal relationship between specific variables, such as distorted thinking, antisocial attitudes or changes in violence.

The role of drug treatments within the public health framework we are considering here is also worth bearing in mind. Pharmaceutical drugs do not feature on the WHO's list of 'best buy' strategies (World Health Organization, 2014). This reflects the emphasis there on population-based prevention measures alongside more focused early intervention with high-risk groups that may not yet have met the threshold for formal designation as 'pathological' in some way. Medication *per se* clearly has a role in some public health strategies as demonstrated by the controversial but widespread prescription of statins in primary care to reduce cholesterol and the addition of fluoride to public water supplies. So there is nothing inherently unthinkable about population-wide prescription of chemical agents to prevent disease. But if the widespread prescription of 'anti-violence' drugs in the same way as fluoride for the whole population was ever proposed, it would be much more controversial, and the recent growth in the targeted use of such drugs for early intervention raises major concerns beyond those generated by the prescription of statins, for example. Violence is a phenomenon with much greater social and political complexity than heart disease or tooth decay, and its treatment significantly complicates issues of both effectiveness and morality.

In particular, the relatively imprecise nature of psychiatric disorders and disputes over what causes and constitutes 'unacceptable' behaviour in society raise huge questions about the pervasive use of any drug prescribed in order to change behaviour. Since individual violence can be a legitimate response to political injustice and structural oppression, anti-violence drugs can be seen as simply a 'chemical cosh': a way of sedating those who might have a justifiable cause for protest. So the significant reduction in physical aggression reported in some studies (e.g. Krakowski et al., 2006) considered below among those prescribed the antipsychotic drug clozapine, for instance, might indeed be due to reduced paranoia as intended by the prescribing psychiatrists. But it may also be due to the drowsiness which is experienced by those taking the drug and which would blunt any capacity for protesting against unfair or oppressive conditions in or beyond an institution. These broader issues must always be borne in mind when focusing on the deceptively simple question of drug effectiveness. Awareness of such social trends should at least warn us against any simplistic interpretation of violence reductions associated with drug interventions. For that reason, much of this chapter is devoted to considering the wider contextual issues around medication prior to examining the actual evidence itself.

To be clear, the biopsychosocial approach to violence includes, by definition, an awareness of the potential importance of biological factors in human aggression, and we have already examined some of the most relevant pathways from brain to behaviour. Genetic factors may some-times play a role through their influence for instance upon the production of key neurotransmitters linked to impulsivity and other high-risk mental states. The likely importance of neurotransmitters in the capacity for violence among some people in some situations then opens up the possibility for targeted violence treatment through the use of drugs which have been shown to be effective in reducing the behaviour. Drugs clearly have a role to play in reducing violence by some individuals who are thus able to live better, safer, and more enriching lives away from hospitals or prisons. However, their full costs must be acknowledged and their true effectiveness should not be exaggerated. This chapter will examine some of the evidence in this area but will first emphasise the wider issues that are particularly pertinent when considering the prescription of drugs to control and treat violent behaviour.

8.2   The Problem of Unintended Side Effects

All prescribed drugs have an intended effect, but, as active chemical agents operating within a live biological system, all will also have unin-tended side effects which are more or less problematic for the individual. As we will discover below, the drugs which have been found to be most effective in reducing a propensity for violence are antipsychotics and anticonvulsants. While there seems to be robust evidence for their effectiveness, it is well known that this effect is accompanied by the potential for side effects which in some cases can be extremely serious. Antipsychotic medications such as clozapine were developed, as the name suggests, to reduce the experience of psychotic symptoms such as delusions and hallucinations. They also have powerful effects on violent behaviour as demonstrated in several rigorous reviews (Hockenhull et al., 2012), but the effectiveness in reducing psychosis and violence is frequently accompanied by minor side effects and sometimes connected to severe unintended reactions. For those on clozapine, decreased appetite, blurred vision, nausea, abnormal sweating, speech impairment and urinary disorders are common side effects, and disorders such as circulatory collapse, pancreatitis, and ketoacidosis have been reported (National Institute for Health and Care Excellence, 2018a). As a result of these and other risks, people prescribed clozapine require regular blood tests throughout their treatment to monitor various characteristics such as blood lipids. At the start of treatment these blood tests are done weekly and close medical supervision is maintained to check that the patient does not collapse because of hypotension or convulsions. For this reason, drug trials rightly gather data on patient safety, which must be balanced against any evidence of improvement.

Similarly, carbamazepine is an anticonvulsant drug designed to reduce the frequency of epileptic seizures but which has also been tested in several trials in terms of its effect on violent behaviour. Again there is a range of common side effects with varying degrees of unpleasantness (National Institute for Health and Care Excellence, 2018b), such as skin reactions, vision disorders, dizziness, nausea and vomiting, and a number of rare reactions such as anaemia, circulatory collapse, and hepatic disorders. One rare side effect of carbamazepine is drowsiness, which, as noted above, confuses any attempt to identify a specific anti-violence effect separate from a general inhibitory or flattening effect, linked to the idea of the 'chemical cosh'. Another rare side effect, paradoxically, is aggression itself. Regardless of how these two responses may be interpreted in terms of anti-violence effectiveness, it is clear from the well-established list of potential side effects that freedom from any tendency to be violent often comes at a high price for those treated in this way.

8.3   Big Pharma, Disease-Mongering, and Violence

An interrogation of the evidence on medication effectiveness is not meaningful without an awareness of the huge profits that can be made from the successful selling of drugs with a direct or indirect anti-violence effect. The evidence considered below consists of rigorous trials meeting all the criteria for high-quality studies and thus, taken at face value, may seem to constitute a solid, reliable base on which medical doctors can make prescribing decisions. But everything we know about the marketing of psychiatric and other medications indicates that maximum caution should be used when interpreting the results. Widely referred to as 'Big Pharma', the very large and super-profitable pharmaceutical industry clearly has a vested interest in marketing drugs for every ailment, including the personal and social 'disease' of violent tendencies. Antipsychotics are the third biggest product class of drugs, after statins and anti-ulcerants, in terms of sales value (Busfield, 2013), generating US $18 billion in revenue worldwide (Frances, 2016). The systematic and well-resourced 'hard sell' used to push these and other types of licensed drugs is well known and documented. These include company representatives targeting medical practices with selective information and sponsoring influential scientific meetings to shape opinions (Mosher et al., 2013). Primary care physicians are increasingly targeted by drug companies and encouraged to detect complex mental health problems among patients who might be amenable to drug treatment (Frances, 2016).

With regard to the research evidence specifically, the distortion of evidence-based medicine by 'marketing-based medicine' includes, for instance, suppressing results from studies which do not show effectiveness, selecting positive findings within a study by ignoring drop-outs or study sites where no effect was observed, and ghost-writing articles by companies in-house which academics then 'co-author' (Spielmans and Parry, 2010). Conflicts of scientific and financial interests are widespread. Research studies with one or more authors who have a declared financial connection to the company producing the drug being tested are nearly five times more likely to report a favourable finding than studies with completely independent authors. 'Success' is eight times more likely if the study itself is funded by the industry (Perlis et al., 2005). Other studies clearly demonstrate distorted reporting of research in this area (Heres et al., 2006; Turner et al., 2008). While, as noted above with risk assessment tools, such biases occur in psychosocial research as well, there is no evidence that it approaches the level of distortion apparent in these analyses.

Violence propensity has a particular role to play in this sophisticated and orchestrated marketing exercise. While they were developed to treat a specific set of psychiatric symptoms within the internal world of the patient, antipsychotics in particular have been marketed at times with explicit reference to their potential to reduce violent behaviour. Nowadays drug companies in the largest market, the United States, also fund 'advocacy' organisations which highlight dangerousness as an alleged feature of untreated schizophrenia (Mosher et al., 2013). Websites with information about schizophrenia that are funded by drug companies are more likely to link violence to a lack of treatment than those which are independent of such funding (Read, 2008). Perhaps partly as a result of these strategies, the prescription of antipsychotics has increased dramatically over the past twenty years. The number of antipsychotic prescription items increased by 60% between 1998 and 2010 in the United Kingdom, and the costs associated with these drugs tripled to a point where they exceeded all other psychoactive drug types including antidepressants (Ilyas and Moncrieff, 2012).

The success of Big Pharma in selling drugs linked more or less explicitly to violence is clear in two areas particularly. While no one is yet advocating the 'fluoride' model of universal violence prevention for all through the water supply, the 'statin' model of early drug intervention with those considered at risk is increasingly common in certain areas, especially for 'problematic' children and young people. On the one hand, this plausibly fits with a public health approach emphasising early detection and prevention. But, given the particular dangers of medication outlined above and the less-than-objective science available on which to base prescribing decisions, this is not a straightforward choice. Early intervention sounds eminently sensible and helpful to all concerned until the commercial imperatives and social control implications are considered.

The spread of medication marketed to deal with 'disruptive behaviour' and aggression over the past two decades, especially to children, young people and the elderly, regardless of a diagnosed disorder, is alarming. Rather than a benign process of early intervention with those 'at risk' of developing a full-blown disorder, some see this as a clear case of 'disease mongering': the invention of new disorders by those with a vested interest in increasing power, influence, and profits. The relentless expansion of mental health diagnostic categories in the latest editions of the influential *Diagnostic and Statistical Manual of Mental Disorders* (DSM-IV and DSM-5) since the 1980s enables increasing aspects of ordinary life to be annexed by the psychiatric profession and defined, thereby, as suitable for medical treatment. Again, violence and disruptive behaviour are complex interpersonal processes with a political dimension, but they have been caught up in this process of diagnostic inflation too (Frances, 2016).

The best-known example of this is concern over the prescription of stimulants such as methylphenidate to children and adults diagnosed with attention-deficit hyperactivity disorder (ADHD). Nearly 700,000 prescriptions for these drugs were issued in the United Kingdom from 1995 to 2015, mainly to children some of whom were aged as young as six years old (Renoux et al., 2016). Impulsiveness and irritability, common proximal factors in aggressive behaviour, are part of the diagnostic profile of ADHD, but they are also normal human characteristics when people are placed in stressful or provoking situations. So it may actually be a person's intolerable situation within and beyond the family which needs addressing, rather than their brain chemistry. The 800% rise in United Kingdom stimulant prescriptions in the decade and a half after 2000 suggests that drugs are increasingly seen as a relatively simple solution to uncontrolled behaviour, but the rise itself could be viewed as part of a process of the 'pharmaceuticalization' of society (Abraham, 2010).

Antipsychotics are also increasingly used in the United States and Europe to manage disruptive behaviour among young people where the disruptiveness is considered to be a manifestation of mental illness. They are also widely prescribed for elderly people, suggesting for some a shift into new populations at a time when the market for prescriptions to working-age adults with psychosis has become saturated (Frances, 2016). For young people, persistent aggressive behaviour can be associated with a formal diagnosis of conduct disorder, which also includes broader antisocial acts such as theft and, even more broadly, serious violations of rules (including truancy or running away). The most recent guidance for the management of conduct disorder in England and Wales (National Institute for Health and Care Excellence, 2017) recommends against the routine use of pharmacology to manage behavioural disorders, although it does permit the occasional use of one specific antipsychotic drug, risperidone, for the short-term management of 'explosive anger' and severe problems in regulating emotions if psychosocial interventions have not worked. The prescription of antipsychotics to one vulnerable group in the United Kingdom, people with an intellectual disability, trebled in the period 2000–2013, and those with aggressive tendencies in this group were particularly targeted, regardless of the presence or absence of psychosis (Brophy et al., 2018). Similarly in the United States, antipsychotic prescriptions for adolescents increased markedly from 2006 to 2010 (Olfson et al., 2015). In an earlier survey of this practice the main recipients of the drugs were boys with an average age of thirteen, and they were twice as likely to receive it for disruptive behavioural disorders as they were for psychotic disorders (Olfson et al., 2006).

Some have expressed deep disquiet at this widening use of major tranquillisers with young people who in most cases do not have the psychotic features for which the drugs were originally developed. Even when psychosis is present or indicated, there are major questions about whether the biochemical theories advanced to explain and justify the prescription are sound (Moncrieff, 2008). The parallel development of early intervention teams for psychosis and the roll-out of 'early detection' systems to teachers in schools (Monducci et al., 2018) reflect a genuine public health approach but assumes psychosis is a reliable and valid diagnostic feature with an immediate chemical cure available. Both these assumptions are questionable and highly damaging if they are incorrect.

At the other end of the life course, the same growth in antipsychotic medication was observed for elderly people with dementia over a number of years after 1990 until concerns were raised over the potentially fatal side effects in this particularly vulnerable population. Fortunately, when alerts were issued by government agencies, the rate of prescribing antipsychotics for this group was successfully and significantly reduced. The confusion, agitation and loss of impulse control which are prominent and progressive features of dementia clearly increase the potential for aggression and other behaviour which is considered disruptive. Medication can be seen as part of the solution to this behavioural problem, though, again, it does not have any therapeutic effect on the underlying disease process. In the 1990s, more than 15% of people with dementia in the United States were receiving antipsychotics (Kales et al., 2011), and several studies from around the world in the United Kingdom, United States, Canada, Spain, and Australia showed that antipsychotic prescribing levels for the general adult population, often including elderly people, increased substantially into the next decade (Verdoux et al., 2010). By 2005, this worrying increase had been identified and action was taken to intervene. In the United States, the Food and Drug Administration issued a 'black box' alert to doctors, and the prescribing rate since then, both there and elsewhere, has reduced. However, there is some evidence that this reduction has been accompanied by an increase in the use of anticonvulsants over the same time period (Kales et al., 2011), which suggests a switch in drug choice rather than a turn to non-pharmacological alternatives which are widely available (British Psychological Society, 2013).

8.4   Enforced Medication

Alongside these issues of unwanted side effects and intense commercial pressures, the use of drugs to manage violence is also particularly problematic because of the potential for compulsion. While participation in psychological and social programmes for sex offenders, substance abusers and domestic violence perpetrators can be mandated for offenders by courts (Parhar et al., 2008), those made subject to such orders always retain an ultimate freedom to withdraw from the treatment and face the consequences. Furthermore, they can also appear to participate ('play the game') while not taking it seriously, a possibility that is frequently monitored by intervention staff. Uniquely, in contrast, psychoactive pharmacological interventions can be physically enforced in a legal way that ultimately makes it impossible to refuse medication in certain circumstances. This again calls for a particular wariness to be applied when scrutinising the research evidence on effectiveness considered below.

In most countries, medication can be enforced for people with mental disorder either in an emergency or as part of a long-term treatment plan under relevant mental health legislation. In one survey, nearly one in ten people admitted to an acute psychiatric treatment unit in the United Kingdom were subjected to enforced intramuscular injections of medication during the first two weeks of their admission (Bowers et al., 2012), and rates in the first two weeks were slightly higher in Italy (12%) and much higher in Greece (38%) (Bowers et al., 2005). Nearly 40% of patients overall in UK services have experienced this at some point in their lives (Whittington et al., 2009). The intervention tends to be in the first twenty-four hours after admission, when a person's distress and agitation is at its peak, rather than later on, suggesting its use is for management of emergencies rather than formal treatment. But some people are subjected to multiple enforced treatments, with a few receiving up to six injections over the first two weeks of admission, presumably as part of an enforced treatment programme to stabilise the patient's mental state. It appears to some observers that 'a few patients [are] clearly locked in battle with the staff over medication, with repeated refusals and repeated coerced injections' (Bowers et al., 2012, pp. 802–803).

The degree of coercion used to enforce these injections varies, with half of them involving the ultimate measure of being held down in a manual restraint. In the other half of episodes, the injection was agreed to without restraint, suggesting that a show of force by staff with no actual 'hands on' has been sufficient to persuade the patient to comply. Notably, in a quarter of these episodes the patient had engaged in only verbal aggression with no violence beforehand, suggesting a significant escalation of the incident by staff initiating physical contact. As suggested by the authors, presumably this verbal aggression either contained specific threats or was believed to be a significant risk sign which needed immediate neutralisation (Bowers et al., 2012).

Being subjected to enforced intramuscular injections is clearly a highly distressing experience, and it is increasingly recognised as a psychologically traumatising event which can re-evoke previous traumas commonly reported by people in contact with mental health services (Huckshorn, 2004). However, while coercion-free mental health services are still an ideal to work toward, patient views on the use of the treatment in comparison to other forms of coercion are mixed. Some threatening situations in hospitals are dealt with alternatively by the use of seclusion (enforced isolation in a room) or, outside the United Kingdom, through mechanical restraint using restrictive belts. Medication was the most disliked coercive measure in a large survey of UK patients, but seclusion was equally disliked by the sample and both were seen as preferable to mechanical restraint (Whittington et al., 2009). Among Dutch patients, on the other hand, enforced medication was felt to be less coercive, less humiliating and less frightening than seclusion (Georgieva et al., 2012), and it is increasingly advocated in the Netherlands as a humane alternative to seclusion (Georgieva et al., 2013). Clearly, individual preferences for 'how I want to be coerced' in the hypothetical or actual likelihood of having to be treated in this way are important, complex and varied. Nevertheless, the suspension and, in some cases, violation of human rights implicit in the act of forced medication set a very high bar for demonstrations of drug effectiveness in this particular area.

8.5   Methodological Challenges in Testing Drugs for Violence

Beyond these complex conceptual, ethical and political issues which are specific to drug evaluations, there are more general scientific challenges in deciding 'what works' in this field. For example, a large systematic review was conducted by ourselves and colleagues which attempted to address the question of effectiveness by examining all relevant well-designed studies of pharmacological, psychological and other interventions published from the 1950s up until the end of 2008 (Hockenhull et al., 2012; Leitner et al., 2006). The studies were included if they collected data on a violence-related outcome even when this was not their primary focus. Many researchers, for instance, were primarily interested in treating psychotic symptoms such as paranoid delusions but, for the reasons discussed above, considered it valuable to also look at violence data as a secondary measure of interest. The review was deliberately wide-ranging in that it was designed to capture all of the relevant research on this topic with all types of violent populations. These included both offenders with a criminal conviction with or without mental illness and patients in hospitals and the community regardless of any offence history in order to try and get an overall view of what works with this problem. Within this overall review, there were more than a hundred drug trials which have taken place since the first formal investigations in the 1970s. Despite this massive research effort, the conclusions it was possible to draw about drugs as a treatment for violent tendencies remained tentative at best. This is for a number of scientific and methodological reasons.

The deliberately broad scope of the review revealed a major weakness in that the apparently large research literature is actually very fragmented with many different drugs being tested in a wide range of different clinical and criminal justice settings. Even when focusing just on people with a mental disorder, the causes of violence associated with dementia noted above, for instance, are likely to be different biologically, psychologically and socially from those which occur among people with schizophrenia. The role of neurotransmitters, the capacity to think clearly and judge situations and the relationships the person has with professional carers and wider society are all likely to vary when comparing these two clinical diagnoses. This is a further reminder to be cautious in any simplistic claim for an association between mental disorder and violence as noted above in Chapter 1.

Such fragmentation makes it difficult to combine the results across studies in order to conclude whether any one particular drug or group of drugs really does have an effect. When this apparently extensive literature is interrogated with specific questions which might be useful to guide clinicians, there is unfortunately little that can meaningfully be concluded (Hockenhull et al., 2015). Policymakers and prescribers need strong scientific evidence to make decisions about how to tackle a problem like violence at the individual or social levels, but scientific evidence is only strong when it is based on effective replication. The same drug needs to be shown to work repeatedly in different but comparable groups to be sure that it is the right approach. Instead, we have many drugs tested in one or two studies, and, even when tested more often, they are often used in different groups that are difficult to compare meaningfully.

As an example, a clinician might want strong evidence to support the prescription of atypical antipsychotics to a person with schizophrenia. If the large collection of studies in the review is examined to find (1) randomized controlled trials (RCTs) evaluating (2) atypical antipsychotics to reduce violence in (3) individuals on the schizophrenic spectrum, using the most stringent design elements of (4) a comparison against another active drug and (5) a robust scale-based violence outcome measure, then only three of the hundred-plus studies in the review could be found which met these criteria (Hockenhull et al., 2015). Furthermore, the atypical antipsychotics category in criterion (2) above is itself a collection of at least six different specific drugs (e.g. fluphenazine, zuclopentixol) with slightly different profiles, which might further complicate the clinical decision.

Not surprisingly, given this finding from an extensive review, other reviews in this area with more traditional, highly specified questions have come up with similar problems. The authoritative UK-based National Institute of Health and Care Excellence (NICE) guidelines on the treatment of aggression associated with antisocial personality disorder (ASPD), for instance (National Institute for Health and Care Excellence, 2013), focused on a single diagnostic group. ASPD is one of the few psychiatric diagnostic categories with an explicit connection to violence propensity and the only one which includes aggressiveness 'indicated by repeated physical fights or assaults' specified as one of the formal diagnostic criteria. If we accept that neurobiological factors have a role in the development of ASPD (Pemment, 2013), then despite the evidence of aggression being a possible side effect of anticonvulsants, there is a rationale for at least considering the use of pharmacology to treat the underlying personality disorder, the aggressiveness, or both.

With regard to pharmacological treatment of aggression linked to ASPD, the NICE review (National Institute for Health and Care Excellence, 2013) identified eight RCTs in this population testing the effect of three different types of drugs. Six of these studies tested anticonvulsants, so the studies were comparable on the first three criteria listed above: they had the same study design, drug group and diagnostic category. Pooled together, they had a combined sample size of more than 400 participants, which is promising as a basis for drawing robust conclusions. But one study recruited imprisoned offenders, while the others were conducted with outpatients who may or may not have been convicted of an offence. Moreover, the ages of those included ranged from nineteen to sixty-seven years. While it is debatable how significant these variations within the comparable studies might be, the reviewers concluded that the statistical measure of this ('heterogeneity') across these six studies was very high and that, despite being RCTs, the quality of the study designs was very low. These are both warning signs that any combined findings must be interpreted with caution.

However, notwithstanding all of these caveats, the people in the treatment groups receiving the anticonvulsants were less violent on average than those in the control groups. Nevertheless, the difference between the groups was small (standardised mean difference = 0.13) and statistically non-significant which implies the possibility of there being higher rates in some members of the control group. In other words, if the results were generalised to the overall population with the relevant diagnosis, there is a non-trivial chance that some people receiving anticonvulsants would be more violent than those who were not. As a result of this, the NICE guidance concludes that 'pharmacological interventions should not be routinely used for the treatment of antisocial personality disorder or the associated behaviours of aggression, anger and impulsivity' (2013, p. 216).

The main reason for this frustrating 'non-conclusion' from both broad and narrow evidence reviews is that running good rigorous trials is a challenging endeavour for those working with both pharmacological and psychosocial interventions. Such trials require large samples, credible measures of violence and sustained follow-ups to be convincing; and all these features are demanding and expensive to implement. In the latter part of the period covered by our review (Hockenhull et al., 2012), at a time when many of these shortcomings were emerging, the average sample recruited into a drug study had fewer than sixty participants, and this small group would obviously have to be split further into at least two study subgroups to enable a controlled comparison to be run. Then, by the end of the study, on average 20% of this initial sample had dropped out for various reasons, making any conclusions about effect-iveness even more tentative.

Measuring aggression consistently within and across studies is also notoriously difficult. Many studies use instruments such as the Modified Overt Aggression Scale (MOAS; Kay et al., 1988) where four types of aggressive behaviour, including self-harm, are scored by observers on a four-point scale according to intensity. Verbal aggression, for instance, is given a score of '2' if the person 'curses viciously, is severely insulting, [or] has temper outbursts'. While such scales are an improvement on unstructured observation in terms of validity, it can be seen that there is still much scope for subjectivity in scoring each item.

Follow-up periods also vary enormously between studies, again making like-for-like comparisons difficult. A drug which stops a person being violent for a year is obviously preferable to one which has an effect for only a month, but paradoxically the latter is more likely to be counted as successful in a test as it has a lower bar to overcome. While a few drug trials have tracked violence in treatment and control groups for more than two years, and one did so for up to five years (Gossop et al., 2005), the average follow-up period for studies is less than three months. A propensity for violence may be a long-term problem, and it is impos-sible to know what to conclude about a person's eventual improvement (or otherwise) from such a brief assessment period.

8.6   Which Drugs Are Effective for Treating Violence?

Despite all of these problems, a large number of studies have been conducted, and some conclusions about the effectiveness of drugs for curtailing violent behaviour can be drawn, however tentatively. When all diagnostic groups were considered together in the broad systematic review (Hockenhull et al., 2012), the most extensively tested group of drugs in this area were antipsychotics, medication intended primarily to reduce the positive symptoms of schizophrenia and related disorders but, as discussed above, widely used in other groups without such symptoms.

Certainly, experiencing symptoms such as delusions and hallucinations can both intensify a sense of being under threat from other people and create an idea that one's behaviour is entirely controlled by outside influences such as alien forces. Therefore medication which successfully reduces paranoia and increases a sense of personal control is likely to reduce violence as well. In the early period of the broad review prior to 2002, haloperidol was the most effective antipsychotic for reducing violence (Leitner et al., 2006). But, like carbamazepine, it can cause excessive drowsiness as a side-effect, which is both undesirable for the patient and confounds any attempt to specify a direct 'anti-violence' effect. Traditional antipsychotics, of which haloperidol is one, also produce a range of unpleasant side effects such as tremor and shuffling, which resemble Parkinson's disease and originate in their effect on neurotransmitters.

The newer generation of 'atypical' antipsychotic drugs such as clozapine and risperidone have the great benefit of not causing these unwanted and disabling effects, although they come with their own undesirable side effects also noted earlier. Overall these drugs are more effective than traditional antipsychotics when the 'old' and 'new' are tested against each other, and this anti-aggressive effect is separate from the antipsychotic effect (Frogley et al., 2012). Antipsychotics of both types are also associated with substantial reductions in violent crime over several years, so they have substantial social as well as clinical benefits (Fazel et al., 2014).

The literature on these drugs suffers less from fragmentation, and some meaningful combining of results can be conducted. When the studies comparing 'old' and 'new' antipsychotics are pooled in a meta-analysis, the likelihood of violence in the 'atypical' medication group is substantially lower than that in control groups treated either with the traditional anti-psychotic haloperidol or a placebo (Hockenhull et al., 2012). In one of these studies (Krakowski et al., 2006), for example, 110 hospitalised patients with schizophrenia who had been physically aggressive during their admission were randomly allocated to receive clozapine, olanzapine or haloperidol. Violent behaviour over a three-month observation period logged using the physical aggression item of the MOAS instrument was 50% lower in the (new, 'atypical') clozapine group than in the (old, 'traditional') haloperidol group. Interestingly, this reduction in aggression was not accompanied by any significant decrease in positive psychotic symptoms generally or hostility in particular. The authors suggest that this apparently specific anti-aggressive effect of clozapine might be attributable to the serotonin pathway discussed in Chapter 3 above.

Beyond antipsychotics, the effectiveness of a huge range of other drugs listed has been tested in this literature. Anticonvulsants have been discussed above with regard to ASPD, but other groups include antidepressants, anxiolytics, anti-manics, beta-blockers, female sex hormones, CNS stimulants, hypnotics, antihypertensives and antihistamines. Not surprisingly given the discussion, above, there is little robust evidence for any of these medications as treatments for violence. Either no significant effect was demonstrated when they were tested, or the studies are too flawed to use the findings to come to a conclusion, or they are too dissimilar to combine meaningfully. This is not to say they have no value for treating either the propensity for violence or any pathologies underlying that propensity. It is rather the fragmented nature of the evidence base which obscures any potentially conclusive finding.

After atypical antipsychotics, the strongest evidence is for anticonvulsants, which achieve a marked reduction when the findings of eight trials are pooled. A third drug group which has not been discussed so far, the antidepressant selective serotonin reuptake inhibitors (SSRIs), have weaker support, with combined evidence from four trials indicating a relatively small reduction. This effect is statistically insignificant, so it cannot be assumed to be relevant much beyond the samples in which it was tested.

We noted above a distinction between pharmacology to treat a long-standing life-limiting tendency to be violent and medication used to manage imminent violence in an emergency situation. 'Rapid tranquillisation' (RT) is the standard procedure in some countries for medicating an acutely disturbed person when oral medication is not possible, and here there is some consensus, despite fragmentation, on the most effective approach which can be adopted. RT involves an injection into muscle tissue as noted above or, exceptionally, directly into veins. This highly risky procedure is a last resort when all other options for calming the person have been exhausted and there is a risk of real danger to other people. The literature in this area is again piecemeal and inconclusive even when narrowly focused on single drug types such as benzodiazepines (Zaman et al., 2017) or specific drugs such as haloperidol (Ostinelli et al., 2017). However, it is particularly important to have some guidance for clinicians in this potentially life-threatening situation despite the weakness of current evidence. The National Institute for Health and Care Excellence (2015) therefore recommends intramuscular lorazepam (an anxiolytic) or the combination of haloperidol and promethazine, both traditional antipsychotics. The choice of drug should take into account, where possible, an awareness of any relevant physical health problems such as heart disease and the person's previously stated preferences. After being subjected to this procedure, the person must be closely monitored to check for side effects. These pharmacological side effects can be fatal especially when, as often happens, the person is physically held down for the injection and for some time afterward. Such restraint, especially when 'face down', has been associated with several patient deaths within mental health services in the past two decades (Paterson et al., 2003; Ridley & Leitch, 2019).

8.7   Conclusion

Medication for violence has both great potential value in specific circumstances, but also many dangers. The power of medication to treat some symptoms of mental illness and distress is clearly demonstrated, and often these symptoms underlie individual acts of violence. The direct effect of some types of medication on violence propensity is more debatable, and its justification as part of a long-term anti-violence treatment programme is more difficult. Nevertheless, in some emergency situations it is the only intervention available to keep the patient and those around them safe. Patients subjected to enforced medication often endorse its use when looking back in time, and many have expressed a preference for it over the isolation of seclusion and what for some is the horror of mechanical restraint. The dangers of medication, however, are extensive. The potentially lethal side effects, the scope for personal violation and the financial contamination of motives for selling and using prescription drugs raise major questions not only about 'what works' but also about whose benefit it is for. The scope for drugs to be a 'quick fix' for behaviour with no underlying pathology but which is designated as problematic by those in authority within institutions such as hospitals and prisons has always been and remains a highly troubling issue. Now, beyond these institutions, the insertion of drugs for 'disruptive behaviour' into the emerging public health approach to violence raises acute questions about what is acceptable behaviour in everyday life and who is suitable for pharmacological treatment rather than psychosocial care or social empowerment. It should also not be used as an attempt to 'medicalise' the idea of public health and its application to the problem of violence. As noted before, public health is based on social science much more than pure medical science and its effects would be attenuated if it did not draw on this much wider and richer approach. Medicine must be only one of the many partners working on a public health strategy for violence reduction if such an approach has any chance of being effective in the years to come.

9 Psychosocial Interventions
The Unlearning of Violence

9.1 Introduction

Pharmacology clearly has its limitations and dangers as a tool for reducing violence, especially as part of a public health approach which casts its net so widely across many groups who are viewed as more or less challenging for society. Since it is clear from much of the evidence discussed in Part I of this book that many other factors beyond biology contribute to the tendencies some people have toward violence, it is vital to consider what psychological and social options are available with the potential to counter that tendency. These can be much more expensive to implement because of the need for greater human resources, and, however great the leverage, the intervention can ultimately be refused or ignored. In addition, they are often more difficult to test in terms of efficacy for reasons similar to those discussed in the previous chapter. However, it is psychosocial interventions which the WHO approach endorses most strongly in its 'best buy' guidance and which therefore need to be examined here in terms of practicality and effectiveness.

In Chapter 4 we considered the main psychological processes which lead individuals toward committing acts of aggression or violence. Does an understanding of these processes provide us with options for intervening and the prospect of reducing the likelihood of repeated, even persistent, violence (though that pattern is relatively rare)? To answer these questions, we need to shift our focus to research on the evaluation of psychosocial interventions designed to achieve such a goal. The psychological approach places great emphasis on how people learn to be violent because of the environment they grow up or live in; so at the broadest level, the emphasis of treatment here is on some form of unlearning or of acquiring alternative patterns of behaviour. There is now, after several decades of sustained scientific effort, a substantial volume of research on what can be done to reduce violence at the individual level. Numerous primary studies have accumulated and there is also a sizable number of reviews of the field, including the 'broad' review conducted by the present authors and others (discussed in the preceding Chapter 8). In this chapter we survey these reviews and highlight some key studies. The available research output can be classified in several ways. For example, studies could be grouped according to the kind of intervention that was tested, or the type of research design employed. We have grouped them here according to the participant population that was included in a study. As a context for making sense of the material to follow, we refer readers to the discussion of evaluation methodology included in Chapter 6.

Use of the research review methods described in Chapter 6 has had a major impact in the field of aggression, violence and criminal justice. As contrasted with the position that prevailed prior to (roughly) 1990, most practitioners and researchers now accept that criminal and other anti-social behaviour can be altered and reduced. Contrary to widespread penal practice, however, that goal is unlikely to be achieved through retribution, punishment, deterrence or other practices that are central to the decisions made by criminal courts. Rather, direct work with offenders, enabling them to acquire new skills or adopt fresh perspectives on their own behaviour, has been found to be more successful, and research on this has informed changes in practice in some countries or legal jurisdictions.

The basis for these revised expectations is the steadily growing volume of results from a large body of research, brought together in a series of reviews employing meta-analysis. By 2012, a total of 100 reviews of this area had been published (McGuire, 2013), and several more have appeared since then (Weisburd et al., 2016; Weisburd et al., 2017). The majority of these studies and the reviews of them were concerned with criminal recidivism in general, meaning any kind of reoffending, and only a portion examined rates of committing new offences of specific types. However, several have analysed the impact of interventions on rates of aggression or violent offending specifically. In contrast to what we might expect, where such data have been reported, meta-analysis has revealed a trend toward larger treatment effect sizes for offences of personal violence and sexual offences than for acquisitive or property crimes (theft, fraud, burglary, criminal damage) or for drug-related offences (Redondo et al., 2002). This difference also appeared in later large-scale follow-up studies of released prisoners who had attended rehabilitation programmes (Travers et al., 2014).

Prior to embarking on any form of intervention with individuals or groups, it is crucial to carry out some detailed *assessment* of the risk factors involved in violent or other antisocial acts. Staff members of the agencies carrying out this work, whether in youth or adult criminal justice or in forensic mental health services, need to interview those who have been convicted of offences. Interviews should include obtaining information on an individual's background, personal circumstances, history of previous problem behaviour, analysis of offences and of the factors operating at the time they were committed, and appraisal of attitudes, cognitions, emotions, levels of self-control, and other variables to assess the combination of them that led to aggressive or violent behaviour. There are numerous structured scales and other methods that can be used to gather further information for this purpose, and many agencies include risk assessment as an integral part of the process, using some of the approaches or inventories described in Chapter 7. In best practice, the results of such assessment would then be the basis for development of a case formulation which would enable practitioners to make informed judgements about allocation to different types of rehabilitation services, and the kinds of interventions most likely to succeed in reducing an individual's likelihood of acting violently on future occasions.

9.2   Reducing Violent Behaviour by Children and Young People

Prevention Programmes at Home and School

Some studies have been reported on work with children who from an early age have shown aggressive tendencies, before they have reached the age of criminal responsibility and are not yet liable to arrest or court proceedings. Antisocial behaviour at an early age is of concern in itself, and also because it can be a forerunner of later delinquency and other problems. Sometimes this work is carried out directly within families, or in child guidance or other care centres. Other interventions have been developed for use in school settings, in attempts to address aggression in school itself, such as fights or bullying. Most studies report multiple outcome measures, for example observations of child behaviour by researchers or teachers, and parents' reports of aggression at home.

Interventions carried out in the home often involve methods such as *behavioural parent training* (BPT). Essentially, the objective of this is to avoid cycles of responding to children that make aggression or other problem behaviour more likely, in effect reversing the coercive family learning process described in Chapter 4 and enabling parents to adopt a different approach to managing their children. Serketich and Dumas (1996) reviewed a set of twenty-six studies of this, eighteen employing random assignment, targeting aggression and related problem behaviour in children on average aged six. The mean effect size for child aggression and related behaviour was 0.86 after 9.5 sessions of training. Using

Cohen's rule of thumb, this is a fairly large effect, but it is based only on changes shortly after the training, as the number of studies reporting follow-up data was not sufficient for analysis.

Positive but weaker effects were reported by Kaminski et al. (2008). Their review of seventy-seven studies addressing a range of child problems included forty-eight concerned with aggression, non-compliance, and hyperactivity, producing a lower mean effect size of 0.25, but the effect for aggression was not reported separately. In contrast, Dretzke et al. (2009) reported a meta-analysis of fifty-seven controlled trials of parenting programmes in families where children had conduct problems. Some compared parent training with no treatment, others with a different type of treatment. The mean effect size here was moderate (0.67) in favour of the intervention.

McCart et al. (2006) compared the relative effect sizes reported in forty-one studies of BPT and thirty of cognitive behavioural therapies (CBT) in reducing aggression and other antisocial behaviour among children and young people across a wide spread of ages up to eighteen. The outcome variables recorded were of physical or verbal aggression or delinquency, and it should be noted that the children in the BPT studies were younger (average age five to six years) than those provided with CBT (eleven to twelve years). Across the full set of studies, the immediate post-treatment mean effect sizes were 0.47 and 0.35 for BPT and CBT, respectively. In the thirteen CBT studies for which longer term follow-up data could be analysed, there was a mean effect size of +0.31 over an average follow-up period of eight months. These are clearly smaller effects than in the other two reviews above, most likely due to the higher average age of the children.

Occasionally, as mentioned earlier, researchers go one step further and carry out a larger-scale task by integrating results not of a series of primary studies but of a collection of reviews. Farrington et al. (2017) have reported an overview of this kind, assembling findings from a total of fifty systematic reviews of the field of *developmental prevention*. This refers to 'community-based programs designed to prevent antisocial behaviour, targeted on children and adolescents, and aiming to change individual, family, or school risk factors' (p. 91). The interventions surveyed included a wide range of services from child skills training to home visiting, foster care arrangements and school-based initiatives. In this review the authors reported the overall effect size as an *odds ratio*, which compares the relative rates of successful and unsuccessful outcomes in experimental and control groups, respectively. The resultant figure was 1.46, which corresponds to a reduction in aggression by one-quarter in those who received interventions as compared to those who did not. As the authors conclude, 'this is not a small effect' (p. 102).

School-based interventions. Beyond the home, there have been numerous studies of interventions carried out in schools, often with a range of targets including improvements in health, reducing substance abuse, or improving relationship skills. Some, however, have examined aggression and violence. Wilson and Lipsey (2007) and Wilson et al. (2003) reviewed findings from 249 studies of interventions designed to reduce aggressive and disruptive behaviour in schools. The selected studies were carried out with participant samples ranging from pre-school to the age of eighteen. Of the comparisons possible between experimental and control groups, just over 40% were derived from randomised designs. Interventions included behavioural strategies, counselling, social skills training programmes, anger management and cognitively based methods. The mean effect size for universal, school-wide interventions at the primary prevention level was 0.21 in favour of experimental groups, and for specifically targeted interventions focused on those involved in bullying it was slightly higher at 0.29. The corresponding figure for nonrandomised designs was +0.16. While these are statistically small effects on the scale proposed by Cohen, 'effect sizes of 0.21 and 0.29 represent reductions from a base rate prevalence of 20% to about 15% and 13%, respectively, that is, 25–33% reductions. The programs of above average effectiveness, of course, produce even larger decreases' (Wilson and Lipsey, 2007, p. S141). Primary prevention through population-wide methods may be likely to have smaller effects given the 'scatter gun' nature of the approach.

Anti-bullying programmes. Within school-based studies, there has been particular interest in the evaluation of anti-bullying programmes (ABPs) and other approaches to tackling this difficulty. Bullying is a form of violence itself and can also be a predictor of later adult violence, so interventions can combine both secondary and tertiary prevention. ABPs typically consist of sessions of skills training provided to those who have been involved in bullying, but in other instances, again, whole-school or 'universal' strategies are employed, giving messages to all students regarding non-aggressive behaviour and values. There has been a mainly positive, but mixed, pattern of findings from reviews of this field. Cantone et al. (2015) reviewed seventeen RCTs of these interventions and found that any positive effects were short-term with no evidence of long-term gains. Better effects were found for universal, whole-school interventions than for those with focused or different and separate components targeting perpetrators themselves. Jiminéz-Barbero et al. (2012) analysed the findings of five other reviews and twenty-seven primary studies on ABPs with a mixture of research designs, separating the latter into four groups according to the methodological quality of the evaluation. In all four categories there was a similar pattern of beneficial effects. Studies covered the full school age range. There were similar patterns of findings across all evidence levels in relation to changes in attitudes, beliefs and behaviours and in the frequency of violent conduct. In a later review of fourteen high-quality RCTs, Jiminéz-Barbero et al. (2016) found a small mean effect size of −0.12 favouring intervention, with programmes that lasted less than a year (as compared with those of longer duration) and those that focused on children younger than ten having larger effects (0.24 and 0.17, respectively). Lee et al. (2015) found thirteen studies with an aggregate sample of 19,619, and reported a mean effect size supporting interventions of −0.15. No interventions had negative effects, but the mean effect size was again comparatively small. Interventions focused on emotional control and peer counselling, and establishing school-wide policies on bullying emerged with larger effect sizes than other approaches. In the largest review of this kind, Ttofi and Farrington (2011) reported a meta-analysis of forty-four studies of ABPs. This review found an overall effect size (also an *odds ratio*) of 1.36 for bullying and 1.29 for victimisation. This corresponds to an overall reduction of 17–23% in bullying events in experimental as compared with control samples. The review provides extensive detail on features of the more effective interventions, and the authors made a number of recommendations, including the establishment of a system of accreditation or quality control process for ABPs. A review by Yeager et al. (2015) of the effects of nineteen studies of the same ABP when administered to different age groups revealed that effect sizes are lower for older adolescents. This may potentially be because, as habits of aggressiveness become more practised, they become more entrenched and less amenable to change.

Prevention of other school violence. Aggression and violence in schools can also take other forms, including fights, and schools sometimes collaborate with police and justice agencies in efforts to pre-empt involvement in violent delinquency, including the formation of gangs. Alford and Derzon (2012), reviewed twenty-four studies of programmes with these objectives, all of which showed some positive effect on reduction of violence or antisocial behaviour. The mean effect sizes obtained were all small: for physical aggression 0.26, antisocial behaviour 0.15, aggressive/disruptive behaviour 0.12, and for general delinquent behaviour a lower figure of +0.08. T. N. Barnes et al. (2014) reported a meta-analysis of twenty-five studies and found a mean effect size across all studies of 0.23 favouring interventions: in 74% of the studies, aggression was lower after treatment. Obviously, this still leaves a quarter with no beneficial effects, but with regard to the spread of interventions this is a positive overall outcome. This study reported a separate estimate of the strength of effects by computing a *file drawer number*. In meta-analysis, this figure (sometimes called the *fail-safe number*) is an estimate of how many unpublished studies with zero effect sizes would be necessary to overturn the observed effect size found in the published studies that have been located and reviewed. In Barnes et al.'s review of twenty-five studies, the figure was 224, suggesting the obtained effect is robust and meaningful.

In a higher-level overview, Matjasko et al. (2012) synthesised findings from fifteen systematic reviews and thirty-seven meta-analyses on youth violence prevention programmes, covering a wide spectrum of approaches that included family-based, school-based and community-based interventions alongside others that were treatment-specific, that is, focused on those who had committed violence. These authors did not compute mean effect sizes across the reviews, given the variety of studies they encompassed, but summarised outcomes in terms of proportions of effects in the ranges specified by Cohen (1988). Among the family-centred reviews, two found strong effects, nine moderate effects, and three weak effects, although all were in favour of the intervention. Evaluations of treatment-specific interventions had on average moderate effects; and most reviews of school-based programmes reported moderate to strong effects on youth violence-related outcomes. In all but three of the fifty-two reviews, studies with stronger designs that incorporated random allocation had larger effects, an outcome usually taken as an indicator that we can have more confidence in the pattern of findings. In a more recent review, Lester et al. (2017) tabulated results from thirty-one studies of interventions to reduce peer aggression in schools, and found that a majority of studies, especially those of 'discrete' as compared with 'whole school' programmes, reported positive effects, though no mean effect size was given. In contrast, and perhaps surprisingly, a meta-analysis of 'positive youth development' interventions found no positive effects on violence prevention. This strategy places emphasis on young people's strengths and assets, as opposed to what is generally called a 'risk reduction' approach. Melendez-Torres et al. (2016) found three RCTs of this type of intervention, but the mean effect size was not significantly different from zero.

A meta-analysis by Sawyer et al. (2015) of sixty-six studies of long-term prevention or therapeutic programmes produced more positive results. Across all the studies and combining different sets of outcome variables there was a mean effect size of +0.31 supporting interventions. The mean effect size for official records of violence was higher at +0.42, while that for parental reports of aggression was lower at +0.16. There were no differences in observed effects between randomised and non-randomised evaluation studies.

A few reviews have brought together studies of interventions delivered in schools and designed to reduce dating, sexual and relationship violence among young people. De La Rue et al. (2014) located twenty-three studies reporting evaluations of programmes designed for this purpose, based in American middle or high schools. There were significant gains reported immediately at post-test in knowledge, altered attitudes and reduced acceptance of rape myths, beliefs that are supportive of male sexual aggression. Only four studies reported longer term follow-up information, but all of these found a significant reduction in dating violence. There have been two reviews of the effectiveness of early prevention of violence in close relationships, attempting to avoid any such pattern before it begins. Whitaker et al. (2013) reviewed studies of schools-based preventive programmes designed for this purpose. De Koker et al. (2014) reviewed nine controlled trials from the United States, Canada and South Africa on prevention programmes for adolescents, designed to reduce later risks of partner violence, as either a perpetrator (likelihood of assaulting a partner) or a victim (preparedness to report being assaulted). While some of these methods were unsuccessful, several had significant beneficial effects, over some long-term follow-up periods.

Overall, while there are variations in the quality of research, the majority of the studies encompassed in reviews of this area employ acceptable designs and have reported positive results. There is sufficient evidence amassed to conclude that aggression and violence with these populations and at these age ranges can be reduced on average by approximately one-quarter to one-third. That scale of outcome is both significant in statistical terms, and meaningful in practical terms.

Interventions with Young People in the Justice System

The research discussed so far has primarily been concerned with interventions provided in homes, schools or other community settings, mainly with young people who have not been arrested or convicted. However, there has also been a substantial amount of research conducted with young people who have already broken the law and have been given community or custodial sentences. As in other contexts, much of the research has reported data on delinquency in general, but a proportion of it has specifically addressed the problem of violent offending.

Lipsey and Wilson (1998) reviewed 200 studies of young people in the age range twelve to twenty who had committed serious offences including violence; eighty-three of these studies were conducted in institutional settings and 117 in the community. Several types of intervention were found to be effective, with programmes in the most consistently effective category having an average impact in reducing recidivism of 40% in community settings and 30% in custodial settings (Lipsey and Wilson 1998). The largest and most consistent effects were for structured counselling (mean effect size +0.46), interpersonal skills training (+0.44), behavioural programmes (+0.42), and teaching family homes (+0.39), in which children are fostered by specially trained parent figures. While slightly different patterns emerged regarding which interventions worked better in community as compared with institutional settings, there are many examples of methods effective in both. Garrido and Morales (2007) later reviewed a further seventeen studies with a cumulative sample size of 6,658, followed up over a median of eighteen months. Their results were broadly similar to those of Lipsey and Wilson, with larger effect sizes relating to more serious types of offence. Thus although the average effect sizes in these studies were moderate in Cohen's terms, they included young people classed as 'chronic' and 'prolific' offenders. As such groups are often responsible for a high proportion of reported crimes, evidence for the benefit of working with them effectively is of considerable practical value.

The broad trend across the studies and reviews considered so far is for there to be somewhat larger effects with younger age groups. This might be expected on the basis that the earlier it is possible to intervene to halt the learning of aggression (or, for that matter, avert most kinds of problem), the likelier it is that we will succeed in doing so. Going against this, however, Limbos et al. (2007) reported a review of forty-one studies and found that the most successful outcomes were actually obtained in tertiary prevention settings. It is worth noting that some of the studies of primary prevention subsumed in their review evaluated a very wide variety of initiatives, such as the use of school-based metal detectors or a martial arts training programme, rather than programmes focused on interactions in families. Within the true tertiary category there were eleven studies, of which eight reported positive outcomes. Only two of these studies involved randomised controlled trials, but both showed positive results of interventions.

9.3   Reducing Violence by Adult Offenders

Turning to work with psychological interventions to reduce violence by adults, there are fewer studies and reviews than of children and youths in families and schools. Nevertheless, a substantial volume of work has been reported in this field and some important conclusions can be drawn. One of the earliest reviews of the effect of interventions on violent reoffending was that of Dowden and Andrews (2000), who integrated results from a series of thirty-four evaluations of interventions to reduce violence. The target offences included general violence, sexual violence, and domestic assaults. Approximately 70% of the studies focused primarily on work with adults. The overall mean effect size was quite low, but there was a sizable spread among the results: effect sizes ranged from a low of 0.22 to a high of +0.63. The effect size for interventions based on the set of principles defined by the *risk-need-responsivity* (RNR) model (Bonta and Andrews, 2017) was 0.12. This corresponds to recidivism rates of 44% for experimental and 56% for control groups. The greater the number of risk-related ('criminogenic') needs that were targeted in interventions, the larger the observed effect size, with a correlation between the two of 0.69. Thus, while some interventions clearly do not work, and some, such as 'Scared Straight' programmes in which young offenders are warned by adults with long criminal careers about the dangers of involvement in crime, can even be harmful (Petrosino et al., 2000), others yield far better results and are associated with significant reductions in subsequent violence.

In an overview of more recent work, McGuire (2017) located a total of twenty-seven systematic reviews or meta-analyses of research on 'what works' to reduce adult violence, all published in the period 2007–2016. These fell into three broad categories. The first included reviews of interventions organised in structured programmatic form, addressing the development of self-control or acquiring other skills for avoiding violence. These were used mainly in prisons or probation services. The second comprised interventions for reducing intimate partner violence (IPV), incorporating methods influenced by feminist theory in criminology, but often containing skills-training and other cognitive behavioural components. These were predominantly delivered in the community. The third consisted of treatment services for offenders with diagnosed mental disorders, usually provided in secure psychiatric units or other forensic mental health settings, or in some cases as part of community-based treatment and supervision.

Skills-Training and Related Methods

Jolliffe and Farrington (2009) reviewed data from a series of twelve studies of interventions with adult male violent offenders. The intervention methods evaluated included anger control training, intensive self-management training, a multi-modal skills programme, electronic monitoring and other specially devised approaches. Nine studies with a conjoint sample of 1,893 offenders were included in a meta-analysis. The average effect size obtained was rather low: a reduction in recidivism of 6–7%, equivalent to a drop from a 50% reconviction rate in comparison groups to 43% in treatment groups. Use of anger control methods, cognitive skills training, role-play and relapse prevention methods were found, in combination, to yield the largest outcome effects. These are more modest changes than for offending in general, but the outcomes are nevertheless both statistically significant and meaningful in practical terms, especially, as in the Lipsey and Wilson (1998) review, if attention is directed toward more high-frequency offenders.

In terms of research with adult offenders, reactive aggression, that which follows directly from feelings of anger, hostility or other strong emotion, which are discharged in response to threat or provocation, has received much more attention than the instrumental type. Several reviews have examined the effectiveness of *anger control training*, a therapeutic intervention specifically designed to help individuals reduce angry reactions which they are finding difficult to control (Novaco, 2013). Saini (2009) reported the most extensive review to date of the effectiveness of anger treatment, locating ninety-six studies, and compared outcomes of several different approaches to anger treatment. The overall average effect size was quite large, a standardized mean difference of 0.76. The strongest effect size (1.40) was for psychodynamic therapy, though this was based on just two studies. Other mean effects ranged from psychoeducational treatment (0.37) to multicomponent programmes (0.93). The average length of follow-up in these studies, however, was quite short, extending over only a few weeks, with limited evidence of durability of effects beyond this. Anger control training has been a widely used strategy for attempting to reduce aggression, and there are also several reviews dealing with its use in working with people with intellectual disabilities (Hamelin et al., 2013; Nicoll et al., 2013). Vereenooghe and Langdon (2013) reported that anger management produced the largest positive effect size of any of the treatments tested with this group, with a large standardised mean difference of 0.82.

In most of these studies, however, the outcome variable was an individual's own report of their experienced anger, which is clearly open to bias. To redress this limitation, other studies have included observational reports or incident records. Novaco and Taylor (2015) found evidence of significant reductions in numbers of violent incidents among people with intellectual difficulties at a twelve-month follow-up, and found this outcome was correlated with changes in mediating factors such as reported anger. This study needs to be interpreted with caution as it did not contain an untreated comparison sample, but a small number of studies reviewed by Ali et al. (2015) with comparator groups did also report positive outcomes.

Of course, reported success in reducing anger does not necessarily translate into success in reducing violent offending, limiting the conclusions that can be drawn for present purposes. The latter issue of reduced offending among adults was examined by Henwood et al. (2015), who reviewed research on cognitive behavioural methods of anger management. They found fourteen outcomes, divided equally between case-control and before-and-after studies, among which six related to violent recidivism. The mean effect size, reported as an odds ratio, was 0.72. This corresponds to a 28% reduction in risk of reconviction for a violent offence. The possibility of selection bias in some studies and variations in the quality of provision of interventions, however, make it difficult to draw unequivocal conclusions about the methods' effectiveness.

Young adults in the age range of eighteen to twenty-five are often considered to be a particularly difficult group to engage in treatment. McGuire (2015) reviewed a series of ten studies of work with this group, several of which reported positive outcomes on general recidivism. With regard to violent reoffending, Braga et al. (2009), for instance, evaluated the *Boston Re-entry Initiative*, which involved the preparation of specially designed release plans for prison inmates, organised through a multi-agency panel. This was formed to address the needs of young adult males classified as 'high risk', three-quarters of whom had two previous convictions for violence. They were assigned caseworkers, attended a range of programmes, were met on release and mentored on return to the community. Relative to an untreated comparison group, there was a statistically significant 32% reduction in overall arrests and a 37% reduction in arrests for violence.

One of the most successful interventions used to date in addressing serious violent crime among young adults is a strategy with several components loosely called 'pulling levers'. This emerged from a pilot project known as *Operation Ceasefire*, a problem-oriented policing initiative concerning gang-related gun homicides committed by youths aged under twenty-four years in Boston (Braga et al., 2001). Police communicated directly with offender groups and made clear to them that there would be swift and overwhelming responses to shootings that would disrupt gangs' other illegal activities. This would be accompanied by additional law-enforcement consequences including stiffer plea bargains and sentences, but also by providing more opportunities of other kinds, for example making more community services available to targeted offenders. The approach was disseminated across several other US cities.

A meta-analysis found a medium to large mean effect size of 0.60 across studies in ten locations, representing a significant drop in key target outcomes, including homicide rates (Braga and Weisburd, 2015).

As discussed in previous chapters, another factor often associated with violent offences is the excessive consumption of alcohol. Attempts to address the relationship between these two problems have taken a variety of forms. McGuire (2018) located studies of interventions which addressed the combined problems of alcohol (or other substance misuse) and violence committed against close or intimate partners. Effective interventions, evaluated using either RCTs or quasi-experimental designs, included *behavioural couples therapy* (Schumm et al., 2009) and a combined *substance abuse/domestic violence programme* (SADV; Scott and Easton, 2010). Both of these combinations had a significant impact in reducing partner violence as reported by both perpetrators and victims.

Two recent meta-analyses provide further confirmation of the effect of structured, mainly skill-centred rehabilitation programmes in reducing rates of violent reoffending by adults. Gannon et al. (2019) undertook a literature review with the aim of discerning whether 'specialised' rehabilitation programmes designed for those who had committed specific types of crime – violent assaults, sexual offences or domestic violence – had an impact in reducing rates of those types of offences. They also tested for any impact on recidivism rates in general. Their review located sixty-eight studies with a total sample of 55,604 offenders. Over an average follow-up period of just over five years (sixty-six months) there was a significant reduction in 'offence-specific recidivism' of 24.3% for violent offences, although this was based on only four studies. The respective results in other areas were 32.6% for sexual offending (forty-four studies), and 36% in domestic violence (fourteen studies). Across all the studies combined, there was a relative decrease of 33.3% in general reoffending rates.

This review, however, poses some problems of interpretation. Very few of the identified studies employed random assignment, and in many others the membership of the comparison group differed in some important ways from those in the experimental condition. There was thus a marked risk of bias in the findings. The authors employed intention-to-treat (ITT) analysis when calculating effect sizes: this involves retaining dropouts from treatment in the assigned experimental group, and is regarded as a robust analytic strategy. But it is not stated in what proportion of the studies such an analysis was used. While the findings are encouraging, the patterning of them needs to be interpreted with some caution.

Clearer results emerged from a review by Papalia et al. (2019), focused solely on offenders convicted of violence and imprisoned as a result. These authors evaluated the effects of intervention programmes both on institutional misconduct and violence while still in custody, and on rates of violent and non-violent recidivism following release. Papalia et al. located twenty-seven studies with a cumulative sample of 7,062 violent offenders, and here checks were conducted as to the equivalence of treatment and comparison groups. The overall effect on general prison misconduct was non-significant; but for studies of prison violence four out of five studies showed beneficial effects. Concerning recidivism after release, on the other hand, there were positive effects on both violent and non-violent recidivism. Within the nineteen studies that analysed violent reoffending, 'the odds of violent recidivism were 31% lower among treated offenders relative to comparison offenders' (Papalia et al., 2019, p. 14). The corresponding figure for non-violent recidivism was a reduction of 35%. There was evidence of larger outcome effects for 'multi-modal' interventions that contained eight to ten treatment components, in other words that targeted several different types of risk factors, than for those with fewer components. These two reviews add further evidence in support of the proposal that violence can be reduced among adult offenders.

Intimate Partner Violence (IPV)

There is now considerable evidence that the prevalence rate of violence between close partners (which in different sources is given different names, including domestic abuse, marital violence or spousal abuse) is far higher than previously believed (Alhabib et al., 2010). A large proportion of it continues to be unreported, primarily because of victims' fears of the consequences of seeking help. This has proved to be a more difficult area in which to secure changes in those who perpetrate such violence, but some positive findings have been reported.

One difficulty is that the longest-established and most widely used approach to working with perpetrators of domestic abuse has not emerged favourably from evaluation research. The *Duluth model* was developed as part of an interagency domestic violence prevention service in Minnesota in the 1980s. This draws fundamentally on an analysis of the exercise of power and control in close relationships, using concepts from feminist theory, but also incorporates some skills-training elements (Bowen, 2011). Other approaches place greater emphasis on the latter methods of skill acquisition.

Nevertheless, some positive findings have been obtained in this area. Feder et al. (2008) examined effects obtained across ten studies of court-mandated 'batterer intervention' programmes. They located four randomized controlled trials and six quasi-experimental evaluations – studies in which treatment and comparison groups are not allocated randomly – of psychoeducational or cognitive behavioural programmes. The mean effect size obtained from the RCTs was +0.26, a small but statistically significant result; results from the quasi-experimental studies were more varied. However, the participants in these studies were assessed as being at low risk of reoffending. Miller et al. (2013) conducted a meta-analysis of nine intervention studies producing eleven effect sizes. In this review, six evaluations of Duluth-model programmes had an average effect size close to zero. But evaluations of four other types of programme showed better results, with a mean effect of a 33% reduction in IPV recidivism.

In contrast, reviews of other studies drew less optimistic conclusions. Intervention programmes in this area often have high levels of attrition ('drop-out'; Jewell and Wormith, 2010) and their outcome effects have been portrayed as 'meagre' (Stover et al., 2009). In a systematic review, Smedslund et al. (2011) located six studies of cognitive behavioural therapy for physically abusive men, but the observed mean effect size was small and the results were uneven.

The difficulty in securing stronger and more consistent effects in this area is most probably a result of the numerous factors that are involved in the origins and maintenance of this particular problem. In the most widely accepted model of causal factors, this type of violence is like other types, thought to be influenced by variables on four different levels: society/cultural, community, relational and individual, reflecting the ecological model we set out in Chapter 1 (Beyer et al., 2015; Heise, 1998). Results of other reviews studies suggest that if interventions can be directed toward 'turning points' in individuals' motivations, and that if the reasons for attrition can be more fully understood, better results could be achieved (Sheehan et al., 2012). Overall, therefore, although there is no sizable body of findings that permits the drawing of clear conclusions on this area, there have been positive outcomes in several studies and notwithstanding some weaknesses in the data, the findings reported by Gannon et al. (2019), outlined above, are also of note. It is certainly not the case that perpetrators of partner violence are immune to treatment efforts.

9.4   Reducing Violence by Offenders with Mental Disorders

In this area of research, given the target population and the settings in which it is conducted, outcome variables are often aspects of mental health and clinical progress rather than violent behaviour per se. This overlap was discussed above in Chapter 8 when looking at pharmaco-logical treatments which targeted either symptoms or violent behaviour. However, several reviews of psychological interventions have located studies that included measurement of changes in aggression or violence or in factors closely associated with them.

Martin et al. (2012) undertook a review of interventions for offenders with major mental illnesses such as psychotic disorders. They meta-analysed outcome effects from a set of twenty-five studies with a com-bined sample size of 15,678 participants. The mean effect size on crim-inal justice outcomes at +0.19 was positive but small. There were significant effects on rates of arrest, time spent in prison, time lapsed before failure, and violent crime, although the impact on reconviction fell just below statistical significance.

Morgan et al. (2012) carried out a similar review of psychological treatment for offenders, analysing studies that addressed either criminal behaviour outcomes, mental illness, or both. Participants in the studies they reviewed had been diagnosed with schizophrenia, bipolar disorder or major depressive disorder. However only four of the twenty-six studies they located provided data on criminal recidivism, yielding a small mean effect size of +0.11. This is very close to the average effect size reported in the general offender treatment–outcome research in the absence of mental disorder. Among those four studies, however, there was a wide range of effects. Three studies reported positive effect sizes, while the fourth showed a large negative result.

The broad review we conducted and discussed in Chapter 8 (Hock-enhull et al., 2012) included patients diagnosed with major mental disorders who were also assessed as presenting a high risk of engaging in violent behaviour. Despite a wide-ranging literature search, only seven RCTs of psychologically based interventions were found. All were limited to evaluating short-term changes such as improvements in anger control, measured by psychometric or observational rating scales. The mean odds ratio of 0.61 in favour of intervention shows there was a practically meaningful decrease in problems and a clear treatment effect. However, the focus on intermediate variables rather than behavioural outcomes such as reduced rates of assault means we cannot conclude violence rates would have fallen as a result.

Ross et al. (2013) carried out a systematic review of ten studies testing interventions to reduce aggressive behaviour in forensic settings. Among them, two were RCTs, six were pre-post studies (no comparator sample) and two were small case series designs. Given the variety of designs employed, coupled with a mixture of outcome variables, it is difficult to detect clear trends among their results. However, eight of the located studies reported reductions in physical aggression, although only one found a drop in violent recidivism at follow-up.

Frazier and Vela (2014) reported a review of the effectiveness of dialectical behaviour therapy (DBT), which has been widely used in work with individuals who have been diagnosed with borderline personality disorder. These authors analysed twelve studies of the impact of DBT on anger and aggression, seven of which were RCTs. No mean effect size was computed, but ten of the studies reported significant reductions on measures of anger or aggressive behaviour, two of them also finding reductions in violent disciplinary infractions in prisons.

As noted earlier, research in the field of mental healthcare is generally more concerned with clinical or therapeutic change, symptom reduction and restoration of healthy functioning, rather than with violence. There is often a larger emphasis on recording and measuring what are called mediating variables such as levels of anger, anxiety and hostility, and it is less common for data to be gathered on more pertinent outcomes such as violent rearrest. The reviews described do find evidence that clinical variables are influenced by treatment, and some have also found effects in terms of aggression and violence. Alongside these, there is evidence from follow-up studies of discharged patients of reductions in rates of both rearrest and rehospitalisation as a result of new offences of a violent nature. Studies pertaining to this have been collated by McGuire and Duff (2018).

In summary, while many questions remain to be answered concerning the potential for violence prevention among children, young people and adults, there is mounting evidence of the possibility of securing reductions in aggression and violence, in some cases with groups that have been previously considered resistant to change or whose problems were believed to be intractable. Claims for the benefits of this should not be overstated, but the pattern of results does not support the view that violence is a fixed and irremediable feature even of those who have frequently resorted to the use of it.

9.5   Methodological Challenges in Researching Psychosocial Interventions

As with the review of evidence for medication effectiveness, it is important to acknowledge the limitations of any claims for effectiveness in the literature on psychological interventions. The problem of evidence fragmentation is not in any way restricted just to drug trials. In fact, it is even more difficult to draw conclusions about which psychological interventions might be effective for violent behaviour. This is because of the much greater complexity and the subjectivity of the key ingredients, the frequent variability in quality of the implementation, the difficulty of 'blinding' people with a placebo equivalent so they do not change their behaviour based on their expectations, and the consequent potential ambiguity in interpretation of the findings. Drugs of the same type are, by design, functionally identical, and while the physiology of the person ingesting them will introduce some variability, it is not of the same order as that encountered at the psychological and social levels. Some psychosocial programme manuals which therapists use to plan and conduct each session with a client are extremely detailed and prescriptive in order to reduce this subjectivity. The challenges of testing complex interventions (Craig et al., 2013) such as psychological and social programmes have been recognised, and special research designs are being developed to capture the effects of as many facets as possible in a single study. Explicit protocols for implementing, say, twelve sessions of cognitive anger management therapy, checklists to ensure that therapists and researchers stick to 'the script', and video monitoring of the quality of delivery can also help to improve the robustness of evaluations (McMurran and Duggan, 2005).

Nevertheless, the pooling of results from a group of studies in meta-analysis to conclude 'what works' is severely hampered by this problem of comparability. Applying the five study selection criteria listed in Chapter 8 for RCTs of antipsychotic medication to cognitive behavioural interventions for sex offenders and domestic violence perpetrators captured in the broad review (Hockenhull et al., 2012) produces four studies that are on the face of it comparable (Hockenhull et al., 2015). However, one of the sex offender programmes had up to seventy-five two-hour sessions over an unspecified period, while another had a forty-five-week assessment and treatment programme of unspecified length. The two other studies had no details at all on the intervention. In comparison, the drug trials in the previous example at least had clearly specified dosages and frequency of treatment in a way that minimises this source of variability. Notwithstanding these limitations, there are several reviews of the effectiveness of some specific types of intervention. As an example, Lipsey et al. (2007) reported a meta-analysis of fifty-eight studies of the impact of cognitive behavioural programmes on offence recidivism.

9.6   Psychopathy, Treatment Resistance, and Responsiveness

Within the perhaps most daunting category of research on offenders with mental illness there are several studies concerned with individuals who are regarded as either 'treatment resistant' or even as virtually 'untreatable', in that it appears difficult to involve them in any therapeutic or other constructive activities, or that the process of doing so meets with little or no success. Individuals certainly vary in their responsiveness to conscious efforts designed to help or induce them to change. Some flatly reject any such attempt. Others begin to engage but stop participating before the process is complete. Still others appear to benefit during treatment, but afterward show no change in their behaviour.

Among younger offenders, there is a small number who have been so badly damaged by their developmental experiences that even in early adolescence they already appear beyond reach, and are very challenging to work with. But there is evidence of effective treatment for even the most troubled of them, including those who have been assessed as showing features of 'psychopathic disorder' at an early age. The Mendota Juvenile Treatment Center in Wisconsin was reserved for young people with histories of repeated violence, who already had several convictions by the age of fourteen and were considered unmanageable in other institutions. Rather than imposing a high level of control, the Center implemented a process of 'decompression' to address the 'cycle of defiance' that had become instilled in these young people, followed by delivery of structured training programmes. In a four-year follow-up evaluation, researchers found a highly significant reduction in violent reoffending among Mendota youths. Comparing 101 in the treatment cohort with 147 untreated youths, their respective violent recidivism rates were 23% and 44%, and rate of violent felonies 18% and 37%, respectively (Caldwell et al., 2007). The Mendota regime was also found to be economically efficient, yielding a benefit–cost ratio of 7:1 (Caldwell et al., 2006). So, for every dollar spent on implementing the intervention, seven dollars were saved by reducing the effects of antisocial behaviour.

Among adults, individuals with similar features are also often regarded as having intractable problems. This is believed to apply to those who have been diagnosed with antisocial or dissocial personality disorder (as classified by the DSM or ICD psychiatric systems), but more so to those assessed as showing features of the more severe pattern classed as 'psychopathic', according to criteria proposed by Hare (1996 Hare and Neumann, 2008). There has been long-standing scepticism regarding the prospect of achieving any positive treatment effects with this group.

However, views even on this apparent 'hard-wired' violence may be gradually changing. While personality disorders have often been regarded as representing a separate type or category, there is an expanding evidence base to the effect that they are better conceptualised as describing persons who are toward one end of a continuum of functioning (Walters et al., 2015, 2016). In this respect, their development, including the emergence of features of psychopathy, can be explained in terms of the same processes that operate in normal development (Shiner, 2009). With reference to treatment, Reidy et al. (2013) have suggested that 'a specifically and carefully crafted intervention may be effective in reducing violence by psychopathic individuals' (p. 536), while Polaschek and Daly (2013) identified a developing consensus that such an intervention can be devised. Evidence supporting that contention remains provisional, however, and this is a very daunting area in which to carry out research; hence the number of studies reported is relatively small.

For example, Skeem et al. (2002) analysed the progress of 871 patients from the MacArthur Violence Risk Assessment Study, who were supervised in a community setting. Within the study population, seventy-two were classed as 'psychopathic' and 195 as 'potentially psychopathic'. Those designated as psychopaths who had attended seven or more sessions were 3.5 times less likely to commit violent offences than those who attended fewer sessions, and those designated as potentially psychopathic were 2.5 times less likely. These patterns held with several other potentially influential variables controlled. Doren and Yates (2008) investigated the relationships between psychopathic personality and sexual offending. In a systematic review they located ten studies of this connection, based on work carried out at four treatment centres. Despite the widespread impression that psychopathic sex offenders are impossible to treat, analysis of data sets in the located studies showed there was a proportion of many participant samples who had responded constructively to intervention. Among those assessed as 'psychopathic', a proportion had taken part in treatment and had shown evidence of treatment progress. Their rate of recidivism then became comparable to that of non-psychopathic individuals. Wong and his colleagues (2012; Olver and Wong, 2013) reported evidence from evaluation of the Clearwater programme, a group-based intervention for high-risk sexual offenders lasting approximately eight months, delivered in a secure psychiatric centre. A proportion of participants were classed as 'psychopathic'. Yet among this group, 73% completed treatment, and following release they had a reoffending rate one-third lower than those who did not (60.6% versus 91.7%). All these findings are at odds with the view that this group is uniformly unsusceptible to treatment and change.

9.7   Conclusion

Surveying the research results that have been discussed in this chapter, we suggest that considerable evidence has now amassed to the effect that rates of aggressive conduct or violent crime can be reduced even among those who have acted repeatedly in this way. In drawing mainly positive conclusions from the research summarised above, we are not seeking to underestimate the difficulties that continue to beset this field. As noted in Chapter 8, although the volume of research done has been substantial, the literature remains highly fragmented. When closely examined, the number of studies that address any single question can prove to be disappointingly small, for example in using high-quality research designs, including comparable study populations or having other features that facilitate the drawing of sound conclusions (Hockenhull et al., 2015). When summarising this area, therefore, a first caveat to bear in mind is that the evidence base, while appearing extensive, remains weak and tentative in some crucial respects. None of that, however, undermines the principal conclusion that sufficient evidence has accumulated to tentatively support efforts to 'unlearn' violence and to contradict the view that violent behaviour is irreversible.

With respect to theory, there are still numerous unanswered questions over the mechanisms of change that are activated when individuals who have established patterns of reacting violently, or who use violence as a means of solving problems, reduce their rate of doing so or even refrain from doing so entirely. Walker et al. (2013) reviewed research on factors associated with desistance from violence. They identified the principal processes operating within this as being age and maturational growth, parts of which may be attributable to alterations in levels of neurotransmitters, changes in levels of 'informal social control' during different phases of life and development of different kinds of relationships, and reductions in 'criminal propensity' due to gradual changes in self-perception over time. These are plausible explanations and probably all those processes are involved. But the analysis offered by Walker et al. appears to leave out of account the importance of other processes that were involved in the initial acquisition of patterns of violent behaviour. Research such as that described in Chapter 4 has thrown considerable light on the mechanisms through which individuals learn habits of aggressiveness. Complementing that work, it seems important to pay attention to the significance of treatment-outcome research literature, which although conducted for its practical utility, can also supply data for evaluating theories of psychological and behavioural change.

The evidence from our review of outcome research in the present chapter reveals findings that are in a sense a corollary of what has been learnt about development. Having acquired a tendency toward aggressiveness, individuals who have learned to resort to violent behaviour can effectively unlearn it or can learn to control it, usually by replacing it with some form of prosocial behaviour. Many individuals desist from violence as part of maturation or other kinds of developmental and personal change, as Walker et al. (2013) suggest. But many can also be influenced toward change by planned interventions of different kinds. Effects are larger at younger age levels, and if, as individuals develop, they experience repeated occasions or situations that generate violent responding, or as other sets of factors come into play, so their responsiveness to efforts toward change will become attenuated. There is still a great deal of further research needed on all these issues, but the evidence gathered so far fits an explanatory model based on learning more closely than any other. This is critically at odds with the notion that violent behaviour is inevitable or that tendencies to resort to it are immutable.

On a larger canvas, communities and entire societies can elect to avoid violence and can set up systems that reduce the likelihood of its occurrence. Within and between families and larger social groups, and between nations, there can be conflict resolution or peace-making processes that have results at a societal or cultural level similar to those that are found with individuals. The next chapter examines those possibilities.

10 Changing Structures
Integrated Interventions for Violence

10.1 Introduction

The comprehensive biopsychosocial approach to violence requires and enables us to ensure the role of social structures is incorporated in explanations of violence and approaches to addressing the problem. Tackling these social formations requires a public health approach which combines many of the interventions we have considered so far but in addition is designed to do so in an integrated programme which coordinates interventions at different levels. There has been significant growth in these integrated interventions over the past twenty years, especially with vulnerable groups in low- and middle-income countries, and we will consider some examples in this chapter. They are integrated in the sense that they often consist of 'bundles' of discrete intervention packages (Yount et al., 2017) operating at distinct levels within and between individuals and across whole societies to tackle violent behaviour both directly and indirectly. These programmes often combine primary prevention through broad structural changes with more direct and focussed interventions with high-risk groups. They may aim, for instance, to equip vulnerable women with the skills necessary to assertively set limits when they are exposed to violent behaviour by their partner. At the same time, they may aim to enhance the status of the same women through providing economic resources which empower them more generally in their relationships with men. The same programmes may also be designed to work with the perpetrators to change both their approach to negotiating with their partner in conflict situations and to change their attitudes toward women more generally. So these integrated programmes operate both on violence itself directly and, for example, on gender relations as an indirect factor associated with premature death from violence and from other avoidable causes such as HIV/AIDS.

10.2 Direct and Structural Violence Revisited

The ecological model for public health set out previously in Figure 1.2 is, like the biopsychosocial model, a way of integrating interventions for

---

Box 10.1   Illustrative multilevel components of an integrated intervention approach for intimate partner violence

- Batterers' programmes (individual level)
- Couples therapy (group level)
- Provision of refuges, victim support (community level)
- Change of law on marital rape (Turquet et al., 2011), growth of #MeToo movement (society level)

---

such a coordinated, multilevel approach. For example, the interventions in Box 10.1 can all be deployed simultaneously in a national programme against intimate partner violence with each tackling the problem at a different social layer. This combines primary, secondary and tertiary prevention efforts with perpetrators and support for victims in conjunction with national action to provide legislative backing at the more macro-levels of the system.

In Chapter 5 we considered the importance of social structure and noted two ways in which it can be linked to violence: directly and structurally. Core social power structures such as gender differentials or wealth distribution provide a solid framework for understanding and running a society, but they can be organised in a way that causes direct physical violence. So, for instance, assumptions that some men have about women can make them more likely to physically assault their female partners. They may feel angry when a woman does not act in a way that they judge to be appropriate, and such anger may lead to violence (Norlander and Eckhart, 2005). These assumptions need to be changed by some form of intervention to reduce the likelihood of direct violence. Similarly, people in a society may feel a sense of injustice when they look at how wealth, power and exposure to risk are distributed between different groups. According to the International Labour Organization (ILO, 2019), for instance, more than 2.78 million people die each year as a result of avoidable or preventable workplace accidents or from diseases contracted through work. These deaths have been found to be clustered in various high-risk jobs which are likely to be low-paid (Brookman and Robinson, 2012). Frustration and resentment at being poor in a society where others are rich has at many times in history underpinned outbreaks of individual and communal violence, including attacks on others to steal possessions or riots where property symbolising the unfairness is destroyed (Robins and Jones, 2009). Such outbreaks can sometimes become celebrated revolutions leading to social progress, while others can end in worse conditions than before. In both these examples, however, gender and wealth as social structures generate direct violence, and thus they can become the focus of structural interventions to reduce violence. They are also intertwined in many societies where men on average have more wealth than women. We will consider some examples below of attempts to actively challenge these two interlinked structures and thus to reduce their potential to underpin violence.

Beyond this idea of violence more or less directly caused by social structures, we considered above also the more radical conception of violence itself embedded within social structures. This is based on Galtung's (1969) idea of structural violence as anything which results in avoidable premature death. In this conception, death from HIV/AIDS due to a lack of available medication is a form of violence against vulnerable populations who could be protected from the disease if resources were made available but who are not protected for various reasons. By the same token, when a worker dies in a factory which is inadequately protected, they are a victim of structural violence. There may be no malevolent individual in the sense of someone consciously intending the deaths in either case nor any visible actor at the scene when each death takes place. But political and economic choices to create or tolerate the relevant social structures have been made, often high up and far away, and the consequences of these choices filter down to impact upon the poorest and least powerful in the world. Such political choices with fatal consequences are made within relatively prosperous societies as well as being imposed on low-income countries by rich countries. There is evidence, for instance, that there were 35,000 more deaths in the United Kingdom following the imposition of relative constraints on healthcare and social care public expenditure after an austerity programme was implemented in 2010 (Watkins et al., 2017). Such deaths by implication would have been avoided with greater expenditure, and thus they are as such manifestations of structural violence. This alternative conceptualisation of structural violence widens the agenda for intervention enormously.

Broadening the perspective to encompass structure in this way reminds us of the dynamic and interrelated nature of social problems. Our focus here is on violence specifically, but the inequality that contributes to violence also causes numerous other health problems such as gaps of up to ten years in longevity and exposure rates for HIV and AIDS. An integrated intervention may have a particular focus but at the same time may also have a ripple effect on multiple linked problems which are also caused by the same factor. Then changes in the cause of the problem may have feedback effects on other causes and other problems as the initial impact plays out over time. So, for example, an intervention which is successful in reducing HIV/AIDS may well also reduce violence at the same time as discussed further below.

The connection between HIV exposure risk and gender-based violence highlights the conflation of structural and direct violence and has been used as a basis for combined and integrated interventions which address both threats. Women in sub-Saharan Africa, for example, are currently faced with a joint epidemic in which early, avoidable death from one or the other threat is widespread (Nikolova and Small, 2018). The causal pathways between social structures such as gender norms and early death from violence or AIDS are highly interconnected. At their core is an entrenched inequality which is both internalised and externally policed through threatened or actual physical and sexual violence. This fear of violence makes it nearly impossible for women in such circumstances to avoid risk by negotiating safe sex practices or by taking up opportunities to attend HIV prevention and treatment programmes. These twin epidemics (Ezer, 2009) are both rooted in the extreme powerlessness of women in some societies. Combined interventions designed to challenge the assumptions of men and to increase the power and confidence of women can enable the two problems to be targeted with an integrated approach.

These interrelationships remind us never to see human violence as an isolated problem unconnected to other forms of human-driven destruction. We discussed in Chapter 5 how environmental damage can be seen as a form of slow violence in itself. Political campaigns and evidence-based interventions to address any of these three challenges – disease, violence and environmental damage – have the potential to be linked up to maximise their impact in changing societies. The individual-focused interventions discussed in the previous chapters in this section can go only so far in tackling these underlying issues. An effective integrated intervention programme will incorporate additional elements beyond these purely psychological approaches for addressing violence-linked structures. We will now consider some potential ways to introduce change at the structural level and conclude with consideration of some examples of integrated interventions.

10.3   Challenges in Changing Structures

The structural element of integrated interventions which targets economic, political, physical or social environments to improve health and life expectancy is in itself not a new idea. Any public health intervention since the reconstruction of urban water supplies system in Britain in the nineteenth century, the first modern example, is a form of structural intervention. Such interventions are not even a new development in relation to reducing violence as such. Slum housing clearances in the twentieth century were partly aimed at reducing antisocial behaviour, and housing improvements today are often seen as an important potential contributor to reducing violence (Bauer, 2010). But the new public health approach epitomised by the WHO programme and awareness of the need for an evidence-based policy has given an impetus to the development and evaluation of integrated interventions which incorporate structural elements alongside more traditional approaches focused on changing individual behaviour directly.

Bringing about change at the structural level is easier in some ways than it is at the individual level but is also harder in other ways. It is easier in the sense that a single act at the national level, such as new laws on gun control as introduced in the United Kingdom and Australia in the 1990s or the legislation on rape and elder abuse, for instance, noted in Chapter 6 can, in theory, have the potential for an immediate and widespread effect across a whole society. But laws have a limited scope, and population-level change requires millions of adaptations at the individual level. There may also be powerful vested interests which favour the current structural arrangements in any given society and which have the capacity to neutralise efforts aimed at upsetting the status quo. This might include blocking the passage of legislation or ensuring insufficient resources are available for a law to be effectively implemented and policed.

The key assumption informing intervention is the importance of the primary structures shaping and patterning individual behaviour. The individual is not completely autonomous but makes good or bad choices as a result of personal history and the structures of their surrounding society. The political locus of the structural approach has also become more complex with the rise of neoliberalism over the past forty years and the mutations in structural violence discussed above. While interest in structural approaches has been rooted in the left wing of politics since Marx, an awareness of the importance of changing environments and shaping individual behaviour indirectly has also been adopted by the political right. Behavioural economics, or 'nudge theory', was enthusiastically adopted by the UK Coalition government after 2010 as a strategy for shaping people's behaviour toward making the 'right' choices with minimal awareness that they were being influenced in any way (Halpern, 2015). This was never fully developed as an approach specifically to reduce violence, but the potential for primary prevention within this approach is clear.

The politics of structural-level interventions for violence are inevitably complex in other ways. The idea of intervention suggests the arrival of external experts on the scene who then organise and implement a new way of dealing with the relevant problems. But structural change ideally should be initiated and 'owned' by those on the ground who must be empowered in a 'bottom up' approach if any truly transformational change is to be sustained. This degree of change is not usually something that can be simply imposed from above.

Structural-level interventions may be implemented within institutions such as schools or hospitals, but these institutions are themselves also embedded within larger social structures (e.g. a health or educational provider organisation), and structural changes will require significant negotiation, debate and conflict resolution to be brought about at multiple organisational levels. Then, as Blankenship et al. (2006, p. 62) point out, 'it is often the structural changes that occur in order to make it possible to implement a program that comprise the structural intervention as much as it is the program itself'. Acceptance and adjustment to the implementation of such interventions, rather than the intervention itself, may make all the difference.

Access to resources is often seen as the core element of many structural interventions, especially based on the core assumption discussed above that economic inequality is both a root cause of direct violence and can become a form of violence itself. Resources facilitate an increased ability to avoid risks or to minimise the effects of a disease process once it has started. But improving access to resources can take different forms, with some being more structural than others. Interventions which involve 'cash transfers' or even lost benefits (Blankenship et al., 2006) have been classified as structural but may be based on a simple behavioural model of individual incentivisation where the desired behaviour is rewarded with short-term financial gain or avoidance of loss. Other economic interventions like microfinancing (the provision of economic resources such as zero-interest loans to people who do not normally have access to them) involve more sustained empowerment and thus are more accurately seen as potentially contributing to a change in the structures which can foster violence.

10.4   Undoing Structural Violence: Theoretical Perspectives

Since an important feature of structural violence is its invisibility, a key first step for interventions using the structural approach is to encourage people to be aware that their accepted assumptions and relationships may be part of the problem of violence. Once this awareness of connections is created, the next step is to tackle any perceptions of immutability. There may be a sense that, while the connections might be acknowledged, nothing can be done to change the way things are. So, as noted above, wealth inequality can be both a form of structural violence, because people die early when they lack access to health services, and a cause of direct violence, because it generates frustration and resentment. But the idea of equality itself is highly contentious, and even democratic societies which openly debate these issues cannot agree on whether or how much to address inequality, let alone whether to do so as part of a campaign to reduce violence.

As a result, structural violence theorists emphasise the need, first of all, to raise awareness about the connection between social structure and violence and, by implication therefore, to develop the idea that potentially everybody within any society is responsible for maintaining or challenging the status quo. As with environmental consciousness-raising, those people in rich and peaceful countries who would never even consider engaging in direct violence need to be persuaded that their everyday actions or inactions are part of a long causal chain which can end up in death and destruction for others elsewhere. Farmer (2005) advocates a process of 'conscientization' which enables people to realise the interconnectedness of their actions and processes across the world. Srikantia (2016) sees the first step in transforming the global systems which enable structural violence as a personal recognition of complicity in those systems, while Nixon (2011) asserts a particular role for the representational power of writer-activists such as Ken Saro-Wiwa and Arundhati Roy. These leaders can make visible the hidden assault of environmental degradation or destruction in impoverished communities far removed from the Western world which consumes the products they are evicted to make way for. Both emphasise that while each of us may never be responsible for direct interpersonal violence, we are all responsible to some extent for structural violence.

Action can take place only when this awareness is achieved. Just as we expect those who have acted violently to acknowledge their actions and their consequences before moving toward a solution, all of us embedded in violent systems must become aware of the consequences of our actions, however remote and unintended those consequences might be. These are inherently political decisions and include, for Srikantia (2016), attempts to 're-localize our ways of life such that they do not engender structural violence; prevent specific instances of violence against communities; and work to transform the operative system level rules and dynamics so these no longer embed structurally violent relations' (p. 249).

Nixon (2011) advocates support for resistance movements among indigenous communities forced to relocate to make way for infrastructure projects. Farmer (2005) sets out a much broader agenda to address structural violence by ensuring health is treated as a human right so that social and economic rights are inherently included in the broader struggle for human rights. He argues for health professionals to engage more in human rights work and for the development of health services based on co-production through working with vulnerable populations and with strong protections built in. This and other calls have fostered the development of a health and human rights movement which fits particularly well with the public health approach and sees the effective promotion of health as dependent on securing basic human rights (Mann, 2006).

These general exhortations for broader engagement and political action are complemented by Galtung's attempts to produce a more focused and pragmatic approach to fostering conflict resolution. The TRANSCEND model (Transcend International, 2018) sets out a three-step approach for effective peace-making comprised of mapping, legitimizing and bridging. *Mapping* involves understanding the perspectives of all parties involved in a conflict, and *legitimizing* is a process of guiding discussions on the basis of human rights as articulated in codes of law and ethics. *Bridging* is a more creative process of enabling connections to be made between all the parties involved in a conflict. A manual to guide the training and development of skills for those engaged in this form of conflict resolution has been produced (United Nations, 2000) (see Box 10.2), which covers a range of topics across the three steps including the role of conflict workers, the nature of dialogue, conflict theory and practice, violence theory and practice, transformation, peace dialogues, conflict transformation and peace transformation. Having started with the idea of structural violence, it is noticeable that this model

---

Box 10.2   Some elements of the TRANSCEND method

- Map the conflict formation: all parties, all goals, and all issues
- Have highly empathic dialogues with all parties singly
- Bring in forgotten goals that may open new perspectives
- Arrive at over-arching goals acceptable to all parties
- Disembed the conflict from where it was
- Bring in forgotten parties, goals
- Help parties meet 'at the table' for self-sustaining process.

Source: United Nations, 2000.

of Galtung's seems more concerned with direct violence albeit between groups within society. It focuses more on resolving actual conflicts that are ongoing rather than on social and political change to prevent the conflicts ever arising. Galtung (2010) claims some successes with this approach but acknowledges some failures with this model in human conflicts at both the interpersonal and societal levels.

10.5   Types of Structural Intervention

Complex social processes are difficult to define and measure, and, as a result, structural-level interventions which seek to change them are also hard to classify. For reducing violence, such interventions can range from changes in the law for setting alcohol prices to implementation of UN human rights conventions for children and other vulnerable groups, and changes to development rules which govern how resources are allocated within a society. In societies emerging after periods of sustained internal conflict, like those noted in Chapter 1, they may consist of national 'truth and reconciliation' processes as conducted in South Africa and Colombia, for instance, or transnational peace-making initiatives such as the International Criminal Tribunals which have sentenced perpetrators from the former Yugoslavia and elsewhere.

Various categorisations of structural-level interventions for both HIV/AIDS and interpersonal violence prevention are set out in Table 10.1. The concept of structural interventions is highly developed in the field of HIV/AIDS, and Auerbach et al. (2011) identify policy-legal changes such as the decriminalisation of homosexuality and environmental enablers such as increasing access to services and condoms as key interventions to

Table 10.1 *Types of structural intervention for HIV/AIDS and violence*

HIV/AIDS	Intimate partner violence	Gender-based violence
• Policy-legal changes	• Economic	Individual level
• Environmental enablers	• Politico-legal	• Economic resources
• Shifting harmful social norms	• Physical	• Human resources
• Catalysis of social and political	environment	• Social resources
change	• Social environment	• Voice and agency
• Empowerment of communities		
and groups		Community level
• Economic interventions		• Community engagement
		• Infrastructure development

Source: Auerbach et al. (2011); Bourey et al. (2015); Yount et al. (2017).

address HIV/AIDS risk. But these authors also highlight broader approaches which tackle harmful social norms and are more overtly political in the activist sense. The latter include encouraging social and political change through, for instance, advocacy, and broader strategies for the empowerment of communities.

Auerbach et al. (2011) further categorise interventions according to where they lie on two dimensions: causal process and unit of change. Interventions, as we have noted above, may be proximal ('downstream') or distal ('upstream') in their causal effect. In other words, they may act directly on the problem or do so remotely via a long chain of intervening steps. Each step may lead to unintended consequences which may dilute the effects of the intervention and which make it difficult to assess any causal effect accurately. Popular movements for social change such as the #MeToo movement, for instance, would be seen as distal in this framework as they are dynamic, unpredictable collectives operating over at least several years before achieving their goals, and many complex social elements will operate between the intervention and the outcome. Conversely, legal reforms, a key element of the WHO prevention approach and which may be the outcome of a popular movement, are proximal as they operate quite directly on the issue. The empowerment and norm-changing interventions discussed below in relation to violence prevention are at the more distal end of this spectrum.

Separate from causality, the second dimension of Auerbach et al.'s (2011) framework is the unit of change upon which the intervention is focused. Interventions vary in terms of the size of the social unit they are designed to change, with some targeting individuals and others targeting entire countries or communities within those countries. Once again, legal reforms which criminalise intimate partner violence are an example of a society-wide intervention, while those which aim to empower people may focus more at the individual level. Other examples were given in relation to intimate partner violence in Box 10.1.

In this context of intimate partner violence, structural interventions have been defined specifically by Bourey et al. (2015, p. 2) as those which aim 'to change … aspects of the economic, politico-legal, physical and social environment that produce and reproduce risk'. An intervention in this field may therefore address any one of these four domains or, since they are clearly interlinked, may combine strategies across two or more domains to maximise their effect.

A third way of categorising structural-level interventions, again with regard to violence, was developed by Yount et al. (2017) in their meta-review of evaluations testing interventions to reduce gender-based violence to girls and young women in low- and middle-income countries.

Like Auerbach et al. (2011), they distinguish interventions based on the level of implementation (individual level, community level or combined) but also on the number of components, since some interventions combine multiple components in complex 'bundles' of intervention. These bundles can consist only of structural elements as discussed here but may also be combined with psychosocial interventions to construct truly integrated interventions. For example, an intervention could address the psychological element of self-efficacy on its own or combine it with money management skills training. The intervention components for individuals identified by Yount et al. (2017) range across four main types, aimed at boosting the following: economic resources (e.g. cash transfers to support school attendance), human resources (e.g. literacy and numeracy classes), social resources (e.g. interaction with older mentors) and what the authors call voice-and-agency (e.g. assertiveness training). Each of these is a form of primary prevention enhancing the status and confidence of the girls and young women at risk and thus transforming, or at least adjusting, the power dynamics of male–female relationships within the targeted community.

Beyond the individual, there is also a range of community-level interventions consisting of either community engagement activities or infrastructure development aimed at influencing local norms about gender and violence and at changing local institutions. It is the latter which are truly structural in the strongest sense of the term. Community engagement activities involve mobilising all those women and men living in a locality to enhance the collective sense of what can be achieved in relation to gender-based violence and to bring about changes in norms relevant to its perpetration subscribed to by all. Examples include convening periodic meetings with parents and community leaders to promote a particular programme and holding participatory village committees for problem-solving. In one study (Devries, 2015), girls were enabled to get together with key stakeholders in their education such as teachers, school administrators and parents, in order to create an action plan for confronting the violence they faced, with celebrations to mark the completion of key goals. In another programme (Mathews, 2016), teachers and school administrators were coached to view gender-based violence as unacceptable and were made aware of local support services that were available. At the same time, school staff, parents, and police officers learned about the relevant laws to protect women against violence and were guided in how to make a safety plan.

Another community-level intervention involved attempts to develop the local infrastructure and included, among other components, teacher training, changes to the school curriculum and improvements to health services. In one violence prevention study, teachers were trained in the HIV/AIDS education curriculum, and the curriculum for young teenagers (twelve to thirteen years old) was adapted to provide more information about variations in HIV rates by age and gender (Duflo et al., 2006).

10.6   Integrated Interventions for Preventing Intimate Partner Violence

With these thoughts in mind, let us consider in more detail some examples of integrated interventions which combine structural and non-structural elements to reduce intimate partner violence specifically. As first discussed in Chapter 1 and building on the review in Chapter 9, violence against women can take many specific forms, and the UN definition encompasses both direct and structural violence within its remit. Direct violence includes child sexual abuse, female genital mutilation, sexual assault from partners and femicide, while examples of structural violence are child marriage, forced marriage and trafficking. Some of the former are committed by previous or current intimate partners and others by strangers or the wider family. The latter are the result of social or cultural institutional structures or of organised crime.

Intimate partners, former or current, present the greatest risk of violence to women. IPV is the most common form of violence against women in terms of frequency, and women are at much greater danger from their partners at home than from strangers in public places. As a result, the majority of interventions to reduce violence against women have been targeted at IPV with an extensive evidence base accumulating about 'best buy' strategies for this specific type of violence. However, much of this research relates to individual-level interventions, and, as with most violence research, the vast majority was conducted in high-income countries. Since many of these countries, in comparison to many low- and middle-income countries, have relatively strong gender equality and human rights safeguards, the structures which underpin some forms of violence have begun to be dismantled. Less developed countries tend to have greater gender inequality (United Nations, 2015), so there is a greater need to tackle the structural aspects of gender violence in those regions (Ellsberg et al., 2015). There is, of course, a contentious issue here, already noted, about the undesirability of imposing external values on relatively powerless societies. As discussed in Chapter 5, apparently benign ideas such as 'development' certainly involve the imposition of one set of cultural values on another and can involve significant physical harm and cultural damage. Srikantia (2016) and others critique the interference of advanced capitalism in well-established sustainable societies and rightly emphasise the largely negative effects of such interference. This should by no means discourage progressive interventions but it should alert the programme designers to be always aware of the context and the potential unintended effects of their intervention. It also emphasises the essential need for local ownership of all innovations.

As with all other forms of violence, when structural factors are examined they are found to play a key role in identifying who is at risk of IPV. Higher socioeconomic status is well established as a protective factor against exposure to IPV with high status groups reporting significantly lower rates than low status groups in surveys across multiple low- and middle-income countries in Asia, South America, Africa, and Europe (Abramsky et al., 2011). But the relationship between prosperity and risk is not straightforward and can be influenced by wider structural factors. Relatively well-off women in rural Bangladesh, for instance, are at a lower risk overall for IPV than poorer women, in line with the overall global trend. However, one group of high-status women, those living in a culturally conservative area, were found actually at greater risk of IPV than those with a low status in the same area. This was thought to be because they were seen as transgressing local gender norms and exceeding the status expectations of their neighbourhood (Abramsky et al., 2011).

The design of interventions for IPV has developed through a number of phases over the past decades, with early programmes focused initially on post-violence interventions supporting women who were escaping from IPV and applying stronger legal sanctions against perpetrators (Ellsberg et al., 2015). Subsequently, a more preventive approach has developed, with both potential perpetrators and targets to avoid the violence in the first place or at least early on in the relationship. For IPV survivors, a range of services have been developed involving, among other things, empowerment through advocacy and psychosocial support and referral to a group education programme for the perpetrators. There have been structural interventions in high-income countries as well, of course. At the structural level, there have been national policy commitments and legislative action such as the Serious Crime Act in England and Wales (UK Parliament, 2015), which created a new offence of controlling or coercive behaviour in intimate or familial relationships. Individual interventions have been implemented in low- and middle-income countries too, but the emphasis has been more on structural and integrated interventions in these regions for the reasons noted above.

A key element of these interventions is an aim to increase the economic resources available to those women at risk of IPV. Microfinance and cash transfer programmes have also been crucial in empowering women eco-nomically. These interventions often go hand-in-hand with those targeting other manifestations of structural violence such as HIV/AIDS prevention programmes, and some include economic and social empowerment approaches which are a core component of the WHO Global Strategy for the prevention of this type of violence. Community mobilisation schemes, for instance, operate at the population level and aim to change public attitudes involving many stakeholders and varied communication channels such as social media.

Despite a lack of extensive research, it is still possible to get some idea of 'what works' in this difficult and complex field now that integrated interventions have been developed, implemented successfully and evalu-ated a number of times in low- and middle-income countries. A recent review (Bourey et al., 2015) tracked down more than twenty of these evaluations from around the world. The evaluations included assessment of economic interventions centred on microfinance and/or cash transfers run in Bangladesh, Uganda, Mexico, and Ecuador; and social interven-tions involving participatory learning programmes, community mobilisation, community-based programming, discussion groups and media campaigns implemented in Uganda, Cote d'Ivoire, Ethiopia, South Africa, China, and India. One of the most effective interventions combined both of these social and economic elements of societies in South Africa.

The key question is whether we can confidently say that introducing one or more of these interventions to a community reduces the amount of IPV across a range of outcomes, and on this question, the evidence is mixed (Bourey et al., 2015). When restricted to the most direct and overt forms of IPV, rather than broader outcomes such as controlling behav-iour, only three evaluations out of more than twenty showed any signifi-cant effect in reducing physical, psychological or sexual manifestations of the problem. This uncertainty may simply reflect the complexity of implementing and evaluating such multi-layered interventions in under-resourced environments, and it is worth noting that, regardless of changes in direct violence, there were significant effects in other aspects such as attitudes toward the acceptability of violence and involve-ment in social networks by members of the communities.

Two of the successful interventions took place in different parts of Africa. The SHARE (Safe Homes and Respect for Everyone) community mobilisation programme in Uganda used an ecological model of violence to underpin a community-level mobilisation programme designed to change attitudes toward IPV and the wider social norms related to it and thus to make the behaviour of the perpetrators seem less acceptable

(Wagman et al., 2015). Such mobilisation programmes have previously been found to be promising when implemented in low- and middle-income countries. They are complex interventions where stakeholders (e.g. teachers, religious leaders) at a range of levels in a community are engaged and a wide variety of techniques are used, including those focused on individual aspects of behaviour (e.g. group skills training). The anti-violence element of the SHARE programme was linked to a broader HIV/AIDS prevention initiative in Uganda and involved a screening programme and a brief intervention intended to improve people's willingness to disclose their HIV status and reduce their risky behaviour as well. This combined approach reflects again the interconnectedness of violence and other social problems (Campbell et al., 2008), which is highlighted by adopting a structural perspective toward violence and which potentially enables a cumulative impact from joint working.

The overall SHARE programme, funded by a range of agencies including the Bill & Melinda Gates Foundation, the US National Institutes of Health and WHO, had eleven strategies, with some designed to tackle HIV and IPV risk together and others specifically targeting IPV alone. The combined strategies included, for instance, peer groups for school-age girls and boys to discuss relationships, communication, gender equality and resolving conflicts. Some of the violence-specific strategies are listed in Box 10.3.

Women involved in this programme reported that they experienced significantly less physical and sexual violence from their partners three

---

Box 10.3   Core SHARE violence prevention activities

1. Advocacy: Leaders, officials, policymakers were informed about IPV and women's rights, then given the opportunity to discuss and make decisions.
2. Capacity building: Police, social welfare officers, healthcare providers, teachers, local and religious leaders, SHARE staff and volunteers completed a community activism course on IPV prevention.
3. Community activism: Community volunteers were appointed and trained as SHARE ambassadors; IPV watch groups and community action groups were formed; village meetings and forums were held.
4. Learning materials: Booklets, brochures, posters, story cards, and other materials were developed and disseminated.
5. Special events: Community-based fairs, marches, campaigns and poster shows were held, and violence prevention newsletters were created and disseminated to community.

Source: Wagman et al., 2015.

Box 10.4   Some key sessions in the Creating Futures livelihood intervention

- Setting medium-term livelihood goals and the need for assets for livelihoods and coping with crises
- Education and learning including past experiences and how to build on these
- Getting and keeping jobs including work expectations and how one's own behaviours may impede or increase our ability to get a job and to keep it
- Income-generating activities and how to identify viable business opportunities
- Saving and coping with shocks including spending patterns and strategies for saving
- Causes and consequences of getting into debt and ways of overcoming debt.

Source: Jewkes et al., 2014.

---

years after the programme was implemented (Wagman et al., 2015). Their male partners also reported that they themselves engaged in less psychological aggression to their partner than before. This is the only programme so far which has reported significant improvements across all three domains of direct physical, psychological, and sexual violence.

A second effective intervention programme in South Africa went beyond the purely social domain and included a specific economic component relevant to the structural elements thought to underpin IPV (Jewkes et al., 2014). In this programme, 'Creating Futures', funded by a range of international agencies and the South African Medical Research Council, the economic component was designed to enhance people's livelihoods and thus increase their access to and ownership of resources. The key components of the two livelihood interventions are set out in Box 10.4.

The women in this study reported significantly less exposure to sexual violence from their partners after the programme was implemented, but the men self-reported no significant change in their tendency to perpetrate sexual violence. However, there was no significant reduction in recorded levels of physical violence. More broadly, the women in the study also reported some significant improvements in their economic well-being and their involvement in social networks.

Several other studies over the past decade have shown tentative evidence of the scope for improving either HIV- or gender violence–related health outcomes or both simultaneously by changing entrenched attitudes and behaviours. Nikolova and Small (2018) conclude that the evidence supports the need to intervene at the community level and to design interventions which target men as well as women. Taboos around different types of sexuality across cultures need to be overcome to ensure that myths do not get in the way of successful changes to reduce deaths from both structural and direct violence.

10.7   Conclusion

There are undoubtedly real difficulties in taking knowledge on the social determinants of violence and using it to develop practical interventions which can be successfully implemented. The idea of structural violence provides a powerful theoretical tool for understanding the problem and, alongside the analysis of social structures, can act as a constant reminder to psychologists and society more generally to look for causes beyond the individual perpetrator. But there remains a disconnection between theory and practice in this area. There would be advantages if social scientists, who generate and test broad theories of structural causation, were to work more closely with epidemiologists, who study trends, to underpin actual interventions (Blankenship et al. 2006). The former can be seen as examining numerous potential factors at such a fundamental level (e.g. capitalism, patriarchy) that their ideas can be used only to propose 'pie in the sky' solutions. The latter tend toward an empirical pragmatism where structure is poorly theorised and may be defined as something so proximate to the actual violent behaviour it could be seen as not structural at all. Bridging the gap between these two approaches, bringing empiricism to lofty theoretical constructs, is a major challenge for the decades ahead. Public health scientists may be turning away from social explanations and thus social interventions because of a frustration with the lack of guidance provided by social theory (Auerbach et al., 2011). If we fail in this task of integration and end up not taking structural factors seriously enough when planning health programmes, the risk is that our individual-level interventions will fail more often than they should do because the environmental and cultural context is ignored (Link and Phelan, 1995). If we can succeed in integrating theoretical and practical approaches, as suggested by the studies considered in this chapter, the scope for a profound reduction in violence at all levels of society comes within closer reach.

Rewiring Our Expectations
Lessons and Prospects

In this book we have posed and attempted to provide answers to a number of questions about the human capacity for violence. The fundamental aim has been to challenge the idea of violence being hard-wired into human nature, and this has led to questions about the potential for 'rewiring'. This rethink has involved interrogating the evidence for and against various theoretical frameworks through which it is understood. It has implications for strategies to change individuals who have acted violently, the situations they might find themselves in and the societies around them. Brecht complained at the start of this book that our vision is skewed when we see only the violent behaviour of dangerous individuals and what we should always do is take a step back and make ourselves aware of the structures which partly created that person. Even more, we should consider whether the structures themselves are inherently violent because they limit and damage the person who inhabits them. We will gain more from remodelling the banks of the river which create and channel the violent torrent than we do from trying to stop the torrent itself.

The biopsychosocial model provides a helpful starting point for a comprehensive understanding of the potential solutions at a range of levels, and we have used it here as a framework to structure the enormously wide variety of approaches to the problem that have been developed and tested in the past thirty years. But beyond its use in this way as a map of the territory, deploying the biopsychosocial approach as a theoretical tool has drawbacks as well as attractions. On the plus side, the approach is broad, integrative and dynamic. It obviously has a breadth which enables the full complexity of the problem to be considered. Its emphasis on integrating competing perspectives ideally should counter any simplistic biological reductionism, and its dynamic properties highlight the interaction of the person and their environment. As a tool for clinicians assessing and treating violent individuals, the biopsychosocial approach is undoubtedly valuable (Steinert and Whittington, 2013). Even its critics concede that its widespread adoption may have contributed to the development of interdisciplinary working among professionals and thus to a more holistic conception of the person (Benning, 2015). However, as a potential 'theory of violence', its very breadth can lead to an eclecticism which ultimately says very little beyond 'everything is potentially relevant'. Such theoretical anarchy (Ghaemi, 2009) can amount to a weak claim that 'anything goes' and enables a standard reductionist explanation to be contextualised but to remain predominant.

This hard-wiring interpretation of the biopsychosocial model implies a one-way street: higher-level psychological and social factors at most merely modify underlying processes rooted in human biology. It focuses on the river's violent torrent rather than the channel which contains it. The superficial equality of the three domains conceals an assumed hierarchy of causal effect in which the biological is primary over the psychological, the relational and the social. This privileging of an apparent biological underpinning encourages the excessive pathologisation and medicalisation of violent behaviour, making of it a form of madness or of blind fate and, as such, preventing any view of it as 'a meaningful and functional response to a life situation' (Johnstone et al., 2018). A reconceptualisation of the biopsychosocial approach, in contrast, emphasises the multidirectional nature of relationships between the biopsychosocial levels and the emergent capacity of a whole to influence its constituent parts (Elder-Vass, 2010).

What we called the standard narrative of a fundamentally violent human nature introduced in Chapter 2 has been challenged on several fronts, as we have considered the evidence from many fields of research to the extent that the concept of it now appears more of an illusion than a scientifically tested reality (Sahlins, 2008). As a result, multiple strategies can be supported once this causal pessimism is overcome. Exploration of the full diversity of human social systems and animal behaviour patterns reveals many models of peaceful and cooperative social formations rather than confirming the idea of an inherent propensity for violence. The epigenetic evidence of cellular-level influences on the expression or silencing of genes from the environment and neurological evidence of brain plasticity calls for a fundamental rewiring of the biopsychosocial model of violence to recognise the multidirectional pathways between domains. In this revision, the psychological and social are no longer mere offshoots from an immutable biological platform. In an age of genetic ascendancy (Plomin, 2018) the clear evidence from studies of child development that, while there may be direct biological influences involved, violence is largely a product of conditions and events in an individual's life remains solid. The propensity for violence is a question of what the child is exposed to, the impact it has upon developing individuals and what they learn from the challenges of growing up. It is true that their initial temperamental predisposition contributes to how readily this occurs, but the process is shaped by the subsequent patterning of experience. While changes at the neural level underpin psychological and behavioural change, in establishing this propensity to violence and later modifying and reducing it, those alterations are a response to learning rather than in any way a direct outcome of evolutionary or genetic influences.

Theories of causation are only the first step to designing models of intervention. In Chapter 1 we posed three questions in particular: Is human violence inevitable? Is it predictable? and Is it preventable? The evidence of success in designing and delivering a range of interventions and strategies supports some confidence for movement toward a positive answer in each of these areas. Violence is indeed avoidable, predictable and preventable. A propensity for violence developing in the first place can be avoided if the right developmental conditions are available and primary prevention strategies are successfully implemented. The risk of future violence among those who have exhibited some degree of dangerousness can be identified with some accuracy, though we need to do more to understand cause–effect relationships at the individual level, and to link effective assessment with suitable interventions as a basis for prevention. And the expression of violence can be defused or at least managed by drawing from an abundance of social, psychological or, if necessary, pharmacological options.

The United Nations first entered this field with the Seville Statement in 1986 that 'violent behaviour is not genetically programmed into human behaviour and is therefore preventable'. In other words, it was arguing that there is nothing in our biology which makes human violent behaviour inevitable. The evidence we have reviewed here indicates that this claim remains justifiable thirty-five years later. In particular, knowledge about genetic influences on human behaviour has grown exponentially over this time, but, if anything, the more we know about genetics the greater the potential scope for interventions which contribute to reduced risk. As we have seen, the emerging science of epigenetics is rooted in the study of how environmental factors influence gene expression. It is obvious that changing these environmental factors will directly influence the psychological and social roots of violence, but now it is becoming clear that it may also influence the biological roots. This means that 'if social environments could impact epigenetic programs in the first place, they might also be reversed by behavioural intervention. The possibility that behavioural interventions could have biochemical consequences … might be a paradigm shift in the social science field' (Szyf, 2009, p. 11). Such environmental and behavioural interventions could be targeted as early as the start of pregnancy and the immediate post-natal period for maximum effect (Tremblay et al., 2018).

Overall, then, the evidence justifies and encourages the development of new strategies for tackling the problem of violence with renewed confidence. The public health perspective provides a framework for delivering interventions where they are needed most, and the adoption of this approach by the WHO enables these interventions to be implemented on a global scale. The current WHO work programme for the period up to 2023 is guided by a 'triple billion' vision which includes, among other priorities, the aspiration of enabling 1 billion more people to enjoy better health and well-being through actions to reduce exposure to and perpetration of violence alongside other harms such as poor nutrition, bad sanitation and tobacco use. Violence against women and children is a key focus, with specific targets of a 20% decrease in the number of children subjected to any violence and a 5% decrease in the proportion of specific groups of women and girls subjected to physical or sexual partner violence. These aims are backed up by clear policy implementation statements on children (INSPIRE; World Health Organization, 2016b) and women and girls (World Health Organization, 2016c) as part of the Global Campaign for Violence Prevention. These statements provide a concrete action plan for taking forward national prevention programmes, which may include some of the evidence-based psychological and social interventions we have considered in this book.

The overall framework for implementation in these documents consists of political, legal and economic elements as well as the selection and implementation of targeted prevention and intervention programmes. As with the National Action Plans discussed in Chapter 6, within each country politicians and policymakers need to establish a national commitment and check the specific needs in their own jurisdiction in order to establish how generic interventions from the international evidence-base might need to be adapted to suit local conditions. Local practitioners are best placed to understand the relevant local context and to decide how interventions tested and developed in other regions might best be adjusted to work in theirs. Such local knowledge will include awareness of both the particular patterns of violence in the chosen setting and how the new intervention might fit with any existing initiatives. They also need to prepare explicit national and local implementation plans, ensure the availability of adequate resources and establish procedures to monitor implementation and outcomes. But a key step is the selection of the right strategies, and some of the ideas covered in this book might inform choices in this area.

The seven strategies recommended for reducing violence against children are broadly psychosocial and reflect many of the themes considered in Chapter 6. They include supporting parents and caregivers to manage conflict within families effectively and addressing the risk factors, motivations, norms and values underlying the behaviour of perpetrators and the responses of victims when exposed to violence. Some examples of the former were discussed in Chapter 9 and examples of the latter in Chapter 10. Other psychosocial strategies are the establishment of safe environments, economic strengthening and improving life skills. As always, underpinning these strategies for individuals and communities, a robust anti-violence legal framework needs to be in place.

The children growing up in societies which adopt these strategies and can successfully implement them in their communities will have a better chance than their parents had to develop free from exposure to violence. They then may be able to take this challenge to the next stage so that future generations have even better chances. Nobody expects the problem to be eradicated soon, and it is not our wish to make naïve or misleading claims. But if we look ahead over the next several decades, the combination of science and public health policy offers us genuine hope for a more peaceful world and better lives for all.

Appendix   Major UN Initiatives to Address Violence, 1986–2018

1980s and 1990s

1986: **Seville Statement: 'violent behaviour is not genetically programmed into human behaviour and is therefore preventable'; adopted by UNESCO in 1989**

1989: UN General Assembly adopted the Convention on the Rights of the Child including a commitment to protect children from 'all forms of physical or mental violence'

1990: UN Guidelines for the Prevention of Juvenile Delinquency adopted

1993: UN General Assembly adopted the Declaration on the Elimination of Violence against Women

1994: UN Special Rapporteur on Violence against Women appointed

1996: World Health Assembly declared violence a 'leading worldwide public health problem' and called upon the WHO Director General to develop a science-based approach to understanding and prevention (WHA49.25)

1996: UN Development Fund for Women established a Trust Fund to Eliminate Violence against Women

1997: UN Office for Drugs and Crime (UNODC) was established to coordinate responses to drug control, crime prevention and international terrorism in relation to sustainable development and human security

2000s

2002: UN Economic and Social Council adopted Guidelines for the Prevention of Crime

2002: World Report on Violence and Health

2003: World Health Assembly called upon member states to appoint an agency within their ministries of health to be the focus for driving forward the World Report (WH56.24)

2004: Handbook for the Documentation of Interpersonal Violence Prevention Programmes

2006: Study on Violence against Children published by the UN Committee on the Rights of the Child

2006: UN Secretary General's in-depth study on all forms of violence against women published

2009: Appointment of the UN Secretary General's Special Representative on Violence against Children

2010 Onward

2010: UN General Assembly adopted Update Model strategies and practical measures on the elimination of violence against women in the field of crime prevention and criminal justice

2010: UN Entity for Gender Equality and the Empowerment of Women established

2010: Violence Prevention: The Evidence

2013: Global Survey on Violence against Children published

2014: Global Status Report on Violence Prevention published

2014: Global Study on Homicide Trends, Contexts, Data (UNODC)

2014: World Health Assembly called upon the WHO Director General to develop a global plan of action to strengthen the role of health systems in addressing interpersonal violence

2014: UNICEF reports published 'Hidden in Plain Sight: A Statistical Analysis of Violence against Children' and 'Ending Violence against Children: Six Strategies for Action'

2014–2015: WHO Reports published 'Preventing Suicide: A Global Imperative' and 'Preventing Youth Violence: Taking Action and Generating Evidence'

2015: UN General Assembly adopted the 2030 Sustainable Goals Agenda linking sustained peace to sustainable development

2015: Preventing Youth Violence: An Overview of the Evidence

2015: Preventing Youth Violence: Launch of Violence Information (http://apps.who.int/violence-info/)

2016: INSPIRE: Seven Strategies for Ending Violence against Children

2016: Global Plan of Action to Prevent Interpersonal Violence (WHA 69.5)

2016: Global Partnership to End Violence against Children

2018: INSPIRE Global Partnership to End Violence against Children launched Implementation Handbook and Indicator Document

2018: WHA General Programme of Work 2019–2023 includes targets to reduce the prevalence of violence against children by 20% and the prevalence of violence against women by 5%

2018: WHO initiates data collection for the second global status report on violence prevention, with a focus on assessing government support for evidence-based interventions to prevent and respond to violence against children.

Note: Bold entries refer to key 'cornerstone' texts which are referenced repeatedly in the text.

Source: World Health Organization, 2014; Lee, 2015; M. Peres and A. Butchart, personal communications.

References

Abraham, J. (2010). Pharmaceuticalization of society in context: Theoretical, empirical and health dimensions. *Sociology*, 44, 603–622.

Abramsky, T., Watts, C. H., Garcia-Moreno, C., Devries, K., Kiss, l., Ellsberg, M., Jansen, H. A. F. M. & Heise, L. (2011). What factors are associated with recent intimate partner violence? Findings from the WHO multi-country study on women's health and domestic violence. *BMC Public Health*, 11, 109.

Adams, D., Barnett, S. A., Bechtereva, N. P., Carter, B. F., Delgado, J. M. R., Díaz, J. L., Eliasz, A., Genovés, S., Ginsburg, B. E., Groebe, J., Ghosh, S.-K., Hinde, R., Leakey, R. E., Malasi, T. M. Martin Ramiréz, J., Mayor Zaragoza, F., Mendoza, D. L., Nandy, A., Scott, J. P. & Wahlström, R. (1994). The Seville Statement on Violence. *American Psychologist*, 49, 845–846.

Ægisdóttir, S., White, M. J., Spengler, P. M., Maugherman, A. S., Anderson, L. A., Cook, R. S., Nichols, C. N., Lampropoulos, G. K., Walker, B. S., Cohen, G. & Rush, J. D. (2006). The meta-analysis of clinical judgment project: Fifty-six years of accumulated research on clinical versus statistical prediction. *The Counseling Psychologist*, 34, 341–382.

Alford, A. A. & Derzon, J. (2012). Meta-analysis and systematic review of the effectiveness of school-based programs to reduce multiple violent and anti-social behavioral outcomes. In S. R. Jimerson, A. Nickerson, M. J. Mayer & M. J. Furlong (eds.), *Handbook of School Violence and School Safety: International Research and Practice*. 2nd edition. Pp. 593–606. New York: Routledge.

Alhabib, S., Nur, U. & Jones, R. (2010). Domestic violence against women: Systematic review of prevalence studies. *Journal of Family Violence*, 25, 369–382.

Ali, A., Hall, I. Blickwedel, J. & Hassiotis, A. (2015). Behavioural and cognitive-behavioural interventions for outwardly-directed aggressive behaviour in people with intellectual disabilities. *Cochrane Database of Systematic Reviews*, Issue 4, Art. No. CD003406.

Allen, G. & Dempsey, N. (2016). *Prison Population Statistics. Briefing Paper*. London: House of Commons Library.

Allen, M. W. (2014). Hunter-gatherer violence and warfare in Australia. In M. W. Allen & T. L. Jones (eds.), *Violence and Warfare among Hunter-Gatherers*. Pp. 97–111. Walnut Creek, CA: Left Coast Press.

Alrababa'h, A., Marble, W., Mousa, S. & Siegel, A. (2019). *Can Exposure to Celebrities Reduce Prejudice? The Effect of Mohamed Salah on Islamophobic Behaviors and Attitudes.* Working Paper No. 19-04, Immigration Policy Lab, Stanford University.

Altheimer, I. (2013a). Cultural processes and homicide across nations. *International Journal of Offender Therapy and Comparative Criminology*, 57, 842–863.

(2013b). Herding and homicide across nations. *Homicide Studies*, 17, 27–58.

Anderson, C. A. (1989). Temperature and aggression: Ubiquitous effects of heat on occurrence of human violence. *Psychological Bulletin*, 106, 74–96.

(2001). Heat and violence. *Current Directions in Psychological Science*, 10, 33–38.

Andrade, J. T., O'Neill, K. & Diener, R. B. (2009). Violence risk assessment and risk management: A historical overview and clinical application. In J. T. Andrade (ed.), *Handbook of Violence Risk Assessment and Treatment: New Approaches for Mental Health Professionals.* Pp. 3–39. New York: Springer.

Andrews, D. A. (1989). Recidivism is predictable and can be influenced: Using risk assessments to reduce recidivism. *Forum on Corrections Research*, 1, 11–18.

Andrews, D. A. & Bonta, J. (2010). *The Psychology of Criminal Conduct.* 5th edition. Cincinnati, OH: LexisNexis/Anderson.

Andrews, D. A. & Dowden, C. (2006). Risk principle of case classification in correctional treatment: A meta-analytic investigation. *International Journal of Offender Therapy and Comparative Criminology*, 50, 88–100.

Andrews, D. A., Bonta, J. & Wormith, J. S. (2006). The recent past and near future of risk and/or need assessment. *Crime & Delinquency*, 52, 7–27.

American Psychiatric Association (2013). *Diagnostic and Statistical Manual of Mental Disorders. DSM-5.* Washington, DC: American Psychiatric Publishing.

Aristotle (2000). *The Politics.* Revised edition. London: Penguin Books.

Auerbach, J. D., Parkhurst, J. O. & Cáceres, C. F. (2011). Addressing social drivers of HIV/AIDS for the long-term response: Conceptual and methodological considerations. *Global Public Health*, 6 (Suppl 3), S293–S309.

Australian Government Department of Social Services (2014). *The National Plan to Reduce Violence against Women and Their Children 2010–2022.* www.dss.gov.au/women/programs-services/reducing-violence/the-national-plan-to-reduce-violence-against-women-and-their-children-2010-2022. Accessed 18 September 2018.

Azevedo F. A. C., Carvalho, L. R. B., Grinberg, L. T., Farfel, J. M., Ferretti. R. E. L., Leite, R. E. P., Filhom W. J., Lent, R. & Herculano-Houzel, S. (2009). Equal number of neuronal and nonneuronal cells make the human brain an isometrically scaled-up primate brain. *Journal of Comparative Neurology*, 513, 532–541.

Baker, L. A., Jacobson, K. C., Raine, A., Lozano, D. I. & Bezdjian, S. (2007). Genetic and environmental bases of childhood antisocial behaviour: A multi-informant twin study. *Journal of Abnormal Psychology*, 116, 219–235.

Baker, L. A., Raine, A., Liu, J. & Jacobson, K. C. (2008). Differential genetic and environmental influences on reactive and proactive aggression in children. *Journal of Abnormal Child Psychology*, 36, 1265–1278.

Baller, R. D., Zevenbergen, M. P. & Messner, S. F. (2009). The heritage of herding and Southern homicide: Examining the ecological foundations of the code of honor thesis. *Journal of Research in Crime and Delinquency*, 46, 275–300.

Bandura, A. (2006). A murky portrait of human cruelty. *Behavioral and Brain Sciences*, 29, 225–226.

Banerjee, S. (2008). Necrocapitalism. *Organization Studies*, 29, 1541–1563.

Bangalore, S. & Messerli, F. H. (2013). Gun ownership and firearm-related deaths. *American Journal of Medicine*, 126, 873–876.

Banks, S., Robbins, P. C., Silver, E., Vesselinov, R., Steadman, H. J., Monahan, J., Mulvey, E. P., Appelbaum, P. S., Grisso, T. & Roth, L. H. (2004). A multiple-models approach to violence risk assessment among people with mental disorder. *Criminal Justice and Behavior*, 31, 324–340.

Barak, G. (2009). *Criminology: An Integrated Approach*. Lanham, MD: Rowman and Littlefield.

Barnes, J. C., TenEyck, M., Boutwell, B. B. & Beaver, K. M. (2013). Indicators of domestic/intimate partner violence are structured by genetic and non-shared environmental influences. *Journal of Psychiatric Research*, 47, 371–376.

Barnes, J. C., Wright, J. P., Boutwell, B. B., Schwartz, J. A., Connolly, E. J., Nedelec, J. L. & Beaver, K. M. (2014). Demonstrating the validity of twin research in criminology. *Criminology*, 52, 588–626.

Barnes, T. N., Smith, S. W. & Miller, M. D. (2014). School-based cognitive-behavioral interventions in the treatment of aggression in the United States: A meta-analysis. *Aggression and Violent Behavior*, 19, 311–321.

Baron, L., Straus, M. A. & Jaffee, D. (1988). Legitimate violence, violent attitudes, and rape: A test of the Cultural Spillover Theory. In R. A. Prentky & V. L. Quinsey (eds.), *Human Sexual Aggression: Current Perspectives*. Annals of the New York Academy of Sciences, 528, 79–110.

Baron, R. A. & Richardson, D. R. (1994). *Human Aggression*. 2nd edition. New York: Plenum Press.

Bateson, P. & Gluckman, P. (2011). *Plasticity, Robustness, Development and Evolution*. Cambridge: Cambridge University Press.

Bauer, B. (2010). *Violence Prevention through Urban Upgrading. Experiences from Financial Cooperation*. Frankfurt am Main: KfW Bankengrupp. www.kfw-entwicklungsbank.de/Download-Center/PDF-Dokumente-Sektoren-Berichte/2010_03_Violence-Prevention_E.pdf.

BBC News (2003, 1 May). Worms survived Columbia disaster. http://news.bbc.co.uk/2/hi/science/nature/2992123.stm.

Beaver, K. M. (2011). Genetic influences on being processed through the criminal justice system: Results from a sample of adoptees. *Biological Psychiatry*, 60, 282–287.

Beaver, K. M., DeLisi, M., Vaughn, M. G. & Barnes, J. C. (2010a). Monoamine oxidase A genotype is associated with gang membership and weapon use. *Comprehensive Psychiatry*, 51, 130–134.

Beaver, K. M., Ferguson, C. J. & Lynn-Whaley, J. (2010b). The association between parenting and levels of self-control. *Criminal Justice and Behavior*, 37, 1045–1065.

Beaver, K. M., Barnes, J. C. & Boutwell, B. B. (eds.) (2015). *The Nurture versus Biosocial Debate in Criminology: On the Origins of Criminal Behavior and Criminality*. Thousand Oaks, CA: Sage.

Beckerman, S., Erickson, P. I., Yost, J., Regalado, J., Jaramillo, L., Sparks, C., Iromenga, M. & Long, K. (2009). Life histories, blood revenge, and reproductive success among the Waorani of Ecuador. *Proceedings of the National Academy of Sciences*, 106, 8134–8139.

Bellis, M.A., Hughes, K., Perkin, C. & Bennett A. (2012). *Protecting People Promoting Health. A Public Health Approach to Violence Prevention for England*. https://assets.publishing.service.gov.uk/government/uploads/system/uploads/attachment_data/file/216977/Violence-prevention.pdf.

Bennett, S. H., Kirby, A. J. & Finnerty, G. T. (2018). Rewiring the connectome: Evidence and effects. *Neuroscience and Biobehavioral Reviews*, 88, 51–62.

Benning, T. B. (2015). Limitations of the biopsychosocial model in psychiatry. *Advances in Medical Education and Practice*, 6, 347–352.

Berger, P. & Pullberg, S. (1965). Reification and the sociological critique of consciousness. *History and Theory*, 4, 196–211.

Berkowitz, L. (1993). *Aggression: Its Causes, Consequences, and Control*. New York: McGraw-Hill.

Bernat, F. P. & Holschuh, C. S. (2015). Is there a war on women or are females fine? An examination of sex, gender, and the criminal justice field. *Women & Criminal Justice*, 25, 6–10.

Beroldi, G. (1994). Critique of the Seville Statement on Violence. *American Psychologist*, 49, 849–848.

Beyer, K., Wallis, A. B. & Hamberger, L. K. (2015). Neighborhood environment and intimate partner violence: A systematic review. *Trauma, Violence, & Abuse*, 16, 16–47.

Blanchard, D. C. & Blanchard, R. J. (2000). Emotions as mediators and modulators of violence: Some reflections on the 'Seville Statement on Violence'. *Social Research*, 67, 683–708.

Blankenship, K. M., Friedman, S., Dworkin, S. & Mantell, J. (2006). Structural interventions: Concepts, challenges and opportunities for research. *Journal of Urban Health*, 83, 59–72.

Boccio, C. M., McBride, M. & Beaver, K. M. (2018). Molecular genetics of aggression and violent crime. In A. T. Vazsonyi, D. J. Flannery & M. DeLisi (eds.), *The Cambridge Handbook of Violent Behavior and Aggression*. 2nd edition. Pp. 187–174. Cambridge: Cambridge University Press.

Boesch, C., Crockford, C., Herbinger, I., Wittig, R., Moebius, Y. & Normand, E. (2008). Intergroup conflict among chimpanzees in Taï National Park: Lethal violence and the female perspective. *American Journal of Primatology*, 70, 519–532.

Bonduriansky, R. & Day, T. (2018). *Extended Heredity: A New Understanding of Inheritance and Evolution*. Princeton, NJ: Princeton University Press,

Bonta, J. (1996). Risk-needs assessment and treatment. In A. T. Harland (ed.), *Choosing Correctional Options That Work: Defining the Demand and Evaluating the Supply*. Pp. 18–32. Thousand Oaks, CA: Sage Publications.

Bonta, J. & Andrews, D. A. (2017). *The Psychology of Criminal Conduct*. 6th edition. London: Routledge.

Bonta, J. & Wormith, S. J. (2008). Risk and need assessment. In G. McIvor & P. Raynor (eds.), *Developments in Social Work with Offenders*. Pp. 131–152. London: Jessica Kingsley.

Borrell-Carrió, F., Suchman, A. L. & Epstein, R. M. (2004). The biopsychosocial model 25 years later: Principles, practice, and scientific inquiry. *Annals of Family Medicine*, 2, 576–582.

Borsboom, D. (2005). *Measuring the Mind: Conceptual Issues in Contemporary Psychometrics*. Cambridge: Cambridge University Press.

Bourey, C., Williams, W., Bernstein, E. & Stephenson, R. (2015). Systematic review of structural interventions for intimate partner violence in low- and middle-income countries: Organizing evidence for prevention. *BMC Public Health* 15, 1165.

Bowen, E. (2011). *The Rehabilitation of Partner Violent Men*. Chichester: Wiley-Backwell.

Bowers, L., Douzenis, A., Galeazzi, G., Forghieri, M., Tsopelas, C., Simpson A. & Allan, T. (2005). Disruptive and dangerous behaviour by patients on acute psychiatric wards in three European centres. *Social Psychiatry and Psychiatric Epidemiology*, 40, 822–828.

Bowers, L., Ross, J., Owiti, J., Baker, J., Adams, C. & Stewart, D. (2012). Event sequencing of forced intramuscular medication in England. *Journal of Psychiatric and Mental Health Nursing*, 19, 799–806.

Boyle, M. (2013). Persistence of medicalisation: Is the presentation of alternatives part of the problem? In S. Coles, S. Keenan & B. Diamond (eds.), *Madness Contested: Power and Practice*. Monmouth: PCCS Books.

Braga, A. A. & Weisburd, D. L. (2015). Focused deterrence and the prevention of violent gun injuries: Practice, theoretical principles, and scientific evidence. *Annual Review of Public Health*, 36, 55–68.

Braga, A. A., Kennedy, D. M., Waring, E. J. & Piehl, A. M. (2001). Problem-oriented policing, deterrence, and youth violence: An evaluation of Boston's Operation Ceasefire. *Journal of Research in Crime and Delinquency*, 38, 195–225.

Braga, A. A., Piehl, A. M. & Hureau, D. (2009). Controlling violent offenders released to the community: Evaluation of the Boston Reentry Initiative. *Journal of Research in Crime and Delinquency*, 46, 411–436.

Braga, T., Gonçalves, L. C., Batso-Pereira, M. & Maia, Â. (2017). Unraveling the link between maltreatment and juvenile antisocial behaviour: A meta-analysis of prospective longitudinal studies. *Aggression and Violent Behavior*, 33, 37–50.

British Psychological Society (2013). *Alternatives to Antipsychotic Medication: Psychological Approaches in Managing Psychological and Behavioural Distress in People with Dementia*. Briefing paper. (Authors: Brechin, D., Murphy, G., James, I. & Codner, J). Leicester: British Psychological Society.

Brookman, F. & Robinson, A. (2012). Violent crime. In M. Maguire, R. M. Morgan & R. Reiner (eds.), *The Oxford Handbook of Criminology*. 5th edition. Pp. 563–594. Oxford: Oxford University Press.

Brophy, S., Kennedy, J., Fernandez-Gutierrez, F., John, A., Potter, R., Linehan, C. & Kerr, M. (2018). Characteristics of children prescribed antipsychotics: Analysis of routinely collected data. *Journal of Child and Adolescent Psychopharmacology*, 28, 180–191.

Brüne, M. (2007). On human self-domestication, psychiatry, and eugenics. *Philosophy, Ethics, and Humanities in Medicine*, 2, 21–29.

Buckner, R. L. & Krienen, F. M. (2013). The evolution of distributed association networks in the human brain. *Trends in Cognitive Sciences*, 1253.

Bulik-Sullivan, B., Finucane, H. K., Anttila, V., Gusev, A., Day, F. R., Loh, P.-R., ReproGen Consortium, Psychiatric Genomics Consortium, Genetic Consortium for Anorexia Nervosa of the Wellcome Trust Case Control Consortium, Duncan, L., Perry, J. R. B., Patterson, N., Robinson, E. B., Daly, M. J., Price, A. L. & Neale, B. M. (2015). An atlas of genetic correlations across human diseases and traits. *Nature Genetics*, 47, 1236–1241.

Buller, D. J. & Hardcastle, V. G. (2000). Evolutionary psychology, meet developmental neurobiology: Against promiscuous modularity. *Brain and Mind*, 1, 307–325.

Burt, C. H. (2015). Heritability studies: Methodological flaws, invalidated dogmas, and changing paradigms. *Advances in Medical Sociology: Health, Genetics, & Society*, 16, 1–44.

Burt, C. H. & Simons, R. L. (2014). Pulling back the curtain on heritability studies: Biosocial criminology in the postgenomic era. *Criminology*, 52, 223–262.

Burt, S. A. (2009). Are there meaningful etiological differences within antisocial behavior? Results of a meta-analysis. *Clinical Psychology Review*, 29, 163–178.

Busfield, J. (2013). The pharmaceutical industry and mental disorder. In S. Coles, S. Keenan & B. Diamond (eds.), *Madness Contested: Power and Practice*. Pp. 90–110. Monmouth: PCCS Books.

Buss, D. M. (2012). The evolutionary psychology of crime. *Journal of Theoretical and Philosophical Criminology*, 1, 90–98.

Butchart, A., Harvey, A. P., Mian, M. & Fürniss, T. (2006). *Preventing Child Maltreatment: A Guide to Taking Action and Generating Evidence*. Geneva: World Health Organization and the International Society for the Prevention of Child Abuse and Neglect.

Butkus, R., Doherty, R. & Bornstein, S. S. (2018). Reducing firearm injuries and deaths in the United States: A position paper from the American College of Physicians. *Annals of Internal Medicine*, 169, 704–707.

Byrd, A. L. & Manuck, S. B. (2014). MAOA, childhood maltreatment, and antisocial behavior: Meta-analysis of a gene–environment interaction. *Biological Psychiatry*, 75, 9–17.

Caldwell, M. F., Vitacco, M. & Van Rybroek, G. J. (2006). Are violent delinquents worth treating? A cost–benefit analysis. *Journal of Research in Crime and Delinquency*, 43, 148–168.

Caldwell, M. F., McCormick, D. J., Umstead, D. & Van Rybroek, G. J. (2007). Evidence of treatment progress and therapeutic outcomes among adolescents with psychopathic features. *Criminal Justice and Behavior*, 34, 573–587.

Campbell, J. C., Baty, M., Ghandour, R., Stockman, J., Francisco, L. & Wagman, J. (2008). The intersection of intimate partner violence against women and HIV/AIDS: A review. *International Journal of Injury Control and Safety Promotion*, 15, 221–231.

Campbell, M. A., French, S. & Gendreau, P. (2009). The prediction of violence in adult offenders: A meta-analytic comparison of instruments and methods of assessment. *Criminal Justice and Behavior*, 36, 567–590.

Cantone, E., Piras, A. P., Vellante, M., Preti, A., Daníelsdóttir, S., D'Aloja, E., Lesinkiene, S., Angermeyer, M. C., Carta, M. G. & Bhugra, D. (2015). Interventions on bullying and cyberbullying in schools: A systematic review. *Clinical Practice & Epidemiology in Mental Health*, 11(Suppl 1: M4), 58–76.

Caspi, A., Henry, B., McGee, R. O., Moffitt, T. E. & Silva, P. A. (1995). Temperamental origins of child and adolescent behavior problems: From age three to age fifteen. *Child Development*, 66, 55–68.

Caspi, A., McClay, J., Moffitt, T. E., Mill, J., Martin, J., Craig, I. W., Taylor, A. & Poulton, R. (2002). Role of genotype in the cycle of violence in maltreated children. *Science*, 297, 851–854.

Cederman, L.-E. (2001). Back to Kant: Reinterpreting the democratic peace as a macrohistorical learning process. *American Political Science Review*, 95, 15–31.

Centers for Disease Control and Prevention (2000). *Biological and Chemical Terrorism: Strategic Plan for Preparedness and Response*. Recommendations of the CDC Strategic Planning Workgroup. Morbidity and Mortality Weekly Reports. April 21; 4, No. RR-4.

  (2018). *Technical Packages for Violence Prevention: Using Evidence-Based Strategies in Your Violence Prevention Efforts*. www.cdc.gov/violenceprevention/pub/technical-packages.html. Accessed 30 September 2018.

Chagnon, N. A. (1988). Life histories, blood revenge, and warfare in a tribal population. *Science*, 239, 985–992.

Charney, E. (2012). Behavior genetics and postgenomics. *Behavioral and Brain Sciences*, 35, 331–358.

Chimpanzee Sequencing and Analysis Consortium (2005). Initial sequence of the chimpanzee genome and comparison with the human genome. *Nature*, 437, 69–87.

Clay, Z. & de Waal, F. B. M. (2015). Sex and strife: Post-conflict sexual contacts in bonobos. *Behaviour*, 152, 313–334.

Coccaro, E. F., Bergeman, C. S., Kavoussi, R. J. & Seroczynski, A. D. (1997). Heritability of aggression and irritability: A study of the Buss-Durkee aggression scales in adult male subjects. *Biological Psychiatry*, 41, 273–284.

Cohen, J. (1988). *Statistical Power Analysis for the Behavioral Sciences*. Hillsdale, NJ: Erlbaum.

Cohen, L. E. & Machalek, R. (1988). A general theory of expropriative crime: An evolutionary ecological approach. *American Journal of Sociology*, 94, 465–501.

Collins, R. (2008). *Violence: A Micro-Sociological Theory*. Princeton, NJ: Princeton University Press.

(2009). The micro-sociology of violence. *British Journal of Sociology*, 60, 566–576.

(2013). Entering and leaving the tunnel of violence: Micro-sociological dynamics of self-entrainment in severe violence. *Current Sociology*, 61, 132–151.

Conroy, M. A. & Murrie, D. C. (2007). *Forensic Assessment of Violence Risk: A Guide for Risk Assessment and Risk Management*. Hoboken, NJ: Wiley.

Conway, K. P. & McCord, J. (2002). A longitudinal examination of the relation between co-offending with violent accomplices and violent crime. *Aggressive Behavior*, 28, 97–108.

Conway, L. G. & Schaller, M. (2002). On the verifiability of evolutionary psychological theories: An analysis of the psychology of scientific persuasion. *Personality and Social Psychology Review*, 6, 152–166.

Cooke, D. J. & Michie, C. (2010). Limitations of diagnostic precision and predictive utility in the individual case: A challenge for forensic practice. *Law and Human Behavior*, 34, 259–274.

Cooper, R. M. & Zubek, J. P. (1958). Effects of enriched and restricted early environments on the learning ability of bright and dull rats. *Canadian Journal of Psychology*, 12, 159–164.

Cornell, D. G., Warren, J., Hawk, G., Stafford, E., Oram, G. & Pine, D. (1996). Psychopathy in instrumental and reactive violent offenders. *Journal of Consulting and Clinical Psychology*, 64, 783–790.

Cosmides, L. & Tooby, J. (2013). Evolutionary psychology: New perspectives on cognition and motivation. *Annual Review of Psychology*, 64, 201–229.

Costandi, M. (2016). *Neuroplasticity*. Cambridge, MA: MIT Press.

Côté, S. M., Vaillancourt, T., LeBlanc, J. C., Nagin, D. S. & Tremblay, R. E. (2006). The development of physical aggression from toddlerhood to pre-adolescence: A nationwide longitudinal study of Canadian children. *Journal of Abnormal Child Psychology*, 34, 71–85.

Coyne, J. (2009). *Why Evolution Is True*. Oxford: Oxford University Press,

Craig, I. W. & Halton, K. E. (2009). Genetics of human aggressive behaviour. *Human Genetics*, 126, 101–113.

Craig, P., Dieppe, P., Macintyre, S. Michie, S., Nazareth, I. & Petticrew, M. (2013). Developing and evaluating complex interventions: The new Medical Research Council guidance. *International Journal of Nursing Studies*, 50, 587–592.

Crick, F. (1970). The central dogma of molecular biology. *Nature*, 227, 561–563.

Cross-Disorder Group of the Psychiatric Genomics Consortium (2013). Identification of risk loci with shared effects on five major psychiatric disorders: A genome-wide analysis. *The Lancet*, 381, 1371–1379.

Crusio, W. E. (2012). Heritability estimates in behavior genetics: Wasn't that station passed long ago? *Behavioral and Brain Sciences*, 35, 361–362.

Czech Republic Government Committee for the Prevention of Domestic Violence (2011). *National Action Plan for the Prevention of Domestic Violence for the Years 2011–2014.* www.mpsv.cz/files/clanky/12194/5_material_NAP_ 15-04-2011_en.pdf. Accessed 18 September 2018.

Daly, M. & Wilson, M. (1985). Child abuse and other risks of not living with both parents. *Ethology and Sociobiology,* 6, 197–201.

(2005). The 'Cinderella effect' is no fairy tale. *Trends in Cognitive Sciences,* 9, 507–508.

De Koker, P., Mathews, C., Zuch, M., Bastien, S. & Mason-Jones, A. J. (2014). A systematic review of interventions for preventing adolescent intimate partner violence. *Journal of Adolescent Health,* 54, 3–13.

De La Rue, L., Polanin, J. R., Espelage, D. L. & Pigott, T. D. (2014). School-based interventions to reduce dating and sexual violence: A systematic review. *Campbell Systematic Reviews,* 2014, 7. Doi: 10.4073/csr.2014.7.

de Vries Robbe, M., de Vogel, V. & Douglas, K. (2013). Risk factors and protective factors: A two sided dynamic approach to violence risk assessment. *Journal of Forensic Psychiatry and Psychology,* 24, 440–457.

Demuth, J. P., De Bie, T., Stajich, J. E., Cristianini, N. & Hahn, M. W. (2006). The evolution of mammalian gene families. *PLOS One,* 1(1): e85. Doi: 10.1371/journal.pone.0000085.

Dentan, R. K. (2004). Cautious, alert, polite, and elusive: The Semai of central peninsular Malaysia. In G. Kemp & D. P. Fry (eds.), *Keeping the Peace: Conflict Resolution and Peaceful Societies around the World.* Pp. 136–151. New York: Routledge.

Derringer, J., Corley, R. P., Haberstick, B. C., Young, S. E. & fifteen others (2015). Genome-wide association study of behavioural disinhibition in a selected adolescent sample. *Behaviour Genetics,* 45, 375–381.

Desmarais, S. L., Johnson, K. L. & Singh, J. P. (2018). Performance of recidivism risk assessment instruments in U.S. correctional settings. In J. P. Singh, D. G. Kroner, J. S. Wormith, S. L. Desmarais & Z. Hamilton (eds.), *Handbook of Recidivism Risk/Needs Assessment Tools.* Pp. 3–29. Hoboken, NJ: Wiley-Blackwell.

Devernik, M., Beck, A., Grann, M., Hogue, T. & McGuire, J. (2009). The use of psychiatric and psychological evidence in the assessment of terrorist offenders. *Journal of Forensic Psychiatry and Psychology,* 20, 508–515.

Devries, K. M., Knight, L., Child, J., Mirembe, A., Nakuti, J., Jones, R., Sturgess, J., Allen, E., Kyegombe, N., Parkes, J., Walakira, E., Elbourne, D., Watts, C. & Naker, D. (2015). The Good School Toolkit for reducing physical violence from school staff to primary school students: A cluster-randomised controlled trial in Uganda. *The Lancet Global Health,* 3, e378–e386.

Dhamija, D., Tuvblad, C. & Baker, L. A. (2016). Behavioral genetics of the externalising spectrum. In T. P. Beachaine & S. P. Hinshaw (eds.), *The Oxford Handbook of Externalizing Spectrum Disorders.* Pp. 105–124. New York: Oxford University Press.

Dick, D. M., Li, T.-K., Edenberg, H. J., Hesselbrock, V., Kramer, J., Kuperman, S., Porjesz, B., Bucholz, K., Goate, A., Numberger, J. & Foroud, T. (2004). A genome-wide screen for genes influencing conduct disorder. *Molecular Psychiatry,* 9, 81–86.

Dick, D. M., Aliev, F., Krueger, R. F., Edwards, A. & thirteen others as part of the SAGE and GENEVA Consortia. (2011). Genome-wide association study of conduct disorder symptomatology. *Molecular Psychiatry*, 16, 800–808.

D'Inverno, A., Kearns, M. & Reidy, D. (2018). The role of public policies in preventing IPV, TDV, and SV. (Introduction to Special Issue). *Journal of Interpersonal Violence*, 33, 3259–3266.

Dishion, T. J., Patterson, G. R. & Kavanagh, K. A. (1992). An experimental test of the Coercion Model: Linking theory, measurement, and intervention. In J. McCord & R. E. Tremblay (eds.), *Preventing Antisocial Behaviour: Interventions from Birth through Adolescence*. Pp. 253–282. New York: Guilford Press.

Dodge, K. A. & Pettit, G. S. (2003). A biopsychosocial model of the development of chronic conduct problems in adolescence. *Developmental Psychology*, 39, 349–371.

Doherty, J. L., O'Donovan, M. C. & Owen, M. J. (2011). Recent genomic advances in schizophrenia. *Clinical Genetics*, October. Doi: 10.1111/j.1399-0004.2011.01773.x.

D'Onofrio, B. M., Slutske, W. S., Turkheimer, E., Emery, R. E., Harden, K. P., Heath, A. C., Madden, P. F. & Martin, N. G. (2007). Intergenerational transmission of childhood conduct problems: A children of twins study. *Archives of General Psychiatry*, 64, 820–829.

Doren, D. M. & Yates, P. M. (2008). Effectiveness of sex offender treatment for psychopathic sexual offenders. *International Journal of Offender Therapy and Comparative Criminology*, 52, 234–245.

Douglas, K. S., Guy, L. & Hart, S. (2009). Psychosis as a risk factor for violence to others: A meta-analysis. *Psychological Bulletin*, 135, 679–706.

Dowden, C. & Andrews, D. A. (2000). Effective correctional treatment and violent reoffending: A meta-analysis. *Canadian Journal of Criminology and Criminal Justice*, 42, 449–467.

Dretzke, J., Davenport, C., Frew, E., Barlow, J., Stewart-Brown, S., Bayliss, S. Taylor, R. S., Sandercock, J. & Hyde, C. (2009). The clinical effectiveness of different parenting programmes for children with conduct problems: A systematic review of randomised controlled trials. *Child and Adolescent Psychiatry and Mental Health*, 3, 7. www.capmh.com/content/3/1/7.

Dubow, E. F., Huesmann, L. R., Boxer, P. & Smith, C. (2016). Childhood and adolescent risk and protective factors for violence in adulthood. *Journal of Criminal Justice*, 45, 26–31.

Duckworth, A. L. & Kern, M. L. (2011). A meta-analysis of the convergent validity of self-control measures. *Journal of Research in Personality*, 45, 259–268.

Duflo, E., Dupas, P., Kremer, M. & Sinei, S. (2006). *Education and HIV/AIDS Prevention: Evidence from a Randomized Evaluation in Western Kenya*. World Bank Policy Research Working Paper No. 4024. World Bank, Washington, DC.

Duke, A. A., Bègue, L., Bell, R. & Eisenlohr-Moul, T. (2013). Revisiting the serotonin-aggression relation in humans: A meta-analysis. *Psychological Bulletin*, 139, 1148–1172.

Duncan, L. E. & Keller, M. C. (2011). A critical review of the first 10 years of candidate gene-by-environment interaction research in psychiatry. *American Journal of Psychiatry*, 168, 1041–1049.

Duntley, J. D. & Shakelford, T. K. (2008). Darwinian foundations of crime and law. *Aggression and Violent Behaviour*, 13, 373–382.

Durrant, R. & Ward, T. (2011). Evolutionary explanations in the social and behavioral sciences: Introduction and overview. *Aggression and Violent Behavior*, 16, 361–370.

Eckert, P. & Newmark, R. (1980). Central Eskimo song duels: A contextual analysis of ritual ambiguity. *Ethnology*, 19, 191–211.

Eisner, M. (2003). Long-term historical trends in violent crime. *Crime and Justice*, 30, 83–142.

(2012). What causes large-scale variation in homicide rates? In H.-H. Kortüm & J. Heinze (eds.), *Aggression in Humans and Primates*. Pp. 137–162. Berlin: de Gruyter.

Eisner, M. &. Nivette, A. E. (2012). How to reduce the global homicide rate to 2 per 100,000 by 2060. In R. Loeber & B. Welsh (eds.), *The Future of Criminology*. Pp. 219–228. New York: Oxford University Press.

Elder-Vass, D. (2010). *The Causal Power of Social Structures*. Cambridge University Press.

Elias, N. (2000). *The Civilising Process: Sociogenetic and Psychogenetic Investigations*. 2nd edition. Chichester: Wiley.

Elliott, P., Wakefield, J. C., Best, N. & Briggs, D. J. (2000). Spatial epidemiology: Methods and applications. In P. Elliott, J. C. Wakefield, N. Best & D. J. Briggs (eds.), *Spatial Epidemiology: Methods and Applications*. Pp. 3–14. Oxford: Oxford University Press.

Ellis, L. (1991). Monoamine oxidase and criminality: Identifying an apparent biological marker for antisocial behaviour. *Journal of Research in Crime and Delinquency*, 28, 227–251.

Ellis, L., Beaver, K. & Wright, J. (2009). *Handbook of Crime Correlates*. Amsterdam: Academic Press.

Ellsberg, M., Arango, D., Morton, M., Gennari, F., Kiplesund, S., Contreras, M. & Watts, C. (2015). Prevention of violence against women and girls: What does the evidence say? *The Lancet*, 385(9977): 1555–1566.

Elman, J. L., Bates, E. A., Johnson, M. H. Karmiloff-Smith, A., Parisi, D. & Plunkett, K. (1996). *Rethinking Innateness: A Connectionist Perspective on Development*. Cambridge, MA: MIT Press.

Ember, C. R. & Ember, M. (1992). Resource unpredictability, mistrust, and war. *Journal of Conflict Resolution*, 36, 242–262.

Engel G. (1977). The need for a new medical model: A challenge for biomedicine. *Science*, 196, 129–136.

Estabrook, V. H. (2014). Violence and warfare in the European mesolithic and paleolithic. In M. W. Allen & T. L. Jones (eds.), *Violence and Warfare among Hunter-Gatherers*. Pp. 49-69. Walnut Creek, CA: Left Coast Press.

European Women's Lobby (Centre on Violence against Women) (2011). *National Action Plans on Violence against Women in the EU*. www.womenlobby.org/IMG/pdf/ewl_barometer_on_vaw_2011_en.pdf.

Ezer, T. (2009). Lessons from Africa: Combating the twin epidemics of domestic violence and HIV/AIDS. *HIV/AIDS Policy & Law Review/Canadian HIV/ AIDS Legal Network*, 13, 57–62.

Falk, Ö., Wallinius, M., Lundström, S., Frisell, T., Anckarsäter, H. & Kerekes, N. (2014). The 1% of the population accountable for 63% of all violent crime convictions. *Social Psychiatry and Psychiatric Epidemiology*, 49, 559–571.

Farmer, P. (2005). *Pathologies of Power: Health, Human Rights and the New War on the Poor.* Berkeley: University of California Press.

Farrell, M. S., Werge, T., Sklar, P., Owen, M. J., Ophoff, R. A., O'Donovan, M. C., Corvin, A., Cichon, S. & Sullivan, P. F. (2015). Evaluating historical candidate genes for schizophrenia. *Molecular Psychiatry*, 20, 555–562.

Farrington, D. P., Jolliffe, D. & Johnstone, L. (2008). *Assessing Violence Risk: A Framework for Practice.* Paisley: Risk Management Authority.

Farrington, D. P., Gaffney, H., Lösel, F. & Ttofi, M. M. (2017). Systematic reviews of the effectiveness of developmental prevention programs in reducing delinquency, aggression, and bullying. *Aggression and Violent Behavior*, 33, 91–106.

Fazel, S., Gulati, G., Linsell, L., Geddes, J. & Grann, M. (2009a). Schizophrenia and violence: Systematic review and meta-analysis. *PLOS Medicine* 6(8): e1000120.

Fazel, S., Philipson, J., Gardiner, L., Merritt, R. & Grann, M. (2009b). Neurological disorders and violence: A systematic review and meta-analysis with a focus on epilepsy and traumatic brain injury. *Journal of Neurology*, 256, 1591–1602.

Fazel, S., Lichtenstein, P., Grann, M., Goodwin, G. & Långström N. (2010). Bipolar disorder and violent crime: New evidence from population-based longitudinal studies and systematic review. *Archives of General Psychiatry*, 67, 931–938.

Fazel. S., Singh, J. P., Doll, H. & Grann, M. (2012). Use of risk assessment instruments to predict violence and antisocial behaviour in 73 samples involving 24 827 people: Systematic review and meta-analysis. *British Medical Journal*, 345, e4692. Doi: 10.1136/bmj.e4692.

Fazel, S., Zetterqvist, J., Larsson, H., Långström, N. & Lichtenstein, P. (2014). Antipsychotics, mood stabilisers, and risk of violent crime. *The Lancet*, 384 (9949), 1206–1214.

Fazel, S., Chang, Z., Fanshawe, T., Langstrom, N., Lichtenstein, P., Larsson, H. & Mallett, S. (2016). Prediction of violent reoffending on release from prison: Derivation and external validation of a scalable tool. *The Lancet Psychiatry*, 3, 535–543.

Feder, L., Wilson, D. B. & Austin, S. (2008). Court-mandated interventions for individuals convicted of domestic violence. *Campbell Systematic Reviews* 2008, 12. Doi: 10.4073/csr.2008.12.

Feldman, M. W. & Ramachandran, S. (2018). Missing compared to what? Revisiting heritability, genes and culture. *Philosophical Transactions of the Royal Society B*, 373, 20170064. Doi.org/10.1098/rstb.2017.0064.

Felson, J. (2014). What can we learn from twin studies? A comprehensive evaluation of the equal environments assumption. *Social Science Research*, 43, 184–199.

Felson, R. B. & Staff, J. (2010). The effects of alcohol intoxication on violent versus other offending. *Criminal Justice and Behavior*, 37, 1343–1360.

Felson, R. B. & Steadman, H. J. (1983). Situational factors in disputes leading to criminal violence. *Criminology*, 21, 59–74.

Ferguson, C. J. (2010). Genetic contributions to antisocial personality and behaviour: A meta-analytic review from an evolutionary perspective. *Journal of Social Psychology*, 150, 160–180.

Ferguson, C. J. & Beaver, K. M. (2009). Natural born killers: The genetic origins of extreme violence. *Aggression and Violent Behavior*, 14, 286–294.

Ferguson, R. B. (2011). Born to live: Challenging killer myths. In R. W. Sussman & C. R. Cloninger (eds.), *Origins of Altruism and Cooperation*. Pp. 249–270. New York: Springer.

(2012). Why evolutionary psychology cannot be true. Paper prepared for the Annual Meeting of the American Anthropological Association, San Francisco.

(2013a). Pinker's list: Exaggerating prehistoric war mortality. In D. P. Fry (ed.), *War, Peace and Human Nature: The Convergence of Evolutionary and Cultural Views*. Pp. 112–131. New York: Oxford University Press.

(2013b). The prehistory of war and peace in Europe and the Near East. In D. P. Fry (ed.), *War, Peace and Human Nature: The Convergence of Evolutionary and Cultural Views*. Pp. 191–240. New York: Oxford University Press.

Ficks, C. A. & Waldman, I. D. (2014). Candidate genes for aggression and antisocial behaviour: A meta-analysis of association studies of the 5HTTLPR and MAOA-uVNTR. *Behavior Genetics*, 22, 427–444.

Foran, H. M. & O'Leary, K. D. (2008). Alcohol and intimate partner violence: A meta-analytic review. *Clinical Psychology Review*, 28, 1222–1234.

Fosse, R., Joseph, J. & Richardson, K. (2015). A critical assessment of the equal-environment assumption of the twin method for schizophrenia. *Frontiers in Psychiatry*, 6, article 62. Doi: 10.3389/fpsyt.2015.00062.

Foster, E., Jones, D. & the Conduct Problems Prevention Research Group. (2006). Can a costly intervention be cost-effective? An analysis of violence prevention. *Archives of General Psychiatry*, 63, 1284–1291.

Frances, A. (2016). *Saving Normal: An Insider's Revolt against Out-of-Control Psychiatric Diagnosis, DSM-5, Big Pharma and the Medicalization of Everyday Life*. London: Harper Collins.

Frazier, S. N. & Vela, J. (2014). Dialectical behaviour therapy for the treatment of anger and aggressive behaviour: A review. *Aggression and Violent Behavior*, 19, 156–163.

Frogley, C., Taylor, D., Dickens, G. & Picchioni, M. (2012). A systematic review of the evidence of clozapine's anti-aggressive effects. *International Journal of Neuropsychopharmacology* 15, 1351–1371.

Fry, D. P. (2011). Human forager model. In R. W. Sussman & C. R. Cloninger (eds.), *Origins of Altruism and Cooperation*. Pp. 227–247. New York: Springer.

(2012). Life without war. *Science*, 339, 879–884.

(ed.) (2013). *War, Peace and Human Nature: The Convergence of Evolutionary and Cultural Views*. New York: Oxford University Press.

Fry, D. P. & Söderberg, P. (2013). Lethal aggression in mobile forager bands and implications for the origins of war. *Science*, 341, 270–273.

Fry, D. P. & Szala, A. (2013). The evolution of agonism: The triumph of restraint in nonhuman and human primates. In D. P. Fry (ed.), *War, Peace and Human Nature: The Convergence of Evolutionary and Cultural Views.* Pp. 451–474. New York: Oxford University Press.

Gadon, L., Johnstone, L. & Cooke, D. J. (2006). Situational variables and institutional violence: A systematic review of the literature. *Clinical Psychology Review*, 26, 515–534.

Galtung, J. (1969). Violence, peace, and peace research. *Journal of Peace Research*, 6, 167–191.

(1980). *The True Worlds: A Transnational Perspective.* New York: Free Press.

(2010). The TRANSCEND Method in conflict mediation across levels. *European Psychologist*, 15, 82–90.

Gannon, L. (2002). A critique of evolutionary psychology. *Psychology, Evolution and Gender*, 4, 173–218.

Gannon, T. A., Olver, M. E., Mallion, J. S. & James, M. (2019). Does specialized psychological treatment for offending reduce recidivism? A meta-analysis examining staff and program variables as predictors of treatment effectiveness. *Clinical Psychology Review*, doi: 10.1016/j.cpr.2019.101752.

Gard, A., Dotterer, H. L. & Hyde, L. W. (2019). Genetic influences on antisocial behaviour: Recent advances and future directions. *Current Opinion in Psychology*, 27, 46–55.

Gardner, D., Lidz, C. W., Mulvey, E. P. & Shaw, E. C. (1996). A comparison of actuarial methods for identifying repetitively violent patients with mental illnesses. *Law and Human Behavior*, 20, 35–48.

Gardner, P. M. (2000). Respect and nonviolence among recently sedentary Paliyan foragers. *Journal of the Royal Anthropological Institute*, 6, 215–236.

Garrido, V. & Morales, L. A. (2007). *Serious (Violent and Chronic) Juvenile Offenders: A Systematic Review of Treatment Effectiveness in Secure Corrections.* Philadelphia: Campbell Collaboration Reviews of Intervention and Policy Evaluations (C2-RIPE). www.campbellcollaboration.org/doc-pdf/Garrido_seriousjuv_review.pdf.

Gat, A. (2015). Proving communal warfare among hunter-gatherers: The quasi-Rousseauan error. *Evolutionary Anthropology*, 24, 111–126.

(2019). Is war in our nature? What is right and what is wrong about the Seville Statement on Violence. *Human Nature*, 30, 149–154.

Gault-Sherman, M. (2012). It's a two-way street: The bidirectional relationship between parenting and delinquency. *Journal of Youth and Adolescence*, 41, 121–145.

Gehlert, S., Sohmer, D., Sacks, T., Mininger, C., McClintock, M. & Olopade, O. (2008). Targeting health disparities: A model linking upstream determinants to downstream interventions. *Health Affairs*, 27, 339–349.

Gender Links for Equality and Justice (2018). *Policy and Action Plans.* http://genderlinks.org.za/what-we-do/justice/policy-and-action-plans/. Accessed 19 September 2018.

Gendreau, P. & Cullen, F. (2008). Martinson redux. *Crime Scene: The Official Organ of Criminal Justice Psychology of the Canadian Psychological Association,* 15, 13–15.

Genovés, S. (1977). Acali, Ra 1, and Ra 2: Some conclusions and hypotheses concerning human friction under isolation and stress, with special reference to intelligence and personality assessment. *Aggressive Behavior,* 3, 163–171.

(1980). *The Acali Experiment.* New York: Times Books.

(1981). The dissemination of information and misinformation on aggression to the public. *Aggressive Behavior,* 7, 371–375.

Georgieva, I., Mulder, C. & Whittington, R. (2012). Evaluation of behavioral changes and subjective distress after exposure to coercive inpatient interventions. *BMC Psychiatry,* 12(1), 54.

Georgieva, I., Mulder, C. & Noorthoorn, E. (2013). Reducing seclusion through involuntary medication: A randomized clinical trial. *Psychiatry Research* 205, 48–53.

Ghaemi, S. (2009). The rise and fall of the biopsychosocial model. *British Journal of Psychiatry,* 195, 3–4.

Gibbons, A. (2009). Ardipithecus ramidus. *Science,* 326, 1598–1599.

Gizer, I. R., Otto, J. M. & Ellingson, J. M. (2016a). Molecular genetic approaches to studying the externalising spectrum. In T. P. Beachaine & S. P. Hinshaw (eds.), *The Oxford Handbook of Externalizing Spectrum Disorders.* Pp. 125–148. New York: Oxford University Press.

(2016b). Molecular genetics of the externalising spectrum. In T. P. Beachaine & S. P. Hinshaw (eds.), *The Oxford Handbook of Externalizing Spectrum Disorders.* Pp. 149–169. New York: Oxford University Press.

Glaser, D. (1987). Classification for risk. In D. Gottfredson & M. Tonry (eds.), *Prediction and Classification: Criminal Justice Decision Making.* Pp. 249–291. Chicago: University of Chicago Press.

Gleditsch, N., Wallensteen, P., Eriksson, M., Sollenberg, M. & Strand, H. (2002). Armed conflict 1946–2001: A new dataset. *Journal of Peace Research,* 39, 615–637.

Godar, S., Fite, P. J., McFarlin, K. M. & Bortolato, M. (2016). The role of monoamine oxidase A in aggression: Current translational developments and future challenges. *Progress in Neuro-Psychopharmacology & Biological Psychiatry,* 69, 90–100.

Goetz, A. T. (2010). The evolutionary psychology of violence. *Psicothema,* 22, 15–21.

Goldstein, J. H. (1989). Beliefs about human aggression. In J. Groebel & R. A. Hinde (eds.), *Aggression and War: Their Biological and Social Bases.* Pp. 10–19. Cambridge: Cambridge University Press.

Gossop, M., Trakada, K., Stewart, D. & Witton, J. (2005). Reductions in criminal convictions after addiction treatment: 5-year follow-up. *Drug and Alcohol Dependence* 79, 295–302.

Gould, S. J. & Lewontin, S. (1979). The spandrels of San Marco and the Panglossian paradigm: A critique of the adaptationist programme. *Philosophical Transactions of the Royal Society B,* 205, 581–598.

Gowdy, J. (1999). Hunter-gatherers and the mythology of the market. In R. B. Lee & R. Daly (eds.), *The Cambridge Encyclopedia of Hunters and Gatherers*. Pp. 391–398. Cambridge: Cambridge University Press.

Graduate Institute of International and Development Studies (2007). *Small Arms Survey 2007: Guns and the City*. Geneva: Graduate Institute. www .smallarmssurvey.org/publications/by-type/yearbook/small-arms-survey-2007 .html.

Graham, K., Bernards, S., Osgood, D. W. & Wells, S. (2006). Bad nights or bad bars? Multi-level analysis of environmental predictors of aggression in late-night large-capacity bars and clubs. *Addiction*, 101, 1569–1580.

Granic, I. & Dishion, T. J. (2003). Deviant talk in adolescent friendships: A step toward measuring a pathogenic attractor process. *Social Development*, 12, 314–334.

Grassi, L., Peron, L., Marangoni, C., Zanchi, P. & Vanni, A. (2008). Character-istics of violent behaviour in acute psychiatric in-patients: A 5-year Italian study. *Acta Psychiatrica Scandinavica*, 104, 273–279.

Griggs, D., Stafford-Smith, M., Gaffney, O., Rockström, J., Öhman, M., Shyamsundar, P., Steffen, W., Glaser, G., Kanie, N. & Noble. I. (2013). Sustainable development goals for people and planet. *Nature*, 495(7441), 305–307.

Grisso, T. & Appelbaum, P. S. (1992). Is it unethical to offer predictions of future violence? *Law and Human Behavior*, 16, 621–633.

Groebel, J. & Hinde, R. A. (eds.) (1989). *Aggression and War: Their Biological and Social Bases*. Cambridge: Cambridge University Press.

Grove, W. M. (2005). Clinical versus statistical prediction: The contribution of Paul E. Meehl. *Journal of Clinical Psychology*, 61, 1233–1243.

Grove, W. M. & Meehl, P. E. (1996). Comparative efficiency of informal (sub-jective, impressionistic) and formal (mechanical, algorithmic) prediction procedures. *Psychology, Public Policy and Law*, 2, 293–323.

Grove, W. M., Zald, D. H., Lebow, B. S., Snitz, B. E. & Nelson, C. (2000). Clinical versus mechanical prediction: A meta-analysis. *Psychological Assess-ment*, 12, 19–30.

Guerra, N. G., Tolan, P. H. & Hammond, W. R. (1994). Prevention and treatment of adolescent violence. In L. D. Eron, J. H. Gentry & P. Schlegel (eds.), *Reason to Hope: A Psychosocial Perspective on Violence and Youth*. Pp. 383–403. Washington, DC: American Psychological Association.

Guilaine, J. & Zammit, J. (2005). *The Origins of War: Violence in Prehistory*. Malden, MA: Blackwell Publishing.

Guo, G., Roettger, M. E. & Shih, J. C. (2007). Contributions of the DAT1 and DRD2 genes to serious and violent delinquency among adolescents and young adults. *Human Genetics*, 121, 125–136.

Guy, L. S. (2008). *Performance indicators of the Structured Professional Judgment approach to assessing risk for violence to others: A meta-analytic survey*. Unpub-lished doctoral dissertation, Simon Fraser University, Vancouver, BC.

Guy, L. S., Packer, I. K. & Warnken, W. (2012). Assessing risk of violence using structured professional judgment guidelines. *Journal of Forensic Psychology Practice*, 12, 270–283.

Haberstick, B. C., Lessem, J. M., Hewitt, J. K., Smolen, A., Hopfer, C. J., Halpern, C. T., Killeya-Jones, L. A., Boardman, J. D., Tabor, J., Siegler, I. C., Williams, R. B. & Harris, K. M. (2014). MAOA genotype, childhood maltreatment, and their interaction in the etiology of adult antisocial behaviours. *Biological Psychiatry*, 75, 25–30.

Halpern, D. (2015). *Inside the Nudge Unit: How Small Changes Can Make a Big Difference*. London: W. H. Allen.

Hamelin, J., Travis, R. & Sturmey, P. (2013). Anger management and intellectual disabilities: A systematic review. *Journal of Mental Health Research in Intellectual Disabilities*, 6, 60–70.

Hanson, R. K. (2009). The psychological assessment of risk for crime and violence. *Canadian Psychology*, 50, 172–182.

Hanson, R. K. & Howard, P. D. (2010). Individual confidence intervals do not inform decision-makers about the accuracy of risk assessment evaluations. *Law and Human Behavior*, 34, 275–281.

Hanson, R. K. & Morton-Bourgon, K. E. (2009). The accuracy of recidivism risk assessments for sexual offenders: A meta-analysis of 118 prediction studies. *Psychological Assessment*, 21, 1–21.

Hare, B. (2017). Survival of the friendliest: *Homo sapiens* evolved via selection for prosociality. *Annual Review of Psychology*, 68, 155–186.

Hare, R. D. (1996). Psychopathy: A clinical construct whose time has come. *Criminal Justice and Behavior*, 23, 25–54.

Hare, R. D. & Neumann, C. S. (2008). Psychopathy as a clinical and empirical construct. *Annual Review of Clinical Psychology*, 4, 217–246.

Harris, G. T., Rice, M. E. & Quinsey, V. L. (2008). Shall evidence-based risk assessment be abandoned? *British Journal of Psychiatry*, 192, 154.

Harris, W. V. (2004). *Restraining Rage: The Ideology of Anger Control in Classical Antiquity*. Cambridge, MA: Harvard University Press

Hart, S. D. & Cooke, D. J. (2013). Another look at the (im-)precision of individual risk estimates made using actuarial risk assessment instruments. *Behavioral Sciences and the Law*, 31, 81–102.

Hart, S. D., Michie, C. & Cooke, D. J. (2007). Precision of actuarial risk assessment instruments: Evaluating the 'margins of error' of group v. individual predictions of violence. *British Journal of Psychiatry*, 190, 60–65.

Hay, D. F., Perra, O., Hudson, K., Waters, C. S., Mundy, L., Phillips, R., Goodyer, I., Harold, G., Thapar, A., van Goozen, S. & the CCDS team (2010). Identifying early signs of aggression: Psychometric properties of the Cardiff Infant Contentiousness Scale. *Aggressive Behavior*, 36, 351–357.

Hay, D. F., Waters, C. S., Perra, O., Swift, N., Kairis, V., Phillips, R., Jones, R., Goodyer, I., Harold, G. Thapar, A. & van Goozen, S. (2014). Precursors to aggression are evident by six months of age. *Developmental Science*, 17, 471–480.

Heilbrun, K. (2003). Violence risk: From prediction to management. In D. Carson & R. Bull (eds.), *Handbook of Psychology in Legal Contexts*. 2nd edition. Pp. 127–142. Chichester: John Wiley & Sons.

Heilbrun, K., Yasuhara, K. & Shah, S. (2010). Violence risk assessment tools. In R. K. Otto & K. S. Douglas (eds.), *Handbook of Violence Risk Assessment*. Pp. 1–17. New York: Taylor & Francis.

Heise, L. L. (1998). Violence against women: An integrated, ecological framework. *Violence against Women*, 4, 262–290.

Hemphill, S. A., Heerde, J. A. & Scholes-Balog, K. E. (2016). Risk factors and risk-based protective factors for violent offending: A study of young Victorians. *Journal of Criminal Justice*, 45, 94–100.

Henwood, K. S., Chou, S. & Browne, K. D. (2015). A systematic review and meta-analysis on the effectiveness of CBT informed anger management. *Aggression and Violent Behavior*, 25, 280–292.

Hepple, B. (2010). The new single Equality Act in Britain. *The Equal Rights Review*, 5, 11–24.

Heres, S., Davis, J., Maino, K., Jetzinger, E., Kisling, W. & Leucht, S. (2006). Why olanzapine beats risperidone, riseridone beats quetiapine, and quetiapine beats olanzapine: An exploratory analysis of head-to-head comparison studies of second-generation antipsychotics. *American Journal of Psychiatry*, 163, 185–194.

Hillebrand, E. (2008). The global distribution of income in 2050. *World Development*, 36, 727–740.

Hines, D. A. & Saudino, K. J. (2004). Genetic and environmental influences on intimate partner aggression: A preliminary study. *Violence and Victims*, 19, 701–718.

Hirata, Y., Zai, C. C., Nowrouzi, B., Beitchman, J. H. & Kennedy, J. L. (2013). Study of the catechol-O-methyltransferase (COMT) gene with high aggression in children. *Aggressive Behavior*, 39, 45–51.

Hockenhull, J. C., Whittington, R., Leitner, M., Barr, W., McGuire, J., Cherry, M. G., Flentje, R., Quinn, B., Dundar, Y. & Dickson, R. (2012). A systematic review of prevention and intervention strategies for populations at high risk of engaging in violent behaviour: Update 2002–8. *Health Technology Assessment*, 16(3), 1–145.

Hockenhull, J. C., Cherry, M. G., Whittington, R., Dickson, R. C., Leitner, M., Barr, W. & McGuire, J. (2015). Heterogeneity in the interpersonal violence outcome research: An investigation and discussion of clinical and research implications. *Aggression and Violent Behavior*, 22, 18–25.

Hoeve, M., Dubas, J. S., Eichelsheim, V. I., van der Laan, P. H., Smeenk, W. & Gerris, J. R. M. (2009). The relationship between parenting and delinquency: A meta-analysis. *Journal of Abnormal Child Psychology*, 37, 749–775.

Hoffman, M., Gneezy, U. & List, J. A. (2011). Nurture affects gender differences in spatial abilities. *Proceedings of the National Academy of Sciences*, 108, 14786–14788.

Hofvander, B., Ossowski, D., Lundström, S. & Anckarsäter, H. (2009). Continuity of aggressive antisocial behaviour from childhood to adulthood: The question of phenotype definition. *International Journal of Law and Psychiatry*, 32, 224–234.

Hollin, C. R. (2002). Risk-needs assessment and allocation to offender programmes. In J. McGuire (ed.), *Offender Rehabilitation and Treatment: Effective Programmes and Policies to Reduce Re-offending*. Pp. 309–332. Chichester: Wiley.

Honderich, T. (2006). *Punishment: The Supposed Justifications Revisited*. Revised edition. London: Pluto Press.

Hood, K. E. (2005). Toward an integrative account of the development of aggressive behaviour. In D. M. Stoff & E. J. Susman (eds.), *Developmental Psychobiology of Aggression*. Pp. 225–251. Cambridge: Cambridge University Press.

Hopkins, W. D., Adams, M. J. & Weiss, A. (2013). Genetic and environmental contributions to the expression of handedness in chimpanzees (*Pan troglodytes*). *Genes, Brain and Behavior*, 12, 446–452.

Horney, J. (2001). Criminal events and criminal careers: An integrative approach to the study of violence. In R. F. Meier, L. W. Kennedy & V. F. Sacco (eds.), *The Process and Structure of Crime: Criminal Events and Crime Analysis*. Advances in Criminological Theory, vol. 9. Pp. 141–167. New Brunswick, NJ: Transaction Publishers.

Horney, J., Osgood, D. W. & Marshall, I. H. (1995). Criminal careers in the short-term: Intra-individual variability in crime and its relation to local life circumstances. *American Sociological Review*, 60, 655–673.

Howard, P. (2018). Offender Group Reconviction Scale. In J. P. Singh, D. G. Kroner, J. S. Wormith, S. L. Desmarais & Z. Hamilton (eds.), *Handbook of Recidivism Risk/Needs Assessment Tools*. Pp. 231–241. Hoboken, NJ: Wiley-Blackwell.

Hsiang, S. M., Burke, M. & Miguel, E. (2013). Quantifying the influence of climate change on human conflict. *Science*, 341, 1235367. Doi: 10.1126/science.1235367.

Huckshorn, K. (2004). Reducing seclusion restraint in mental health use settings: Core strategies for prevention. *Journal of Psychosocial Nursing and Mental Health Services* 42, 22–33.

Hughes, K., Bellis, M., Hardcastle, K., Butchart, A., Dahlberg, L., Mercy, J. & Mikton, C. (2014). Global development and diffusion of outcome evaluation research for interpersonal and self-directed violence prevention from 2007 to 2013: A systematic review. *Aggression and Violent Behavior*, 19, 655–662.

Human Security Report Project (2013). *The Decline in Global Violence: Evidence, Explanation and Contestation (Human Security Report 2013)*. Vancouver: Simon Fraser University.

Hyman, S. (2010). The diagnosis of mental disorders: The problem of reification. *Annual Review of Clinical Psychology*, 6, 155–179.

Iga, M. (1996). Cultural aspects of suicide: The case of Japanese oyaki shinj [ubar] (parent–child suicide). *Archives of Suicide Research*, 2, 87–102.

Ilyas, S. & Moncrieff, J. (2012). Trends in prescriptions and costs of drugs for mental disorders in England, 1998–2010. *British Journal of Psychiatry*, 200, 393–398.

Imrey, P. B. & Dawid, A. P. (2014). A commentary on statistical assessment of violence recidivism risk. *Statistics and Public Policy*, 2, 25–42.

Institute for Policy Studies (2017). *Global inequality*. http://inequality.org/global-inequality/. Accessed 3 May 2019.

International Labour Organization (ILO) (2019). *Safety and Health at the Heart of the Future of Work: Building on 100 Years of Experience*. Geneva: International Labour Office.

Iofrida, C., Palumbo, S. & Pellegrini, S. (2014). Molecular genetics and anti-social behavior: Where do we stand? *Experimental Biology and Medicine*, 239, 1514–1523.

Jablonka, E. & Lamb, M. J. (2005). *Evolution in Four Dimensions: Genetic, Epigenetic, Behavioral and Symbolic Variation in the History of Life*. Cambridge, MA: MIT Press.

Janka, C., Gallasch-Nemitz, F., Biedermann, J. & Dahle, K.-P. (2012). The significance of offending behavior for predicting sexual recidivism among sex offenders of various age groups. *International Journal of Law and Psychiatry*, 35, 159–164.

Janskepp, J. & Janskepp, J. B. (2000). The seven sins of evolutionary psychology. *Evolution and Cognition*, 6, 108–131.

Jewell, L. M. & Wormith, J. S. (2010). Variables associated with attrition from domestic violence treatment programs targeting male batterers: A meta-analysis. *Criminal Justice and Behavior*, 37, 1086–1113.

Jewkes, R., Gibbs, A., Jama-Shai, N., Willan, S., Misselhorn, A., Mushinga, M., Washington, L., Mbatha, N. & Skiweyiya, Y. (2014). Stepping Stones and Creating Futures intervention: Shortened interrupted time series evaluation of a behavioural and structural health promotion and violence prevention intervention for young people in informal settlements in Durban, South Africa. *BMC Public Health* 14, 1325.

Jha, P., Kester, M. A., Kumar, R., Ram, F., Ram, U., Aleksandrowicz, L., Bassani, D. G., Chandra, S. & Banthia, J. K. (2011). Trends in selective abortion of female foetuses in India: Analysis of nationally representative birth histories from 1990 to 2005 and census data from 1991 to 2011. *The Lancet*, 377, 1921–1928.

Jiminéz-Barbero, J. A., Hernández, J. A., Esteban, B. L. & García, M. P. (2012). Effectiveness of antibullying school programmes: A systematic review by evidence levels. *Children and Youth Services Review*, 34, 1646–1658.

Jiminéz-Barbero, J. A., Hernández, J. A. R., Llor-Zaragoza, L., García, M. P. & Llor-Esteban, B. (2016). Effectiveness of anti-bullying programs: A meta-analysis. *Children and Youth Services Review*, 61, 165–175.

Johansson, A., Santtila, P., Corander, J., Alanko, K. Jern, P., von der Pahlen, B. & Sandnabba, N. K. (2010). Genetic effects on anger control and their interaction with alcohol intoxication: A self-report study. *Biological Psychology*, 85, 291–298.

Johnstone, L. & Boyle, M. with Cromby, J., Dillon, J., Harper, D., Kinderman, P., Longden, E., Pilgrim, D. & Read, J. (2018). *The Power Threat Meaning Framework: Towards the Identification of Patterns in Emotional Distress, Unusual Experiences and Troubled or Troubling Behaviour, as an Alternative to Functional Psychiatric Diagnosis*. Leicester: British Psychological Society.

Jolliffe, D. & Farrington, D. P. (2009). *Effectiveness of Interventions for Adult Male Violent Offenders*. Stockholm: Swedish National Council for Crime Prevention. www.bra.se.

Jones, A. (2017). *Genocide: A Comprehensive Introduction*. 3rd edition. Abingdon: Routledge.

Jones, T. L. & Allen, M. W. (2014). The prehistory of violence and warfare among hunter-gatherers. In M. W. Allen & T. L. Jones (eds.), *Violence and Warfare among Hunter-Gatherers*. Pp. 353–371. Walnut Creek, CA: Left Coast Press.

Joseph, J. (2015). *The Trouble with Twin Studies: A Reassessment of Twin Research in the Social and Behavioral Sciences*. London: Routledge.

Kagan, J. (1998). *Galen's Prophecy: Temperament in Human Nature*. Boulder, CO: Westview Press.

Kagan, J. & Snidman, N. (2004). *The Long Shadow of Temperament*. Cambridge, MA: Belknap Press of Harvard University Press.

Kagan, J., Snidman, N., Khan, V. & Towsley, S. (2007). The preservation of two infant temperaments into adolescence. *Monographs of the Society for Research in Child Development*, 72, 1–95.

Kaighobadi, F., Shakelford, T. K. & Goetz, A. T. (2009). From mate retention to murder: Evolutionary psychological perspectives on men's partner-directed violence. *Review of General Psychology*, 13, 327–334.

Kaldor, M. (2013). *New and Old Wars: Organized Violence in a Global Era*. 3rd edition. London: Cambridge: Polity Press.

Kales, H., Zivin, K., Kim, H., Valenstein, M., Chiang, C., Ignacio, R., Ganoczy, D., Cunningham, F., Schneider, L. & Blow, F. (2011). Trends in antipsychotic use in dementia 1999–2007. *Archives of General Psychiatry*, 68, 190–197.

Kaminski, J. W., Valle, L. A., Filene, J. H. & Boyle, C. L. (2008). A meta-analytic review of components associated with parent training program effectiveness. *Journal of Abnormal Child Psychology*, 36, 567–589.

Kamphuis, J., Meerlo, P., Koolhaas, J. M. & Lancel, M. (2012). Poor sleep as a potential causal factor in aggression and violence. *Sleep Medicine*, 13, 327–334.

Kaplan, D. (2000). The darker side of the 'Original Affluent Society'. *Journal of Anthropological Research*, 56, 301–324.

Kay, S., Wolkenfeld, F. & Murrill, L. (1988). Profiles of aggression among psychiatric patients: I. Nature and prevalence. *The Journal of Nervous and Mental Disease*, 176, 539–546.

Keller, E. F. (2015). The postgenomic genome. In S. R. Richardson & H. Stevens (eds.), *Postgenomics: Perspectives on Biology after the Genome*. Pp. 9–31. Durham, NC: Duke University Press.

Kelly, R. C. (2005). The evolution of lethal intergroup violence. *Proceedings of the National Academy of Sciences*, 102, 15294–15298.

Kennedy, L. W. & Baron, S. W. (1993). Routine activities and a subculture of violence: A study of violence on the street. *Journal of Research in Crime and Delinquency*, 30, 88–112.

Kennedy, L. W. & Forde, D. R. (1996). Pathways to aggression: A factorial study of 'routine conflict'. *Journal of Quantitative Criminology*, 12, 417–438.

Khiroya, R., Weaver, T. & Maden, T. (2009). Use and perceived utility of structured violence risk assessments in English medium secure forensic units. *Psychiatric Bulletin*, 33, 129–132.

Killias, M. & Markwalder, N. (2012). Firearms and homicide in Europe. In M. C. A. Liem & W. A. Pridemore (eds.), *Handbook of European Homicide*

Research: Patterns, Explanations and Country Studies. Pp. 261–272. Springer Science + Business Media. Doi: 10.1007/978-1-4614-0466-8_16.

Kim, B. K. E., Gilman, A. B., Hill, K. G. & Hawkins, D. J. (2016). Examining protective factors against violence among high-risk youth: Findings from the Seattle Social Development Project. *Journal of Criminal Justice*, 45, 19–25.

Kingdom of Cambodia (2018). *National Action Plan to Prevent Violence against Women 2014–18.* https://drive.google.com/file/d/0By4DrHxo3C94Skx4Vm ZUN2JoMmc/view?pli=1. Accessed 18 September 2018.

Klusemann, S. (2010). Micro-situational antecedents of violent atrocity. *Sociological Forum*, 25, 272–295.

(2012). Massacres as process: A micro-sociological theory of internal patterns of mass atrocities. *European Journal of Criminology*, 9, 468–480.

Knauft, B. M. (2011). Violence reduction among the Gebusi of Papua New Guinea – And across humanity. In R. W. Sussman & C. R. Cloninger (eds.), *Origins of Altruism and Cooperation.* Pp. 203–225. Developments in Primatology: Progress and Prospects, 36. New York: Springer.

Knauft, B. M., Daly, M., Wilson, M., Donald, L., Morren, G. E. E., Otterbein, K. F., Ross, M. H., Thoden, H. U. E. & van Wetering, W. (1987). Reconsidering violence in simple human societies: Homicide among the Gebusi of New Guinea. *Current Anthropology*, 28, 457–500.

Knopik, V. S., Neiderhiser, J. M., DeFries, J. C. & Plomin, R. (2017). *Behavioral Genetics.* 7th edition. New York: Worth Publishers.

Koenig, M. A., Ahmed, S., Hossain, M. & Mozumder, A. (2003). Women's status and domestic violence in rural Bangladesh: Individual- and community-level effects. *Demography*, 40, 269–288.

Krakowski, M., Czobor, P., Citrome, L., Bark, N. & Cooper, T. (2006). Atypical antipsychotic agents in the treatment of violent patients with schizophrenia and schizoaffective disorder. *Archives of General Psychiatry*, 63, 622–629.

Krieger, N. (2008). Proximal, distal, and the politics of causation: What's level got to do with it? *American Journal of Public Health*, 98, 221–230.

Kroner, D. G., Mills, J. F. & Reddon, J. R. (2005). A coffee can, factor analysis, and prediction of antisocial behavior: The structure of criminal risk. *International Journal of Law and Psychiatry*, 28, 360–374.

Krug, E. G., Mercy, J., Dahlberg, L. & Zwi, A. (2002). The World Report on Violence and Health. *The Lancet*, 360(9339), 1083–1088.

Krützen, M., Willems, E. P. & van Schaik, C. P. (2011). Culture and geographic variation in orangutan behavior. *Current Biology*, 21, 1808–1812.

Kuin, N., Masthoff, E., Kramer, M. & Schreder, E. (2015). The role of risky decision-making in aggression: A systematic review. *Aggression and Violent Behavior*, 25, 159–172.

Ladyman, J. (2002). *Understanding Philosophy of Science.* London: Routledge.

Laland, K. N. & Brown, G. R. (2011). *Sense and Nonsense: Evolutionary Perspectives on Human Behaviour.* 2nd edition. Oxford: Oxford University Press.

(2018). The social construction of human nature. In E. Hannon & T. Lewens (eds.), *Why We Disagree about Human Nature.* Pp. 127–144. Oxford: Oxford University Press.

Laland, K. N., Uller, T, Feldman, M. W., Sterelny, K., Müller, G. B, Moczek, A., Jablonka, E. & Odling-Smee, J. (2015). The extended evolutionary synthesis: Its structure, assumptions and predictions. *Proceedings of the Royal Society B*, 282, 20151019. Doi: 10.1098/rspb.2015.1019.

Lansford, J. E., Miller-Johnson, S., Berlin, L. J., Dodge, K. A., Bates, J. E. & Pettit, G. S. (2007). Early physical abuse and later violent delinquency: A prospective longitudinal study. *Child Maltreatment*, 12, 233–245.

Larsson, H., Andershed, H. & Lichtenstein, P. (2006). A genetic factor explains most of the variation in the psychopathic personality. *Journal of Abnormal Psychology*, 115, 221–230.

LeBlanc, S. & Register, K. E. (2003). *Constant Battles: Why We Fight*. New York: St. Martin's Press.

Lee, B. X. (2015). Causes and cures I: Toward a new definition. *Aggression and Violent Behavior*, 25, 199–203.

Lee, L., Kim, C.-J. & Kim, D. H. (2015). A meta-analysis of the effect of school-based anti-bullying programs. *Journal of Child Health Care*, 19, 136–153.

Lehman, B. J., David, D. M. & Gruber, J. A. (2017). Rethinking the biopsychosocial model of health: Understanding health as a dynamic system. *Social & Personality Psychology Compass*, 11: e12328. Doi.org/10.1111/spc3.12328.

Leitner, M., Jones, S, Barr, W., Whittington, R. & McGuire, J. (2006). *Systematic Review of Prevention and Intervention Strategies for Populations at High Risk of Engaging in Violent Behaviour*. Final project report to the NHS National Forensic Mental Health R&D Programme.

Leschied, A., Chiodo, D., Nowicki, E. & Rodger, S. (2008). Childhood predictors of adult criminality: A meta-analysis drawn from the prospective longitudinal literature. *Canadian Journal of Criminology and Criminal Justice*, 435–467.

Lester, S., Lawrence, C. & Ward, C. L. (2017). What do we know about preventing school violence? A systematic review of systematic reviews. *Psychology, Health & Medicine*, 22, 187–223.

Levitt, M. (2013). Perceptions of nature, nurture and behaviour. *Life Sciences, Society and Policy*, 9, 1–11.

Lewens, T. (2015). *Cultural Evolution: Conceptual Challenges*. Oxford: Oxford University Press.

Lewis, R. (2011). *Human Genetics: The Basics*. London: Routledge.

Lewis, T., Leeb, R., Kotch, J., Smith, J., Thompson, R., Black, M. M., Pelaez-Merrick, M., Briggs, E. & Coyne-Beasley, T. (2007). Maltreatment history and weapon carrying among early adolescents. *Child Maltreatment*, 12, 259–268.

Lewontin, S. (2006). The analysis of variance and the analysis of causes. *International Journal of Epidemiology*, 35, 520–525. [Originally published in the *American Journal of Human Genetics* (1974), 26, 400–411.]

Lien, Y.-J., Chen, W. J., Hsiao, P.-C. & Tsuang, H.-C. (2015). Estimation of heritability for varied indexes of handedness. *Laterality*, 20, 469–482.

Lim, S. S., Vos, T., Flaxman, A & 206 others (2012). A comparative risk assessment of burden of disease and injury attributable to 67 risk factors and risk factor clusters in 21 regions, 1990–2010: A systematic analysis for the Global Burden of Disease Study 2010. *The Lancet*, 380(9859), 2224–2260.

Limbos, M. A., Chan, L. S., Warf, C., Schneir, A., Iverson, E., Shekelle, P. & Kipke, M. D. (2007). Effectiveness of interventions to prevent youth violence: A systematic review. *American Journal of Preventive Medicine*, 33, 65–74.

Lindvall, D. (2018). Editorial Issue 85. *Film International*, 16(3), 4-5. Doi: 10.1386/fiin.16.3.4_2.

Link, B. G. & Phelan, J. (1995). Social conditions as fundamental causes of disease. *Journal of Health and Social Behavior*, Extra Issue, 80–94.

Linquist, S., Machery, E., Griffiths, P. E. & Stotz, K. (2011). Exploring the folkbiological concept of human nature. *Philosophical Transaction of the Royal Society B*, 366, 444–453.

Lipsey, M. W. & Wilson, D. B. (1998). Effective intervention for serious juvenile offenders: A synthesis of research. In R. Loeber & D. P. Farrington (eds.), *Serious and Violent Juvenile Offenders: Risk Factors and Successful Interventions*. Pp. 313–345. Thousand Oaks, CA: Sage Publications.

Lipsey, M. W., Landenberger, N. A. & Wilson, S. J. (2007). Effects of cognitive-behavioral programs for criminal offenders. *Campbell Systematic Reviews*. Doi: 10.4073/csr.2007.6.

Litwack, T. R. (1993). On the ethics of dangerousness assessments. *Law and Human Behavior*, 17, 479–482.

Locke, D. P., Hillier, L. W., Warren, W. C. & 98 others (2011). Comparative and demographic analysis of orang-utan genomes. *Nature*, 469, 529–533.

Loeber, R., Pardini, D., Homish, D. L., Wes, E. H., Crawford, A. M., Farrington, D. P., Stouthamer-Loeber, M., Creemers, J., Koehler, S. A. & Rosenfeld, R. (2005). The prediction of violence and homicide in young men. *Journal of Consulting and Clinical Psychology*, 73, 1074–1088.

Loeber, R., Farrington, D. P., Stouthamer-Loeber, M. & White, H. R. (2008). *Violence and Serious Theft: Development and Prediction from Childhood to Adulthood*. New York: Routledge.

LoParo, D. & Waldman, I. (2014). Twins' rearing environment similarity and childhood externalizing disorders: A test of the equal environments assumption. *Behavior Genetics*, 44, 606–613.

Lowenkamp, C. T., Latessa, E. J. & Holsinger, A. M. (2006). The risk principle in action: What have we learned from 13,676 offenders and 97 correctional programs? *Crime & Delinquency*, 52, 77–93.

Loza, W. (2003). Predicting violent and nonviolent recidivism of incarcerated male offenders. *Aggression and Violent Behaviour*, 8, 175–203.

Lozano, R., Naghavi, N., Foreman, K. & 188 others (2012). Global and regional mortality from 235 causes of death for 20 age groups in 1990 and 2010: A systematic analysis for the Global Burden of Disease Study 2010. *The Lancet*, 380(9859), 2095–2128.

Lu, Y.-F. & Menard, S. (2017). The interplay of MAOA and peer influences in predicting adult criminal behaviour. *Psychiatric Quarterly*, 88, 115–128.

Luckenbill, D. F. (1977). Criminal homicide as a situated transaction. *Social Problems*, 25, 176–186.

(1981). Generating compliance: The case of robbery. *Urban Life (Journal of Contemporary Ethnography)*, 10, 25–46.

Lysova, A. (2018). Challenges to the veracity and the international comparability of Russian homicide statistics. *European Journal of Criminology*, https://doi .org/10.1177/1477370818794124.

Maas, C., Herrenkohl, T. I. & Sousa, C. (2008). Review of research on child maltreatment and violence in youth. *Trauma Violence Abuse*, 9, 56–67.

Machery, E. (2018). Doubling down on the nomological notion of human nature. In E. Hannon & T. Lewens (eds.), *Why We Disagree about Human Nature*. Pp. 18–39. Oxford: Oxford University Press.

MacLean, E. L., Hare, B., Nunn, C. L. et al. (2014). The evolution of self-control. *Proceedings of the National Academy of Sciences of the United States*, E2140–E2148. www.pnas.org/cgi/doi/10.1073/pnas.1323533111.

Maimon, D. & Browning, C. R. (2010). Unstructured socializing, collective efficacy, and violent behaviour among urban youth. *Criminology*, 48, 443–474.

Maniglio, R. (2009). Severe mental illness and criminal victimization: A systematic review. *Acta Psychiatrica Scandinavica*, 119, 180–191.

Mann, J. (2006). Health and human rights. If not now, when? *American Journal of Public Health*, 96, 1940–1943.

Manolio, T. A., Collins, F. S., Cox, N. J., Goldstein, D. B. & 23 others (2009). Finding the missing heritability of complex diseases. *Nature*, 461, 747–753.

Marks, J. (2002). *What It Means to Be 97% Chimpanzee*. Los Angeles: University of California Press.

Marshall, I. & Summers, D. (2012). Contemporary differences in rates and trends of homicide among European nations. In M. Liem & W. Pridemore (eds.), *Handbook of European Homicide Research: Patterns, Explanations, and Country Studies*. Pp. 39–69. New York: Springer.

Martin, M. S., Dorken, S. K., Wamboldt, A. D. & Wootten, S. E. (2012). Stopping the revolving door: A meta-analysis on the effectiveness of interventions for criminally involved individuals with major mental disorders. *Law and Human Behavior*, 36, 1–12.

Mason, D. A. & Frick, P. J. (1994). The heritability of antisocial behaviour: A meta-analysis of twin and adoption studies. *Journal of Psychopathology and Behavioral Assessment*, 16, 301–323.

Mathews, C., Eggers, S., Townsend, L., Aarø, L., de Vries, P., Mason-Jones, A., De Koker, P., McClinton Appollis, T., Mtshizana, Y., Koech, J., Wubs, A. & De Vries, H. (2016). Effects of PREPARE, a multi-component, school-based HIV and Intimate Partner Violence (IPV) prevention programme on adolescent sexual risk behaviour and IPV: Cluster randomised controlled trial. *AIDS and Behavior*, 20, 1821–1840.

Matjasko, J. L., Vivolo-Kantro, A. M., Massetti, G. M., Holland, K. M., Holt, M. K. & Dela Cruz, J. (2012). A systematic meta-review of evaluations of youth violence prevention programs: Common and divergent findings from 25 years of meta-analyses and systematic reviews. *Aggression and Violent Behavior*, 17, 540–552.

Matsueda, R. L. & Anderson, K. (1998). The dynamics of delinquent peers and delinquent behaviour. *Criminology*, 36, 269–308.

Mattick, J. S. (2011). The central role of RNA in human development and cognition. *FEBS Letters*, 585, 1600–1616.

McAdams, T. A., Neiderhiser, J. M., Rijsdijk, F. V., Narusyte, J., Lichtenstein, P. & Eley, T. C. (2014). Accounting for genetic and environmental confounds in associations between parent and child characteristics: A systematic review of children-of-twins studies. *Psychological Bulletin*, 140, 1138–1173.

McCall, G. S. & Shields, N. (2008). Examining the evidence from small-scale societies and early prehistory and implications for modern theories and aggression and violence. *Aggression and Violent Behavior*, 13, 1–9.

McCart, M. R., Priester, P. E., Davies, W. H. & Azen, R. (2006). Differential effectiveness of behavioural parent-training and cognitive-behavioral therapy for antisocial youth: A meta-analysis. *Journal of Abnormal Child Psychology*, 34, 527–543.

McGue, M., Zhang, Y., Miller, M. B., Basu, S., Vrieze, S., Hicks, B., Malone, S. Oetting, W. S. & Iacono, W. G. (2013). A genome-wide association study of behavioural disinhibition. *Behavior Genetics*, 43, 363–373.

McGuire, J. (2004). Minimising harm in violence risk assessments: Practical solutions to ethical problems? *Health, Risk and Society*, 6, 327–345.

(2008). A review of effective interventions for reducing aggression and violence. *Philosophical Transactions of the Royal Society B*, 363, 2577–2597.

(2013). 'What works' to reduce reoffending: 18 years on. In L. Craig, J. Dixon & T. A. Gannon (eds.), *What Works in Offender Rehabilitation: An Evidence Based Approach to Assessment and Treatment*. Pp. 20–49. Chichester: Wiley-Blackwell.

(2015). *What Works in Reducing Reoffending in Young Adults? A Rapid Evidence Assessment*. Analytical Summary. London: National Offender Management Service.

(2017). Evidence-based practice and adults: What works? What works best? In P. Sturmey (ed.), *The Wiley Handbook of Violence and Aggression*. Pp. 803–814. New York: Wiley.

(2018). *Understanding Prison Violence: A Rapid Evidence Assessment*. Analytical Summary. London: HM Prison and Probation Service.

(2019). Interventions to reduce alcohol-related offending. In D. Polaschek, A. Day & C. R. Hollin (eds.), *The Handbook of Psychology and Corrections*. Pp. 543–557. Chichester: Wiley.

McGuire, J. & Duff, S. (2018). *Forensic Psychology: Routes through the System*. London: Palgrave.

McLaren, N. (1998). A critical review of the biopsychosocial model. *Australian and New Zealand Journal of Psychiatry*, 32, 86–92.

McLernon, H., Feiger, J. & Schug, R. (2018). Neuroimaging evidence of violence and aggression. In A. T. Vazsonyi, D. J. Flannery & M. DeLisi (eds.), *The Cambridge Handbook of Violent Behavior and Aggression*. 2nd edition. Pp. 106–124. Cambridge: Cambridge University Press.

McManus, I. C., Moore, J., Freegard, M. & Rawles, R. (2010). Science in the making: Right hand, left hand. III: Estimating historical rates of left-handedness. *Laterality*, 15, 186–208.

McMurran, M. & Duggan, C. (2005). The manualization of a treatment programme for personality disorder. *Criminal Behaviour and Mental Health*, 15, 17–27.

Medland, S. E., Duffy, D. L., Wright, M. J., Geffen, G. M., Hay, D. A., Levy, F. L., van-Beijsterveldt, C. E. M., Willemsen, G., Townsend, G. C., White, V., Hewitt, A. W., Mackey, D. A., Bailey, J. M., Slutske, W. S., Nyholt, D. R., Treloar, S. A., Martin, N. G. & Boomsma, D. I. (2009). Genetic influences on handedness: Data from 25,732 Australian and Dutch twin families. *Neuropsychologia*, 47, 330–337.

Meehl, P. E. (1954). *Clinical and Statistical Prediction: A Theoretical Analysis and Review of the Evidence*. Minneapolis: University of Minnesota Press.

Mehta, P. H., Goetz, S. M. & Carré, J. M. (2013). Genetic, hormonal, and neural underpinnings of human aggressive behavior. In D. D. Franks & J. H. Turner (eds.), *Handbook of Neurosociology*. Pp. 47–65. New York: Springer.

Meier, R. F., Kennedy, L. W. & Sacco, V. F. (2001). Crime and the criminal event perspective. In R. F. Meier, L. W. Kennedy & V. F. Sacco (eds.), *The Process and Structure of Crime: Criminal Events and Crime Analysis*. Advances in Criminological Theory, vol. 9. Pp. 1–27. New Brunswick, NJ: Transaction Publishers.

Melendez-Torres, G. J., Dickson, K., Fletcher, A., Thomas, J., Hinds, K., Campbell, R., Murphy, S. & Bonell, C. (2016). Systematic review and meta-analysis of effects of community-delivered positive youth development interventions on violence outcomes. *Journal of Epidemiology and Community Health*, 70, 1171–1177.

Melton, G. B., Petrila, J., Poythress, N. G. & Slobogin, C. (2007). *Psychological Evaluations for the Courts: A Handbook for Mental Health Professionals and Lawyers*. 3rd edition. New York: Guilford Press.

Melton, G. B., Petrila, J. Pothress, N. G., Slobogin, C., Otto, R. K., Mossman, D. & Condie, L. O. (2018). *Psychological Evaluations for the Courts: A Handbook for Mental Health Professionals and Lawyers*. 4th edition. New York: Guilford Press.

Mercy, J. A., Rosenberg, M., Powell, K., Broome, C. & Roper, W. (1993). Public health policy for preventing violence. *Health Affairs*, 12, 7–29.

Meyer-Lindenberg, A., Buckholtz, J. W., Kolachana, B., Hariri, A. R., Pezawas, L., Blasi, G., Wabnitz, A., Honea, R., Verchinski, B., Callicott, J. H., Egan, M., Mattay, V. & Weinberger, D. R. (2006). Neural mechanisms of genetic risk for impulsivity and violence in humans. *Proceedings of the National Academy of Sciences*, 103, 6269–6274.

Mielke, H. W. & Zahran, S. (2012). The urban rise and fall of air lead (Pb) and the latent surge and retreat of societal violence. *Environment International*, 43, 48–55.

Miles, D. R. & Carey, G. (1997). Genetic and environmental architecture of human aggression. *Journal of Personality and Social Psychology*, 72, 207–217.

Miller, M., Drake, E. & Nafziger, M. (2013). *What Works to Reduce Recidivism by Domestic Violence Offenders?* Document No. 13-01-1201. Olympia: Washington State Institute for Public Policy.

Milner, G. R. (2015). Review of 'Violence and Warfare among Hunter-Gatherers'. *American Antiquity*, 80, 787–788.

Moffitt, T. E. (2005). Genetic and environmental influences on antisocial behaviours: Evidence from behaviour-genetic research. *Advances in Genetics*, 55, 41–104.

Moffitt, T. E. & Caspi, A. (2007). Evidence from behavioural genetics for environmental contributions to antisocial conduct. In. J. E. Grusex & P. D. Hastings (eds.), *Handbook of Socialisation: Theory and Research*. Pp. 96–123. New York: Guilford Press.

Monahan, J. (1981). *The Clinical Prediction of Violent Behavior*. Washington, DC: Government Printing Office.

(1984). The prediction of violent behaviour: Towards a second generation of theory and policy. *American Journal of Psychiatry*, 141, 10–15.

Monahan, J., Steadman, H. J., Silver, E., Appelbaum, P. S., Robbins, P. C., Mulvey, E. P., Roth, L. H., Grisso, T. & Banks, S. (2001). *Rethinking Risk Assessment: The MacArthur Study of Mental Disorder and Violence*. New York: Oxford University Press.

Moncrieff, J. (2008). *The Myth of the Chemical Cure: A Critique of Psychiatric Drug Treatment*. Basingstoke: Palgrave Macmillan.

Monducci, E., Battaglia, C., Forte, A., Masillo, A., Telesforo, L., Carlotto, A., Piazzi, G., Patanè, M., De Angelis, G., Romano, A., Fagioli, F., Girardi, P., Cocchi, A., Meneghelli, A., Alpi, A., Pafumi, N., Moreno Granados, N., Preti, A., Masolo, F., Benzoni, S., Cavenaghi, S., Molteni, I., Salvadori, L., Solbiati, S., Costantino, A., Di Lauro, R., Piccinini, A., Collins Eade, A., Holmshaw, J. & Fiori Nastro, P. (2018). Secondary school teachers and mental health competence: Italy–United Kingdom comparison. *Early Intervention in Psychiatry*, 12, 456–463.

Moore, D. S. (2015). *The Developing Genome: An Introduction to Behavioral Epigenetics*. New York: Oxford University Press.

Moore, J. H. (1990). The reproductive success of Cheyenne war chiefs: A contrary case to Chagnon's Yanomamo. *Current Anthropology*, 31, 322–330.

Morgan, R. D., Flora, D. B., Kroner, D. G., Mills, J. F., Varghese, F. & Steffan, J. S. (2012). Treating offenders with mental illness: A research synthesis. *Law and Human Behavior*, 36, 37–50.

Mosher, L., Gosden, R. & Beder, S. (2013). Drug companies and 'schizophrenia': Unbridled capitalism meets madness. In J. Read & J. Dillon (eds.), *Models of Madness. Psychological, Social and Biological Approaches to Psychosis*. Pp. 125–140. 2nd edition. Hove: Routledge.

Mossman, D. (1994). Assessing predictions of violence: Being accurate about accuracy. *Journal of Consulting and Clinical Psychology*, 62, 783–792.

(2013). Evaluating risk assessments using receiver operating characteristics analysis: Rationale, advantages, insights, and limitations. *Behavioral Sciences and the Law*, 31, 23–39.

(2015). From group data to useful probabilities: The relevance of actuarial risk assessment in individual instances. *Journal of the American Academy of Psychiatry and Law*, 43, 93–102.

Mossman, D. & Sellke, T. (2007). Avoiding error about 'margins of error'. *British Journal of Psychiatry*, 191, 561.

Mueller, J. E., (2004). *The Remnants of War*. Ithaca, NY: Cornell University Press.

Nasrullah, M., Haqqi, S. & Cummings, K. J. (2009). The epidemiological patterns of honour killings of women in Pakistan. *European Journal of Public Health*, 19, 193–197.

National Confidential Inquiry into Suicide and Homicide by People with Mental Illness (2014). *Annual Report*. Manchester: University of Manchester.

National Institute for Health and Care Excellence (2013). *Antisocial Personality Disorder. Prevention and Management*. Clinical Guideline CG77. National Collaborating Centre for Mental Health.

(2015). *Violence and Aggression. Short-Term Management in Mental Health, Health and Community Settings*. NICE Guideline NG10. National Collaborating Centre for Mental Health.

(2018a). *Clozapine*. https://bnf.nice.org.uk/drug/clozapine.html. Accessed 18 September 2018.

(2018b). *Carbamazepine*. https://bnf.nice.org.uk/drug/carbamazepine.html. Accessed 18 September 2018.

Nell, V. (2006). Cruelty's rewards: The gratifications of perpetrators and spectators. *Behavioral and Brain Sciences*, 29, 211–257.

Nelson, R. J. & Trainor, B. C. (2007). Neural mechanisms of aggression. *Nature Reviews Neuroscience*, 8, 536–546.

Newton-Fisher, N. E. & Thompson, M. E. (2012). Comparative evolutionary perspectives on violence. In T. D. Shackelford & V. A. Weekes-Shackelford (eds.), *The Oxford Handbook of Evolutionary Perspectives on Violence, Homicide and War*. Pp. 41–60. Oxford: Oxford University Press.

Nicholls, T. L., Pritchard, M. M., Reeves, K. A. & Hilterman, E. (2013). Risk assessment in intimate partner violence: A systematic review of contemporary approaches. *Partner Abuse*, 4, 76–168.

Nicholls, T. L., Petersen, K. L. & Pritchard, M. M. (2016). Comparing preferences for actuarial versus structured professional judgment violence risk assessment measures across five continents: To what extent is practice keeping pace with science? In J. P. Singh, S. Bjorkly & S. Fazel (eds.), *International Perspectives on Violence Risk Assessment*. Pp. 127–149. New York: Oxford University Press.

Nichols, S. (2011). Media representations of youth violence. In C. Barter & D. Berridge (eds.), *Children Behaving Badly: Peer Violence between Children and Young People*. Pp. 167–179. Chichester: Wiley-Blackwell.

Nicoll, M., Beail, N. & Saxon, D. (2013). Cognitive behavioural treatment of anger in adults with learning disabilities: A systematic review and meta-analysis. *Journal of Applied Research in Intellectual Disabilities*, 26, 47–62.

Nikolova, S. P. & Small, E. (2018). Review of the evidence of gender-focused interventions including men to reduce HIV risk and violence against women in sub-Saharan Africa. *Journal of HIV/AIDS & Social Services*, 17, 87–117.

Nisbett, R. E. & Cohen, D. (1996). *Culture of Honor: The Psychology of Violence in the South*. Oxford: Westview Press.

Niv, S. & Baker, L. A. (2012). Genetic markers for antisocial behaviour. In C. R. Thomas & K. Pope (eds.), *The Origins of Antisocial Behavior: A Developmental Perspective*. Pp. 3–38. New York: Oxford University Press.

Nivette, A. E. (2011). Cross-national predictors of crime: A meta-analysis. *Homicide Studies*, 15, 103–131.

Nixon, R. (2011). *Slow Violence and the Environmentalism of the Poor*. Cambridge, MA: Harvard University Press.

Norlander, B. & Eckhardt, C. (2005). Anger, hostility, and male perpetrators of intimate partner violence: A meta-analytic review. *Clinical Psychology Review* 25, 119–152.

Norman, R. E., Byambaa, M., De, R., Butchart, A., Scott, J. & Vos, T. (2012). The long-term health consequences of child physical abuse, emotional abuse, and neglect: A systematic review and meta-analysis. *PLOS Medicine*. https://doi.org/10.1371/journal.pmed.1001349.

Novaco, R. W. (2013). Reducing anger-related offending. In L. Craig, J. Dixon & T. A. Gannon (eds.), *What Works in Offender Rehabilitation: An Evidence Based Approach to Assessment and Treatment*. Pp. 211–236. Chichester: Wiley-Blackwell.

Novaco, R. W. & Taylor, J. L. (2015). Reduction of assaultive behaviour following anger treatment of forensic hospital patients with intellectual disabilities. *Behaviour Research and Therapy*, 65, 52–59.

Ocklenburg, S., Betse, C. & Arning, L. (2014). Handedness genetics: Considering the phenotype. *Frontiers in Psychology*, 5. Doi: 10.3389/fpsyg.2014.01300.

Office for National Statistics (2015). *Life Expectancy at Birth and at Age 65 by Local Areas in England and Wales: 2012 to 2014*. www.ons.gov.uk/people populationandcommunity/birthsdeathsandmarriages/lifeexpectancies/bulletins/ lifeexpectancyatbirthandatage65bylocalareasinenglandandwales/2015-11-04. Accessed 6 May 2019.

   (2016). *UK Statistics Authority Assessment*. http://webarchive.nationalarchives .gov.uk/20160105191751/www.ons.gov.uk/ons/guide-method/method-qual ity/specific/crime-statistics-methodology/uk-statistics-authority-assessment/ index.html. Accessed 6 May 2019.

   (2019). www.ons.gov.uk/peoplepopulationandcommunity/crimeandjustice/bul letins/crimeinenglandandwales/yearendingmarch2019. Accessed 17 October 2019.

Olfson, M., Blanco, C., Liu, L., Moreno, C. & Laje, G. (2006). National trends in the outpatient treatment of children and adolescents with antipsychotic drugs. *Archives of General Psychiatry*, 63, 679–685.

Olfson, M., King, M. & Schoenbaum, M. (2015). Treatment of young people with antipsychotic medications in the United States. *JAMA Psychiatry*, 72, 867–874.

Olver, M. E. & Wong, S. C. P. (2013). A description and research review of the Clearwater Sex Offender Treatment Programme. *Psychology, Crime & Law*, 19, 477–492.

Olweus, D. (1988). Environmental and biological factors in the development of aggressive behaviour. In W. Buikhuisen & S. A. Mednick (eds.), *Explaining Criminal Behaviour*. Pp. 90–120. Leiden: E. J. Brill.

Ostinelli, E. G., Brooke-Powney, M., Li, X. & Adams, C. (2017). Haloperidol for psychosis-induced aggression or agitation (rapid tranquillisation). *Cochrane Database of Systematic Reviews*, Issue 7, Art. No. CD009377. Doi: 10.1002/14651858.CD009377.pub3.

Otto, R. K. (2000). Assessing and managing violence risk in outpatient settings. *Journal of Clinical Psychology*, 56, 1239–1262.

Oxfam (2018). *Reward Work, Not Wealth*. Oxfam Briefing Paper. www-cdn .oxfam.org/s3fs-public/file_attachments/bp-reward-work-not-wealth-220118-en.pdf.

Panofsky, A. (2015). From behaviour genetics to postgenomics. In S. R. Richardson & H. Stevens (eds.), *Postgenomics: Perspectives on Biology after the Genome*. Pp. 150–173. Durham, NC: Duke University Press.

Papalia, N., Spivak, B., Daffern, M. & Ogloff, J. R. P. (2019). A meta-analytic review of the efficacy of psychological treatments for violent offenders in correctional and forensic mental health settings. *Clinical Psychology, Science and Practice*, 26: e12282.

Pappa, I., St. Pourcain, B., Benke, K., Cavadino, A. & 39 others (2015). A genome-wide approach to children's aggressive behavior: The EAGLE consortium. *American Journal of Medical Genetics Part B*, 171B, 562–572.

Pardoe, C. (2014). Conflict and territoriality in Aboriginal Australia: Evidence from biology and ethnography. In M. W. Allen & T. L. Jones (eds.), *Violence and Warfare among Hunter-Gatherers*. Pp. 112–132. Walnut Creek, CA: Left Coast Press.

Parhar, K. K., Wormith, J., Derkzen, D. & Beauregard, A. (2008). Offender coercion in treatment: A meta-analysis of effectiveness. *Criminal Justice and Behavior*, 35, 1109–1135.

Parsons, K. A. (2007). Structural violence and power. *Peace Review*, 19, 173–181.

Paterson, B., Bradley, P., Stark, C., Saddler, D., Leadbetter, D. & Allen, D. (2003). Deaths associated with restraint use in health and social care in the UK. The results of a preliminary survey. *Journal of Psychiatric and Mental Health Nursing*, 10, 3–15.

Patrick, C. J. (2008). Psychophysiological correlates of aggression and violence: An integrative review. *Philosophical Transactions of the Royal Society B*, 363, 2543–2555.

Patterson, G. R. (1982). *Coercive Family Process*. Eugene, OR: Castalia.

Patterson, G. R., Dishion, T. J. & Bank, L. (1984). Family interaction: A process model of deviancy training. *Aggressive Behavior*, 10, 253–267.

Pemment, J. (2013). The neurobiology of antisocial personality disorder: The quest for rehabilitation and treatment. *Aggression and Violent Behavior* 18, 79–82.

Perlis, R., Perlis, C., Wu, Y., Hwang, C., Joseph, M. & Nierenberg, A. (2005). Industry sponsorship and financial conflict of interest in the reporting of clinical trials in psychiatry. *American Journal of Psychiatry*, 162, 1957–1960.

Petrosino, A., Turpin-Petrosino, C. & Finckenauer, J. O. (2000). Well-meaning programs can have harmful effects! Lessons from experiments of programs such as Scared Straight. *Crime and Delinquency*, 46, 354–379.

Pfohl, S. J. (1979). From whom will we be protected? Comparative approaches to the assessment of dangerousness. *International Journal of Law and Psychiatry*, 2, 55–78.

Pickett, K. & Wilkinson, R. (2010). *The Spirit Level: Why Greater Equality Makes Societies Stronger*. New York: Bloomsbury.

Pim, J. E. (2013). Man the singer: Song duels as an aggression restraint mechanism for nonkilling conflict management. In D. P. Fry (ed.), *War, Peace and Human Nature: The Convergence of Evolutionary and Cultural Views.* Pp. 514–540. New York: Oxford University Press.

Pinker, S. (1997). *How the Mind Works.* New York: W. W. Norton.

(2011). *The Better Angels of Our Nature: The Decline of Violence in History and Its Causes.* London: Penguin Books.

Piquero, A. L., Jennings, W. C. & Barnes, J. C. (2012). Violence in criminal careers: A review of the literature from a life-course developmental perspective. *Aggression and Violent Behavior,* 17, 171–179.

Plomin, R. (2013). Child development and molecular genetics: 14 years later. *Child Development,* 84, 104–120.

(2018). *Blueprint: How DNA Makes Us Who We Are.* London: Allen Lane.

Plomin, R., Corley, R., Caspi, A., Fulker, D. W. & DeFries, J. (1998). Adoption results for self-reported personality: Evidence for nonadditive genetic effects? *Journal of Personality and Social Psychology,* 75, 211–218.

Polaschek, D. & Daly, T. E. (2013). Treatment and psychopathy in forensic settings. *Aggression and Violent Behavior,* 18, 592–603.

Polaschek, D. L. L., Wilson, N. J., Townsend, M. R. & Daly, L. R. (2005). Cognitive-behavioral rehabilitation for high-risk violent offenders: An outcome evaluation of the violence prevention unit. *Journal of Interpersonal Violence,* 29, 1611–1627.

Polderman, T. J. C., Benyamin, B., de Leeuw, C. A., Sullivan, P. F., van Bochoven, A., Visscher, P. M. & Posthuma, D. (2015). Meta-analysis of the heritability of human traits based on fifty years of twin studies. *Nature Genetics,* 47, 702–709.

Polman, H., de Castro, B. O., Koops, W., van Boxtel, H. W. & Merk, W. W. (2007). A meta-analysis of the distinction between reactive and proactive aggression in children and adolescents. *Journal of Abnormal Child Psychology,* 35, 522–535.

Portnoy, J., Gao, Y., Glenn, A. L., Niv, S., Peskin, M., Rudo-Hutt, A., Schug, R. A., Yang, Y. & Raine, A. (2013). The biology of childhood crime and antisocial behavior. In C. L. Gibson & M. D. Krohn (eds.), *Handbook of Life-Course Criminology: Emerging Trends and Directions for Future Research.* Pp. 21–42. New York: Springer.

Potvin, L., Gendron, S., Bilodeau, A. & Chabot, P. (2005). Integrating social theory into public health practice. *American Journal of Public Health,* 95, 591–595.

Pressman, D. E. & Flockton, J. (2012). Calibrating risk for violent political extremists and terrorists: The VERA 2 structured assessment. *British Journal of Forensic Practice,* 14, 237–251.

Provençal, N., Booij, L. & Tremblay, R. E. (2015). The developmental origins of chronic physical aggression: Biological pathways triggered by early life adversity. *Journal of Experimental Biology,* 218, 123–133.

Prüfer, K. & 40 others (2012). The bonobo genome compared with the chimpanzee and human genomes. *Nature,* 486, 527–532. Doi: 10.1038/nature11128.

Qayyum, A., Zai, C. C., Hirata, Y., Tiwari, A. K., Cheema, S., Nowrouzi, B., Beitchman, J. H. & Kennedy, J. L. (2015). The role of the catechol-o-methyltransferase (COMT) gene Val158Met in aggressive behavior: A review of genetic studies. *Current Neuropharmacology*, 13, 802–814.

Quigley, B. M., Leonard, K. E. & Collins, R. E. (2003). Characteristics of violent bars and bar patrons. *Journal of Studies on Alcohol*, 64, 765–772.

Ramirez, J. M. (2013). Biology does not condemn humanity to violence. *Medunarodne studije [International Studies]*, 13(3–4), 21–31.

Rautiainen, M.-R., Paunio, T., Repo-Tiihonen, E., Virkkunen, M., Ollila, H. M., Sulkava, S., Jolanki, O., Palotie, A. & Tiihonen, J. (2016). Genome-wide association study of antisocial personality disorder. *Translational Psychiatry*, 6: e883. Doi:10.1038/tp.2016.155.

Read, J. (2008). Schizophrenia, drug companies and the internet. *Social Science & Medicine* 66, 99–109.

Reader, S. M. & Laland, K. N. (2002). Social intelligence, innovation, and enhanced brain size in primates. *Proceedings of the National Academy of Sciences*, 99, 4436–4441.

Rebellon, C. J. (2006). Do adolescents engage in delinquency to attract the social attention of peers? An extension and longitudinal test of the social reinforcement hypothesis. *Journal of Research in Crime and Delinquency*, 43, 387–411.

Redondo, S., Sánchez-Meca, J. & Garrido, V. (2002). Crime treatment in Europe: A review of outcome studies. In J. McGuire (ed.), *Offender Rehabilitation and Treatment: Effective Programmes and Policies to Reduce Re-offending*. Pp. 113–141. Chichester: John Wiley & Sons.

Reid, J. B., Patterson, G. R. & Snyder, J. (2002). *Antisocial Behavior in Children and Adolescents: A Developmental Analysis and Model for Intervention*. Washington, DC: American Psychological Association.

Reidy, D. E., Kearns, M. C. & DeGue, S. (2013). Reducing psychopathic violence: A review of the treatment literature. *Aggression and Violent Behavior*, 18, 527–538.

Renoux, C., Shin, J.-Y., Dell'Aniello, S., Fergusson, E. & Suissa, S. (2016). Prescribing trends of attention-deficit hyperactivity disorder (ADHD) medications in UK primary care, 1995–2015. *British Journal of Clinical Pharmacology*, 82, 858–868.

Reuter, M. (2010). Population and molecular genetics of anger and aggression: Current state of the art. In M. Potegal, G. Stemmler & C. Spielberger (eds.), *International Handbook of Anger*. Pp. 27–37. Bonn: Springer.

Rhee, S. H. & Waldman, I. D. (2002). Genetic and environmental influences on antisocial behaviour: A meta-analysis of twin and adoption studies. *Psychological Bulletin*, 128, 490–529.

Ridley, J. & Leitch, S. (2019). *Restraint Reduction Network Training Standards*. Birmingham: BILD Publications.

Rilling, J. K. (2014). Comparative primate neuroimaging: Insights into human brain evolution. *Trends in Cognitive Sciences*, 18, 46–55.

Roberts, D. (2008). *Human Insecurity: Global Structures of Violence*. London: Zed Books.

Robins, N. A. & Jones, A. (eds.) (2009). *Genocides by the Oppressed: Subaltern Genocide in Theory and Practice*. Bloomington: Indiana University Press.

Romero, T., Catsellano, M. A. & de Waal, F. B. M. (2010). Consolation as possible expression of sympathetic concern among chimpanzees. *Proceedings of the National Academy of Sciences*, 107, 12110–12115.

Rose, G. (1981). Strategy of prevention: Lessons from cardiovascular disease. *British Medical Journal*, 282, 1847–1851.

Rose, S. P. R. (2006). Commentary: Heritability estimates – Long past their sell-by date. *International Journal of Epidemiology*, 35, 525–527.

Rosell, D. R. & Siever, L. J. (2015). The neurobiology of aggression and violence. *CNS Spectrums*, 20, 254–279.

Ross, J., Quayle, E., Newman, E. & Tansey, L. (2013). The impact of psychological therapies on violent behaviour in clinical and forensic settings: A systematic review. *Aggression and Violent Behavior*, 18, 761–773.

Rossegger, A., Gerth, J., Seewald, K., Urbaniok, F., Singh, J. P. & Endrass, J. (2013). Current obstacles in replicating risk assessment findings: A systematic review of commonly used actuarial instruments. *Behavioral Sciences and the Law*, 31, 154–164.

Roth, G. & Dicke, U. (2005). Evolution of the brain and intelligence. *Trends in Cognitive Sciences*, 9, 250–257.

Roth, T. L. (2012). Epigenetics of neurobiology and behavior during development and adulthood. *Developmental Psychobiology*, 54, 590–597.

Rothbart, M. K. (2011). *Becoming Who We Are: Temperament and Personality in Development*. New York: Guilford Press.

Sabates, R. & Dex, S. (2012). *Multiple Risk Factors in Young Children's Development*. CLS Cohort Studies, Working paper 2012/1. London: Centre for Longitudinal Studies, Institute of Education, University of London.

Sahlins, M. (1972/2004). *Stone Age Economics*. London: Tavistock.

   (2008). *The Western Illusion of Human Nature*. Chicago: University of Chicago Press.

Saini, M. (2009). A meta-analysis of the psychological treatment of anger: Developing guidelines for evidence-based practice. *Journal of the American Academy of Psychiatry and the Law*, 37, 473–488.

Salvatore, J. E., Edwards, A. C., McClintock, J. N., Bigdeli, T. B., Adkins, A., Aliev, F., Edenberg, H. J., Foroud, T., Hesselbrock, V., Kramer, J., Numberger, J. I., Schukit, M., Tischfield, J. A., Xuei, X. & Dick, D. M. (2015). Genome-wide association data suggest ABCB1 and immune-related gene sets may be involved in adult antisocial behavior. *Translational Psychiatry*, 5, e558. Doi: 10.1038/tp.2015.36.

Salzberger, T. (2013). Attempting measurement of psychological attributes. *Frontiers in Psychology*, 4. Doi: 10.3389/fpsyg.2013.00075.

Salzinger, S., Rosario, M. & Feldman, R. S. (2007). Physical child abuse and adolescent violent delinquency: The mediating and moderating roles of personal relationships. *Child Maltreatment*, 12, 208–219.

Sameroff, A. (2009). The transactional model. In A. Sameroff (ed.), *The Transactional Model of Development: How Children and Contexts Shape Each Other*. Pp. 3–21. Washington, DC: American Psychological Association.

Sanday, P. R. (1981). The socio-cultural context of rape: A cross-cultural study. *Journal of Social Issues*, 37, 5–27.

(2004). *Women at the Center: Life in a Modern Matriarchy*. Ithaca, NY: Cornell University Press.

Sapolsky, R. M. (2006). A natural history of peace. *Foreign Affairs*, 85, 104–120.

Sawyer, A. M., Borduin, C. M. & Dopp, A. R. (2015). Long-term effects of prevention and treatment on youth antisocial behavior: A meta-analysis. *Clinical Psychology Review*, 42, 130–144.

Sawyer, J. (1966). Measurement and prediction, clinical and statistical. *Psychological Bulletin*, 66, 178–299.

Sayers, K., Raghanti, M. A. & Lovejoy, C. O. (2012). Human evolution and the chimpanzee referential doctrine. *Annual Review of Anthropology*, 41, 119–138.

Scally, A., Dutheil, J. Y., Hillier, L. D. & 68 others (2012). Insights into hominid evolution from the gorilla genome sequence. *Nature*, 483, 169–175.

Schinkel, W. (2010). *Aspects of Violence. A Critical Theory*. Basingstoke: Palgrave Macmillan.

Schlüter, T., Winz, O., Henkel, K., Eggerman, T., Mohammadkhani-Shali, S., Dietrich, C., Heinzel, A., Decker, M., Cumming, P., Zerres, K., Piel, M., Mottaghy, F. M. & Vernaleken, I. (2016). MAOA-VNTR polymorphism modulates context-dependent dopamine release and aggressive behavior in males. *NeuroImage*, 125, 378–385.

Schumm, J. A., O'Farrell, T. J., Murphy, C. M. & Fals-Stewart, W. (2009). Partner violence before and after couples-based alcoholism treatment for female alcoholic patients. *Journal of Consulting and Clinical Psychology*, 77, 1136–1146.

Schwitalla, A. W., Jones, T. L., Pilloud, M. A., Codding, B. F. & Wiberg, R. S. (2014). Violence among foragers: The bioarchaeological record from central California. *Journal of Anthropological Archaeology*, 33, 66–83.

Science Daily (2009). Warrior gene' predicts aggressive behaviour after provocation. www.sciencedaily.com/releases/2009/01/090121093343.htm.

Scott, J. P. & Ginsburg, B. E. (1994). The Seville Statement on Violence revisited. *American Psychologist*, 49, 849–850.

Scott, M. C. & Easton, C. J. (2010). Racial differences in treatment effect among men in a substance abuse and domestic violence program. *American Journal of Drug and Alcohol Abuse*, 36, 357–362.

Searle, J. R. (1995). *The Construction of Social Reality*. London: Penguin Books.

Séguin, J. R., Booij, L. & Lilienfeld, S. O. (2018). The neuropsychology of violence. In A. T. Vazsonyi, D. J. Flannery & M. DeLisi (eds.), *The Cambridge Handbook of Violent Behavior and Aggression*. 2nd edition. Pp. 135–158. Cambridge: Cambridge University Press.

Serketich, W. J. & Dumas, J. E. (1996). The effectiveness of behavioural parent training to modify antisocial behaviour in children: A meta-analysis. *Behavior Therapy*, 27, 171–186.

Seung, S. (2012). *Connectome: How the Brain's Wiring Makes Us Who We Are*. London: Allen Lane.

Shakelford, T. K. & Weekes-Shakelford, V. A. (eds.) (2012). *The Oxford Handbook of Evolutionary Perspectives on Violence, Homicide, and War*. New York: Oxford University Press.

Shears, T. (2012). The standard model. *Philosophical Transaction of the Royal Society A*, 370, 805–817.

Sheehan, K. A., Thakor, S. & Stewart, D. E. (2012). Turning points for perpetrators of intimate partner violence. *Trauma, Violence, & Abuse*, 13, 30–40.

Sheeran, P., Gollwitzer, P. & Bargh, J. (2013). Nonconscious processes and health. *Health Psychology* 32, 460–473.

Shepherd, S. M. & Sullivan, D. (2017). Covert and implicit influences on the interpretation of violence risk instruments. *Psychiatry, Psychology and Law*, 24, 292–301.

Shiner, R. L. (2009). The development of personality disorders: Perspectives from normal personality development in childhood and adolescence. *Development and Psychopathology*, 21, 715–734.

Silberg, J. L., Maes, H. & Eaves, L. J. (2012). Unraveling the effect of genes and environment in the transmission of parental antisocial behaviour to children's conduct disturbance, depression and hyperactivity. *Journal of Child Psychology and Psychiatry*, 53, 668–677.

Simons, R. L. & Lei, M. K. (2013). Enhanced susceptibility to context: A promising perspective on the interplay of genes and the social environment. In C. L. Gibson & M. D. Krohn (eds.), *Handbook of Life-Course Criminology: Emerging Trends and Directions for Future Research*. Pp. 57–67. New York: Springer.

Simons, R. L., Lei, M. K., Stewart, E. A., Beach, S. R. H., Brody, G. H., Philibert, R. A. & Gibbons, F. X. (2012). Social adversity, genetic variation, street code, and aggression: A genetically informed model of violent behavior. *Youth Violence and Juvenile Justice*, 10, 3–24.

Simopoulos, A., (2011). Evolutionary aspects of diet: The Omega-6/Omega-3 ratio and the brain. *Molecular Neurobiology*, 44, 203–215.

Singh, J. P. (2013). Predictive validity performance indicators in violence risk assessment: A methodological primer. *Behavioral Sciences and the Law*, 31, 8–22.

Singh, J. P. & Fazel, S. (2010). Forensic risk assessment: A metareview. *Criminal Justice and Behavior*, 37, 965–988.

Singh, J. P., Grann, M. & Fazel, S. (2011). A comparative study of violence risk assessment tools: A systematic review and metaregression analysis of 68 studies involving 25,980 participants. *Clinical Psychology Review*, 31, 499–513.

Singh, J. P., Desmarais, S. L. & Van Dorn, R. A. (2013). Measurement of predictive validity in violence risk assessment studies: A second-order systematic review. *Behavioral Sciences and the Law*, 31, 55–73.

Singh, J. P., Desmarais, S. L., Otto, R. K., Nicholls, T. L., Petersen, K. L. & Pritchard, M. M. (2016). The International Risk Survey: Use and perceived utility of structured violence risk assessment tools in 44 countries. In J. P. Singh, S. Bjorkly & S. Fazel (eds.), *International Perspectives on Violence Risk Assessment*. Pp. 101–126. New York: Oxford University Press.

Skeem, J. L., Monahan, J. & Mulvey, E. P. (2002). Psychopathy, treatment involvement, and subsequent violence among civil psychiatric patients. *Law and Human Behavior*, 26, 577–603.

Smedslund, G., Dalsbø, T. K., Steiro, A., Winsvold, A. & Clench-Aas, J. (2011). Cognitive behavioural therapy for men who physical abuse their female partner. *Cochrane Database of Systematic Reviews*, Issue 2. Art. No. CD006048.

Smith, R. C., Fortin, A. H., Dwamena, F. & Frankel, R. M. (2013). An evidence-based patient-centered method makes the biopsychosocial model scientific. *Patient Education and Counselling*, 91, 265–270.

Somers, M., Ophoff, R. A., Aukesm, M. F., Cantor, R. M., Boks, M. P., Dauwan, M., de Visser, K. L., Kahn, R. S. & Sommer, I. E. (2015). Linkage analysis in a Dutch population isolate shows no major gene for left-handedness or atypical language lateralization. *Journal of Neuroscience*, 35, 8730–8736.

Spielman, R. S., Bastone, L. A., Burdick, J. T., Morley, M., Ewens, W. J. & Cheung, V. G. (2007). Common genetic variants account for differences in gene expression among ethnic groups. *Nature Genetics*, 39, 226–231.

Spielmans, G. I. & Parry, P. (2010). From evidence-based medicine to marketing-based medicine: Evidence from internal industry documents. *Journal of Bioethical Inquiry*, 7, 13–29.

Spierenburg, P. (2012). Long-term historical trends of homicide in Europe. In M. C. A. Liem & W. A. Pridemore (eds.), *Handbook of European Homicide Research: Patterns, Explanations, and Country Studies*. Pp. 25–38. New York: Springer.

Sporns, O., Tononi, G. & Kötter, R. (2005). The human connectome: A structural description of the human brain. *PLOS Computational Biology*, 1, e42. Doi: 10.1371/journal.pcbi.0010042.

Srikantia, J. (2016). The structural violence of globalization. *Critical Perspectives on International Business*, 12, 222–258.

Staub, E. (1999). The roots of evil: Social conditions, culture, personality, and basic human needs. *Personality and Social Psychology Review*, 3, 179–192.

  (2000). Genocide and mass killing: Origins, prevention, healing and reconciliation. *Political Psychology*, 21, 367–382.

Stearns, S. C. & Hoekstra, R. F. (2005). *Evolution: An Introduction*. 2nd edition. Oxford: Oxford University Press.

Steinert T. & Whittington R. (2013). A bio-psycho-social model of violence related to mental health problems. *International Journal of Law and Psychiatry*, 36, 168–175.

Sterelny, K. (2018). Sceptical reflections on human nature. In E. Hannon & T. Lewens (eds.), *Why We Disagree about Human Nature*. Pp. 108–126. Oxford: Oxford University Press.

Stetler, D., Davis, C., Leavitt, K., Schriger, I., Benson, K., Bhakta, S., Wang, L. C., Oben, C., Watters, M., Haghnegahdar, T. & Bortolato, M. (2014). Association of low-activity MAOA allelic variants with violent crime in incarcerated offenders. *Journal of Psychiatric Research*, 58, 69–75.

Stewart, L. A., Gabora, N., Kropp, P. R. & Lee, Z. (2014). Effectiveness of risks-needs-responsibility-based family violence programs with male offenders. *Journal of Family Violence*, 29, 151–164.

Stöckl, H., Devries, K., Rotstein, A., Abrahams, N., Campbell, J., Watts, C. & Moreno, C. G. (2013). The global prevalence of intimate partner homicide: A systematic review. *The Lancet*, 382(9895), 859–865.

Stotz, K. & Griffiths, P. (2018). A developmental systems account of human nature. In E. Hannon & T. Lewens (eds.), *Why We Disagree about Human Nature*. Pp. 58–75. Oxford: Oxford University Press.

Stover, C. S., Meadows, A. M. & Kaufman, J. (2009). Interventions for intimate partner violence: Review and implications for evidence-based practice. *Professional Psychology: Research and Practice*, 40, 223–233.

Striedter, G. F. (2005). *Principles of Brain Evolution*. Sunderland, MA: Sinauer Associates.

Sullivan, C. J. & Newsome, J. (2015). Psychosocial and genetic risk markers for longitudinal trends in delinquency: An empirical assessment and practical discussion. *Criminal Justice Studies*, 28, 61–83.

Sullivan, P. F., Agrawal, A., Bulik, C. M., Andreassen, O. A., Børglum, A. D., Breen, G., Cichin, S., Edenberg, H. J., Faraone, S. V., Gelernter, J., Mathews, C. A., Nievergelt, C. M., Smoller, J. W. & O'Donovan, M. C. for the Psychiatric Genomics Consortium (2018). Psychiatric genomics: An update and an agenda. *American Journal of Psychiatry*, 175, 15–27.

Surbeck, D., Boesch, C., Crockford, C., Thompson, M. E., Furuichi, T., Fruth, B., Hohmann, G., Ishizuka, S., Machanda, Z., Muller, M. N., Pusey, A., Sakamaki, T., Tokuyama, N., Walker, K., Wrangham. R., Wroblewski, E., Zuberbühler, K., Vigilant, L. & Langergraber, K. (2019). Males with a mother living in their group have higher paternity success in bonobos but not chimpanzees. *Current Biology*, 29, R354–R355.

Sussman, R. W. (2013). Why the legend of the killer ape never dies: The enduring power of cultural beliefs to distort our view of human nature. In D. P. Fry (ed.), *War, Peace and Human Nature: The Convergence of Evolutionary and Cultural Views*. Pp. 97–111. New York: Oxford University Press.

Swain, J. E. (2006). Epigenetic effects of child abuse and neglect propagate human cruelty. *Behavioral and Brain Sciences*, 29, 242–243.

Szmukler, G., Everitt, B. & Leese, M. (2011). Risk assessment and receiver operating characteristic curves. *Psychological Medicine*, 42, 895–898.

Szmukler, G. & Rose, N. (2013). Risk assessment in mental health care: Values and costs. *Behavioral Sciences and the Law*, 31, 125–140.

Szyf, M. (2009). Implications of a life-long dynamic epigenome. *Epigenomics*, 1, 9–12.

Tardiff, K. & Hughes, D. M. (2011). Structured and clinical assessment of risk of violence. In E. Y. Drogin, F. M. Dattilio, R. L. Sadoff & T. G. Gutheil (eds.), *Handbook of Forensic Assessment: Psychological and Psychiatric Perspectives*. Pp. 335–359. Hoboken, NJ: Wiley.

Taxman, F. S. (2018). Risk assessment: Where do we go from here? In J. P. Singh, D. G. Kroner, J. S. Wormith, S. L. Desmarais & Z. Hamilton (eds.),

Handbook of Recidivism Risk/Needs Assessment Tools. Pp. 271–284. Chichester: Wiley-Blackwell.

Taylor, A. & Kim-Cohen, J. (2007). Meta-analysis of gene–environment interactions in developmental psychopathology. *Development and Psychopathology,* 19, 1029–1037.

Taylor, C. A., Manganello, J. A., Lee, S. J. & Rice, J. C. (2010). Mothers' spanking of 3-year-old children and subsequent risk of children's aggressive behaviour. *Pediatrics,* 125, e1057–e1066. Doi: 10.1542/peds.2009-2678.

Temcheff, C. E., Serbin, L. A., Martin-Stoyey, A., Stack, D. M., Hodgins, S., Ledingham, J. & Schwartzman, A. E. (2008). Continuity and pathways from aggression in childhood to family violence in adulthood: A 30-year longitudinal study. *Journal of Family Violence,* 23, 231–242.

Theofanopoulou, C., Gastaldon, S., O'Rourke, T., Samuels, B. D., Messner, A., Martins, P. T., Delogu, F., Alamri, S. & Boeckx, C. (2017). Self-domestication in *Homo sapiens*: Insights from comparative genomics. *PLOS One,* 12 (10): e0185306.

Thornberry, T. P., Knight, K. E. & Lovegrove, P. J. (2012). Does maltreatment beget maltreatment? A systematic review of the intergenerational literature. *Trauma, Violence, & Abuse,* 13, 135–152.

Thornhill, R. & Palmer, C. T. (2000). *A Natural History of Rape: Biological Bases of Sexual Coercion.* Cambridge, MA: MIT Press.

Tielbeek, J. J., Medland, S. E., Benyamin, B., Byrne, E. M., Heath, A. C., Madden, P. A. F., Martin, N. G., Wray, N. R. & Verweij, K. J. H. (2012). Unraveling the genetic etiology of adult antisocial behavior: A genome-wide association study. *PLOS One,* 7(10), E45086. Doi: 10.1371/journal.pone.0045086.

Tielbeek, J. J. & 38 others for the Broad Antisocial Behavior Consortium (2017). Genome-wide association studies of a broad spectrum of antisocial behaviour. *JAMA Psychiatry.* Doi: 10.1001/jamapsychiatry.2017.3069.

Tiihonen, J., Rautianen, M.-R., Ollila, H. M., Repo-Tiihonen, E. R., Virkkunen, M., Palotie, A., Pietiläinen, O., Kristiansson, K., Joukamaa, M., Lauerma, H., Saarela, J., Tyni, S., Vartiainen, H., Paananen, J., Goldman, D. & Paunio, T. (2015). Genetic background of extreme violent behavior. *Molecular Psychiatry,* 20, 786–792.

Tombs, S. (2007). 'Violence', safety crimes and criminology. *British Journal of Criminology,* 47, 531–550.

Tomlinson, M. F., Brown, M. & Hoaken, P. N. S. (2016). Recreational drug use and human aggressive behavior: A comprehensive review since 2003. *Aggression and Violent Behavior,* 27, 9–29.

Tooby, J. & Cosmides, L. (1992). The psychological foundations of culture. In J. Barkow, L. Cosmides & J. Tooby (eds.), *The Adapted Mind: Evolutionary Psychology and the Generation of Culture.* Pp. 19–136. New York: Oxford University Press.

Transcend International (2018). *A Peace Development Environment Network.* www.transcend.org. Accessed 19 September 2018.

Travers, R., Mann, R. E. & Hollin, C. R. (2014). Who benefits from cognitive skills programs? Differential impact by risk and offense type. *Criminal Justice and Behavior,* 41, 1103–1129.

Tremblay, R. E., Japel, C., Pérusse, D., McDuff, P., Boivin, M., Zoccolilli, M. & Montplaisir, K. (1999). The search for the age of 'onset' of physical aggression: Rousseau and Bandura revisited. *Criminal Behaviour and Mental Health*, 9, 8–23.

Tremblay, R. E., Nagin, D. S., Séguin, J. R., Zoccolillo, M., Zelazo, P. D., Boivin, M., Pérusse, D. & Japel, C. (2004). Physical aggression during early childhood: Trajectories and predictors. *Pediatrics*, 114, e43–e50.

Tremblay, R. E., Vitaro, F. & Côté, S. M. (2018). Developmental origins of chronic physical aggression: A bio-psycho-social model for the next generation of preventive interventions. *Annual Review of Psychology*, 69, 383–407.

Tryon, R. C. (1930). Studies in individual differences in maze ability. I. The measurement of the reliability of individual differences. *Journal of Comparative Psychology*, 11, 145–170.

(1931). Studies in individual differences in maze ability. IV. The constancy of individual differences: Correlation between learning and relearning. *Journal of Comparative Psychology*, 12, 303–345.

(1940). Genetic differences in maze-learning ability in rats. *Yearbook of the National Society for Studies in Education*, 39, 111–119.

Trzaskowski, M., Dale, P. S. & Plomin, R. (2013). No genetic influence for childhood behaviour problems from DNA analysis. *Journal of the American Academy of Child and Adolescent Psychiatry*, 52, 1048–1056.

Ttofi, M. M. & Farrington, D. P. (2011). Effectiveness of school-based programs to reduce bullying: A systematic and meta-analytic review. *Journal of Experimental Criminology*, 7, 27–56.

Ttofi, M. M., Farrington, D. P., Piquero, A. R. & DeLisi, M. (2016). Protective factors against offending and violence: Results from prospective longitudinal studies. *Journal of Criminal Justice*, 45, 1–3.

Tully, R. J., Chou, S. & Browne, K. D. (2013). A systematic review on the effectiveness of sex offender risk assessment tools in predicting sexual recidivism of adult male sex offenders. *Clinical Psychology Review*, 33, 287–316.

Turkheimer, E., Haley, A., Waldron, M., D'Onofrio, B. & Gottesman, I. I. (2003). Socioeconomic status modifies the heritability of IQ in young children. *Psychological Science*, 14, 623–628.

Turner, E. H., Matthews, A. M., Linardatos, E., Tell, R. A. & Rosenthal, R. (2008). Selective publication of antidepressant trials and its influence on apparent efficacy. *New England Journal of Medicine*, 358, 252–260.

Turquet, L., Seck, P., Azcona, G., Menon, R., Boyce, C., Pierron, N. & Harbour, E. (2011). *Progress of the World's Women 2011–2012*. New York: UN Women (United Nations Entity for Gender Equality and the Empowerment of Women).

Tuvblad, C., Raine, A., Zheng, M. & Baker, L. A. (2009). Genetic and environmental stability differs in reactive and proactive aggression. *Aggressive Behavior*, 35, 437–452.

UK Parliament (2015). *Serious Crime Act*. London: The Stationery Office:

UN Women (2012). *Handbook for National Action Plans on Violence against Women*. www.un.org/womenwatch/daw/vaw/handbook-for-nap-on-vaw.pdf.

United Nations (2000). *Conflict Transformation by Peaceful Means (the Transcend Method)*. Participants' Manual/Trainers' Manual. United Nations Disaster Management Training Programme (DMTP). Geneva, Switzerland. www .transcend.org/pctrcluj2004/TRANSCEND_manual.pdf.

(2015). *Human Development Reports: Gender Inequality Index.* http://hdr.undp .org/en/composite/GII. Accessed 6 May 2019.

(2016). *Sustainable Development Goals. 17 Goals to Transform Our World.* www .un.org/sustainabledevelopment/. Accessed 6 May 2019.

University of Alabama at Birmingham (2019). *Peaceful Societies: Alternatives to Violence and War.* https://cas.uab.edu/peacefulsocieties/ Accessed 8 April 2019.

Vassallo, S., Edwards, B. & Forrest, W. (2016). Childhood behaviour problems and fighting in early adulthood: What factors are protective? *Journal of Criminal Justice*, 45, 85–93.

Vassos, E., Collier, D. A. & Fazel, S. (2014). Systematic meta-analyses and field synopsis of genetic association studies of violence and aggression. *Molecular Psychiatry*, 19, 471–477.

Vaughn, M. G., DeLisi, M., Beaver, K. M. & Wright, J. P. (2009). DAT1 and 5HTT are associated with pathological criminal behavior in a nationally representative sample of youth. *Criminal Justice and Behaviour*, 36, 1113–1124.

Verdoux, H., Tournier, M. & Bégaud, B. (2010). Antipsychotic prescribing trends: A review of pharmaco-epidemiological studies. *Acta Psychiatrica Scandinavica*, 121, 4–10.

Vereenooghe, L. & Langdon, P. E. (2013). Psychological therapies for people with intellectual disabilities: A systematic review and meta-analysis. *Research in Developmental Disabilities*, 34, 4085–4102.

Verendeev, A. & Sherwood, C. C. (2017). Human brain evolution. *Current Opinion in Behavioral Sciences*, 16, 41–45.

Viding, E., Hanscombe, K. B., Curtis, C. J. C., Davis, O. S. P., Meaburn, E. L. & Plomin, R. (2010). In search of genes associated with risk for psychopathic tendencies in children: A two-stage genome-wide association study of pooled DNA. *Journal of Child Psychology and Psychiatry*, 51, 780–788.

Vieraitis, L. M., Britto, S. & Morris, R. (2015). Assessing the impact of changes in gender equality on female homicide victimization: 1980–2000. *Crime & Delinquency*, 61(3), 428–453.

Vila, B. (1994). A general paradigm for understanding criminal behaviour: Extending evolutionary ecological theory. *Criminology*, 32, 311–359.

Wade, D. T. & Halligan, P. W. (2017). The biopsychosocial model of illness: A model whose time has come. *Clinical Rehabilitation*, 31, 995–1004.

Wagman, J. A., Gray, R., Campbell, J., Thoma, M., Ndyanabo, A., Ssekasanvu, J., Nalugoda, F., Kagaayi, J., Nakigozi, G., Serwadda, D. & Brahmbhatt, H. (2015). Effectiveness of an integrated intimate partner violence and HIV prevention intervention in Rakai, Uganda: Analysis of an intervention in an existing cluster randomised cohort. *The Lancet Global Health*, 3(1): e23–e33.

Walker, K., Bowen, E. & Brown, S. (2013). Psychological and criminological factors associated with desistance from violence: A review of the literature. *Aggression and Violent Behavior*, 18, 286–299.

Walker, P. L. (2001). A bioarchaeological perspective on the history of violence. *Annual Review of Anthropology*, 30, 573–596.

Waller, J. (2007). *Becoming Evil: How Ordinary People Commit Genocide and Mass Killing*. 2nd edition. Oxford: Oxford University Press.

Waller, R., Dotterer, H. L., Murray, L. & Hyde, L. W. (2018). Neural substrates of youth and adult antisocial behavior. In A. T. Vazsonyi, D. J. Flannery & M. DeLisi (eds.), *The Cambridge Handbook of Violent Behavior and Aggression*. 2nd edition. Pp. 736–755. Cambridge: Cambridge University Press.

Walsh, E., Moran, P., Scott, C. & McKenzie, K. (2003). Prevalence of violent victimisation in severe mental illness. *British Journal of Psychiatry*, 183, 233–238.

Walters, G. D. (1992). A meta-analysis of the gene–crime relationship. *Criminology*, 30, 595–613.

Walters, G. D., Ermer, E., Knight, R. A. & Kiehl, K. A. (2015). Paralimbic biomarkers in taxometric analyses of psychopathy: Does changing the indicators change the conclusion? *Personality Disorders: Theory, Research, and Treatment*, 6, 41–52.

Walters, G. D., Knight, R. A., Looman, J. & Abracen, J. (2016). Child molestation and psychopathy: A taxometric analysis. *Journal of Sexual Aggression*, 22, 379–393.

Warrier, V., Toro, R., Chakrabarti, B., The iPSYCH-Broad Autism Group, Grove, J., Borglum, A. D., The 23andMe Research Team, Hinds, D. A., Bourgeron, T. & Baron-Cohen, S. (2018). Genome-wide analyses of self-reported empathy: Correlations with autism, schizophrenia, and anorexia nervosa. *Translational Psychiatry*, 8, 35. Doi: 10.1038/s41398-017-0082-6.

Watkins, J., Wulaningsih, W., Da Zhou, C., Marshall, D. C., Syliantend, G. D. C., Dela Rosa, P. G., Miguel, V. A., Raine, R., King, L. P. & Maruthappu, M. (2017). Effects of health and social care spending restraints on mortality in England: A time trend analysis. *BMJ Open*, 7 e017722.

Watts, D. P. & Mitani, J. C. (2000). Infanticide and cannibalism by male chimpanzees at Ngogo, Kibale National Park, Uganda. *Primates*, 41, 357–365.

Weaver, I. C. G., Cervoni, N., Champagne, F. A., D'Alessio, A. C., Sharma, S., Seckl, J. R., Dymov, S., Szyf, M. & Meaney, M. J. (2004). Epigenetic programming by maternal behaviour. *Nature Neuroscience*, 7, 847–854.

Webb, S. (1995). *Paleopathology of Aboriginal Australians: Health and Disease across a Hunter-Gatherer Continent*. Cambridge: Cambridge University Press.

Weeland, J., Overbeek, G., Orobio de Castro, B. & Matthys, W. (2015). Underlying mechanisms of gene–environment interactions in externalizing behaviour: A systematic review and search for theoretical mechanisms. *Clinical Child and Family Psychology Review*, 18, 413–442.

Weinstein, D. (2016). The 'make love, not war' ape: Bonobos and late twentieth-century explanations for war and peace. *Endeavour*, 40, 256–267.

Weisburd, D., Farrington, D. P. & Gill, C. (eds.) (2016). *What Works in Crime Prevention and Rehabilitation: Lessons from Systematic Reviews*. New York: Springer.

Weisburd, D., Farrington, D. P., Gill, C., Ajzenstadt, M., Bennett, T., Bowers, K., Caudy, M. S., Holloway, K., Johnson, S., Lösel, F., Mallender, J., Perry,

A., Tang, L. L., Taxman, F., Telep, C., Tierney, R., Ttofi, M. M., Watson, C., Wilson, D. B. & Wooditch, A. (2017). What works in crime prevention and rehabilitation: An assessment of systematic reviews. *Criminology & Public Policy*, 16, 415–449.

Welsh, E., Bader, S. & Evans, S. E. (2013). Situational variables related to aggression in institutional settings. *Aggression and Violent Behavior*, 18, 792–796.

Whitaker, D. J., Murphy, C. M., Eckhardt, C. I., Hodges, A. E. & Cowart, M. (2013). Effectiveness of primary prevention efforts for intimate partner violence. *Partner Abuse*, 4, 175–195.

Whittington, R., Bowers, L., Nolan, P., Simpson, A. & Neil, L. (2009). Approval ratings of inpatient coercive interventions in a national sample of mental health service users and staff in England. *Psychiatric Services*, 60, 792–798.

Whittington, R., Hockenhull, J. C., McGuire, J., Leitner, M., Barr, W., Cherry, M. G., Flentje, R., Quinn, B., Dundar, Y. & Dickson, R. (2013). A systematic review of risk assessment strategies for populations at high risk of engaging in violent behaviour: Update 2002–8. *Health Technology Assessment*, 17(50), 1–128.

Widom, C. S. (1989). The cycle of violence. *Science*, 244, 160–166.

Williams, H., Chitsabesan, P., Fazel, S., McMillan, T., Hughes, N., Parsonage, M. & Tonks, J. (2018). Traumatic brain injury: A potential cause of violent crime? *The Lancet Psychiatry*. http://dx.doi.org/10.1016/S2215-0366(18)30062-2.

Wilson, M. L. (2013). Chimpanzees, warfare, and the invention of peace. In D. P. Fry (ed.), *War, Peace and Human Nature: The Convergence of Evolutionary and Cultural Views*. Pp. 361–388. New York: Oxford University Press.

Wilson, M. L. & Wrangham, R. W. (2003). Intergroup relations in chimpanzees. *Annual Review of Anthropology*, 32, 363–392.

Wilson, M. L., Boesch, C., Fruth, B. et al. (2014). Lethal aggression in *Pan* is better explained by adaptive strategies than human impacts. *Nature*, 513, 414–417.

Wilson, R. K. (1999). How the worm was won: The *C. elegans* genome sequencing project. *Trends in Genetics*, 15, 51–58.

Wilson, S. J. & Lipsey, M. W. (2007). School-based interventions for aggressive and disruptive behaviour: Update of a meta-analysis. *American Journal of Preventive Medicine*, 33, S130–S143.

Wilson, S. J., Lipsey, M. W. & Derzon, J. H. (2003). The effects of school-based intervention programs on aggressive behaviour: A meta-analysis. *Journal of Consulting and Clinical Psychology*, 71, 136–149.

Winstanley, S. & Whittington, R. (2004). Aggression towards health care staff in a UK general hospital: Variation among professions and departments. *Journal of Clinical Nursing*, 13, 3–10.

Witt, K., van Dorn, R. & Fazel, S. (2013). Risk factors for violence in psychosis: Systematic review and meta-regression analysis of 110 studies. *PLOS One*, 8, e55942.

Wolf, A., Gray, R. & Fazel, S. (2014). Violence as a public health problem: An ecological study of 169 countries. *Social Science & Medicine*, 104, 220–227.

Wong, S. C. P., Gordon, A. & Gu, D. (2007). Assessment and treatment of violence-prone forensic clients: An integrated approach. *British Journal of Psychiatry*, 190, S66–S74.

Wong, S. C. P., Olver, M. E. & Stockdale, K. C. (2009). The utility of dynamic and static factors in risk assessment, prediction, and treatment. In J. C. Andrade (ed.), *Handbook of Violence Risk Assessment and Treatment: New Approaches for Mental Health Professionals*. Pp. 83–118. New York: Springer.

Wong, S., Gordon, A., Gu, D., Lewis, K. & Olver, M. E. (2012). The effectiveness of violence reduction treatment for psychopathic offenders: Empirical evidence and a treatment model. *International Journal of Forensic Mental Health*, 11, 336–349.

World Health Organization (1996). *Violence: A Public Health Priority*. WHO Global Consultation on Violence and Health. WHO/EHA/SPI.POA.2.

World Health Organization (2002). *World Report on Violence and Health*, eds. E. Krug, L. Dahlberg, J. Mercy, A. A. Zwi & R. Lozano. Geneva: World Health Organization. https://apps.who.int/iris/bitstream/handle/10665/42495/92415 45615_eng.pdf.

(2004). *Preventing Violence: A Guide to Implementing the Recommendations of the 'World Report on Violence and Health'*. Geneva: World Health Organization. https://apps.who.int/iris/bitstream/handle/10665/43014/9241592079.pdf.

(2013a). *Global and Regional Estimates of Violence against Women: Prevalence and Health Effects of Intimate Partner Violence and Non-Partner Sexual Violence*. Geneva: World Health Organization. https://apps.who.int/iris/bitstream/ handle/10665/85239/9789241564625_eng.pdf.

(2013b). *Handbook for the Readiness Assessment for the Prevention of Child Maltreatment (RAP-CM)*. Geneva: World Health Organization. www.who.int/ violence_injury_prevention/violence/child/handbook_rap_cmp.pdf.

(2014). *Global Status Report on Violence Prevention*. Geneva: World Health Organization. www.who.int/violence_injury_prevention/violence/status_ report/2014/report/report/en/.

(2016a). *Global Health Observatory Data Repository: Life Expectancy Data by WHO Region*. http://apps.who.int/gho/data/view.main.SDG2016LEXREGv? lang=en. Accessed 17 January 2017.

(2016b). *INSPIRE. Seven Strategies for Ending Violence against Children*. Geneva: World Health Organization. https://apps.who.int/iris/bitstream/ handle/10665/207717/9789241565356-eng.pdf.

(2016c). *Global Plan of Action to Strengthen the Role of the Health System within a National Multisectoral Response to Address Interpersonal Violence, in Particular against Women and Girls, and against Children*. Geneva: World Health Organization. https://apps.who.int/iris/bitstream/handle/10665/252276/978924151 1537-eng.pdf.

(2018). *The Top Ten Causes of Death 2016*. www.who.int/mediacentre/fact sheets/fs310.pdf. Accessed 6 May 2019.

(2019a). *Global Campaign for Violence Prevention*. www.who.int/violence_ injury_prevention/violence/global_campaign/en/. Accessed 6 May 2019.

(2019b). *ICD-11. International Classification of Diseases. The Global Standard for Diagnostic Health Information.* https://icd.who.int/en/. Accessed 6 May 2019.

Wrangham, R. (2019). *The Goodness Paradox: How Evolution Made Us More and Less Violent.* London: Profile Books.

Wrangham, R. & Peterson, D. (1996). *Demonic Males: Apes and the Origins of Human Violence.* New York: Houghton Mifflin.

Wrangham, R. W., Wilson, M. L. & Muller, M. N. (2006). Comparative rates of violence in chimpanzees and humans. *Primates,* 47, 14–26.

Wright, J. P. & Beaver, K. M. (2005). Do parents matter in creating self-control in their children? A genetically informed test of Gottfredson and Hirschi's theory of low self-control. *Criminology,* 43, 1169–1202.

Yang, M., Wong, S. C. P. & Coid, J. (2010). The efficacy of violence prediction: A meta-analytic comparison of nine risk assessment tools. *Psychological Bulletin,* 136, 740–767.

Yang, Y. & Raine, A. (2009). Prefrontal structural and functional brain imaging findings in antisocial, violent, and psychopathic individuals: A meta-analysis. *Psychiatry Research: Neuroimaging,* 30, 81–88.

Yeager, D. S., Fong, C. J., Lee, H. Y. & Espelage, D. L. (2015). Declines in efficacy of anti-bullying programs among older adolescents: Theory and a three-level meta-analysis. *Journal of Applied Developmental Psychology,* 37, 36–51.

Yount, K. M., Krause, K. & Miedema, S. (2017). Preventing gender-based violence victimization in adolescent girls in lower-income countries: Systematic review of reviews. *Social Science & Medicine,* 192, 1–13.

Yu, R., Geddes, J. & Fazel, S. (2012). Personality disorders, violence, and antisocial behavior: A systematic review and meta-regression analysis. *Journal of Personality Disorders,* 26, 775–792.

Zai, C. C., Ehtesham, S., Choi, E., Nowrouzi, B., De Luca, V., Stankovich, L., Davidge, K., Freeman, N., King, N., Kennedy, J. L. & Beitchman, J. H. (2012). Dopaminergic system genes in childhood aggression: Possible role for DRD2. *World Journal of Biological Psychiatry,* 13, 65–74.

Zaman, H., Sampson, S., Beck, A., Sharma, T., Clay, F., Spyridi, S., Zhao, S. & Gillies, D. (2017). Benzodiazepines for psychosis-induced aggression or agitation. *Cochrane Database of Systematic Reviews,* 12. Art. No.: CD003079. Doi: 10.1002/14651858.CD003079.pub4.

Zumkley, H. (1994). The stability of aggressive behavior: A meta-analysis. *German Journal of Psychology,* 18, 273–281.

Index

295

Lightning Source UK Ltd.
Milton Keynes UK
UKHW020703160222
398639UK00013B/307